Death of the Public University?

Higher Education in Critical Perspective: Practices and Policies

Series editors:
Susan Wright, Aarhus University
Penny Welch, Wolverhampton University

Around the globe, universities are being reformed to supply two crucial ingredients of a purported 'global knowledge economy': research and graduates. Higher education's aims, concepts, structures and practices are all in process of change. This series provides in-depth analyses of these changes and how those involved – managers, academics and students – are experimenting with critical pedagogies, reflecting upon the best organization of their own institutions, and engaging with public policy debates about higher education in the twenty-first century.

Volume 1
Learning Under Neoliberalism: Ethnographies of Governance in Higher Education
Edited by Susan Brin Hyatt, Boone W. Shear, and Susan Wright

Volume 2
Creating a New Public University and Reviving Democracy: Action Research in Higher Education
Morten Levin and Davydd J. Greenwood

Volume 3
Death of the Public University?: Uncertain Futures for Higher Education in the Knowledge Economy
Edited by Susan Wright and Cris Shore

Death of the Public University?
Uncertain Futures for Higher Education in the Knowledge Economy

◆◆◆

Edited by

Susan Wright and Cris Shore

berghahn
NEW YORK • OXFORD
www.berghahnbooks.com

Published in 2017 by
Berghahn Books
www.berghahnbooks.com

© 2017, 2019 Susan Wright and Cris Shore
First paperback edition published in 2019

All rights reserved. Except for the quotation of short passages for the purposes of criticism and review, no part of this book may be reproduced in any form or by any means, electronic or mechanical, including photocopying, recording, or any information storage and retrieval system now known or to be invented, without written permission of the publisher.

Library of Congress Cataloging-in-Publication Data
A C.I.P. cataloging record is available from the Library of Congress
LCCN 2017003364, https://lccn.loc.gov/2017003364

British Library Cataloguing in Publication Data

A catalogue record for this book is available from the British Library

ISBN 978-1-78533-542-6 (hardback)
ISBN 978-1-78920-091-1 (paperback)
EISBN 978-1-78533-543-3 (ebook)

Contents

List of Illustrations, Figures and Tables	vii
Acknowledgements	viii
Preface	ix

Introduction Privatizing the Public University: Key Trends, Countertrends and Alternatives 1
Cris Shore and Susan Wright

Part I: Redefining the Mission and Meaning of the University

Chapter 1 Universities in Britain and the Spirit of '45 31
John Morgan

Chapter 2 Managing the Third Mission: Reform or Reinvention of the Public University? 47
Nick Lewis and Cris Shore

Chapter 3 Universities in the Competition State: Lessons from Denmark 69
Susan Wright and Jakob Williams Ørberg

Chapter 4 Leadership in Higher Education: A Critical Feminist Perspective on Global Restructuring 90
Jill Blackmore

Part II: Performing the New University – New Priorities, New Subjects

Chapter 5 Science/Industry Collaboration: Bugs, Project Barons and Managing Symbiosis 117
Birgitte Gorm Hansen

Chapter 6 On Delivering the Consumer-Citizen: New Pedagogies and Their Affective Economies 138
Barbara M. Grant

Chapter 7 Tuning Up and Tuning In: How the European Bologna Process Is Influencing Students' Time of Study   156
Gritt B. Nielsen and Laura Louise Sarauw

Part III: Managing the Risk University – Research, Ranking and Reputation

Chapter 8 The Causes, Mechanisms and Consequences of Reputational Risk Management of Universities and the Higher Education Sector   175
Roger Dale

Chapter 9 The Rise and Rise of the Performance-Based Research Fund?   193
Bruce Curtis

Chapter 10 Evaluating Academic Research: Ambivalence, Anxiety and Audit in the Risk University   213
Lisa Lucas

Chapter 11 The Ethics of University Ethics Committees: Risk Management and the Research Imagination   229
Tamara Kohn and Cris Shore

Part IV: Reviving the Public University – Alternative Visions

Chapter 12 Who Will Win the Global Hunger Games? The Emerging Significance of Research Universities in the International Relations of States   253
Christopher Tremewan

Chapter 13 Resistance in the Neoliberal University   275
Sandra Grey

Chapter 14 The University as a Place of Possibilities: Scholarship as Dissensus   296
Sean Sturm and Stephen Turner

Chapter 15 Crisis, Critique and the Contemporary University: Reinventing the Future   312
Susan L. Robertson

Index   334

Illustrations, Figures and Tables

Illustrations

Illustration 2.1 Poster on the university library door advertising programmes in Innovation and Entrepreneurship. 61
Illustration 5.1 (A) *Lotus corniculatus*; (B) mature six-spotted burnet moth; (C) larva of a six-spotted burnet moth. 127
Illustration 7.1 Posters promoting the acquisition of employment skills in the common room, Faculty of Humanities, Copenhagen University. 163
Illustration 14.1 What is a Really Open University? 298
Illustration 14.2 *The Invisible College of the Rosy Cross Fraternity* by Theophilus Schweighardt, 1604. 300

Figures

Figure 12.1 Scholarly output (2015) and field-weighted citation impact (2015). 259

Tables

Table 9.1 Quality scores of PBRF Review Panels and the percentage of New Zealand-trained academics from the 2006 Quality Evaluation. 198
Table 9.2 Subject area by quality score (QS) from the 2006 Quality Evaluation. 199
Table 9.3 Changes to average quality scores and percentage of eligible staff between the 2003 and 2006 Quality Evaluations. 203
Table 9.4 Ten top subject areas from the 2006 and 2012 Quality Evaluations. 207
Table 9.5 Subject-area weightings. 208
Table 10.1 Profile of Interviewees. 220

Acknowledgements

There are too many people who have worked to make this book possible to thank them all by name. However, special mention should be given to Viktoria Hofbauer for her work in standardizing the chapters and copyediting the manuscript, and to Miri Davidson for her work in organizing the conferences and symposiums that provided much of the impetus for this volume.

Preface

This book has its origins in a four-year research project entitled 'University Reform, Globalisation and Europeanisation' (or 'URGE', to use its EU acronym). URGE was a multidisciplinary programme of knowledge exchange funded jointly by the European Commission (FP7 IRSES, 2009-247565) and the New Zealand Ministry of Research Science and Technology (MoRST). It examined how processes of regionalization and globalization were redefining the nature, scope and mission of universities. The partners were the Danish School of Education, Aarhus University, Denmark (Project Coordinator Professor Sue Wright), Graduate School of Education, University of Bristol, U.K. (Coordinator Professor Susan Robertson) and the European Institute, Auckland University (Coordinator Professor Cris Shore). Part of its aim was to make comparison between Europe and Australasia, especially New Zealand, and ask, what is actually going on in apparently similar processes of university reform? Are processes of creating a European Higher Education Area not only preparing Europe for global competition but also acting as a model and motor for globalization in other regions? How do academics engage with such processes of university reform? How are these processes affecting their conduct, their work and their ideas of the very purpose of universities?

Starting in January 2010 and lasting for four years, URGE involved twenty-five members of staff from the three universities in a series of visits, workshops, conferences, publications and future research initiatives aimed at exchanging knowledge and forging long-lasting research partnerships. The project was highly successful and generated twenty-four research seminars, five Ph.D. courses and eleven conferences and workshops, resulting in nine working papers and over forty published articles. This volume, in many respects, represents the culmination of that project. Five of those working papers were of particular importance in advancing the ideas and methodologies that frame the book and so deserve particular mention:[1] 'Toward a New Conceptual Framework' (WP 20), by Susan Robertson et al., set out a theoretical framework for mapping and tracking the key changes that are reshaping higher education globally; 'Methodologies for Studying University Reform and Globalization: Combining Ethnography and Political

Economy', by Cris Shore and Miri Davidson et al. (WP 21), explored how to bring together macro-level perspectives of university reform with more micro-level analyses based on empirical and often experiential research; 'European Coordination and Globalisation' (WP 22), by Roger Dale, looked at the Bologna Process and its ripple effects within and beyond Europe; 'Shooting Arrows – Disruptions, Intersections and Tracing Lines in Gender Research' (WP 23), by Kirsten Locke, explored the gender dimensions of university reform and globalization; and 'Research Assessment Systems and their Impacts on Academic Work' (WP 24), by Susan Wright et al., made in-depth comparisons of the various research evaluation systems and their effects on universities. Together, these working papers provided the bedrock for the ideas with which this book engages, taking them in new directions. The URGE project officially ended in 2014 but the ideas and collaborations that it created have continued, including under the auspices of a new EU-funded Ph.D. training network (or ITN) entitled 'Universities in the Knowledge Economy' (UNIKE).[2]

Notes

1. See http://edu.au.dk/forskning/projekter/afsluttede-projekter/urge/
2. See http://unike.au.dk.

INTRODUCTION
Privatizing the Public University
Key Trends, Countertrends and Alternatives

CRIS SHORE AND SUSAN WRIGHT

◆◆◆

Since the 1980s, public universities have undergone a seemingly unending series of reforms designed to make them more responsive both to markets and to government priorities. Initially, the aim behind these reforms was to render universities more economic, efficient and effective. However, by the 1990s, prompted by the Organization for Economic Cooperation and Development (OECD 1998) and other international agencies, many national governments adopted the idea that the future lay in a 'global knowledge economy'. To these ends, they implemented policies to repurpose higher education as the engine for producing the knowledge, skills and graduates to generate the intellectual property and innovative products that would make their countries more globally competitive. These reforms were premised on neoliberal ideas about turning universities into autonomous and entrepreneurial 'knowledge organizations' by promoting competition, opening them up to private investors, making educational services contribute to economic competitiveness, and enabling individuals to maximize their skills in global labour markets. These policy narratives position universities as static entities within an all-encompassing market economy, but alternatively, the university can be seen as a dynamic and fluid set of relations within a wider 'ecology' of diverse interests and organizations (Hansen this volume; Wright 2016). The boundaries of the university are constantly being renegotiated as its core values and distinctive purpose rub up against those predatory market forces, or what Slaughter and Leslie (1997) term 'academic capitalism'. Under pressure to produce 'excellence', quality research and innovative teaching, improve world rankings, forge business links and attract elite, fee-paying students, many universities struggle to maintain their traditional mandate to be 'inclusive', foster social cohesion, improve social mobility and challenge received wisdom – let alone improve the poor records on gender, diversity and equality.

This book examines how public universities engage with these dilemmas and the implications for the future of the public university as an ideal and set of institutional practices. The book has arisen from a four-year programme of knowledge exchange between three research groups in Europe and the Asia Pacific, which focused on the future of public universities in contexts of globalization and regionalization.[1] The groups were based in the U.K. and Denmark, chosen as European countries whose public universities have quite different histories and current reform policies, and New Zealand, as a country at the forefront of developing 'entrepreneurial' public universities, and with networks to other university researchers in Australia and Asia. Through a series of six workshops, four conferences and over thirty individual exchange visits, the project developed an extended discussion between the three groups of researchers. This enabled us to generate a new approach and methodology for analysing the challenges facing public universities. As a result, this book asks:

- How are higher education institutions being reconfigured as 'entrepreneurial' and as 'knowledge' organizations, and with what effects?
- In what ways are new management systems and governance regimes transforming the culture of academia?
- How are universities responding to these often contradictory policy agendas?
- How are national and international reforms impacting on the social purposes of the university and its relationship to society?
- What possibilities are there for challenging current trends and developing alternative university futures?

Mapping the Major Trends

Nowhere are the above trends more evident than in the English-speaking universities, particularly in the U.K., Australia and New Zealand. These countries have been a laboratory for testing out a new model of the neoliberal entrepreneurial university. At least seven key features characterize these reforms.

1. State Disinvestment in Universities – or Risk-free Profits for Private Providers?

The first feature is a progressive withdrawal of government support for higher education. In the U.K., for example, the Dearing Report (1997) showed that during the previous twenty years, a period of massive university expansion, state funding per student had declined by 40 percent. While Tony Blair's New Labour government of 1997 proclaimed 'education, education, education' as its key priority, it did so by introducing cost-sharing, in the form of student tuition fees, as a way to reduce the annual deficit in the funding of university teaching. In 2010, the British Conservative–Liberal government under David Cameron went even further by removing all state funding for teaching except in the STEM subjects (science, technology, engineering and mathematics). Instead, students were now to pay fees of £9,000 per annum (a three-fold increase) for which state-funded loans were made available. From the government's perspective, the genius of this shifting of state funding from teaching to loans was that private for-profit education providers could now access taxpayers' money – and this transfer of funds was further justified ideologically as providing competition and creating a 'level playing field' between public and private education providers.

Other countries have also decided to withdraw state funding for higher education. For example, in September 2015, Japan's education minister Hakobyan Shimomura wrote to all of the country's eighty-six national universities calling on them to 'take active steps to abolish [social science and humanities] organizations or to convert them to serve areas that better meet society's needs' (Grove 2015b). These measures echo the wider global trend set by advocates of Milton Friedman and the Chicago School's brand of neoliberal economics. In the 1980s, the 'Chicago boys' carried out their most radical experiments in Chile, removing the state's direct grants to universities, funding teaching only through students' tuition fees, and making government loans available to students so that they could pay those fees (Bekhradnia 2015). In the United States, the same policies have been adopted. For example, in California between 1984 and 2004, state spending per capita on higher education declined by 12 percent. Significantly, in the same period per capita spending on prisons increased by 126 percent (Newfield 2008: 266). Between the 1970s and 1990s there was a 400 percent increase in charges in tuition, room and board in U.S. universities and tuition costs have grown at about ten times the rate of family income (ibid.). What these instances highlight is not just the state's retreat from direct funding of higher education but also a calculated initiative to enable private companies to capture and profit from tax-funded student loans.

2. New Regimes for Promoting Competitiveness

A second major trend that has reshaped higher education has been the creation of funding and assessment regimes designed to increase productivity and competition between universities, both nationally and globally. What began in the 1980s as an exercise to assure the 'quality' of research in British universities had morphed, by the end of the 1990s, into ever-more invasive systems for ranking institutions, disciplines, departments, and even individuals. The results were used to allocate funds to those institutions that performed best in what has become a fetishistic quest for ever-higher ratings and 'world class' status, or what Hazelkorn (2008: 209) has termed the 'rankings arms-race'. Where some rankings are focused on research performance (such as the U.K.'s Research Excellence Framework, the Excellence in Research for Australia, and New Zealand's Performance Based Research Framework), others rank whole institutions (the Shanghai Jiao Tong Index, the QS and THE World University Rankings). Significantly, these ranking systems have especially negative impacts on minority groups and women (see Blackmore, Curtis, Grant and Lucas, this volume). This obsession with auditing and measuring performance also includes systems for evaluating teaching quality, surveying student satisfaction and measuring student engagement.[2] Even though vice chancellors and university managers ridicule ranking methodologies, they have learned to their cost to take them extremely seriously, as the financial viability of a university increasingly hinges on the reputational effects of these measures of performance (Sauder and Espeland 2009; Wright 2012).

3. Rise of Audit Culture: Performance and Output Measures

Third, running alongside the growth of these ranking systems has been the proliferation of performance and output measurements and indicators designed to foster transparency, efficiency and 'value for money'. This is part of a wider phenomenon called 'audit culture' and its growing presence throughout the public and private sectors, including higher education (Shore and Wright 2015; Strathern 2000). Driven by financial imperatives and the rhetoric of 'value for money' – and justified by a political discourse about the virtues of transparency and accountability – these technologies have been particularly instrumental in promoting the logics of risk management, financialization and managerialism (see Dale, and Lewis and Shore, this volume). In Denmark, time has become a key metric and instrument for the efficient throughput of students and the accountability of institutions, but as Nielsen and Sarauw (this volume) show, these measures affect the very nature of education. Audits do not simply or passively measure performance; they actively reshape the institutions into which they are introduced (Power 1997; Shore and Wright 2015). When a measurement becomes a target, institutional environments are restructured so that they focus their resources and activities primarily on what 'counts' to funders and governors rather than on their wider professional ethics and societal goals (see Kohn and Shore, this volume).

4. Administrative Bloat, Academic Decline

The fourth key development during this period has been the extraordinary growth in the number and status of university managers and administrators. For the first time in history, as figures from the U.K.'s Higher Education Statistics Agency (HESA) show, support staff now outnumber academic staff at 71 percent of higher education institutions (Jump 2015). In Denmark, there has been an equally large increase in the number of administrators and the increased percentage of annual expenditure on administrators in just five years alone was equivalent to 746 new lectureships (Wright and Boden 2010). The figures from the U.S. are even more dramatic. Federal figures for the period 1987 to 2011/2012 show that the number of college and university administrators and professional employees has more than doubled in the last twenty-five years; an increase of 517,636 people – or an average of eight-seven new administrators every working day (Marcus 2014). The recruitment of administrators has far outpaced the growth in the number of faculty – or even students. Meanwhile, universities claim to be struggling with budget crises that force them to reduce permanent academic posts, and the temporarily employed teaching assistants – the 'precariat' – have undergone a massive increase in numbers.

This astonishing increase in management and administration is partly due to the pressures universities now face to produce data and statistics for harvesting by the ranking industries. Universities themselves often attribute the growth of their administrative and technical units to the enormous rise in government regulations. As the President of the American Association of University Administrators recently explained, 'there are "thousands" of regulations governing the distribution of financial aid alone' and every university that is accredited probably has at least one person dedicated to that. However, the proliferation of administrators and managers has also been fuelled by the universities themselves, as they have taken on new functions and pursued new income streams. This is particularly evident in the U.S.:

> Since 1987, universities have also started or expanded departments devoted to marketing, diversity, disability, sustainability, security, environmental health, recruiting, technology and fundraising, and added new majors and graduate and athletics programs, satellite campuses, and conference centers (Marcus 2014).

These trends are captured with exceptional clarity in Benjamin Ginsberg's book, *The Fall of the Faculty* (2011a). Ginsberg's thesis is that the new professional managers 'make administration their life's work', to the detriment of the universities' core functions. They have little or no faculty experience and promoting teaching and research is less important than expanding their own administrative domains: 'under their supervision, the means have become the end' (ibid.: 2). Every year, writes Ginsberg:

> hosts of administrators and staffers are added to college and university payrolls, even as schools claim to be battling budget crises that are forcing them to reduce the size of their full-time faculties. As a result, universities are filled with armies of functionaries—vice presidents, associate vice presidents, assistant vice presidents, provosts, associate provosts, vice provosts, assistant provosts, deans, deanlets, deanlings, each commanding staffers and assistants—who, more and more, direct the operations of every school. Backed by their administrative legions, university presidents and other senior administrators have been able, at most schools, to dispense with faculty involvement in campus management and, thereby to reduce the faculty's influence in university affairs (Ginsberg 2011a: 2).

One of the weaknesses in these statistics is that they fail to distinguish between administrative staff who support the teaching and research and those who do not. Support staff are crucial to enabling academics to carry out effective research, teaching and scholarship – the traditional mission of the university. Likewise, universities need managers who support academics in fulfilling these key functions of the university, but the statistics are rarely sufficiently refined to make these distinctions. Interestingly, many universities have dropped the term 'support staff' in favour of terms like 'senior administrators' and 'professional staff'. This move reflects the way that many university managers now see their role – which is no longer to provide support for academics but, rather, to manage them as 'human capital' and a resource. From the perspective of many university managers and human resources (HR) departments, academics are increasingly portrayed as a reluctant, unruly and undisciplined workforce that needs to be incentivized or cajoled to meet management's targeted outputs and performance indicators.

5. Institutional Capture: the Power of the 'Administeriat'

The budgetary reallocation from academic to administrative salaries is linked to a fifth major trend: the rise of the 'administeriat' as a new governing class and the corresponding shift in power relations within the university. Whereas in the past the main cleavage in universities was between the arts and the sciences, or what C.P. Snow (1956) famously termed 'the two cultures', today the main division is between academics and managers. Collini (2013) attributes this shift in power to the way all university activities are now reduced to a common managerial metric. As he puts it, the 'terms that suit [managers'] activities are the terms that have triumphed'. Scholars now spend increasing amounts of their working day accounting for their activities in the 'misleading' and 'alienating' language and categories of managers. This 'squeezing out' of the true use-value of scholarly labour accounts for the 'pervasive sense of malaise, stress and disenchantment within British universities' (Collini 2013).

Professor of Critical Management Studies Rebecca Boden compares the way that university managers expand their increasingly onerous regulations to the way that 'cuckoos lay their eggs in the nests of other birds, and how the young cuckoos then evict the nest-builders' offspring' (cited in Havergal 2015). This cuckoo-in-the-nest metaphor might seem somewhat overblown, but it highlights the important fact that managers and administrators have usurped power in what were formerly more collegial, self-governing institutions. Yet many of these managers would not succeed as professionals in industry. Levin and Greenwood (2016) argue that, if universities were indeed business corporations, they would soon collapse, as their work organization currently violates nearly every one of the practices that characterize successful and dynamic high-tech areas and service industries. It is a short step from here to managers' appropriation of the identity of the university, with managers increasingly claiming not only to speak for the university but to be the university (Ørberg 2007; Readings 1996; Shore and Taitz 2010). Today, rather than being treated as core members of a professional community, academics are constantly being told by managers and senior administrators what 'the university' expects of them, as if they were somehow peripheral or subordinate to 'the university'.

6. New Income Streams and the Rise of the 'Entrepreneurial University'

Faced with diminishing state funding and year-on-year cuts to national budgets for higher education, universities have been compelled to seek alternative income streams. This has entailed fostering more lucrative and entrepreneurial partnerships with industry; conducting commissioned research for businesses and government; partnering up with venture capitalists; commercializing the university's intellectual property through patents and licences; developing campus spin-out (and spin-in) companies; engaging proactively in city development programmes; and maximizing university assets including real estate, halls of residence, conference facilities and industrial parks. Equally important has been the raising of student tuition fees and the relentless drive to recruit more high-fee-paying international students. This project has given rise to the moniker 'export education', a sector of the economy and foreign-currency earner of growing importance to many countries. For example, in Canada, expenditures of international education students (tuition, accommodation, living costs and so on) infused $6.5 billion into the Canadian economy, surpassing exports of coniferous lumber (CAN$5.1 billion) and coal (CAN$6.1 billion) and gave employment to 83,00 Canadians (Roslyn Kunin and Associates, Inc 2009). Similarly, 'educational services' has become one of Australia's leading export industries such that, by 2008, it had become Australia's third-largest generator of export earnings with over AU$12.6 billion (Olds 2008). Along with Australia and Canada, the U.S.A., U.K. and New Zealand dominate the trade in international students (OECD 2011; chart 3.3) and the global demand for international student places is estimated to rise to 5.8 million by 2020 (Bohm et al. 2004).

The relentless pursuit of these new income streams has had a transformative effect on universities. Almost two decades ago Marginson and Considine (2000) coined the term the 'enterprise university' to describe the model in which:

> the economic and academic dimensions are both subordinated to something else. Money is a key objective, but it is also the means to a

more fundamental mission: to advance the prestige and competitiveness of the university as an end in itself (ibid. 2000: 5).

However, it would be misleading to suggest that all these changes are simply a consequence of the pressures that governments have placed on universities to refashion themselves as pseudo-business corporations. Some of the more entrepreneurially hawkish university rectors, vice chancellors and presidents have enthusiastically welcomed these changes. Many have benefitted from the enormous executive salaries that have become the norm for university 'CEOs', and they undoubtedly enjoy their vaulted status and the opportunities this provides to mingle with world leaders at prestigious summits and receptions, airport VIP lounges and gala fundraising events. For example, the *Times Higher Education* annual review of vice chancellors' pay shows that average salary and benefits for university vice chancellors in the U.K. rose by between £8,397 and £240,794 in 2013–2014. This constituted a 3.6 percent rise, whereas in the same period, other university staff received an increase of only 1 per cent (Grove 2015a). A study by economists Bachan and Reilly (2015), from Brighton Business School, found that in the past two decades, vice chancellors have seen their salaries soar by an eye-watering 59 percent (Henry 2015), but concluded that these increases could not be justified in terms of their university's performance criteria, such as widening participation or bringing in income such as grants for teaching and research and capital funding. Rather, the study found that the presence of other high-paid administrative staff was pushing up vice chancellors' pay. Both the U.K.'s House of Commons' Public Accounts Committee and the former Minister for Business and Employment, Vince Cable, have condemned this 'substantial upward drift' of salaries among vice chancellors. However, this annual ritual of chastisement has little perceivable impact.

7. Higher Education as Private Investment Versus Public Good

The seventh major trend is recasting university education as a private and positional investment rather than a public good. The idea that gained prominence in the post-war era was that higher education was a public investment that benefits the economy and society as well as contributing to personal growth and social mobility (Morgan this volume). In the 1990s, this idea – and the Keynesian model that sustained it – was displaced by the Chicago School's economic doctrine and the notion that individuals, not the state, should take responsibility for repeatedly investing in their education and skills in order to sustain and improve their position in a fast-changing competitive and global labour market. This is what the OECD termed 'new human capital theory' (Henry et al. 2001), an idea that came to dominate government thinking about growth and investment. However, several recent studies challenge the premises upon which this model is based (Ashton, Lauder and Brown 2011; Wright and Ørberg this volume).

Arising from this new way of conceptualizing higher education as a private individual good and the reduction of government funding for the sector, has been the replacement of student grants with loans. This has been coupled with a massive hike in student fees – or what is euphemistically called 'cost-sharing' by ministers and World Bank experts. There are several bizarre paradoxes in this way of financing higher education. First, as McGettigan (2013) shows, government funding of student loans to pay fees is likely to cost the taxpayer more than the previous system of funding universities directly for their teaching. Second, as Vernon (2010) points out, most students and their families can only afford to pay for the costs of their higher education through the kinds of debt-financing that governments across the world now condemn as reckless and inappropriate for themselves. Third, whereas the scale of national debt in many countries has become so severe that it has required emergency austerity measures to combat, the level of household debt is even more perilously high, peaking to 110 percent of GDP in 2009 in the U.K. (Jones 2013). This was before the government transferred even more of the costs of higher education to families and tripled university fees. These policies are justified on the grounds that degree-holders gain a lifetime premium in earning: hence the catchphrase 'learn to earn'. In New Zealand, however, which has the seventh-highest university fees among developed countries, the OECD survey found that the value of a university degree in terms of earning power is the lowest in the world. The net value of a New Zealand tertiary education for a man is just $63,000 over his working life (compared with $395,000 in the U.S.). For a woman, it is even lower: $38,000 over her working life (Edmunds 2012). As Brown and Hesketh (2004) also show for the U.S., graduates' imagined future incomes are largely illusory. Yet students and parents are encouraged to take out what is effectively a 'subprime loan', in the gamble that it will eventually pay off by enhancing their future job prospects and earning power: it is a 'hedge against their future security' (Vernon 2008). In other words, higher education is now being modelled on the same types of financial speculation that produced the 2010 global financial crisis.

The Death of the Public University?

Do the seven trends outlined above spell the end of the public university? From the earliest beginnings of these developments, there has been an extensive literature foretelling the demise of the university. According to historians Sheldon Rothblatt and Bjorn Wittrock (1993: 1), the university is the second-longest unbroken institution in Western civilization, after the Catholic Church. Today, however, the university – or what John Henry Newman termed the 'idea of a university' – does indeed look broken. Or is this an unduly pessimistic conclusion? Jean-Francoise Lyotard set the agenda with his provocative book *The Postmodern Condition: A Report on Knowledge*. Noting the collapse of the university's traditional authority in producing legitimate knowledge, he wrote:

> The question (overt or implied) now asked by the professionalist student, the State, or institutions of higher education is no long 'Is it true?' but 'What use is it?' In the context of the mercantilization of knowledge, more often than not this question is equivalent to: 'Is it saleable?' And in the context of power-growth: 'Is it efficient?' (Lyotard 1994: 51).

Following this line of reasoning, Bill Readings' book *The University in Ruins* (1996), noted both the decline of the university as the cultural arm of nation building and the administrators' eclipse of the scholar-teacher as the central figure in the university story. As he gloomily argued, the grand narrative of the university 'centred on the production of a liberal reasoning subject is no longer readily available to us (1996: 9). If, for Readings, the university was in a state of 'ruin', for David Mills, writing in 2003, it is locked in a state of permanent 'scaffolding'; an ongoing and ambiguous project of both maintenance and repair, construction and demolition. Thus 'crumbling bastions of social and intellectual elitism' are combined 'with shiny new campuses espousing lifelong access to 24/7 education for all' (Mills 2003). These contradictory trends have both positive and negative dimensions for universities and the project of higher education. On the one hand, access to universities has been massively increased and technological innovations, including Mass Open Online Courses (MOOCs), have allowed more distance learning. But on the other hand, universities and their staff have been subjected to an almost continuous process of reforms and restructurings designed both to recast higher education institutions as transnational business corporations and to open up the sector to more private-sector involvement.

The complaint often voiced by academics is that universities – like hospitals, libraries and other local community services – are undergoing a process of 'death by a thousand cuts'. But chronic underfunding of public institutions also reflects a wider and arguably more purposeful political agenda that aims to fundamentally transform the public sector. One of the greatest threats to the university today lies in the 'unbundling' of its various research, teaching and degree-awarding functions into separate, profit-making activities that can then be outsourced and privatized. This agenda is articulated clearly in the recent report entitled 'An Avalanche is Coming: Higher Education and the Revolution Ahead' (Barber et al. 2013), published by the London-based think tank, the Institute for Public Policy Research. Its principal authors are Sir Michael Barber, Chief Education Advisor for Pearson PLC (a British-owned multinational education provider and publisher) and two of Pearson's executive directors. The report's central argument, captured in its 'avalanche' metaphor, is that the current system of higher education is untenable and will be swept away unless bold and radical steps are taken:

> The next 50 years could see a golden age for higher education, but only if all the players in the system, from students to governments, seize the initiative and act ambitiously. If not, an avalanche of change will sweep the system away. Deep, radical and urgent transformation is required in higher education. The biggest risk is that as a result of complacency, caution or anxiety the pace of change is too slow and the nature of change is too incremental. The models of higher education that marched triumphantly across the globe in the second half of the 20th century are broken (Barber, Donnelly and Rizvi 2013: 5).

A series of forces that lie 'under the surface' threatens to transform the landscape of higher education. These include: a changing world economy in which the centre of gravity is shifting towards the Asia-Pacific region; a global economy still struggling to recover from the trauma of the global financial crash of 2007–2008; and the escalating costs of higher education, which are vastly outstripping inflation and household income. These are coupled with the declining value of a degree and a technological shift that makes information ubiquitous. Universities no longer hold a monopoly over knowledge production and distribution and face growing competition from the emergence of new universities and from 'entirely new models of university' that Pearson itself has been spearheading to exploit the new environment of globalization and the digital revolution (ibid. 2013: 9–21).

The Barber report is part of a growing literature which seeks to 'remake the university' as an altogether different kind of institution (see Bokor 2012). Epochal and prophetic in tone and often claiming to be diagnostic and neutral, this literature proposes solutions that are anything but impartial or disinterested. Pearson, for example, makes no secret of its ambition to acquire a larger share of the higher education market and the rents that can be captured from its various activities. In 2015, Pearson sold off its major publishing interests to restructure the company around for-profit educational provision both in England and worldwide. Pearson also has a primary listing on the London Stock Exchange and a secondary listing on the New York Stock Exchange. Writing in the preface to the Barber reports, former president of Harvard University Lawrence Summers underscores its central ambition when he writes that in this new 'phase of competitive intensity', all of the university's core functions can be 'unbundled and increasingly supplied, perhaps better, by providers that are not universities at all' (Barber 2013: 1). As John Morgan (this volume) shows, higher education has long been – and continues to be – a site of ideological struggle between competing interests and their vision of society.

Towards the Privatization of English Universities

In England, these processes have been taken to an extreme. Events since the Conservative–Liberal coalition took office in 2010 suggest a tipping point may have been reached in the transformation of the public university. Research by the legal firm Eversheds (2009) revealed that no legislation was needed for public universities to be transferred to the private for-profit sector, either by a management buyout or by outside interests buying-in (Wright 2015). London Metropolitan University was an early contender. It advertised a tender worth £74 million over five years for a partner who would create a for-profit 'special services vehicle' to deliver all the university's functions and services – everything except academic teaching and the Vice Chancellor's powers. Such 'special services vehicles' are a way for private investors to buy into the university's activities. This plan was only stymied because civil servants found major administrative failings, and the resulting fines and repayments pushed the university close to bankruptcy. But this 'special services vehicle' model has been implemented by other universities, including Falmouth and Exeter, where a private company runs not only catering, estate maintenance and services on the two campuses, but also its entire academic support services (libraries, IT, academic skills and disability support services) (University and College Union 2013).

London Metropolitan's near-bankruptcy opened the possibility of a second method of privatization; a 'fire sale' of a university and its prized degree-awarding powers, to one of the many U.S. for profit education providers that had been seeking entry into the market (Wright 2015). Privatization was only avoided thanks to the successful actions of its new Vice Chancellor. However, one university with a charter and degree-awarding powers has been transferred to the for-profit sector. In 2006, the Department of Business, Innovation and Science rushed through approval to give the College of Law in London degree-awarding powers and university status. This was just in time for its sale to finance company Montagu Private Equity. To maintain that university's charitable (tax-favourable) status and provide bursaries for students, the institution divided itself into a for-profit company with all the education and training activities, and an educational foundation. Montagu Private Equity made a leveraged buyout of the university: £177 million of the £200 million purchase price was borrowed and then put on the university's balance sheet, making it responsible for paying the debt and interest from its cash flow. A few years later, Montagu announced it was selling the university's buildings, in what was a clear case of asset stripping. The legal firm Eversheds recommended that other public universities follow this model and either sell stakes in their institution or be sold outright to financiers. As the University of Law example shows, such investors' prime interest is the short-term extraction of profit and liquidization of assets, rather the long-term future of higher education. Indeed, in June 2015, Montagu sold the University of Law to Aaron Etingen, founder and chief executive officer of Global University Systems (GUS), which owns a network of for-profit colleges worldwide (Morgan 2015).

The Etingen family is in the forefront of a third model for privatizing English higher education. This relies on access to the state-funded loans for student tuition fees. From 2010, private colleges were authorized to provide two-year, subdegree level courses, which made their students eligible to access student loans up to £6,000 per annum. The number of such courses rose from 157 in 2009–2010 to 403 in 2011–2012 and the cost of loans for students at private colleges rose from £30 million in 2010 to £1 billion in 2014. The Etingen family's Global University

Systems owns two such colleges. St Patrick's International College was too small in 2011–2012 to register for student loans. However, a year later it had 4,000 students delivering an income of £11 million in publicly funded loans. Its other college, the London School of Business and Finance (LSBF) had 1,354 students on publicly backed loans. To get international students LSBF made a financial arrangement with Glyndwr University in Wales (which had acquired university status in 2008, and three other English universities. Glyndwr sponsored its students' immigration visas and the LSBF provided the teaching and collected tuition fees. However, a Home Office investigation of visa fraud found 230 students sponsored by Glyndwr had invalid results, resulting in the suspension of the English-language testing company it had used. Tax records revealed that 290 foreign students at LSBF had been working instead of studying. It also found that 57 private colleges and several universities that had set up branch offices in London were misusing their licenses to sponsor students. An ensuing fraud investigation resulted in 63 colleges subsequently losing their designation and thus their students' access to loans. Government then gave Pearson the task of finding new institutions for the students affected by the de-designation of their courses – even though it was Pearson that had validated one quarter of these subdegree courses in the first place (Morgan 2014a and b).

Another key player is the private equity fund Sovereign Capital, whose cofounder John Nash (a former chairman of the British Venture Capital Association and cofounder of a charity sponsoring the development of privatized academies), advised the government on public sector reform. In 2013, he was appointed Parliamentary Under-secretary of State for Schools and elevated to a peerage as Baron Nash in the House of Lords. Sovereign Capital bought Greenwich School of Management in 2011, expanding its operation from 496 students to 3,366 students in 2012–2013, and growing its income from government-backed student loans to £11 million. The main qualifications for students at these two-year colleges were the Edexcel exam board – which is owned by Pearson. Building on income from these exam fees, Pearson set up its own college and then added a third year, which was recognized for degrees by Royal Holloway, London University. Without passing any legislation, public higher education in England is thus being stealthily privatized – either through taxpayer-funded risk-free capitalism or by asset stripping – as global capital seeks out new sources of revenue and investment (Wright 2015).

Challenges to Privatization

The explosive growth of private universities in the United States is based on a similar model of the private capture of publicly funded student loans. According to recent Federal figures, for-profit colleges enrolled only 12 percent of the country's students, but they accounted for almost half of all student loan defaults in 2013 (Gillespie 2015). The University of Phoenix has arguably the most rapacious and notorious business model. Owned by the Apollo Education Group, Phoenix was the United States' largest for-profit university. Its business model involved strenuous selling to socially disadvantaged and underqualified people eager to gain a degree to improve their life chances. A scathing 2004 U.S. Department of Education investigation castigated its 'high pressure sales culture' that rewarded recruiters who 'put most arses in classes' (Hotson 2011). Despite such criticism, Phoenix continued these practices. Having paid their fees and started classes, many students were unable to cope and dropped out, thereby acquiring a lifelong student debt rather than a qualification. Between 2008 and 2010, for example, 60.5 percent of Phoenix's students dropped out and, in 2008, 20.8 percent had defaulted on their loans (United States Senate Committee 2012: 285). To keep wages down, an astonishing 96 percent of faculty were part-time (ibid: 290) and their contracts were not confirmed until the dropout period was over. A course at Phoenix cost $24,500 compared to $4,087 for an equivalent course at a community college (U.S. Senate 2012: 281). In 2009, Phoenix spent only $892 on each student', whereas $2,225 went on marketing and recruitment and $2,535 profit was made (ibid: 289); this allowed $8.6 million remuneration for founder and chairman John Sperling – a sum thirteen times greater than the salary of the president of the University of Arizona (2012: 279).

Phoenix has been a focus of continuous criticism. For example, a U.S. federal jury in 2008 found Apollo guilty of 'knowingly and recklessly' misleading investors and instructed the group to pay shareholders $280 in reparations (Hotson 2011). A U.S. accreditation body later put the university on probation because the Apollo Group had given Phoenix insufficient autonomy to 'assure the university's integrity', 'exercise its fiduciary responsibilities' and 'fulfil its mission' (*Times Higher Education* 2013). The damning conclusion of the U.S. Senate report was that 'Apollo had prioritized financial success over student success' (2012: 292).

By 2015, with private providers unable to shake off such criticisms, President Obama announced an initiative to make community colleges, their main competitor, free of charge for the first two years (Executive Office of the President 2015; Smith 2015). Even before the America's College Promise Act was passed, eleven states had proposed similar legislative initiatives, thus torpedoing the business model of the for-profit providers. Phoenix's recruitment swiftly fell from 460,000 students in 2010 to 213,000 by 2015, and Apollo Education Group's revenues fell from $5 billion in 2010 to around $2.7 billion (Gillespie 2015). The path towards privatization, it seems, is not without bumps and upheavals.

The move to privatize higher education is not universal either. In Europe, Norway has enshrined free higher education in law. In Germany, after the Federal Constitutional Court ruled in 2005 that moderate fees were permissible, seven of Germany's ten federal states (*Länder*) introduced tuition fees in 2006–2007. Yet within one electoral cycle, this seemingly inevitable and inexorable change has been overturned – largely as a result of student demonstrations supported by voters' ensuring that those politicians who favoured the policy lost office. Now the *Länder* have passed legislation banning tuition fees (Hotson 2014).

In Chile, once 'the canary in the privatisation coalmine' (González 2013), a process is now underway to bring higher education back under public control. During the 1980s and 1990s, Chile's military government introduced the by-now familiar neoliberal formula of opening the sector to private, for-profit providers, differentiating and ranking institutions, and transferring the cost of state-financed institutions to students (Brunner 1993). In 2011, students took to the streets to demonstrate against increasing tuition fees and high interest rates on loans as well as the highly segmented and underfunded system that the free market had produced. Students and school children sustained their protests for over a year. As a result, thorough reforms of the whole education system from universities to preschools became one of the key promises of a new government, which vowed a 'paradigm shift' to overturn the Chicago-inspired neoliberal reforms. Two of the student leaders were elected as members of parliament and one of them helped lead the parliamentary committee charged with devising Chile's new system of public education, while dissatisfied students, taking to the streets, have continued to keep up the pressure for free quality education (Mackenzie 2014).

These developments – and the increasing level of dissatisfaction with neoliberal 'solutions' to the financial challenges facing universities – suggest that 'reports of the university's death have been greatly exaggerated'. However, if the public university has proved resilient to the more extreme predations of global capitalism (at least in some countries), it also appears increasingly vulnerable. For some authors, the 'death of the university' is a misleading aphorism, as the public university cannot be allowed to die; rather, it must continue to operate in order to keep generating income for its new stakeholders and owners. Dislocated, dismembered and progressively unbundled, the public university today exists in a state of chronic fragility, servitude and uncertainty that has left it if not 'dead', then permanently moribund and drained of autonomy and agency. This argument has been extensively developed in Andrew Whelan, Ruth Walker and Christopher Moore's (2013) recent book, *Zombies in the Academy: Living Death in Higher Education*. In what is a humorous yet also serious study, the authors use 'zombification' (or 'zombiedom') as a powerful metaphor for thinking about the changing conditions of university life. In the corporatized university environment shaped by narrowly defined metrics, instrumental research, and mind-numbing standardization, the language of zombie culture seems particularly appropriate: the universities have been overrun by a plague of managerialism and a virulent and seemingly unstoppable strain of 'administrivia' (Blackmore this volume). Academics operate under a kind of siege mentality that echoes the 'fall-behind-and-get-eaten' trope of the classical zombie movie.

Rethinking University Futures: Alternatives Models

Despite the many critiques of the demise of the public university and its privatization, there have been relatively few attempts to posit serious alternatives to the current neoliberal policy agenda and its seemingly inevitable trajectory (but see Robertson this volume). In countries where neoliberal rhetorics about choice and affordability have become doxic, even many students and parents have come to accept student loans and lifelong debt as an unavoidable fact of life. However, as McGettigan (2013) shows, the direction of English university reform represents a dangerous gamble with the national economy, a valued institution and, more importantly, the hopes and futures of younger generations. Yet this need not be the case. Gray (this volume) offers an alternative vision for organizing higher education based on benchmarks of equality, democracy and sustainability. There are numerous alternative ways to conceptualize and organize the university, from cooperatives, trusts and mutuals, to free universities and MOOCs. While some of these draw inspiration from Gibson-Graham's (2006) vision of a 'post-capitalist' future, not all of these alternatives require radical change to existing institutions.

One of the oldest cooperative universities is Mondragon in northern Spain, which started in 1997. While Mondragon arose from a highly particular regional cooperative movement, it nevertheless highlights some of the general features of what distinguishes a cooperative university (Wright, Greenwood and Boden 2011). These include: a flat rather than hierarchical structure in which each faculty is a cooperative nested within a wider university cooperative, with a small central administration of only six full-time employees; each employee is also a partner, who invests some of their income in the institution. Every employee is part of decision-making each year on how to distribute any surplus or deficit: should they increase their salaries or invest in new programmes to develop the university, and so on? This creates a very different engagement with the institution from that of the top-down, steered self-management of the 'responsibilized' neoliberal subject. In Britain, a network of academics is formulating ideas for a cooperative university drawing on that country's long-standing cooperative movement. At Lincoln University, the Social Science Centre is developing a model for a cooperative university, including a pedagogical framework, business plan, constitutional rules and a model for creating a federation of cooperative universities (Neary and Wynn 2015). The Manchester-based Cooperative College's commissioned report on 'Realising the Cooperative University' concluded that existing universities could be made into cooperatives without major changes to existing rules, although a wide 'cultural gulf' needs to be crossed for that to happen (Cook 2013). Even the U.K. Cabinet Office is now exploring how public sector employees can turn their activities into spin-offs organized as mutuals. However, its £10 million fund seems more designed to further unbundle and privatize public institutions along the lines criticized above, while appropriating the positive cache surrounding the term 'mutual'.

The trust university model, in this respect, is perhaps more robust than the cooperative model as cooperatives can easily be 'de-mutualized' – as witnessed in the realization of U.K. building societies' assets and their conversion into banks during the 1990s. This model is inspired by the U.K.'s highly successful commercial retail business, the John Lewis Partnership, with over 87,000 employees. 'Trust' has three meanings. First, a nonrevocable trust is a legal form of ownership which makes the assets inalienable (so it cannot be privatized, asset stripped or de-mutualized). Second, trust between management and workers is fostered through a clearly defined purpose and shared structures of governance. In the case of John Lewis, the goals of the organization do not mention making a profit; rather, the ultimate purpose is 'the happiness of all its members through their worthwhile and satisfying employment in a successful business' (John Lewis Partnership 2015). All employees are beneficiaries ('partners') of the trust and, via a substantial and formalized system of representative democracy, the employees are directly responsible for the success of the institution. Restraints on pay differentials between the highest- and lowest-paid employees prevent managers from rewarding themselves excessive salaries and appropriating the wealth of the organization. Unlike privatized businesses, trusts and cooperatives do not squander their organization's surpluses in the form of executive bonuses or shareholder dividends. Third, trust entails a different kind of social contract with the surrounding society, one that recognizes the public service role and responsibilities of academics (Boden, Ciancanelli and Wright 2012). Tremewan (this volume) provides an example of how universities could be much more proactive in fulfilling their social responsibilities by using their research to address points of conflict and build trust between countries.

Another alternative to the corporate business model are 'free universities'. These universities have sprung up at different times and places – including the University of California, Berkeley in the 1960s and more recently in Europe, Australia and North America – both in opposition to conventional institutions and forms of education and with an impetus to experiment with radical new modes of learning. Notable examples include the 'Really Open University' (Sturm and Turner, this volume), and the Ragged Universities in Glasgow and Manchester, which define themselves as being not about certificates, CVs or making money but about 'valuing knowledgeable people, exploring what is possible and creating something' using free knowledge exchange. Their venues include pubs, cafes, museums, libraries and other public spaces. Similarly, the 'IF Project' in London treats the capital as a 'giant lecture hall', collating free resources and events, and adding the best online lectures from internationally acclaimed academics. It targets nongraduates from eighteen to thirty, enlisting academics to contribute 'shards' of their time to lecturing, tutoring or mentoring its humanities foundation course. In some respects, this resembles the University of the Third Age (U3A), but free universities usually have a more political agenda and experiment with pedagogies that seek to 'prefigure' the creation of a better (post-capitalist) world (Thompsett, forthcoming).

At present, these alternative higher education projects that attempt to make education free and open for everyone are small, disparate and precariously funded. While they exist outside of the university and have freed themselves from the blight of entrepreneurialism, managerialism and administrative bloat, they are often dependent on input from salaried academics. They are also no substitute for a properly funded public university system. However, they do illustrate some of the advantages of an education system freed from commercial imperatives: they inspire enthusiasm, are run collaboratively, are able to engage in creative, participatory teaching and learning, and are unencumbered by concerns about performance indicators and profit. In this respect, they highlight a fourth possible meaning of the word 'trust': a commitment to, and confidence in, higher education as a vehicle for creating a better future for all. As our examples illustrate, the for-profit and overmanaged corporatized public universities are typically 'low-trust' organizations characterized by a corrosive pessimism and exhausted progressive impulses. Perhaps all four meanings of the term 'trust' are needed to revive the public university: it may not be dead, but it cannot be allowed to continue in its zombified state.

Conclusion

In identifying current trends and challenges facing the public university, this introduction has already made reference to the chapters in the four sections that follow. The first section explores how the mission of the public university has been redefined in Europe and Australasia. Starting with a historical account and then focusing on contemporary developments, this section shows how the very meaning and boundaries of the public university are in the process of change. The second section analyses how the policy priorities for public universities generate new subject positions for academics and students, and four ethnographic studies show how these offer some people new opportunities and benefits for research and teaching while, for others, these changes are deeply contested. The third section explores the tasks of managing the competitive, entrepreneurial, efficient and flexible public university as an ever-increasing multitude of 'risks' become measurable and costed. University managers are faced with navigating their institutions' reputation, rankings and research performance and ensuring ethics procedures protect against any possible legal challenge. This section explores how these management instruments have developed in different countries, and how academics have engaged with these changes to their work and sense of professionalism. The final section brings together a growing number of initiatives to revive the public university, not by harking back to a golden-age-that-never-was, but by looking forwards to alternative visions for the role, organization and core research, teaching and public service activities of the university. As the concluding chapter argues, the challenge is to imagine and create alternative futures for universities whose purposes and outcomes are geared towards more societal rather than economic ends. Together, these chapters engage with global trends and discourses about university reform. They develop new ways of combining large-scale analysis of the political economy of universities in different regions with detailed local and ethnographic insights into the way that managers, academics and students engage with and contest these processes of change. These ethnographies show how academics and students not only have occasional success in resisting measures that they consider herald the death of the public university, but are also developing their own visions for what the public university of the future might look like.

◆

Cris Shore (D.Phil. in social anthropology, Sussex) is Professor of Social Anthropology at the University of Auckland, having previously worked at Goldsmiths College, London. His research interests include political anthropology, the study of organizations, power and corruption, higher education, the European Union and the anthropology of policy. Cris was founding editor of *Anthropology in Action*, founding director of Auckland University's Europe Institute and, with Sue Wright, is editor of Stanford University Press's book series, *Anthropology of Policy*. Current research includes a study of the 'Crown' in post-colonial settler societies and a book exploring how indicators and ranking are reassembling society.

Susan Wright (D.Phil. in social anthropology, Oxford) is Professor of Educational Anthropology at Aarhus University. She studies people's participation in large-scale processes of political transformation, working with concepts of audit culture, governance, contestation and policy. She coordinated the EU project 'University Reform, Globalisation and Europeanisation' and the EU ITN project 'Universities in the Knowledge Economy' in Europe and the Asia-Pacific Rim. She coedits (with Penny Welch) the journal *LATISS (Learning and Teaching: International Journal of Higher Education in the Social Sciences)* and recently published *Policy Worlds: Anthropology and the Anatomy of Contemporary Power* (coedited with Cris Shore and Davide Però, 2011, Berghahn).

Notes

1. The project, called URGE (University Reform, Globalization and Regionalization) was funded by the EU FP7 Marie Curie IRSES action, project number 247565, 2010–2014. The records of the URGE project and the URGE working papers are available at http://edu.au.dk/forskning/projekter/afsluttede-projekter/urge/
2. A notable countermeasure is the EU's 'U-Multirank' system which was specifically designed not to produce an overall ranking: instead, students choose their own criteria for finding the university that best meets their expectations.

References

Ashton, D., H. Lauder and P. Brown. 2011. *The Global Auction: The Broken Promises of Education, Jobs, and Incomes*. Oxford: Oxford University Press.

Bachan, R. and B. Reilly. 2015. 'Is UK Vice Chancellor Pay Justified by University Performance?', *Fiscal Studies* 36(1): 51–73.

Barber, M., K. Donnelly, and S. Rizvi. 2013. 'An Avalanche is Coming: Higher Education and the Revolution ahead', London: Institute for Public Policy Research, March 2013. Retrieved 10 February 2016 from http://www.studynet2.herts.ac.uk/intranet/lti.nsf/0/684431DD8106AF1680257B560052BCCC/$FILE/avalanche-is-coming_Mar2013_10432.pdf.

Bekhradnia, B. 2015. 'Chile steps back from bitter market fruits', *Times Higher Education*, 15 January. https://www.timeshighereducation.com/comment/opinion/chile-steps-back-from-bitter-market-fruits/2017895.article

Boden, R., P. Ciancanelli and S. Wright. 2012. 'Trust Universities? Governance for Post-Capitalist Futures', *Journal of Cooperative Studies* 45(2): 16–24.

Bohm, A., et al. 2004. *Vision 2020: Forecasting International Student Mobility. A UK Perspective*. London: British Council.

Bokor, J. 2012. 'University of the Future: A thousand year old industry on the cusp of profound change.' *Ernst and Young report. Australia: Ernst and Young*.

Brown, P., and A. Hesketh. 2004. *The Mismanagement of Talent: Employability and Jobs in the Knowledge Economy*. Oxford: Oxford University Press.

Brunner, J.J. 1993. 'Chile's Higher Education: Between Market and State', *Higher Education* 25(1): 35–43.

Collini, S. 2013. 'Sold Out', *London Review of Books* 35(20): 3–12. Retrieved 10 February 2016 from http://www.lrb.co.uk/v35/n20/stefan-collini/sold-out.

Cook, D. 2013 'Realising the Co-operative University: A consultancy report for The Co-operative College, September.' Retrieved 27 October 2016 from http://josswinn.org/wp-content/uploads/2013/12/realising-the-co-operative-university-for-disemmination.pdf.

Dearing, R. 1997. 'Higher Education in the Learning Society', Report of the National Committee of Enquiry into Higher Education, Norwich: HMSO.

Edmunds, S. 2012. 'Our Degrees Don't Repay Their Cost', *New Zealand Herald*, 30 September. Retrieved 10 February 2016 from http://www.nzherald.co.nz/business/news/article.cfm?c_id=3&objectid=10837419.

Executive Office of the President. 2015. 'America's College Promise: A Progress Report on Free Community College', September. Retrieved 10 February 2016 from https://www.whitehouse.gov/sites/default/files/docs/progressreporton communitycollege.pdf.
Gibson-Graham, J.K. 2006. *A Postcapitalist Politics*. Minneapolis: University of Minnesota Press.
Gillespie, P. 2015. 'University of Phoenix has lost half its students', *CNN Money*, 25 March, Retrieved 8 February 2016 from http://money.cnn.com/2015/03/25/investing/university-of-phoenix-apollo-earnings-tank/.
Ginsberg, B. 2011a. *The Fall of the Faculty: The Rise of the All-Administrative University and Why it Matters*. Oxford: Oxford University Press.
González, C. 2013. 'Higher education: A canary in a privatisation coalmine', *University World News* 295 (November). Grove.
Grove, J. 2015a. 'Times Higher Education Pay Survey 2015', *Times Higher Education*, 2 April. Retrieved 8 February 2016 from https://www.timeshighereducation.com/features/times-higher-education-pay-survey-2015/2019360.article.
———. 2015b. 'Social sciences and humanities faculties "to close" in Japan after ministerial intervention', *Times Higher Education*, 14 September. Retrieved 10 February 2016 from https://www.timeshighereducation.com/news/social-sciences-and-humanities-faculties-close-japan-after-ministerial-decree.
Havergal, C. 2015. '"Cuckoo managers" are throwing out academy traditions', *Times Higher Education*, 21 May. Retrieved 21 January 2016 from https://www.timeshighereducation.com/news/cuckoo-managers-are-throwing-out-academy-traditions/2020315.
Hazelkorn, E. 2008. 'Learning to Live with League Tables and Ranking: The Experience of Institutional Leaders', *Higher Education Policy* 21(2): 193–215.
Henry, J. 2015. '"Eye-watering" salary rises for university chiefs cannot be justified, says report', *The Guardian*, 15 March. Retrieved 20 December 2015 from http://www.theguardian.com/education/2015/mar/15/rises-for-university-chiefs-cannot-be-justified.
Henry, M. et al. 2001. *The OECD, Globalisation and Education Policy*. Oxford: Pergamon Press.
Hotson, H. 2011. 'Short Cuts', *London Review of Books*, *33*(11): 19. Retrieved 10 February 2016 from http://www.lrb.co.uk/v33/n11/howard-hotson/short-cuts.
———. 2014. 'Germany's Great Tuition Fees U-turn', *Times Higher Education* 13 February. Retrieved 26 September 2016 from https://www.timeshighereducation.com/features/germanys-great-tuition-fees-u-turn/2011168.article.
John Lewis Partnership. 2015. 'Our Principles'. Retrieved 9 February 2016 from http://www.johnlewispartnership.co.uk/about/our-principles.html.
Jones, J. 2013. 'Dominic Raab reveals Britain's true debt burden', *The Spectator*, 4 May. Retrieved 10 February 2016 from http://blogs.spectator.co.uk/coffeehouse/2013/05/dominic-raab-reveals-britains-true-debt-burden/.
Jump, P. (2015) 'Academics in the minority at more than two-thirds of UK universities', *Times Higher Education*, 3 September. Retrieved 10 February 2016

from https://www.timeshighereducation.com/news/academics-minority-more-two-thirds-uk-universities.

Levin, L., and D.J. Greenwood. 2016. *Creating a New Public University and Reviving Democracy: Action Research in Higher Education*. Oxford: Berghahn.

Lyotard, J.-F. 1994 *The Postmodern Condition: A Report on Knowledge*. Minnesota: University of Minnesota Press.

Mackenzie, C. 2014. 'Chilean student protests keep marching through Bachelet's reforms', *Latin Correspondent* 14 July. Retrieved 19 December 2015 from http://latincorrespondent.com/2014/07/chilean-student-protests-marching-bachelet-education-reforms/.

Marcus, J. 2014. 'New Analysis Shows Problematic Boom in Higher Ed Administrators', *Huffington Post,* 6 February. Retrieved 20 December 2015 from http://www.huffingtonpost.com/2014/02/06/higher-ed-administrators-growth_n_4738584.html.

Marginson, S., and M. Considine. 2000. *The Enterprise University: Power, Governance and Reinvention in Australia*. Cambridge: Cambridge University Press.

McGettigan, A. 2013. *The University Gamble: Money, Markets and the Future of Higher Education*. London: Pluto.

Mills, D. 1993. 'The University in scaffolding or What do we do with benchmarks?' *Anthropology Matters Journal,* Vol 5, No. 1. Retrieved 29 November 2016 from http://www.anthropologymatters.com/index.php/anth_matters/issue/view/24.

Morgan, J. 2014a. 'Private colleges investigated amid fears of fraud', *Times Higher Education*, 19 June. Retrieved 26 September 2016 from https://www.timeshighereducation.com/news/private-colleges-investigated-amid-fears-of-fraud/2014015.article.

_____. 2014b. 'Pearson Rehomes Private Outcasts', *Times Higher Education*, 28 August. Retrieved 26 September 2016 from https://www.questia.com/read/1P3-3420635861/pearson-rehomes-private-outcasts.

_____. (2015) 'University of Law sold to Global University Systems', *Times Higher Education*, 2 June. Retrieved 8 February 2016 from https://www.timeshighereducation.com/content/university-law-sold-global-university-systems.

Neary, M., and J. Wynn, J. 2015. 'Beyond public and private: a model for co-operative higher education', *Krisis. Journal for Contemporary Philosophy* 2: 114–20.

Newfield, C. 2008. *Unmaking the Public University*. Cambridge, Mass.: Harvard University Press.

OECD. 1998. *Redefining Tertiary Education*. Paris.

_____. 2011. *Education at a Glance; OECD Indicators*. Paris.

Olds, K. 2008. 'Analysing Australia's global higher ed export industry', *GlobalHigherEd*, 24 June. Retrieved 20 December 2015 from https://globalhighered.wordpress.com/2008/06/24/australias-global-highered-export-industry/.

Ørberg, J. 2007. 'Who Speaks for the University? Legislative Frameworks for Danish University Leadership 1970–2003', EPOKE Working Paper no. 5, May

2007. Retrieved 10 February 2016 from http://edu.au.dk/forskning/omraader/epoke/publikationer/workingpapers/.

Power, M. 1997. *The Audit Society: Rituals of Verification*. Oxford: Oxford University Press.

Readings, B. 1996. *The University in Ruins*. Cambridge, MA: Harvard University Press.

Roslyn Kunin and Associates, Inc. 2009. 'Economic Impact of International Education in Canada. Final report presented to Foreign Affairs and International Trade Canada', Vancouver.

Rothblatt, S., and B. Wittrock (eds). 1993. *The European and American University Since 1800: Historical and Sociological Essays*. Cambridge: Cambridge University Press.

Sauder, M. and Espeland, W. 2009. 'The discipline of rankings: tight coupling and organisational change.' *American Sociological Review*, 74 (1): 63–82.

Shore, C., and M. Taitz. 2012. 'Who Owns the University? Institutional Autonomy and Academic Freedom in an Age of Knowledge Capitalism', *Globalisation, Societies and Education* 10(2): 201–19.

Shore, C., and S. Wright. 2015. 'Audit Culture Revisited: Rankings, Ratings and the Reassembling of Society', *Current Anthropology* 56(3): 421–39.

Slaughter, S., and L. Leslie. 1997. *Academic Capitalism: Politics, Policies, and the Entrepreneurial University*. Baltimore, MD: Johns Hopkins University Press.

Smith, A. 2015. 'Obama Steps Up Push for Free', *Inside Higher Ed*, 9 September. Retrieved 6 February 2016 from https://www.insidehighered.com/news/2015/09/09/obama-unveils-new-push-national-free-community-college.

Snow, C.P. 1956. 'The Two Cultures', *The New Statesman and Nation*, 52 (1334): 413–14.

Strathern, M. (ed.). 2000. *Audit Cultures: Anthropological Studies in Accountability, Ethics, and the Academy*. London: Routledge.

Thompsett, F. Forthcoming. 'Study without End: Free Universities as Sites for the Radical Re-imagination of Learning', *LATISS, Learning and Teaching: International Journal of Higher Education in the Social Sciences*.

The Times Higher Education Supplement. 2013. 'BPP Title Fight Nears End as US Sibling Struggles', 11 July.

United States Senate Committee on Health, Education, Labor, and Pensions. 2012. 'For Profit Higher Education: The Failure to Safeguard the Federal Investment and Ensure Student Success', 30 July. Washington: U.S. Government Printing Office. Retrieved 10 February 2016 from https://www.gpo.gov/fdsys/pkg/CPRT-112SPRT74931/pdf/CPRT-112SPRT74931.pdf.

University and College Union. 2013. 'FX Plus – Sharing out the Pain', 8 March. Retrieved 8 February 2016 from http://southwestregion.web.ucu.org.uk/2013/03/08/fx-plus-sharing-out-the-pain/.

Vernon, J. 2010. 'The end of the public university in England', *GlobalHigherEd*, 27 October. Retrieved 30 September 2015 from https://www.insidehighered.com/blogs/globalhighered/the_end_of_the_public_university_in_england.

Whelan, A., Walker, R. and Moore C. (eds). 2013. *Zombies in the Academy: Living Death in Higher Education*. Chicago: University of Chicago Press.

Wright, S. 2012. 'Ranking Universities Within a Globalised World of Competition States: to what Purpose, and with what Implications for Students?', in H.L. Anderson and J.C. Jacobsen (eds), *Uddannelseskvalitet I det 21. Aahundrede [Quality in Higher Education in the 21st Century]*. Frederiksberg: Samfundslitterature, pp. 79–100.

_____. 2015. 'The "Imaginators" of English University Reform', in S. Slaughter and B.J. Taylor (eds), *Higher Education, Stratification and Workforce Development: Competitive Advantage in Europe, the US, and Canada*. New York: Springer: 127–50.

_____. 2016. 'Universities in a knowledge economy or ecology? Policy, contestation and abjection', *Critical Policy Studies*, 10 (1): 59–78.

Wright, S. and R. Boden. 2010. 'Follow the Money: An interim report on Danish University funding prepared for Dansk Magisterforening' *Working Papers in University Reform* no. 16, Copenhagen: Danish School of Education, October. Retrieved 29 November 2016 from http://edu.au.dk/fileadmin/www.dpu.dk/forskning/forskningsprogrammer/epoke/workingpapers/WP_16.pdf.

Wright, S., D. Greenwood and R. Boden. 2011. 'Report on a Field Visit to Mondragon University: a Cooperative Experience/Experiment', *LATISS* 4(3): 38–56.

PART I

Redefining the Mission and Meaning of the University

CHAPTER 1
Universities in Britain and the Spirit of '45
JOHN MORGAN

The Spirit of '45

For two successive evenings after the election of a Conservative government in the British elections of 7 May 2015, I watched Ken Loach's film *The Spirit of '45*, which was being broadcast on BBC's Knowledge channel. The film, which is unashamedly nostalgic, is a film of two halves. In the first, the focus is on the vision and practical activities of the Labour governments in the aftermath of the Second World War. The second part shows the unravelling of that vision, and its active dismantling by the Thatcher governments that were equally radical in their ambitions in the 1980s. The film uses historical footage and interviews to build a strong sense of, to borrow Peter Laslett's (1965) apposite phrase, 'the world we have lost'. The message that comes through is the overwhelming sense of a loss of ambition, and a failure of imagination and of faith in the power of people to build a just society.

The Spirit of '45 is an impressive film. It is, though, a piece of political ideology, and one that focuses on a particular moment of the Labour Party's history. It is, after all, the one part of the Labour record in government that the New Labour governments of 1997–2010 were prepared to remember (as opposed to, for example, the Wilson and Callaghan governments of the 1970s, whose record, in historical terms, does not compare so badly as is often portrayed). In the context of the policies of austerity, which have characterized the years after 2010, the 1945–1951 Labour government acts as an important reservoir of memories for the 'left', and reminds us of what can be achieved with political will and imagination (Kynaston 2007).

These questions of historical memory are important because they help us to understand the debates of the present. These are my own concerns: I am interested in the question of why the 'educational left' has failed to offer alternatives to what has been termed the Conservative hegemony of the past three decades (at the time of writing, it is too early to assess the possible impact of a new 'left-wing' Labour leader). In what follows, I first set out a general framework in which these debates can be understood, before going on to examine the specific case of university expansion in post-war Britain. In this period, there existed a number of competing and overlapping narratives or stories about the importance of education, and the breakdown in the social settlement led to the replacement of one vision of the university with another. The chapter finally returns to the questions I have raised in this introduction about the meaning of '1945' and its continued importance in discussions of the purposes of universities.

Post-war Stories

The framework that I use here is borrowed from Alan Sinfield's (1989) impressive study, *Literature, Politics and Culture in Postwar Britain*. In terms of 'literary theory', Sinfield is a 'cultural materialist' (Eagleton 1983; Brannigan 1998): he insists that literary criticism should abandon the concept of 'idealism' that lies at its heart. Idealist readings of literary and cultural texts suggest that they contain an inner truth that resides in and stems from the genius of the author or artist. Against this, materialist readings stress the importance of understanding the economic, political and social contexts in which texts are produced. This is not to say that we can understand the meaning of a text simply by knowing the social origins of its author, but it does mean we have to take seriously the conditions under which texts were produced, distributed and consumed. The importance of cultural materialism is that it suggests that, because we live in societies where meanings matter, we need to pay close attention to the types of 'stories' or representations that help us to make sense of our experience – or give meaning to our lives. Sinfield decides that the term 'stories' gets us close to this, and suggests that stories are all around us, and help to give meaning to our experiences. There are, of course, more powerful or dominant stories, and ones that are less widely circulated and recognized, and the exact arrangement of these stories into hierarchies is the outcome of cultural struggle. Where a powerful story comes to assume the status of 'common sense', then it can be seen to be ideological. Use of the word 'ideology' is always guaranteed to raise an eyebrow or a 'knowing nod' amongst post-modern and post-structuralist sophisticates, since it usefully serves to locate the author as a simple-minded determinist. Indeed, in the years following the publication of Sinfield's book, it became very fashionable to dismiss the view that stories or texts can, in any sense, be seen to represent in any simple way the interests of particular groups in society. This move may be seen variously in the shift from the Barthes of *Mythologies* (1957) to the Barthes *of S/Z* (1970), Foucault's insistence on the notion of 'discourse', or Derrida's oft-stated claim that 'there is nothing beyond the text', which itself drew from Pierre Macherey's (1978) pithy aphorism that 'the text says what it does not say'. Despite this, and setting my account against intellectual fashion, I want to insist that there is an urgent need to revisit the type of 'ideology critique' found in the work of cultural materialists such as Sinfield, simply because, as has become clear since the global financial crisis of 2008, there has been an intense struggle (conducted at the level of culture) to narrate or tell a convincing story about the meanings of that event. At a more general level, it is clear that writers such as Sinfield can in no sense be accused of simple determinism or 'textual reductionism'. Indeed, *Literature, Politics and Culture in Postwar Britain* remains a detailed and nuanced account of the cultural struggles of the period.

So, what was the 'story' that became dominant in the years following the Second World War? Sinfield states it succinctly:

> To win the war, people were encouraged to believe that there would not be a return to widespread injustice and poverty. The war exemplified (though not without contest) a pattern of state intervention and popular co-operation to organise production for a common purpose. And its successful conclusion afforded a rare opportunity to recast British society. Full employment and the welfare state created, for a while, the sense of a society moving towards fairness, in which remaining 'pockets of poverty' would soon be eliminated. (Sinfield 1997: 1)

If this was a founding story, then Sinfield seeks to show how it was constructed, how it became the post-war consensus, and why, in the 1980s, it was replaced so successfully by another – that is, what led to the rejection of this 'New Jerusalem' and the belief that socialism is a failed and redundant ideology. Though Loach's *The Spirit of '45* focused its attention on housing and the health service, Sinfield reminds us that it was widely accepted that the 'benefits that the upper classes had customarily arranged for itself would now be generally available' (ibid.: 2) and extended to 'good' culture too:

> what had hitherto been, in the main, the culture of the leisure class was proclaimed (to the discomfort of that class) as a universal culture. Literature and the arts were made to embody the spiritual and human values that consumer capitalism and 'mass' culture seemed to slight and, at the same time, were deployed as indicators of educational success and social mobility. (Sinfield 1997: 2)

Sinfield points out that this struggle over culture is one of the important sites where the dominant story about equality and justice was disputed. For example, in the early post-war period it can be seen in the novels of Evelyn Waugh (for example, *Brideshead Revisited* 1945) in which it is imagined that the 'good taste' and 'culture' of the upper classes would be sullied by allowing access to 'ordinary people', or in the arguments about English culture associated with T.S. Eliot (1948), who saw the existence of two classes and no room for their overlap.

Education was a key institution in and around which these stories were produced and circulated. The 1944 Education Act had its origins in the Beveridge Report of 1942 – the publication of which led to overnight queues outside HMSO offices in Holborn, making it, as Timmins (2001) wryly notes, possibly the most bought and least read book until the publication of Stephen Hawking's (1988) *A Brief History of Time*. The general project of educational expansion was accepted across the political spectrum, so much so that the 1944 Education Act was passed with little argument or debate (but, as critics point out, it failed to nationalize 'private schools', thus leaving intact a major source of class division). The ideology of expansion based on the idea of equality of opportunity was the basis for consensus for the next quarter of a century. In this time the notion of genetic intelligence was increasingly challenged, the notion of the 'scholarship boy' (working-class boys who gained places at grammar schools and experienced a kind of cultural dislocation) gained widespread attention, and in 1964 the Labour government made electoral gains with its promise to aspirational middle-class parents about the development of comprehensive schools designed to 'level the playing field' (it is worth noting that the 'scholarship girl' gained much less literary attention, as explored by Carolyn Steedman in her 1986 book, *Landscape for a Good Woman*, which I discuss later). In this period, the idea that more schooling for more children for longer was a good thing reigned supreme. And it was in this context that we should understand the emergence of calls for the expansion of university education.

It is crucial to understand the specific development of British universities within the 'structure of feeling' based around post-war affluence and expansion. As a starting point it will be useful to provide some factual evidence about the development of universities in the post-war period the proportion of school leavers who attended university each year increased significantly in the period after the Second World War. Whilst just 0.8 percent of school leavers went on to university in 1900, the figure was 3.2 percent in 1954 and 4.0 percent in 1962. In the post-war period there were three phases of expansion: the immediate boom after 1945 as soldiers returned from the front, another boom in the mid 1950s and again in mid to late 1960s. This process of university expansion was largely spontaneous and unplanned; it reflected an idealistic mix of fairness, democracy and citizenship, along with the fact of a growing, youthful population (although in this chapter I am arguing that these developments are significant, it is worth noting that Britain was not unique amongst European nations in its educational expansion). It was in line with the dominant ideology of post-war Britain, based around welfare capitalism, which held that the 'good' things in life (healthcare, decent housing, culture and education) should be available to all social classes, and that the role of the state was to intervene to lessen the vicissitudes of the market. Increased numbers of school leavers provided an increasing supply of potential students and, in 1960, the Anderson Committee favoured universal national entitlement to a place at university and financial support for all those who met the entry requirements; the subsequent Robbins Report (1963) argued for a place for all who wanted to take it up. Funding – with the mandatory (universal) student grant – by world standards was generous, and there was a low dropout rate. As Richard Hoggart summarized it in his 1995 book *The Way We Live Now*, the widely accepted common-sense features of the British university were established at this time: relatively generous funding of university entrants through a grant system; the provision of bespoke, on-campus student accommodation; the continuance of small-group teaching; the belief that tutors should be in loco parentis; the low failure rate as compared with most developed countries; and the idea that academics should run their own institutions, not hand them over to professional administrators or accept interference by central government.

University expansion was linked to a broader notion of 'welfare capitalism' and its attendant idea of 'left culturalism', which tended to regard the products of the market as pandering to the lowest common denominator, and the role of state-sponsored culture to provide access to quality experiences and the education of taste. In line with this, it was held that the state should seek to regulate the market, limit the spread of advertising and maintain standards in broadcasting, as well as sponsor the arts, theatre, libraries and so on.

There is another interpretation of these developments, which resists the tendency, widely found in educational studies, to assume the relative autonomy of educational processes from wider questions of political economy. Thus, against the 'liberal' reading of the Anderson and Robins reports, which regards them as part of the story of expansion and opportunity, a more critical reading would relate them to the growing concern throughout the late 1950s and into the 1960s about the underlying weaknesses of the British economy and the need for restructuring. This was eventually expressed by the Wilson government of the 1960s with its much vaunted 'white heat' of the 'scientific revolution' (Wilson 1964). This was in line with a general 'upskilling thesis' about the future needs of the British economy. Thus, educational expansion at all levels was predicated on a general model of human capital formation, though there was little or no analysis of the actual skill requirements. This in itself reflected the relative weakness of the British state to intervene and direct the economy, and forms an important part of the story to follow.

Notes towards a Literary History of University Life

Having set out a framework for analysing the stories that society has told itself about educational change and provided some brief background to the expansion of university education in the decades after the Second World War, I want now to turn to some specific examples drawn from the literature of this period. The overall question or problem that I am attempting to get at in this (and other) work is how we can understand the relative rapidity with which the educational settlement became unhinged and unravelled in the 1970s and 1980s, to be replaced by a new settlement based on market logics.

One way to approach this is offered by Bruce Robbins (2007) in his book *Upward Mobility and the Common Good* which has as its subtitle *Toward a Literary History of the Welfare State* – a phrase that Robbins suggests was little used before the 1930s. Robbins takes on board an insight from Daniel T. Rodgers' study of the emergence of New Deal Progressivism in the United States. Rodgers argues that the seeds of the New Deal, which reached its fruition in the 1930s, were planted much further back, in the 1870s, in the break with laissez-faire policy in

Germany. What this suggests, Robbins thinks, is that we might be able to detect the 'slow, diffuse cultural preparation' that eventually makes it possible to break with the stories which have come to assume the status of common sense. Thus, in the post-war era there emerged a large body of 'academic fiction' which explored the ambiguities and contradictions of the welfare state. On the one hand there was concern about the pace of social change and the idea that things were not moving fast enough, but, on the other, there were also concerns about the notion of state patronage – that people were gaining advantage because of political support rather than on their own merit. As James F. English (2006) has argued, novels that dealt with the experience of university life in the post-war period were, in effect, novels about the welfare state. As English concludes, 'at no time in British history has education occupied such a privileged place in political discourse, or carried such a burden of societal hopes and expectations'. At the centre of concerns about education was the issue of social mobility, experienced as a sense of the upper classes moving over and allowing a new set of people to have their turn. These 'new' people tended to come from working-class backgrounds, and often from the unfashionable regions and places of Britain – 'the North', including cities such as Hull and Huddersfield. In many ways these texts were part of a more general trend for literature to document '[s]cenes from provincial life', to borrow the title of William Cooper's fond depiction of Leicester. Thus, Phillip Larkin's *Jill* is about a young boy from Huddersfield who goes to Oxford and is torn between his lower-middle-class roots and the new world that Oxford opens up; and Malcolm Bradbury's (1975) *The History Man* focuses on the upward mobility of Barbara and Howard Kirk, who come from 'the grimmer, tighter north, in respectable upper-working class cum lower-middle class backgrounds'. Howard Kirk is that stock anti-hero – a left-wing, Marxist sociologist – and the book gains much of its satire from this, especially as Howard is exposed as hypocritical and sexually predation. Barbara Kirk calls her husband a 'radical poseur' who follows trends rather than being true to his roots and moral commitments. The novel hints at the changed sexual cultures surrounding the expansion of higher education, but also raises more general questions about the whole project of university expansion, such as whether it allows for self-transformation, and whether it will allow for the democratic redistribution of educational benefits. An important feature of these texts is their ambivalence towards the whole project of expansion, social mobility and, by extension, the whole ideology of the welfare state, with its promise to confer benefits on a 'deserving' class of people.

Such ambivalence is found in Kingsley Amis's (1954) *Lucky Jim*. As Amis explained in a public discussion, Jim Dixon:

> is supposed to be the son of a clerk, an office worker (like myself). He is a Labour Party socialist and probably took part in student politics when younger (like myself). One is meant to feel that he did well enough in his student academic career to make it natural for him to become a history lecturer, which he did without much thought. Though he finds the academic world decreasingly to his taste, he sticks at it because he does think university teaching an important job, and also because he is afraid of venturing out on his own. I think he is a plausible figure in his world: there are certainly many like him in that they are the first generation in their families to have received a university education, they have won their way up by scholarships all through, they are not the conventional Oxford-Cambridge academic type, they don't embrace the manners, customs and pastimes of that type (sherry, learned discussion tea-parties with the Principal's wife, chamber concerts) but stick to their own, to the ones their non-academic contemporaries share (beer, arguments in pubs, amorous behaviour at – and outside – dances, jazz). Dixon has seen, throughout his life, power and position going to people who (he suspects) are less notable for their ability than their smooth manners, their accents, the influence they or their fathers can wield. The money thing is less important; Dixon is hard-up himself, and is a bit suspicious of the rich, but is far more so of Oxford-accented 'culture' (Amis, cited in Kynaston 2009: 360).

Stories such as this are indicative of a set of shifts in the class-inflected social landscape of Britain in the middle of the twentieth century. They point to the ways in which established marks of distinction were being maintained and challenged, and how codes of sexual morality and behaviour were being interrogated and at times disrupted. That they are fictional representations does not diminish their value in helping to understand something of the 'structure of feeling' of the period, though it is important to try to sort fact from fiction when it comes to the role of education in advancing the social mobility of the working class. As Sinfield states, 'the preoccupation with upward mobility through education was a story that society, or parts of it, wanted to tell itself, not a record of experience' (Sinfield 1997: 234) It might be added that this is still a story that society wants to tell itself. Most upward movement was not because the class system was weaker but because there were more 'middle class' jobs (in teaching, local government, social work, media, management and so on) as a result of the expansion of the economy and the growth of the welfare state. Family circumstances remained the major factor determining educational attainment, and by 1972 the effect of parental class on education had actually grown since 1945. This argument is worth remembering, as Selina Todd has recently argued:

> Focusing on social mobility as an educational goal leads to a narrowing of everyone's horizons. Schools and universities cannot create job opportunities, yet students are urged to believe that they can and must (Todd 2015: 391).

An important feature of British fiction in the 1970s was the discussion of the middle classes in the light of a straightened economic situation and a period of political retrenchment. Universities reflected this too, and the sense of social and cultural decay was palpable. This was a crisis of welfare capitalism. It is captured in Margaret Drabble's (1977) *The Ice Age*, published in the aftermath of Britain becoming the first advanced industrial nation to require assistance from the IMF, and before the turning point of the election of the first Thatcher government in 1979. Three years later, Drabble's (1980) *The Middle Ground* explores the post-feminist, post-progress experience of Kate Hoey. Kate is, in many ways, the archetypical success story of the welfare state. Despite attending an 'ordinary' school, and not going to university, she was clearly able, and was a respected figure. As a feminist writer, Kate was at home in the liberal left milieu that flourished in the 1960s. She says of one of her a dinner-party guests:

> her pieces on middle-class manipulation of the health service, on rows about underprivileged gifted children and the preponderance of black children were classics of their kind, and warmly welcomed, for in those days people were still willing to hear the humane, sensible left-wing view, the so-called 'progressive' view. She and Ted came from backgrounds not dissimilar ... both in their own way seeking the egalitarian millennium, which would bring security, opportunity and prosperity to all, while rewarding its faithful and elect (such as themselves) (Drabble 1980: 43).

As the novel progresses, it is clear that this middle-class milieu is under threat, and Kate is plagued with doubts about the meaning and possibility of sustaining a holistic and complex view of society. This is, of course, the point at which a Conservative prime minister informed readers of *Woman's Own* that there is 'no such thing as society'. In

Drabble's fiction of this time, we see the unravelling of a (particular) middle-class worldview, in which the assumptions of gradual progress, the betterment of individuals, and the legitimacy of the state (and the public sector) are brought into question. Tew (2004) points out, though, that this sense of being decentred, having no fixed moorings, and thus viewing the world as a smorgasbord of contingent opportunities, is very much in line with a middle-class view of mobility and choice, one that was to increasingly gain the ascendancy in the neoliberal era (Skeggs 2004). The unravelling of the social democratic settlement paved the way for the mobile, cosmopolitan middle-class identities of the 1990s, where class no longer seemed to matter (for an interesting set of reflections on how this 'middle-classlessness' was reflected in films produced in the New Labour era, see Neville 2010).

Not everyone could engineer an easy escape from the binds of class and location though, as evidenced by the ambivalence to the welfare state recorded in Carolyn Steedman's (1986) autobiographical *Landscape for a Good Woman*. The book is focused on Steedman's relationship with her working-class mother, who had 'dreamt of marrying a prince' (i.e. achieving 'everything and anything'). Her dreams had been largely unfulfilled and her inability to realize her ambition is a source of anger. Steedman, however, has achieved 'upward social mobility', in the form of state-sponsored education and a job in academia, whose salary is paid by the taxpayer. Steedman is aware of the way that a 'benevolent state', through intervening in her own development as a child, has made her what she has become but, at the same time, she recognizes the 'hidden injuries of class' that accompany the philanthropy or charity of the state (the visits from the health visitor or the truancy officer). Steedman's own career started out as a teacher in a primary school (as 'a suitable job for a woman', this fact has its own resonance), and her own ambivalence about the role of the state in the provision of education is recorded in *The Tidy House* (1982), which is an extraordinary analysis of a story collectively written over three afternoons by three working-class eight-year-old girls. The story reveals the ways in which, from an early age, working-class girls are aware of the gender politics of the family and community, the roles expected of them, and their likely futures.

Steedman recognizes the genuine achievement that education for all represented, even if, as a teacher, she is acutely aware of the disappointments that awaited the majority of working-class children. In a comment that encapsulates the failures of 'welfare capitalism', Steedman writes:

> in the last weeks of the summer term there is frequently a specific concern added to the general anxiety of many children in working-class primary schools: they do not know what is going to happen to them in September. It is the policy in some schools not to tell the children which class they will be in next year, nor which teacher will be theirs, until the last day of term ... So when Lindie asked me which class the three of them were going to be in next year and I replied, 'I really don't know', I was, quite simply, lying. (Steedman 1982: 9)

Steedman evades the question of which class students will be in next year because she knows that children, even at a young age, are able to recognise how they 'rank' in the educational hierarchy, and wishes to avoid telling working-class children too early the unpalatable truth about their educational and occupational fates. Quite simply, it is difficult for teachers on an individual level to publicly acknowledge what they know to be true, that many of the children they teach are destined for educational failure.

I hope that these few examples are able to offer a sense that Robbin's argument about the need for a 'literary history of the welfare state' is productive, and that examining the written responses to living in a society that, in Steedman's words, 'poured so much milk and orange juice down the throats of its children' (Steedman 1986: 122) may shed light on the contradictions and experiences. In part, we might speculate that it was these experiences, these little grievances, which provided the conditions for the eventual loss of faith in the welfare state, and the growing appeal of the 'new right' with its promise to reward individual thrift and hard work. Basically, as the 'new right' was developing its economic analysis of the failures of British capitalism, it tended to see the university as a site of perverse sexuality, lifestyle experimentation and drug use. This was reflected in Prime Minister Margaret Thatcher's stormy relationship with academics, of whom she was suspicious, apart from a few prized right-wing academics (Harrison 1994). For the new right, the university, as an archetypal institution of the welfare state, was in need of reform.

Whilst much of the literature associated with academic life during the 1960s was concerned with the fine-graded differentiations of the British class system (with special attention to the middle-class habitus), throughout the 1970s the economic aspects of university life became more prominent. This is an important reminder that university expansion – and the higher status and rewards it allowed for academics

– was linked to the need to raise the U.K.'s productivity through science and technology. After the period of initial expansion, universities faced a funding crisis, as the proportions of direct fee-paying students declined, and there were reduced funds from donations and endowments. Universities sought commercial and industrial funding, a trend which reached its height in the publication in 1970 E.P. Thompson's *Warwick University Ltd*, which criticized the extent to which the Pro Vice Chancellor had welcomed the overtures of industrial capital. By today's standards of corporate involvement in universities, these interventions seem positively restrained. However, this was part of a wider legitimation crisis for many academics in universities.

It is interesting, therefore, that there is no sign of this legitimation crisis in the first of David Lodge's 'campus novels' – *Changing Places* – published in 1975. However, by the time that the third instalment of his trilogy was published, in 1988, the question of what a university is for and its relationship to the circuits of the national economy loom large. *Nice Work* offers readers a sceptical industrialist's view of cutting-edge work in the humanities. Set in the West Midland's city of Rummidge (a thinly disguised Birmingham) in the context of rising unemployment and the declining manufacturing industries, it provides a commentary on Britain's decline ('how we lost the peace') and the re-emergence of the north–south divide explored in Elizabeth's Gaskell's novel *North and South* (1855). Indeed, in *Nice Work* (1988), Robyn Penrose, a literary scholar, is an expert on the nineteenth-century industrial novel, and an expert in 'deconstruction'. In her role, she is charged with developing enterprise links with local engineering firms, and it is here she meets Vic Gaitskell, a hard-nosed industrialist with a strong analysis of Britain's industrial failings. As the novel develops, the two seemingly opposing characters come to recognize each other's perspective. The book draws upon and gives literary expression to the argument developed in popular historical texts such as Martin Weiner's (1981) *English Culture and the Decline of the Industrial Spirit*, which argues that the lack of a full-blown bourgeois revolution has led to the continuance of an aristocratic culture that is anti-industrial in its outlook and attitudes. These longer term attitudes and trajectories are overlaid by a shorter term narrative that is critical of the relative insulation of the university (and education in general) from the 'hard-nosed' realities of economic life. As one of the characters says:

> You and I, Robyn, grew up in a period when the state was smart: state schools, state universities, state-subsidised arts, state welfare,

state medicine – these were things progressive, energetic and people believed in. It isn't like that anymore (ibid.: 167).

These types of arguments and statements became increasingly common in the 1980s as universities were urged to encourage 'enterprise', and in Lodge's novel we see a working-out of the tension in British culture between what John Corner and Sylvia Harvey (1991) call 'enterprise' and 'heritage'.

An illustration of what is at stake in these accounts of the changing social landscape can be found in the fourth volume of the popular historian Dominic Sandbrook's (2012) tetralogy of Britain between 1958 and 1979. *Seasons in the Sun* (which covers the years 1974–1979) offers a revisionist view of the educational politics of the 1970s. Sandbrook's stock rhetorical device is to interrupt the hubris of widely accepted historical accounts (for instance he reminds us that, in 1968, at the supposed height of radicalism and the 'new Britain' of the Beatles and the Rolling Stones, the top-selling album was the soundtrack to *The Sound of Music*). In *Seasons in the Sun*, Sandbrook mocks the politicized forms of knowledge of the 1970s, with thinly veiled pokes at Steven Rose ('[t]he Open University biology professor who insisted that scientists needed to fight against the "undemocratic" nature of their discipline') or 'bearded' young lecturers who eagerly discussed 'hegemony' or 'false consciousness' (Sandbrook 2012: 299). Sandbrook's point is that these people were out of touch with reality, noting that the early 1970s were 'surprisingly good years' for the U.K.'s universities. Politicians agreed that increased university education was crucial to Britain's economic success, signalled by the fact that the new Education Secretary, Margaret Thatcher's, 1972 White Paper envisaged an 'ambitious expansion of 60 percent in just nine years' (ibid.: 293). Although these forecasts did not materialize and capital spending cuts combined with stagnant pay left 'many academics with an acute sense of decline' (ibid.: 294), Sandbrook argues that there was no doubt that campuses were 'livelier, busier more diverse places'(ibid.: 294). For students, who benefitted from generous government grants, life was 'not bad at all' (ibid.: 294). Sandbrook is mocking of the student activism of the period, noting the contradictions between students at elite institutions and the workers for whose rights they espoused (not a particularly original observation, we might add). He points to evidence that students were 'far more interested in putting away a few pints of Watneys, listening to grandiose concept albums, passing their exams and getting decent jobs than in smashing the system or having more representatives on the university council' (ibid.: 296).

Sandbrook's account of this period (whose status as an 'unreliable witness' is, to my mind, revealed by his extraordinary comment that popular music did not really play much of a role in the lives of working-class young people in this period) raises the question of how we should make sense of the stories told about this period. There is little doubt that the 1960s and 1970s represent seminal moments in understanding the development of post-war Britain, and thus, attempts to make authoritative claims about their meaning and significance need to be treated with a critical eye. As David Marquand and Anthony Seldon (1996) note in *The Ideas that Shaped Post-war Britain*, there is, as yet, no settled agreement about the historiography of this period. In the final section of this chapter, I want to briefly consider some other narratives that came to prominence in the aftermath of the collapse of the social democratic settlement.

Different Stories

In this chapter, I have argued that the expansion of state-funded university provision was one of the 'ideas that shaped post-war Britain'. As a product of that expansion – someone whose parents benefitted from post-war 'affluence' to achieve 'lower middle class' status and whose children could get jobs in the expanding welfare state – I have taken for granted that this is a 'good thing'. That is, perhaps, why I found *The Spirit of '45* so compelling (and so moving) – it is the story I was told when I was growing up, yet it is one that I find hard to believe in now. As I watched it, another cinematic image kept presenting itself to me, this time the final scene of Mike Leigh's *High Hopes*, in which an elderly woman is assisted to the top of the towering block of council flats in which she lives (a building that clearly no longer meets her physical needs), to take a panoramic view of the area around King's Cross in central London. Eight years into the Thatcher era, King's Cross is becoming increasingly divided and gentrified, the material expression of the processes depicted in the film as three couples come to terms with the economic and social changes associated with an increasingly materialistic and divided society. 'Families' (which, as Leigh shows, are themselves fragile and flawed) seem to be the only thing left to cling on to as the idea of 'society' crumbles. The elderly lady has seen the austerity of the war and its aftermath, the building of the 'New Jerusalem' (of which the council-provided flats are a symbol), and its rapid disintegration (soon after, large crowds would gather to witness the detonation of such tower blocks, widely seen as symbols of the failure of the 'welfare state').

Leigh's film seems to suggest that the moment of 'high hopes' has passed, and a new realism is in the air. There can be no going back. Interestingly, Sinfield (whose work has informed this chapter), in his introduction to the third edition of *Literature, Politics and Culture in Postwar Britain* appears to recognize as much. Reflecting on the conditions that created the social democratic welfare state, and the space that this created for a radical politics in universities, Sinfield notes that today, 'student culture is located elsewhere, in music, video and the internet, offering realms of engagement that may outdistance the personal and political potential of traditional cultures' (1989: xvi). Whether or not that student culture will contribute to a radical renewal of social democratic politics remains to be seen.

◆

John Morgan is Professor of Education at the University of Auckland, having previously worked at the Institute of Education (London, U.K.) and the University of Bristol (U.K.). His primary discipline is geography. He also has an interest in the cultural and political economy of education, and his latest work explores the implications of the economic 'crisis' for the future of capitalist education.

References

Amis, K. 1954. *Lucky Jim*. Harmondsworth: Penguin.
Barthes, R. (1972 [1957]). *Mythologies*. New York: Hill and Wang.
_____. (1970). *S/Z*. Seuil: Paris.
Bradbury, M. 1975. *The History Man*. London: Arrow Books.
Brannigan, J. 1998. *New Historicism and Cultural Materialism*. Basingstoke: Macmillan.
Corner, J. and Harvey, S. 1991. *Enterprise and Heritage: Crosscurrents in National Culture*. London: Routledge.
Drabble, M. 1977. *The Ice Age*. Harmondsworth: Penguin.
_____. 1980. *The Middle Ground*. London: Wiedenfeld and Nicolson.
Eagleton, T. 1983. *Literary Theory: An Introduction*. Oxford: Basil Blackwell.
Eliot, T.S. 1948. *Notes Towards a Definition of English Culture*. London: Faber.
English, J.F. 2006. 'What the porter saw: on the academic novel', in J.F. English (ed.), *A Concise Companion to Contemporary British Fiction*. Oxford: Basil Blackwell, pp. 248–66.
Gaskell, E. (2012 [1855]). *North and South*. London: Penguin.

Harrison, B. 1994. 'Mrs Thatcher and the intellectuals', *Twentieth Century British History* 5(2): 206–45.
Hoggart, R. 1995. *The Way We Live Now*. London: Pimlico.
Kynaston, D. 2007. *Austerity Britain 1945–51*. London: Bloomsbury.
_____. 2009. *Family Britain 1951–57*. London: Bloomsbury.
Larkin P. (1946) *Jill*. London: The Fortune Press
Laslett, P. 1965. *The World We Have Lost*. London: Methuen and Co.
Lodge, D. 1975. *Changing Places*. Harmondsworth: Penguin.
_____. 1988. *Nice Work*. London: Penguin.
Macherey, P. 1978. *A Theory of Literary Production*. London: Verso.
Marquand, D., and A. Seldon (eds). 1996. *The Ideas that Shaped Post-war Britain*. London: Fontana.
Neville, R. 2010. *Classless*. Zero Books.
Robbins, B. 2007. *Upward Mobility and the Common Good: Toward a Literary History of the Welfare State*. Princeton, NJ: Princeton University Press.
Sandbrook, D. 2012. *Seasons in the Sun: The Battle for Britain 1974–1979*. London: Allen Lane.
Sinfield, A. 1997. *Literature, Politics and Culture in Postwar Britain*. 2nd Edn. London: Athlone Press.
Skeggs, B. 2004. *Class, Self, Culture*. London: Routledge.
Steedman, C. 1982. *The Tidy House*. London: Virago.
_____. 1986. *Landscape for a Good Woman*. London: Virago.
Tew, P. 2004. *The Contemporary British Novel*. London: Continuum.
Timmins, N. 2001. *The Five Giants: A Biography of the Welfare State*, 2nd edn. London: Harper Collins.
Thompson, E.P. 1970. *Warwick University Ltd*. Harmondsworth: Penguin.
Todd, S. 2015. *The People: The Rise and Fall of the Working Class 1910–2010*, London: John Murray.
Waugh, E. 1945. *Brideshead Revisited*. London: Chapman and Hall.
Wiener, M. 1981. *English Culture and the Decline of the Industrial Spirit*. Harmondsworth: Penguin.
Wilson, H. (1964) 'Labour's Plan for Science'. Speech delivered at Annual Labour Party Conference, Scarborough (October 1st). Available at: http://nottspolitics.org/wp-content/uploads/2013/06/Labours-Plan-for-science.pdf (last accessed 17th November 2016).

CHAPTER 2
Managing the Third Mission
Reform or Reinvention of the Public University?

NICK LEWIS AND CRIS SHORE

═══ ◆◆◆

Introduction: Strategic Hiring and Institutional Capture

The rise of the 'third mission' represents one of the most important facets of the globalization of universities over the past fifteen years. Typically, third mission activities are geared towards commercializing universities' intellectual property and establishing externally referenced research institutes that bring business and government more directly into the routine activities of universities. These trends are thought to be having a major impact not only on research and the work of academics and their relations to each other, but also on the organizational architecture of universities, the nature of the knowledge they produce, and the very meaning and mission of the public university. Drawing on a two-year research project that explored the rise of the third mission in New Zealand, this chapter examines these claims and the implications of these developments for university futures. We begin, however, with a brief ethnographic vignette that both illustrates and contextualizes the themes of the chapter.

Strategic Hiring and Academic Autonomy

After months of protracted negotiations with management, the Dean finally agreed to appoint a new junior lecturer in anthropology. Although the department had already lost two academic staff in the past few years and was about to lose one of its longest-serving professors due to retirement, this was strictly not a replacement position, we were told. University managers had decreed that all new appointments had to be based on a sound business case. This particular case had taken months to craft and included detailed forecasts of student enrolments, teaching gaps, programme development, and calculations of future competitive research performance funding. However, a week before the new post was to be advertised, the Vice Chancellor announced a university-wide job freeze, following publication of declining enrolment figures. The head of school passed on the grim news: there would be no new appointments for the foreseeable future. Yet the following week the Dean let it be known that a new 'strategic appointment process' had been created that would allow for select appointments, but only in areas deemed to be of 'strategic' value to the university. These appointments were based on a previous model of recruiting 'strategic chairs' to provide academic leadership, but in this case appointees were to be 'early- to mid-career high-fliers' with 'at least three to four years of post-doctoral experience'.

Whereas previously faculties and departments largely determined the areas of expertise required for their research and teaching needs, this new model was based on 'capacity gaps' where the Research Office and Auckland UniServices Ltd[1] perceived potential funding opportunities. These included 'agri-technology', 'brain and neuro-science', 'epidemiology/biostatistics', 'data analytics and visualization', 'environmental/sustainability', 'personalized health care', 'translational medicine', 'digital economy', 'Infrastructure engineering/urban design' and 'Vision Maturaanga (sic) Capability' (Harding 2015). A very different business case now had to be made; these new appointments would be tied to future 'sustainable funding of the post in a capped funding environment'; they were not to be tied to calculations about student numbers ('EFTS') but successful candidates had to have 'demonstrated capacity or high potential to win external research income'. Under this new model, the university centre (rather than individual faculties or schools), would 'underwrite the costs of the new appointment for a fixed period of up to five years, tapering from year three, after which the new staff member would be expected to be integrated into the usual faculty budget process'. In other words, appointees would be expected to generate their own salary and overhead costs within five years, otherwise they would need to take on teaching roles or become a burden on the department's finances.

The ideal candidates for these new positions were young, highly successful expatriate New Zealand scientists with post-doctoral positions in prestigious overseas universities who might be attracted 'home', and who would be likely to stay. Applications were to be made by deans to the Vice Chancellor's 'Strategic Appointment's Committee' comprising members of the Senior Leadership Team. As one Head of

Department put it, 'they are basically looking to poach expat high-fliers from Australia; junior academics who are likely to score a 'B' or even an 'A' in the next Performance-Based Research Fund exercise'.[2]

* * *

This vignette reveals several key changes in the management of the modern university and the way public universities are being reinvented in response to the pressures of the global knowledge economy. Firstly, it indicates the shifting priorities of university managers, their vision of what a university is (and is for) and the changing patterns of investment this gives rise to. Reflected here too is the familiar emphasis placed on STEM subjects and corresponding relegation of the arts and humanities. Second, it hints at the presence of a new and emerging organizational architecture that is profoundly reshaping the borders and boundaries of the public university. By this we mean the proliferation of new functions and employment opportunities within the university (fund-raising, communications, HR, risk management, technology transfer and commercialization offices, property services, alumni relations, and so on) that have little to do with teaching or research. Third, it reveals the increasing extent to which senior managers, administrators and commercialization officers now intervene in academic matters and the corresponding decline of disciplinary authority and collegial practices. Fourth, it illustrates a new or emerging model of academic labour and the contractual apparatus that underpins it. Finally, it also demonstrates how university managers are subverting established employment practices surrounding the recruitment of public employees.

These five developments, which vice chancellors typically frame as necessary responses to sustained government underfunding of higher education, are indicative of what we term 'the rise of the third mission'. In using this term, we do not seek to reify the third mission but rather to use the concept as an analytical category in order to understand how universities are being repurposed in response to the imperatives to face outwards and engage more proactively with industry, commerce and other external stakeholders. If teaching and research were the university's traditional missions, understanding these developments as the third mission highlights just how fundamental these changes have become in defining the contemporary university. The increasing emphasis on third mission activities is producing a raft of new material forms, from investment flows, designer buildings, entrepreneurial research institutions and public-private partnerships, to new labour relations, hiring practices and forms of academic subjectivity.

Our focus on the idea of the third mission, and its relations to the first and second missions, provides a useful alternative to the more commonly used terms such as the 'entrepreneurial university', 'managerialism' or 'academic capitalism' as it draws attention to the contradictions between the established missions of the university and the imperatives now driving university reform, and to the everyday practices that mediate these contradictions. In saying this, we note that the term 'third mission' is used very differently in Europe and the U.K., where it was first coined to describe (and foster) a wide range of different relationships between universities and their communities and 'stakeholders', including participation in policymaking and involvement in social and cultural life (Etzkowitz et al. 2000; Etzkowitz and Leydesdorff 1997; Molas-Gallart et al. 2002).[3] As our research discovered, the third mission is a term not commonly used in New Zealand (Shore and McLauchlan 2012). By using the unfamiliar term in our conversations with university managers, however, we have found that it has disturbed their taken-for-granted reduction of external relationships to commercialized funding relations. It has helped to highlight that, in New Zealand, external partnerships and stakeholder engagement are much more narrowly concerned with the overriding imperatives of generating external income, building commercial relationships and stimulating economic transformation. It has also helped us to point out surreptitiously that, in other national settings, other forms of community engagement are valued.

Drawing on a series of interviews with strategic leaders in six of New Zealand's eight universities, and some of the external stakeholders shaping the flow of external income, this chapter sets out to examine these trends and reflect on their implications for academia and the future of the public university.[4] New Zealand offers a particularly useful site for analysing these processes partly because of the country's small scale, and institutional transparency, but also because of its well-developed history of economic nationalism, its reputation as a 'neoliberal laboratory '(Kelsey 1995; Bruneau and Savage 2002), and its repeated government-led attempts to reinvent universities as 'drivers' of the knowledge economy (Clark 2001; Larner and Le Heron 2005; Narayan 2012; Shore 2010; Universities New Zealand 2011).

Shifting Priorities of University Leaders

A key indicator of how 'third mission' agendas are reshaping the operation of the university can be seen in changing language use, particularly in the articulation of university vision statements, strategic plans and annual reports. A striking feature of these is the desire of university leaders to please government. As the 2011 Universities New Zealand 'Briefing' document on 'contributing to government goals' declares:

> [t]he eight universities, represented by Universities New Zealand – TePokai Tara, constitute a unique resource with which our government could partner to achieve its goals. No other group of public organizations is as well equipped to assist the government in achieving its targets as are the universities, yet at present that capability is not being engaged to the greatest extent possible (Universities New Zealand 2011: 2).

Far from advocating institutional autonomy, academic freedom and international research excellence, New Zealand's vice chancellors are re-narrating (and reorganizing) their institutions to suit government calls for more applied science and skills-based learning that will boost economic growth, create high value jobs and grow the 'export education' sector. Indeed, commercialization and business development have become central to the way New Zealand universities narrate themselves. The same Universities New Zealand document justifies the university sector's contribution to New Zealand primarily in financial terms: Universities, we read, are now 'responsible for contributing NZ$10–12 billion to the national economy; over NZ$800 million to Research and Development, over NZ$500 million in contract research revenue, and over NZ$860 million in the market capitalization of their home-grown start-up companies. Virtually no mention is made of the contribution universities make to fundamental research, scholarship or education for citizenship, or of their role as democratic institutions in an institutionally thin democracy (see Mulgan 1994). As the University of Auckland's director of research partnerships summed it up:

> It's no longer research – it's innovation. It's no longer a grant – it's an investment. It's no longer about you – it's a team activity. It's not an exploration – it's about making a difference. It's not about research outputs – it's about societal impacts, risk management and performance monitoring (Smart 2013).

Typically, vice chancellors assert that the purpose of commercializing university intellectual property and engaging in ever-more elaborate revenue-raising activities is to enable the university to continue to invest in its core business of teaching and research. However, this particular document suggests the opposite: that raising external revenue is becoming an end in itself. Indeed, one informant confirmed that the costs of pursuing the marginal benefits of certain revenue-raising activities commonly outweighed the returns that these activities generate (Interviews with Pro-VC Research, University A; 2014). The perverse economic rationality of this pursuit of additional income is exemplified by university responses to New Zealand's five-yearly research assessment exercise, the Performance-Based Research Fund (PBRF). The exercise absorbs enormous amounts of institutional resources and largely uncosted academic staff time to capture relatively small additional increments (Curtis 2008 and this volume). Even the otherwise positive formal reviews of the PBRF point to the problem of compliance costs relative to marginal gains (see, for example, Adams 2008). There are also ample grounds to be sceptical of the resources consumed in the direct commercialization of science through royalties, patents, licences and spin-out companies. The failure of universities to provide evidence of the net profits of these activities means that there is never any basis upon which to allay this scepticism or to be confident that resources are not being diverted from publicly funded teaching and research to revenue raising for its own sake (Ciancanelli 2008).

The University of Auckland (UoA)'s Strategic Plan 2013–2020 lists 'the development and commercialization of enterprise based on the university's research and creative works' as one of its seven key objectives, and the words 'commercialization', 'investment' and 'entrepreneurship' feature prominently in the text (University of Auckland 2013a: 6, 12). Objective 10 is to produce 'high quality research that has the greatest possible impact on and value for New Zealand and the world'. However, the 'key actions' for translating this into practice entail engaging 'proactively with key industry partners to ensure that we maximize opportunities to support their business development through commercialization and contract research, and through skills development via research degree students and placements'. It also includes 'supporting industry-facing commercial innovation' and maximizing 'synergies between the University and UniServices to ensure that barriers to commercialization are minimized'.

These commercial imperatives are no longer peripheral to the university but have become deeply institutionalized and embedded in a number of its organizational structures. Most notable in this respect is the University of Auckland's new 'Leadership Framework' adopted in 2013. This was a set of management-led policies and practices aimed at transforming the culture of the university and aligning staff behaviour with the university's strategic plan. Starting from the premise that all staff have a key role to play in leadership, this goes on to outline how leadership will be distributed and embodied in university structures. According to the guiding document, the ideal university-professor-as-leader is someone who 'sets direction', who 'displays an understanding of the international and commercial context in which the University operates' and who:

> demonstrates an understanding of the competitive global environment and key market drivers ... and uses this understanding to create and seize opportunities, expand into new markets and deliver programmes ....; displays behaviours of a leader who demonstrates global and commercial acumen; leads and inspires innovation, pursues ambitious ventures [and] advocates and clearly articulates the University's aspirations, objectives and values (University of Auckland 2013b: 8).

These imperatives to generate revenue and display commercial entrepreneurship – criteria over which the Vice Chancellor fought a bitter and personal battle with the academic union (Shore and Taitz 2012) – have now become fully incorporated into the university's promotions criteria and annual performance review process (Amsler and Shore 2015). Being entrepreneurial, it would seem, is compulsory for any academic who aspires to a position of leadership.

Third Mission Organizational Architectures

In March 2015, funding for the University of Auckland's Thematic Research Initiatives (or TRIs) came to an end. A five-year experiment, the three TRIs were created to build university-wide capability in selected fields (bio-pharmaceuticals, transforming cities, and indigenous knowledge) by establishing cross-disciplinary research networks that would identify and secure future external funding opportunities. Each TRI was tasked to build cross-disciplinary teams and relationships with funding agencies, conduct small-scale research projects in targeted areas, and encourage academics to be more 'go-getting' and proactive in seeking funding. Each had a Directorate and a corporate form complete with web presence and office space. Never fully corralled into performing what their architects wanted, they were a gamble, and unpopular with senior academics who resented the diversion of funds from established internal funding streams. While the TRIs achieved interesting results, they failed to build the envisaged platform for proactive, team-based and competitive external research gathering.

The vignette at the start of this chapter draws attention to the challenges of organizing and institutionalizing the third mission within traditional university structures, and the tactics used for its implementation. It highlights the way managers seek to make visible, corporatize, experiment with, and take control of the research capabilities of the university. The Research Office and commercialization unit officials were appointed to steering groups and governance boards of the TRIs, took responsibility for managing the KPIs of research directors, and participated in their key outward-facing initiatives. Universities have long been organized by discipline-based administrative units, run by disciplinary leaders and based upon disciplinary identities and research practices. In short, the TRIs were an experiment in breaking down that model by building multidisciplinary teams and research clusters more amenable to managerial and entrepreneurial logics and business opportunities. They were tasked with assembling research expertise into measurable and calculable units that might identify fields for investment and better realize the commercial value of that expertise.

The TRIs were one initiative among many launched by New Zealand universities in their struggles to design and implement a coherent alternative to the discipline-siloed university, which might integrate third mission research, teaching and scholarship. The most prominent have been the research institutes and centres that have proliferated over the last twenty years. In early 2015, a web search of New Zealand universities revealed that, apart from Lincoln University near Christchurch, they had at least twenty of these centres or institutes across multiple spheres. Set up by opportunistic and/or entrepreneurial academics, or would-be 'project barons' (see Gorm Hanson, this volume), these centres took different forms and had multiple agendas largely focused on supporting academic research and scholarship. These new institutional forms allowed academics to be more entrepreneurial in developing their research programmes: to cultivate reputation, source external funding and leverage internal funding, overcome the strictures of university budget cycles, leverage supervision revenues, and be independent of departments and faculties.

These centres ranged from loose clusters of academics and their interests to the tightly held fiefdoms of particular project barons, but more often than not pursued a third mission to underwrite some field of fundamental scholarship. For this reason and that of their idiosyncratic and opportunistic formation, they were seldom structured in ways that made them amenable to centralized university management. These institutes were formed in a range of different parts of the various universities, with mixed terms of reference with respect to the university's strategic priorities. Indeed, both authors of this chapter established and directed one of these centres for several years (the Wine Industry Research Institute and the Europe Institute, respectively) – two very different opportunistic interventions, both with the intention to secure a trans-disciplinary research agenda at arm's length from disciplinary administrative units. Like other institutes and centres across the country, they drew on a mixture of support from university grants, external public-good funding, commercial contracts, and academic labour supported by Vote Education (i.e. government tertiary education funding). However, while many have survived, only a few have been truly successful in becoming self-funded.[5] Each university reports having had to rein in these initiatives periodically and reorganize the rules under which they were constituted, and five of the universities now have very clearly defined hierarchies of units laid out on their websites. In short, universities have struggled to get right the organizational model for the third mission.

A central feature of this emerging organizational architecture is the research office and university commercialization units. These manage grant processes and the relationships between academics, funding agencies and commercial funders. They are structured differently across the universities but share certain common characteristics: they sit outside the disciplines, answer to the university DVC (Deputy Vice Chancellor) Research, and are staffed increasingly by professional research managers. As they have grown, and become increasingly professionalized, these offices have begun to create and administer databases to make visible areas of expertise that are aligned with applied or 'translational' research categories. They also foster and promote the type of entrepreneurial sensibilities and subjectivities envisaged in the Leadership Framework mentioned earlier. Research Office staff now use their databases to target academics and exhort them to apply for particular funding opportunities. The databases allow senior university leaders to imagine specific research capabilities that can be 'commanded' to respond to external research opportunities, or even, as one Vice Chancellor puts it, a 'university project':

> So the key really was to get a university project and begin to try and connect people to it. ... Universities used to be convenient organizations for individuals called academics who were independent contractors in their own minds to come to work each day to do what they wanted to do. ... But what we know now in an internationalizing

environment, the university has to have some distinct offer ... we always say to people we're not going to tell you what to do, but we would prefer that once you've done your own thing that you begin to think about how it links to the project in some way, to ask what you can contribute to it.

In performing these roles, research offices operate alongside the new commercialization units. While again, commercialization units take very different forms across the country, the general model is that they seek to commercialize university research through patents, licenses and royalties. They also support spin-in and spin-out companies, and the incubation of new ventures centred on discoveries and innovations. In general, they leave contract research and public-good research within the domains of university research offices. The exception, however, is Auckland University's UniServices Ltd, New Zealand's first and largest university commercialization unit. A wholly owned subsidiary of the university, it handles contract research as well as the commercialization functions associated with bringing scientific discoveries to market. As a result, UniServices is able to claim a far greater revenue stream, and in doing so makes very visible the full extent of commercial and commercializing activities in the modern university.

Another growing role of research offices is to respond to the changing research environment and opportunities created by government. So-called 'public good' research in New Zealand is channelled through four primary avenues, each funded from a different government source: the blue-skies Marsden fund; targeted research initiatives administered by the Ministry of Business, Innovation and Employment (MBIE); Centres of Research Excellence; and the National Science Challenges. All are now understood to provide investment rather than grants (Smart 2013). Both the Centres of Research Excellence (CoREs) and National Science Challenges (NSCs) are modelled on similar initiatives introduced into Australia and Canada during the 1990s (Cooper 2011). The National Science Challenges is a government initiative to create ten multidisciplinary areas to direct research funding into 'questions of broad societal relevance to New Zealand' (Witze 2013). Brainchild of the Chief Science Advisor to the Prime Minister and one of the country's leading advocates of research commercialization, Sir Peter Gluckman, the eleven 'challenges' are an attempt to direct science investment into the areas of health, environment and economic growth.

Each challenge is to be achieved by national research teams organized around a programme of funded projects. The teams are designed to integrate researchers from universities, Crown Research Institutes, and private and other public sector organizations. The research programme is overseen by both science and stakeholder boards. The effect of this is to tie academics into a funding regime dominated by applied scientific and technological research that is geared towards national development. According to the Minister for MBIE (whose portfolio includes higher education), these challenges represent 'a more strategic approach to [New Zealand's] science investment' (Joyce 2013). In early 2015, a senior official from MBIE articulated a ministry view of universities as actors in the innovation process ('providing skills for innovation, generating knowledge for economic and social development, exchanging knowledge and strengthening pathways to impact, facilitating international knowledge exchange and collaboration, and regional innovation systems and competitive advantage'). His presentation to the UNIKE (Universities in the Knowledge Economy) conference questioned how well New Zealand universities were performing this role, observing that 'many of our academic specializations are not well matched to areas of current or future economic comparative advantage'.

This combination of the word 'strategic', with 'science', 'innovation', 'investment' and national 'competitive advantage' mirrors the approach of the university research office and its rationale for taking control over the academic appointment process. For the universities, this results in ever-greater emphasis on third mission activities, including new categories of staff (such as National Science Challenge teams in research offices), new pressures on academics to participate in the challenges, and new strategic hires of potential challenge leaders. As a result, the boundaries between universities, government science laboratories and private research providers are blurred as research becomes increasingly steered towards addressing government-defined research goals. As Gluckman describes it, the challenges are 'a novel experiment in many ways, in terms of how best a small country must do science' (cited in Witze 2013).

New Labour Practices

The third mission funding regime is influencing not only research-support functions but also the selection of academic staff and what it means to be an academic. Our opening vignette of the new strategic appointment agenda is a case in point. Whereas in the past the public university had relatively few research-only positions, and those that existed were mostly confined to distinguished academics leading major projects or engaged in key frontiers of research and scholarship, the third mission is characterized by a growing separation of research from teaching. Research-only positions are increasingly being offered to relatively junior academics, while academics are incentivized – or coerced – to pursue external funding in order to buy themselves out of teaching responsibilities. With the devaluing of teaching and scholarship, the cornerstone of the traditional research-based teaching university is being eroded. In the new taxonomies of human resources planning and the third mission more generally, academics are reclassified as 'researchers' rather than as specialists and practitioners of a particular field of knowledge. One effect of this is to transform academics from disciplinary-based scholars into generic subjects for management; malleable, auditable, interchangeable, replaceable and able to be aggregated into clusters or teams as required by research office managers.

The other side of this 'will to unbundle' is the creation of 'teaching only' positions, often at reduced salaries and status, and with a different set of contractual obligations and manageable attributes: the Senior Tutor or Professional Teaching Fellow both of which tend to be more precarious and casualized roles. The third mission requires that academics become undisciplined so that they can be redisc18iplined according to the managerialist logics of research offices and technology transfer offices. This is also reflected in the drive towards schooling, centralization, interdisciplinarity and the breakup of departments as semi-autonomous units in the reformed organizational architecture of the third mission university.

In the New Zealand context, such 'teaching only' lectureships undermine and arguably contradict the legislative requirement of the 1989 Education Amendment Act (S162(4)). This states that one of the fundamental characteristics of New Zealand universities is that 'their research and teaching are closely inter-dependent, and most of their teaching is done by people who are active in advancing knowledge'. The decoupling of teaching from research also exposes departments and faculties to new risks. As our opening vignette confirms, junior academics are being explicitly hired for the commercializable potential of their research, as defined by research office professionals who are often remote from actual research trajectories and the cutting edges of knew knowledge. These officials are gambling on the basis of how the existing intellectual property of the university can be adapted to what they imagine to be the needs of future research funders. Traditional disciplinary hiring practices are based on the idea that universities should seek out candidates capable of developing new questions rather than demonstrating a capacity to provide answers to preset questions. This is one of the core principles behind the advance of robust scientific knowledge and the benefits that it generates: we cannot know what we do not yet know, or that which we may one day need to know.

Finally, these junior academics are hired with the expectation that they will fund not only their own salaries, but also the growing overhead costs of the university, which include the ballooning salaries of university administrators and managers. In some universities, particularly the University of Auckland, senior leaders and HR managers have rewritten the academic grades and standards policies to make entrepreneurialism and 'commercial acumen' explicit and measurable criteria for academic promotion (Amsler and Shore 2015). All of this places an extra burden on those junior staff as their positions are secured or ring-fenced for only a few years. What happens after the initial three or five years if the strategic appointee is unable to leverage their own salary and overheads? Then the cost of sustaining the appointment falls to the academic unit. In short, the risk is borne not by the managers who set the strategy, but by the departments and the academic body at large, who must pay that salary within their capped budgets. In practical terms this means that they will be unable to make any further hires to maintain their core teaching programmes and they may have to take on greater teaching responsibilities themselves, or persuade/coerce the strategic appointee into teaching, for which they may not have the appropriate expertise. The alternative is that teaching programmes become altered to suit the expertise of the now underperforming appointee, with the result that university teaching and knowledge is reshaped around these supposedly strategic themes (like 'personalized health care', 'agri-technology' or 'vision Matauranga') that managers, some five years earlier, had deemed important. Few developments more clearly symbolize the takeover of the university by the new managerial class or the ascendancy of its interests.

The Third Mission and Entrepreneurial Pedagogy

One frequently heard complaint from our academic research participants concerns the perceived erosion of academic values in contemporary university pedagogy. Here, the rise of new courses associated with the third mission university is seen as dovetailing with wider efforts to popularize curricula so as to attract students. All six of the eight universities we visited now teach entrepreneurship programmes (usually at graduate level), have established professorships in areas such as 'innovation', 'entrepreneurship' and 'leadership', and have created centres of entrepreneurship. A good example of this is the University of Auckland's one-year Masters in Commercialization and Entrepreneurship (MCE). Run out of the Business School's Centre for Innovation and Entrepreneurship (CIE), this course promises students they will acquire jobs, skills and knowledge that 'will unlock the secrets of success in starting up your own business'. As Director of Auckland UniServices acknowledged, 'there's an awful lot of attention in the Business School to creating a more entrepreneurial set of graduates, and a more business-savvy environment' (Dr Andy Shenk, interviewed 2013). This expertise is applied directly to the teaching of the third mission in the MCE, which along with more generic commercial nous promises to teach students 'the core knowledge and skills needed to commercialize and take to market new products, services and processes based on research discoveries, inventions, innovations and new ideas', and how to 'obtain funding and sell research-related innovations into national and global markets'.

The CIE (2014) boasts having created a 'unique entrepreneurial ecosystem' that 'supports New Zealand value creation through enterprise and innovations'.[6] This has, apparently, enabled the university to make a 'real impact on the New Zealand economy through supporting the creation and growth of New Zealand companies'. Postgraduate students, who may be in a position to have some knowledge of how to commercialize, are invited into the CIE ecosystem to attend short courses. Ph.D. students were invited to a two-day course in May 2014 to learn how 'to harness knowledge for wealth creation' from 'academic entrepreneurs', develop 'strategies for creating and capturing value from science', describe their ideas in an investment proposal, and workshop 'potential commercial applications' from their research (CIE 2014). The second day would help students to take 'a peek in the academic entrepreneur's toolbox'. Closely connected to the CIE in terms of its genesis, is Auckland University's Institute of Innovation in Biotechnology (IIB), which is actually contracted by the university to run a Masters in Bioscience Enterprise programme. As its Director Joerg Kistler explained, 'we're breaking down the barriers between industry and academia, so increasingly the university becomes more commercially oriented, the research becomes more translational' (Kistler, interviewed 2013).

There is nothing particularly exceptional about business schools running graduate programmes to teach skills in commerce or how to

Illustration 2.1: Poster on the university library door advertising programmes in Innovation and Entrepreneurship (Photo: Cris Shore 2016).

meet the needs of industry. What is unusual, perhaps, is the focus on the third mission itself as the object of study, as well as the extension of these programmes to students and parts of the university that previously had little to do with business or commerce, and the way these programmes are lionized by university leaders. Even the doors of the university library now carry posters proclaiming the importance of learning to become more entrepreneurial (see Illustration 2.1).

It seems that all disciplines and programmes are now required to think of themselves through the lens of commercialization and address the question: 'What contribution are you making to the university's entrepreneurialism and New Zealand's economic prosperity?'

New Contractualism and the Third Mission University

One of the interesting features of the University of Auckland's 'Strategic Appointments – Proposal for Implementation' document (Harding 2015), which outlines the criteria and process for appointing staff, is the carefully calculated attention that it pays to public sector hiring practices at the same time as it seeks to flout them. The document explicitly states that 'standard employment practices, including the requirement for continuation are essential'. It also insists that the strategic case for these new appointments is not to be based on arguments around student numbers (or EFTS). The implication one can draw from this is that these appointments are ring-fenced from public funding and thus immune from the requirements for open advertising, equal opportunities legislation and legal due process, as well as academic conventions. In short, these are 'exceptional hires' that do not require the rigour or transparency required for normal academic recruitment. There can therefore be no claims of discriminatory practice or unfair treatment and no appeal against any decision made under these 'special circumstances'. Candidates are approached individually and informally and invited to submit a Curriculum Vitae. The Head of School and senior academics fashion these details into a convincing business case, the Dean takes this to the Deputy Vice Chancellor (Research) and the DVC (Research) eventually informs the faculty of his or her committee's decision. This process has contradictory implications. On the one hand, it can appear as a wonderful opportunity for those departments that are able and willing to play the game, or that need to replace retiring staff under conditions of a university-wide hiring freeze. On the other hand, it is an extraordinarily divisive and high-risk strategy that tends to encourage patronage, cronyism, short-termism and opportunism; such hiring practices erode academic values and disciplines and undermine the links between local academic units and university management.

These strategic appointment initiatives are not isolated from other key shifts in contractual relations within the university. While each of New Zealand's universities has undergone periodic administrative restructurings, leading to redundancies, reassignments and new job specifications, our research confirms that none of these match the scale and intensity of the Faculty Administrative Review process (FAR) carried out at Auckland University in 2014.

Conclusion

Rather than serving the first and second missions of the university, the third mission is increasingly superseding them as the principal purpose of the university in its strategic thinking, managerial logics and daily practices. Our opening vignette points to one of the sites where the colonizing force of the third mission is most apparent and potent

– where it threatens to disentangle (or unbundle) research from teaching, overthrow disciplinary conventions and public-service defences of the democratic function of university, and lock teaching and scholarship into the priorities of commercialization. The rest of the chapter provides ample evidence to suggest that the third mission is becoming the mission of the university, not just contingently or even by stealth, but through a full-on frontal assault on hiring practices, promotions processes, internal investment in research and the organization of functions. In short, from strategic policy to new investment priorities, technologies of governance and daily routines, the new business of the university is displacing its traditional missions. While vice chancellors continue to justify the emphasis on revenue-raising and commercialization as a necessary expedient to support teaching and scholarship, our evidence suggests that the third mission is becoming the main purpose of the university.

However, while the pressures to which we point are real, powerful and certainly changing the university, our narrative also points to ongoing struggles and a set of traditions, academic values and democratic potential that are not yet completely lost. At several key sites where the third mission comes into conflict with the other two missions, there remain contest and opportunities to mount a politics that might evade some of its colonizing force. Those keys sites where the third mission is contested include the traditions of investigator-led research, the formation of research institutes, research-based teaching, and the research assessment exercise (PBRF) where performance is assessed with reference to disciplinary excellence rather than external revenue raising. These are sites where university leaders use the rhetoric and rationale of the third mission to actively and strategically reinvent the university as they try to marshal resources and manoeuvre academics into research teams and fields that are deemed to be more commercializable or relevant to business, while government seeks to define new social impact metrics for the PBRF. Yet third mission advocates are far from always sure what to do, let alone always winning.

Academics are proving adept at developing their own metrics, altering their publishing practices and often strategically double-counting to subvert the metrics of the new grades and standards (see Curtis, this volume) – and we await the first lawsuit that uses the metrics to contest a promotion denied. Both authors have become entangled in strategic appointment debates, one in crafting a case for a new hire in terms that made the appointment appear 'strategic' and the other in successfully contesting alongside colleagues the disruptive consequences on a discipline and teaching programme of a prospective appointment. More generally, the academic's expertise is embodied in the individual and resists easy aggregation into manageable teams or disaggregation into manageable units of 'skills'. In many respects, the competitive advantage of the university in commercialized research markets remains its mystique, its reputation, and the training of its employees to imagine new questions. This resists managerial models. Finally, the academic subject remains formed around the freedom to think and learn within the disciplines of their particular discipline. This is the appeal of the profession and the great privilege for which academics forgo other prospective careers. All is as yet not lost.

We wish to conclude by asking what might be done to grasp any potential to practice a politics of the university in the name of its primary missions. In this we are given some perverse optimism by a conversation with an administrator based in our university's Research Office. He tells us that within the Research Office, academics, and their disciplines, teaching and scholarly activities are referred to colloquially as 'faculty land' (interviews carried out in 2015). The term suggests a dismissive lack of understanding of what is the substance and social and economic value of the university enterprise, as well as an 'us and them' logic in which the Research Office positions itself at the core of the university. While there is much in this to critique, not least the image of a Monday morning meeting room full of managers being briefed on the week's plans to bring 'faculty land' to heel, there is also much to suggest that they are some distance away from being able to fully break into the wild terrain of teaching and scholarship, discipline the academics into manageable and controllable teams of researchers, and muzzle their ornery habits. There is something in the use of the disparaging sobriquet that speaks of a grudging recognition of how difficult it remains to tame the wilds, even if it also suggests an arrogant and ignorant sense of inevitable victory.

It used to be argued that the main tension within the university was between the arts and the sciences (what C.P. Snow termed 'two cultures'). Today, the main dividing lines are increasingly set between academics and managers. For the new cadre of managers, academics are constructed as an unruly workforce that needs to be cajoled and incentivized into ever-higher productivity and 'performance'. Yet they do not yet know how to do this. For managers, academics are as mysterious as they are irritating and seemingly ungovernable, yet in the context of the university, academics are both the workforce that produces capital for the knowledge economy and, in many respects, that capital itself. Despite this, those branches of the university that are growing most rapidly are its administrative and managerial branches, not 'faculty land'. We have now reached the astonishing point in the history of the university where the majority of university employees have no direct link with either teaching or research.

The task for a progressive politics of the university today is to begin the process of reclaiming academic ownership of the university. How can we do this? We can start by contesting so-called 'strategic hires' and adopting a more sceptical stance towards the promises of vice chancellors and senior leadership teams whose motivations are based on very different Key Performance Indicators. We can also make university management and governance foci for critical academic research and scholarship in order to highlight the costs of managerialism and to show the alternatives that are possible. Above all, we need to ensure that faculty land continues to be a wild and undomesticated space.

◆

Nick Lewis is Associate Professor in geography at the University of Auckland. Nick's research interests lie primarily in the fields of economic and political geography and are focused on economic governance. He is interested in the visible hand of the market and in how economies are made. Nick is currently investigating the commercialization of higher education, but has previously studied industry-building initiatives in high fashion, wine, and international education. He has an ongoing interest in ideas of constructive critique and is beginning a new project on how an innovation economy is being brought into being in New Zealand.

Cris Shore (D.Phil. in social anthropology, Sussex) is Professor of Social Anthropology at the University of Auckland, having previously worked at Goldsmiths College, London. His research interests include political anthropology, the study of organizations, power and corruption, higher education, and the European Union and the anthropology of policy. Cris was founding Editor of *Anthropology in Action*, founding Director of Auckland University's Europe Institute and, with Sue Wright, is Editor of Stanford University Press's book series, *Anthropology of Policy*. Current research includes a study of the 'Crown' in post-colonial settler societies and a book exploring how indicators and ranking are reassembling society.

Notes

1. The university's commercialization unit. See http://www.uniservices.co.nz/ for a full description.

2. The Performance-Based Research Fund is a competitive, five-yearly research assessment exercise, similar to the U.K.'s former Research Assessment Exercise (RAE) and the Australian Excellence in Research for Australia (ERA).
3. The most widely cited and accepted definition of what such activities encompass, as set out in the 2002 Science Policy Research Unit Report to the Russell Group of universities, is those that are 'concerned with the generation, use, application and exploitation of knowledge and other university capabilities outside academic environments' (Molas-Gallart et al. 2002)
4. The research underpinning this chapter was funded by the University of Auckland's cross-faculty research initiatives fund, a fund established to support third-mission-like activities. The project (2013–2014) involved researchers in the Faculties of Science, Arts, Education, and Business (Nick Lewis, Cris Shore, John Morgan and Nigel Haworth). Its objective was to map the third mission in New Zealand universities.
5. In our fieldwork we visited several of these, including the Centre for Sustainability at Otago University, the Auckland Bioengineering Institute at Auckland University, and the Agricultural Economics Research Unit at Lincoln University.
6. The Business School's 'entrepreneurial ecosystem' for students includes its annual Spark Prize for young entrepreneurs, its 'Icehouse' business incubator, and its 'Entrepreneur's Challenge' initiative.

References

Adams, P. 2008. *Strategic Review of the Performance-Based Research Fund: The Assessment Process*. Leeds: Evidence Ltd.

Amsler, M., and C. Shore. 2015. 'Responsibilisation and Leadership in the neoliberal university: a New Zealand perspective', *Discourse: Studies in the Cultural Politics of Education*, published online: DOI: 10.1080/01596306.2015.1 104857.

Bruneau, W., and D. Savage. 2002. *Counting out the Scholars: How Performance Indicators Undermine Universities and Colleges*. Toronto: J. Lorimer.

Ciancanelli, P. 2008. 'The business of teaching and learning: an accounting perspective', *Learning and Teaching* 1(1): 155–83.

CIE (Centre for Innovation and Entrepreneurship). 2014. 'PhD Research Innovation and Commercialisation Course', The University of Auckland, 12–13 May. Retrieved 1 October 2015 from http://www.gsm.auckland.ac.nz/cie/programmes/phd.

Clark, H. 2001. 'Knowledge Wave conference: statement from the co-chairs', 3 August. Retrieved 10 February 2016 from http://www.beehive.govt.nz/node/11379.

Cooper, D. 2011. *The University in Development: Case Studies of Use-Oriented Research*. Cape Town: Human Sciences Research Council.

Crabtree, P. 2015. 'The National Research Environment: Emerging Pressures and New Possibilities?', *Universities in the Knowledge Economy Conference:*

Transforming Higher Education in the Asia-Pacific Rim and Europe, 10–13 February 2015. Auckland: University of Auckland.
Curtis, B. 2008. 'The Performance-Based Research Fund: research assessment and funding in New Zealand', *Globalisation, Societies and Education* 6(2): 179–94.
Etzkowitz, H., and L. Leydesdorff (eds). 1997. *Universities in the Global Economy: A Triplehelix of University–Industry–Government Relations*. London: Cassell Academic.
Etzkowitz, H., et al. 2000. 'The Future of the University and the University of the Future: Evolution of Ivory Tower to Entrepreneurial Paradigm', *Research Policy* 29: 313–30.
Harding, J. 2015. 'Strategic Appointments – Proposal for Implementation', internal document, February 2015. Auckland: University of Auckland.
Wellington Parliamentary Counsel Office. 1989. 'New Zealand Education Amendment Act 1989 S162(4)'. Wellington. Retrieved 10 February 2016 from http://www.legislation.govt.nz/act/public/1989/0080/latest/DLM175959.html.
Joyce, S. 2013. 'Budget 2013: National Science Challenges Announced', 1 May. Retrieved 12 January 2016 from http://www.beehive.govt.nz/release/budget-2013-national-science-challenges-announced---budget-boost-735m.
Kelsey, J. 1995. *The New Zealand Experiment: A World Model for Structural Adjustment?* Auckland: Auckland University Press.
Larner, W., and R. Le Heron. 2005. 'Neo-liberalizing Spaces and Subjectivities: Reinventing New Zealand Universities', *Organization* 12(6): 843–62.
Molas-Gallart, J., et al. 2002. *Measuring Third Stream Activities*. Brighton: SPRU.
Mulgan, R. 1994. *Politics in New Zealand*. Auckland: Auckland University Press.
Narayan, A.K. 2012. 'The Role of Government and Accounting in the Development of Academic Research Commercialization: The New Zealand Experience', *Accounting History* 17(3-4): 311–29.
Shore, C. 2010. 'The Reform of New Zealand's University System: "After Neoliberalism"', *(LATISS) Learning and Teaching: International Journal of Higher Education in the Social Sciences* 3(1): 1–31.
Shore, C., and L. McLauchlan. 2012. '"Third mission" activities and academic entrepreneurs: commercialisation and the remaking of the university', *Social Anthropology/Anthropologie Sociale* 20(3): 267–86.
Shore, C., and M. Taitz. 2012. 'Who Owns the University? Institutional Autonomy and Academic Freedom in an Age of Knowledge Capitalism', *Globalisation, Societies and Education* 10(2): 201–19.
Smart, J. 2013. 'University Research Strategies', *The University in 2Q30 Conference, 2 April 2013*. Auckland: University of Auckland.
Universities New Zealand. 2011. 'Universities New Zealand Briefing: Contributing to Government Goals'. Universities New Zealand: Wellington. Retrieved 10 February 2016 from http://www.universitiesnz.ac.nz/files/Briefing%20for%20the%20Incoming%20Government%20Dec%202011%20.pdf.
University of Auckland. 2013a. 'University of Auckland Strategic Plan 2013–2020'. Auckland. Retrieved 10 February 2016 from https://cdn.auckland.ac.nz/

assets/central/about/equal-opportunities/strategic-plan-2013-2020_web-version.pdf.

_____. 2013b. 'Guide to the University of Auckland Leadership Framework', internal document. Auckland: University of Auckland.

Witze, A. 2013. 'New Zealand Aims High with National Science Challenges', *Nature*, 28 June. Retrieved 10 February 2016 from http://www.nature.com/news/new-zealand-aims-high-with-national-science-challenges-1.13253.

CHAPTER 3
Universities in the Competition State
Lessons from Denmark

SUSAN WRIGHT AND JAKOB WILLIAMS ØRBERG

━━ ◆◆◆

In 2003 Denmark passed a radical law reforming its universities' functions, management and governance and giving them a so-called autonomous, 'self-owning' status. In the following decade, further reforms brought bibliographic indicators for calculating publication output and allocating funding competitively, a new budgeting and inspection system, mergers between universities and government research institutes and the foundation of a Sino-Danish Centre in Beijing. Education programmes were simultaneously changed from a progressive, discipline-based approach to the acquisition of competences through modules, the introduction of a new programme accreditation regime, and later a system for institutional accreditation. These changes were accompanied by significantly increased university budgets. The aim of these reforms was not to hasten the death of Danish public universities; rather, the opposite. It was to restore politicians' trust and make universities and their graduates contribute more actively to the society and economy.[1]

These reforms created numerous tensions in the higher education environment: they envisioned universities having multiple interactions with society, but how would this be facilitated by a new top-down governance regime? What was the role and public purpose of the university to be? What kind of organization should it be? What was the purpose of higher education and what kind of attributes should graduates have? Opponents of the reforms published a death notice:

> The Free University (1479–2003) departed this life at Parliament's third reading on 8 May. You will be missed. We will remember you for your self-government and independence. Your involuntary death will leave a large void in our everyday life. The Bereaved (*ForskerFORUM* 2003: 1, authors' translation).

The Minister of Science Technology and Innovation also claimed that the 2003 law was the most significant thing to happen to Danish universities since the creation of the University of Copenhagen, but rejected claims that he had killed the public university. Whereas opponents argued there was nothing wrong prior to 2003 that needed fixing, quoting bibliometrics to show Danish academics consistently ranked second most productive among OECD countries, the Minister said the reforms were to reposition universities in a new context. That context was depicted as the inevitable arrival of a 'global knowledge economy', which necessitated not only reforming the university, but also the state itself. The state's role was to mobilize resources and deploy them to competitive advantage in the global economy. Universities produced the two main raw materials to be mined by this imagined new form of capitalism: knowledge and graduates. Danish competitiveness was said to reside in, first, the speed with which knowledge could be turned into innovative products and technologies ('From thought to invoice' was the Minister's catchphrase) and, second, in the production of a highly skilled workforce, with up-to-date knowledge, international networks, and the transferable 'soft' skills to move smoothly into industrial employment as 'knowledge workers'.

Drawing on government papers, lobbying documents and academic reports leading up to the 2003 University Law, this chapter traces how arguments about becoming a competition state in a global knowledge economy took shape in Denmark and mobilized changes to its higher education sector. We then explore how contradictions emerged in the ways in which universities were conceptualized as 'knowledge organizations' and how graduates were expected to benefit from being 'knowledge workers' in this new context. While universities were to drive Denmark's competitiveness by being more receptive to the demands of the economy and society, they were also being tied ever closer to the state's priorities. The government's emphasis on steering students towards degrees relevant for society first made universities responsible for moulding knowledge workers and then pushed this responsibility onto the student themselves.

The Changing Context – Universities and the Global Knowledge Economy

The 1970s oil price hike by OPEC is often quoted as the first shock that disturbed the post-war economic and political settlement and, by 1979, Denmark's Minister of Finance claimed that Denmark 'was heading for the abyss' (Østergaard 1998: 12–13). This financial crisis produced two strands of reform concerning the global political economy and the role of the state.

Discussions about how to gain competitive advantage and attract 'footloose capital' gained currency in policy circles, particularly in Denmark, where the Finance Ministry used arguments by Michael Porter, Harvard Business School Professor and influential government advisor, to change industrial policy in the 1990s (Pedersen 2011: 57). In *The Competitive Advantage of Nations,* Porter (1989) argued that the primary responsibility for competitiveness shifted from national firms to nations themselves. Competitiveness was a problem of state governance: how to gear state policies to improve the capacity of 'national' flagship firms to innovate and compete with foreign ones.

The question in Denmark was, 'Which firms?' In the early 1990s the Danish industrial sector had few very large companies but a large number of small and medium-sized enterprises (SMEs). Large companies were strong innovators and relied on using knowledge produced by universities. Seventy-five percent of large manufacturing firms in the government's prioritized fields – pharmaceuticals, biotechnology, engineering, and information and communication technology – successfully translated universities' specialized scientific knowledge into new products (Graversen, Lauridsen and Mortensen 2003: 48, 59). Such firms benefitted from universities' long-term scientific research, which enabled industry to avoid 'high risk' investments and to develop new materials and products shielded from market competition (Schmidt 2008: 632). In contrast, SMEs only engaged in incremental, low-risk innovations, rather than developing new products, operations and markets. SME managers often did not hire university graduates and did not understand how to use university research (Schmidt 2003, 2008: 627). Bengt-Åke Lundvall, Professor of Business at Aalborg University, found that only 11 percent of Danish SMEs with fewer than fifty members of staff had a graduate employee; and those firms were twice as likely to cooperate with research institutions (Lundvall 2006: 10–11, 14). In work for the OECD, World Bank and EU, and in advice to the Danish government, he proposed a 'learning economy' approach that focused on facilitating the employment of graduates in SMEs (ibid.: 13–15).

The Confederation of Danish Industry (DI) and the industry think tank Academy for Technical Sciences (ATV 1997, 1998, 2001) argued that Denmark's success as a knowledge economy depended on the ability of certain manufacturing firms with a global reach to translate research into innovative products and modes of organizing. They produced reports and lobbied vigorously to set the terms of the policy debate in the 1990s. Keeping a focus on the interest of large corporations, they wanted universities to concentrate their activities on sectors where the transfer of scientific and technical knowledge into industrial innovation could secure the future competitiveness of Danish industry (ATV 1998: 42; 2001: 29). DI calculated that private investment in research and development needed to grow by 30 percent to reach the OECD average (DI 1997a: 23) and public funding also needed to increase, especially because of serious underinvestment in universities. They deflected blame for low levels of industrial research and development away from industry, claiming that universities were responsible because they focused on academic publications rather than converting knowledge into business possibilities and industrial value creation (DI 1997b: 9, 18).They called for universities to have a 'third wing', a statutory role of 'obligatory collaboration' with industry (ATV 1998; DI 1997b: 20). Redefining universities as one of industry's 'knowledge suppliers', DI demanded that higher education be aligned with industry's future needs (DI 1997b:13) and claimed that '[a] national knowledge base that has no applicability to industry or society has no value' (ibid.: 43).

Industrial lobbyists wanted increased government funding of universities so that industries could reap the benefits of publicly funded research, arguing that this was for the public good, as industry funded Denmark's high-cost welfare society (ATV 2001; DI 1997b: 7). Between them, DI and ATV set out their members' recommendations as if they would benefit all industry. Lundvall criticized the 'tendency to ... use those exceptions as the basis for general strategies to change the universities' and argued that it was not realistic to make 'whole industry' cooperate with 'whole university' (Lundvall 2006: 9). But government adopted the discourse, saying 'universities' should collaborate with 'industry'. In a final shift in the discourse, the narrow industrial interests that would benefit from the reforms referred to themselves as the 'surrounding society' (DI 2000: 13, 15). The 'problem' of universities' weak links with 'surrounding society' became a central justification for the 2003 University Law.

An influential OECD report (1995) portrayed the new 'global economy' – whose central commodity was 'knowledge' – as an inevitable and fast-approaching future in which competitive advantage lay in converting knowledge into innovative products or new ways of organizing operations. The OECD set out to collect best practice and create checklists of policy actions for governments to use in preparing their states to compete in this knowledge economy. The OECD urged its thirty-four members to become 'knowledge economies' so as to retain their position as the world's richest countries. They were to 'head' a global economy, while outsourcing repetitive, dirty and dangerous work to 'hands' in the rest of the world. The World Bank subsequently produced its own knowledge economy index arguing that, if poorer countries engaged in knowledge work and reforms of their higher education sectors, they could leapfrog stages in development and compete successfully with the richest countries.

Competition States and Their Universities

Whilst one section of the OECD impelled members to follow a programme that would bring the 'global knowledge economy' into being, another section, the Public Management Committee (PUMA) worked on reforming the role and steering of the state. PUMA's reports adopted a tone of 'naked urgency', arguing that governments were faced with such fiscal pressures, economic competition, declining public trust, political turbulence and 'ever-faster, multi-fronted change' that nothing short of a paradigm shift to a new way of ordering the state was required (Pal 2008: 60–63). PUMA also developed toolkits, checklists and best-practice guides, identified successful countries for others to follow, and created templates to assess and rank countries' progress. Denmark and other countries in turn fed their ideas and experience into PUMA's formulations of public-sector reform and actively adopted and shaped New Public Management as the image of the 'ideal modern state' (ibid.: 72; Sahlin-Andersson 2000: 2, 18).

PUMA influenced the Danish Ministry of Finance from 1980 onwards (Østergaard 1998) and inspired Denmark's Modernization Programme. Denmark also played a strong role in the OECD's policy development, culminating in a top Danish civil servant becoming head of PUMA (Ejersbo and Greve 2005: 10). The Danish Modernization Programme was a result of a commission to improve the state system for appropriation set up by the Social Democrat government in 1982, but its results were implemented under the Conservative government in 1983. The programme aimed to decentralize the public sector, create incentives for efficiency, simplify the appropriation system and gain more local control over spending (Østergaard 1998: 13). By the 1990s, privatization and liberalization of the public sector were firmly entrenched and governments of different hues passed the reforms between one another, simply shifting the 'political spotlight' within roughly the same overall agenda (Ejersbo and Greve 2005: 1, 9).

Cerny (1990), one of the authors most influential in the OECD and Denmark, argued that 'at the heart of globalization' was the transformation of nation-states into 'competition states'. Cameron and Palan (2004) developed this further by identifying the 'competition state' as the actor that must reconcile the market requirements of globalization with society's demands for economic opportunities and social cohesion (Cameron and Palan 2004: 109). The role of the 'competition state' was no longer to apply universal welfare services to a homogeneous population but rather to mobilize productive resources and deploy them to competitive advantage (Pedersen 2011). To promote national prosperity, states should provide the legal, regulatory and financial framework for opening up new frontiers for capital in global markets and reform the organization of educational and other services so that they contribute to economic competitiveness. In *The Work of Nations*, Reich (1991) added that the use of redistributive taxation should counter social inequalities and, through education, enable every individual to leave the archipelago of 'exclusion', optimize their skills and join the globalized labour market. In this way of conceiving the world, every state, institution and person is imagined as mobilized in the global competition. If states can incentivize institutions and individuals to activate capacities that maximize their own income, their position (in labour markets, league tables and so on) and their share of markets and services, then the whole country prospers.

Where states traditionally took certain economic activities out of the market and used labour-market regulation and universal services to maintain some sense of a public good, the state was now converting its own administration and services into competitive entities. As Cerny argued, the state was drawn into becoming a market actor itself:

> The post-modern irony of the state is that rather than being undermined by inexorable forces of globalization, the competition state is becoming both the engine room and the steering mechanism of political globalization itself (Cerny 1997: 274).

In 1996, the Danish Ministry of Finance published a review of the way its PUMA-aligned 'modernization' reform, called 'Aim and Frame Steering', had transformed the state (Ministry of Finance 1996). This report divided the public sector into three categories: 'political leadership' (ministers and local authority leaders); administration (*forvaltning*) (leading civil servants and public administration managers); and producers (*producenter*) (those who deliver public services). In the pre-reform (1960s) phase, all three categories were integrated into a bureaucratic 'command and control' system, where political leaders assumed that their decisions were carried out down the hierarchy. But, the report argued, this was not necessarily the case, and the size and cost of the public sector had risen out of control. The reform engaged politicians in what Osborne and Gaebler (1992) called a shift from 'rowing' to 'steering' the public sector. Instead of managing the detailed allocation of funding and tasks, political leaders would focus on setting the overall political aims and budget, leaving civil servants to achieve the desired results in negotiation with service deliverers. At this stage, the reform had three main components, reflecting Cerny's argument that the state commodified itself. First, from 1985 onwards, budgets for each service were fixed. Managers were given greater autonomy over budgets and personnel and reporting was simplified to an annual account of performance (Thorn and Lyndrup 2006: 2, 3). Second, ministries were divided into 'departments' where policymaking and evaluation were carried out, and independent entities called 'agencies' were responsible for policy implementation and administration. Following Pollitt et al.'s (2001) 'principal–agent' theory, if a commissioning department (principal) was separated from an 'agency' responsible for policy implementation, the latter was expected to organize itself much more effectively. Third, in keeping with this principal–agent theory, departments steered the 'agencies' through contracts whose performance targets reflected the political aims for their work – for example, demanding they rationalize their work processes and improve productivity and quality (Ministry of Finance 1996: section 1.2).

The reform's final phase divided the bureaucracy between 'administration' and 'service deliverers' and extended Aim and Frame Steering to relations between them. This involved giving local managers of 'service delivery' organizations (such as education institutions or social care facilities) greater control. But they would also be more responsive to political targets, by shifting from input to output funding and by introducing a number of 'quasi-market mechanisms' under the rubric of 'citizens' choice' and competition between service providers. Each ministry or local authority selected aspects of these reforms to implement in their own way. Whereas some parts of the public service delivery were converted into public corporations, in 1991 the Ministry of Education converted technical schools into 'self-owning institutions' with a governing board, control over their own budgets and the ability to allocate funds according to political priorities (Thorn and Lyndrup

2006: 2). To induce technical schools to compete for students and improve their pass rates, state funding was changed to 'output payments': the school clocked up a unit of funding every time a student passed an exam – the so-called taximeter system. A similar system of 'taximeter' output funding was later introduced more widely: for example, to hospitals and, in 1994, to universities (Drumaux in Pedersen et al. 2006; Wright and Ørberg 2015).

The 2003 University Law turned universities into 'self-owning institutions' and brought them fully under Aim and Frame steering (Ørberg 2006). The same law reconfigured universities to operate in the three imagined spaces of a globalized world. First, they were to position themselves as corporations in the 'offshore' global space, competing to project themselves globally and attract international faculty and a share of the international trade in students and research contracts. Second, they were to service the national economy by providing industry with knowledge that could be turned into innovations, and students who had the knowledge, networks and skills needed to be self-starting, team-working, mobile 'knowledge workers'. Third, by retaining free tuition and educational opportunities in every region, universities might overcome the inherently divisive effects of the 'high skills' economy by being open to all on meritocratic grounds. In less than twenty years, universities shifted from being institutions ring-fenced from economic and political interests, to institutions 'driving' the global knowledge economy by providing knowledge for innovation and highly skilled knowledge workers, and being part of that global economy themselves.

What Kind of Organization?

These two issues – getting universities to drive Denmark's competitiveness and aligning them with the Aim and Frame Steering agenda – required reforms to the organization and leadership of Denmark's universities. But the two issues implied different forms of organization that were not necessarily compatible.

A government-commissioned report on the 'Leadership, organization and competences' needed by Danish companies in the twenty-first century (Arbejdsministeriet et al. 1997) depicted a network of knowledge organizations operating in a knowledge economy. Old, stable hierarchical structures were outdated because companies are continually changing. They needed 'a flat decision-making system, self-managing groups, cross-disciplinarity, and leadership based on values rather than steering and control' (ibid.: 12). To become such 'flexible' organizations, firms would need close relations with their surroundings and to be part of a network of consultants, educators, researchers and collaboration partners so as to keep developing new competences, products and forms of organization (ibid.:14). The report argued that to be a knowledge resource for surrounding society, higher education institutions should be part of this network of flexible organizations with more mobility of researchers, teachers, students, managers and employees between them and industry (ibid.: 9, 28–29, 32).

One company considered a model for such networked, flat organizations was Bang and Olufsen, where, as Krause-Jensen's (2010) ethnography shows, each employee was expected to draw on their own extensive network of people in other companies to solve problems or form project teams. This networking organization was described by Reich (1991), who influenced policymakers in the United States and Europe, especially when he became President Clinton's Secretary of State for Labor (1993–1997). Reich described the organizational structure for high-value knowledge-based production as a spider's web: 'an array of decentralized groups and subgroups which are continuously contracting with similarly diffuse groups and working units all over the world' (Reich 1991: 89). At each point of connection a small number of 'problem identifiers' and 'problem solvers' create profitable links to other webs and, in the centre, strategic brokers bind the threads together, make resources available for initiatives, and ensure there is a return to the 'bottom line'. Mobility and networking make boundaries hard to discern. Unlike old-style corporations, there is no 'inside' and 'outside'; it is rather an enterprise web, with different distances from the strategic centre.[2] This resembles one view of the university as the sum total of individual academics' networks and the activities that these generate. Management's role is, then, to encourage academics to look outwards and use their networks to generate new research questions and ideas for teaching; to spot promising ideas; and to make sure resources and work conditions facilitate their development. The main difference from other knowledge organizations is that a university needs forums for academics to discuss their networking initiatives and to generate a collective awareness, and sometimes judgements, on how to protect the research freedom, independence and ethics of the institution.

Reports by pressure groups presented a less coherent picture of the university as a knowledge organization. DI clearly wanted universities to have a flatter structure with which to interact with firms and respond flexibly to their needs:

> The form of management has changed from a stratified hierarchy to a flatter organization with many self-steering and cross-disciplinary groups. The individual worker is increasingly required to be 'self-supporting' and able to create results in groups on the basis of an understanding of the overall aims of the company (DI 1997b: 30, authors' translation).

Before the reform, Danish academics arguably already had flexible, networked and self-managing groups with flat governance structures and elected decision-making boards and leaders. But DI argued that universities also needed stronger leadership to overcome their inward focus; leaders who could direct resources to research areas needed by industry and with whom industry could do business. To become flexible organizations, they needed a new management that was not dependent on collegial rule. The idea of a university having a strong, central decision maker contradicted the 'flat' characteristics of a networked knowledge organizations, as employees would have to look up to the leadership to whom they were accountable, and not outwards to 'surrounding society'. Later the academic unions and concerned individual academics made these arguments, but in the 1990s they did not participate in this debate.

The 'Aim and Frame' model did not see the university as a flat organization with a spider's web of flexible networking in surrounding society. In this model, the university would no longer be protected/controlled by the ministry and would be 'set free' as a discrete entity, or 'agent', led by a strategic manager who would organize relations with other individual entities in 'surrounding society' through contracts. Ministries, industry, health, education and other public agencies, local authorities and community groups could all legitimately make demands on the university for education and research services. It was up to the university as a 'free agent' to negotiate these demands and enter into contracts about what it promised to deliver. Importantly, the university had a statutory requirement to make periodic contracts with the ministry, with performance targets through which it would be closely bound to government policy and held accountable for its efficient use of public funding. This system needed a hierarchy of leaders at each level of the organization who could sign contracts and be held to account. Both the PUMA reports and the OECD's higher education unit projected a new heroic role for these managers (Wright and Ørberg 2011: 284–86). New Public Management reforms were challenging and dangerous, fraught with uncertainty and disastrous if done incorrectly, and reforming managers had an urgent and exciting vocation, making hard political choices and steeling their will to ride through employees' resistance to change, which was seen as an understandable but thoughtless and irrational universal reflex (Pal 2008: 70–71). These ideas of public sector reform depicted universities as organizations with a strong boundary against 'surrounding society' and a coherent and hierarchical internal structure focused on delivering performance targets upwards through tiers of strong leaders and ultimately to the ministry. Exponents of performance management argued that an emphasis on strong leadership was compatible with the empowerment of employees because, if employees 'owned' the targets set in performance contracts, this would induce 'a more relaxed and flexible performance regime that focuse[d] more on output and outcome and less on internal processes' (Thorn and Lyndrup 2006: 9). But such co-option is not the same as self-managed academics generating their own initiatives through engagement with widespread networks. In performance management, the attention of academics is focused not outwards, but upwards and in the opposite direction to a networked knowledge organization.

The tension between these different ideas of organization and leadership – fluid/networked versus discrete/coherent organizations, flat versus hierarchical structures, self-managed versus controlled by external governing boards, collegial versus strategic leaders – was hotly debated during the 1990s (ATV 1997; Danish Council for Research Policy 1999; DI 2000; DI and CO-Industri 2001). The government eventually appointed a Danish Research Commission (2001) to resolve this issue. Business leaders on the commission looked askance at the newly introduced hierarchical structure at the Danish Technical University, with an appointed rector and upwardly accountable line management. They viewed a centralized system of control responsible to the ministry as making universities less responsive to industry. They needed a university leadership that would facilitate cooperation with industry, that was able to prioritize, make decisions, and deal with the apocryphal stories of a scandalous waste of resources, whilst also listening to academics and encouraging their networking and knowledge exchange.

An organizational researcher on the Danish Research Commission (Jensen 2010) argued that a university has two coexisting organizational forms: a professional bureaucracy for fairly standardized teaching operations and case administration; and for research, an 'adhocracy' of independent experts responding to a dynamic environment. The Danish Research Commission (2001) recommended a mix of strong leadership and collegiality: governing boards with a majority of external members and appointed rectors and deans; but departments should have elected leaders and research groups should be free to choose their organizational form. The government rejected this compromise, establishing instead a model based on governing boards with a majority of external members, appointed leaders at every level, and no forums for academic input into decision making beyond 'academic councils' responsible for quality control. It was, as a high-level ministry official told us, a model free from 'fuss'. Of the previous elected system, only 'study boards' of academics and students continued to review education programmes (Wright and Ørberg 2015). The legislation stated that the university should be both strategically led and outward looking, but the ministry's use of Aim and Frame to steer and curb the freedom of universities meant that industry continued to complain that the universities still did not engage sufficiently with 'surrounding society'.

What Kind of Knowledge Workers?

Universities' other 'core' contribution to society, the formation of 'knowledge workers' through research-based teaching – was debated alongside university organization. A series of reports and lobbying documents detailed what kinds of students they should be producing and what education reforms were needed in a competition state and knowledge economy. Pedersen (2011) explains that each historical formation of the state entails a vision of the way that citizens should see themselves and conduct themselves. Whereas in the welfare state students' education was thought to also benefit society, in the competition state individuals are responsible for their own prospects. It is up to each individual to invest in their education and acquire the skills needed for employment and to market themselves through their CV. According to 'new human capital theory' (Brown et al. 2011), which developed alongside the 'global knowledge economy' and 'competition state' discourse, individuals should continually invest in lifelong learning as a personal and positional good to keep themselves employed in a fast-moving labour market. Much of this language was evident in Danish policies, but as Danish higher education is free and supported by a grant for living costs, students' private 'investment' referred to time and effort rather than money. Nor was labour market information made available for students to steer their choice, as the English phrase goes, on where to 'learn to earn'. Instead, government retained a key role in steering universities to make students 'employable' in a knowledge economy.

Denmark was in the vanguard of the Bologna Process to harmonize higher education and develop a European Higher Education Area. The Ministry of Science, Technology and Innovation issued a Danish Qualifications Framework (VTU 2003) long before the ministers in the Bologna Process committed to doing so (EC 2005). Whereas the European Qualifications Framework stressed a broad and advanced knowledge base, democratic participation, and competences intended to make students employable in the knowledge economy, the Danish guidelines mainly focused on competences for employability (Sarauw 2011). Previously, government reports had emphasized that students were to gain a deep disciplinary knowledge and experience of democratic and critical citizenship as well as employability, but a Ministry of Education report (1997c) stated that students were expected to have already been formed as democratic citizens in the lower levels of the education system. From 1997 the focus was on competence-oriented higher education geared to the envisioned future needs of industry, and the other purposes of higher education were sidelined (Ørberg 2008: 7, 22). In its reports on the knowledge economy, DI argued that universities should be required to document how their education aligned with needs in the labour market (DI 1997a: 13) and predicted that knowledge-intensive industries needed 3–4,000 more engineers each year, 50 percent more graduates (but far fewer humanities graduates) and double the number of doctorates (DI 1997a: 16, 9; 1997b: 12, 32–3). The Ministry of Education (1997a and b) and Ministry of Finance (1997) argued that future knowledge workers needed faster throughput to gain their degrees and enter the labour market with competences that would make them employable.

By 2003, however, the idea that competition states needed a highly skilled population to succeed in the global knowledge economy was already being questioned by business gurus. These ideas originally stemmed from Reich (1991) and business consultant, Peter Drucker (1993). Central to Reich's image of knowledge organizations as a network of projects were 'symbolic analysts' with high cognitive skill, able to interpret and present information in diagrams, graphs, tables and texts that communicate with different colleagues and clients. They needed to be self-starters and team players, with a boundary-less devotion to work, skilled in intercultural communication, and forever expanding their capacities and researching new topics. They were envisaged as working flexibly in short-term project teams, using their networks to get recruited into new projects, and building up their CVs as 'portfolio workers'. A college degree was a crucial starting point for such knowledge workers, and Reich envisaged a future of infinite expansion of knowledge work, promising increasing numbers of Americans joining the middle class. Drucker (1993), who coined the term 'knowledge worker', projected a similar image of a creative and innovative, highly skilled workforce and shared this promise of infinite expansion of knowledge work in the future. He argued that, when the prosperity of individuals, companies and nations depended on the application of knowledge, there would be a power shift in favour of knowledge workers. The owners of capital and employers would become dependent on knowledge workers as they owned the 'means of production' – the knowledge – in their heads (Drucker 1993: 57).

By the late 1990s, this promise looked doubtful. Stewart (1997) argued that companies do not need a mass of knowledge workers but a small number with exceptional talent. Then the company's problem is how to systematize their knowledge and gain proprietorial control of it, as knowledge workers are very mobile and, when they leave, the firm loses its main resource. Stewart foresaw that other work, previously associated with knowledge workers, could be standardized and outsourced to parts of the world with cheaper (and sometimes better) graduates. Brown et al. (2011) went further, calling the Western image of infinitely expanding highly paid knowledge work a 'false promise'. Their study of 200 managers and executives of leading transnational companies and policymakers in the United States, Britain, Germany, South Korea, China and India revealed that the Euro-American idea of a new affluence based on knowledge work was a chimera. They showed that there had been a doubling of university enrolment in the world in a decade. In Western countries, young people had to gain a degree as a basic credential to enter the labour market, which became 'congested' as a result: the problem was not the employability of graduates, but that employment opportunities for knowledge workers had not expanded as predicted. Furthermore, the market for knowledge jobs was now a 'global auction'. China had more university students than the United States, and produced more engineers and scientists than the West. Increasingly, Western companies were engaging in 'digital Taylorism' – standardizing technical, managerial and professional knowledge work and outsourcing it to high quality, low cost Indian and Chinese graduates. Asian companies were also competing higher up the value chain.

Brown et al. (2011) also challenged the assumption that a highly skilled workforce would earn high wages and expand the middle class and thus the prosperity of the country. In what they called the 'War for talent' companies looked to the top universities for 'exceptional talent' and they were indeed highly paid. For others, the link between learning and earning was broken, and they joined the over-supply of graduates in the global labour market, bringing wages down. A study of U.S. college graduates between 1973 and 2007 showed that the highest-earner category of men and women had experienced significant growth in real income and since 1989 had accelerated away from the rest (ibid.: 118). Middle- and low-income earners had not improved their wages in real terms over this period, showing that the promised graduate premium had failed to deliver. A similar picture was evident in the U.K. between 1994 and 2006, with increased benefits for a bachelor degree at the top end of the wage distribution, but a sharp decrease at the bottom end, with evidence of graduates taking low paid jobs for which a college education was not required. A third of students who had taken government loans to pay tuition fees since 1998 had not repaid anything, mainly because their earnings were below the repayment threshold (ibid.: 117–18). As the differential between the highly paid elite and a high-skill low-pay workforce widens, the latter, would join those marginalized by globalization as Cameron and Palan predicted.

While a high-skill low-pay workforce has not been created to the same degree in Denmark, recent unemployment rates for some groups of the highly educated have been above the national average and debates about graduates' precarious career paths have intensified (Produktivitetskommissionen 2013: 42, Figure 4.3). Sarauw and Nielsen (2012) see this reflected in the discourse on graduate employability, which once more pushes the responsibility for successful outcomes of higher education down towards the student. All students are expected to become employable in the knowledge economy, but the characteristics of the knowledge worker have changed. The idea that students need to acquire a predefined list of competences is criticized for being a mechanical and instrumental idea of knowledge that impedes students' creativity and motivation. 'Entrepreneurialism' is now on the government's agenda (FIVU 2012) and the ideas of Saras Sarasvarthy, Professor in Business Administration, have 'a foothold on Danish education from school to university' (Sarauw and Nielsen 2012: 44). Rather than starting with predefined goals, this approach gets the student to ask, Who am I? Who do I know? What can I do? In other words, through steered self-reflection, self-development and self-efficacy, students find out what they can 'effectuate' (in Sarasvarthy's jargon) through 'concrete actions' in the world. Students are increasingly encouraged to see themselves as sites of boundless potential and to take responsibility for learning as a process of self-realization that internalizes enterprise as a personal competence. Brown (2004) identified a similar move in business recruitment and human resource management (HRM) away from a list of abstract competences and towards applicants' 'personal capital', that is their personal capacities and the narrative used to sell them. The 'selling point' of this kind of knowledge worker, as Bovbjerg (2011) identified, is a willingness to commit oneself 100% to a task and constantly work on oneself to optimize one's creativity and productivity in ways that align personal development with the company's profit maximization.

Sarauw and Nielsen note that Denmark's new entrepreneurial education elides a classic humanities conception of emancipation with an idea of self-realization as individual prosperity and national economic growth. This elision loses sight of the political aspect of emancipation, which is to develop a critical stance to free oneself from constraining aspects of social and economic systems. Instead, the 'self as entrepreneur' intensifies the responsibilization of the individual who now absorbs risks previously carried by the firm and by society. In this way the competition state pushes responsibility onto individuals, who must develop and deploy their personal capital, and deflects attention from structural factors, including lack of employment opportunities, a congested local labour market and a global auction for knowledge workers.

Conclusion

Universities have been pressed to produce increasing numbers of knowledge workers in the right fields (STEM subjects, not humanities) and with the relevant, prescribed competences. However, if industry only needs relatively small numbers of graduates with 'exceptional talent' and leadership abilities, the rest will have to settle for low competence work or precarious jobs. The move to 'entrepreneurial education' and the promotion of one 'undisciplined' leadership type suggests that universities are intensifying the focus on the individual student's responsibility to make him or herself employable and deflecting attention from structural weaknesses in the labour market. The inability of policymakers and university leaders to define a successful relationship between universities and industry over the production of graduates pushes responsibility for finding solutions onto students, who must bridge these seemingly incompatible poles. In effect, graduates are asked to become 'competition citizens' to compensate for inadequacies in the competition state.

The 2003 University Law's aim to mobilize what were envisioned as universities' two major contributions to society – research and graduates – has played out in ambiguous ways. The tension between two different ideas of organization and leadership remains unresolved: should universities be flat organizations concentrating on networking with surrounding society; or should they be hierarchical, with strongly bounded and tightly managed units? This dilemma was also highlighted in the law itself, which required universities, as agencies of the competition state, to orient towards the 'surrounding society' and better serve its needs. But to make universities accountable to the competition state and align their activities with the Minister of Science, Technology and Innovation's priorities, a very tight budgetary and supervisory framework was developed that instead oriented universities towards the state's hierarchy of contracts and incentives. Since 2003, attempts to balance Ministry requirements with incentives to engage with industry and society have been largely unsuccessful, as evidenced by continual restatement of the 'problem' that the reform was meant to remedy. What the policy is moving towards is the subjugation of the purpose of the Danish university to the shifting requirements of the competition state – an extremely narrow, impoverished and instrumental notion of the meaning of the public university.

◆

Susan Wright (D. Phil. in social anthropology, Oxford) is Professor of Educational Anthropology at Aarhus University. She studies people's participation in large-scale processes of political transformation, working with concepts of audit culture, governance, contestation and policy. She coordinated the EU project 'University Reform, Globalisation and Europeanisation' and the EU ITN project 'Universities in the Knowledge Economy' in Europe and the Asia-Pacific Rim. She coedits (with Penny Welch) the journal *LATISS (Learning and Teaching: International Journal of Higher Education in the Social Sciences)* and recently published *Policy Worlds: Anthropology and the Anatomy of Contemporary Power* (coedited with Cris Shore and Davide Però, 2011, Berghahn).

Jakob Williams Ørberg (MSc in anthropology, University of Copenhagen) is researching Indian higher technical education as a Ph.D. Fellow at Aarhus University, Danish School of Education. He has a background in policymaking from the Danish Ministry of Higher Education and Research and was a research assistant in the project 'New Management, New Identities? Danish University Reform in an International Perspective (NewMI)' led by Susan Wright. He is coauthor (with Susan Wright) of 'Autonomy and control: Danish university reform in the context of modern governance' (in *Learning Under Neoliberalism*, 2015, Berghahn), 'The double shuffle of University Reform – The OECD/ Denmark policy interface' (in *Academic Identities – Academic Challenges?*, 2012, Cambridge Scholar Press) and 'Paradoxes of the self: self-owning universities in a society of control' (in *The Politics of Self-Governance*, 2009, Ashgate).

Notes

1. This research was part of the project 'New Management, New Identities: Danish University Reform in International Context' funded by the Danish Research Council grant no. 09-058690/FSE.
2. Wright is grateful to Xuan Nguyen, a student on the Masters for Lifelong Learning, Aarhus University, for working with her on these ideas and helping to refine them.

References

Arbejdsministeriet, Erhvervsministeriet, Forskningsministeriet, Undervisningsministeriet. 1997. *Ledelse, organisation og kompetence: Mod bedre produktivitet, velfærd og innovation i danske virksomheder i det 21. Århundrede*. Copenhagen: Statens Information.

ATV. 1997. *Den vanskelige balance – en bog om forskningsledelse*. Lyngby: Akademiet for de Tekniske Videnskaber.

———. 1998. *Bedre vilkår for videnbaserede virksomheder: En ATV-rapport om elementer af en dansk forsknings-, teknologi- og innovationspolitik*. Lyngby: Akademiet for de Tekniske Videnskaber.

———. 2001. *Viden og velfæred – visioner for dansk forskning*. Lyngby: Akademiet for de Tekniske Videnskaber.

Bovbjerg, K.M. (ed.). 2011. *Motivation og mismod*. Aarhus: Aarhus Universitetsforlag.

Brown, P., and A. Hesketh. 2004. *The Mismanagement of Talent*. Oxford: Oxford University Press.

Brown, P., H. Lauder and D. Ashton. 2011. *The Global Auction*. Oxford: Oxford University Press.

Cameron, A., and R. Palan. 2004. *The Imagined Economies of Globalization*. London: Sage.

Cerny, P. 1990. *The Changing Architecture of Politics: Structure, Agency and the Future of the State*. London: Sage.

———. 1997. 'Paradoxes of the Competition State: The Dynamics of Political Globalization', *Government and Opposition* 32(2): 251–74.

Danish Council for Research Policy. 1999. *Ledelse af universiteterne – Oplæg fra Danmarks Forskningsråd*. Copenhagen: Danish Council for Research Policy.

Danish Research Commission. 2001. *Report volume 1*. Copenhagen: IT and Research Ministry.

DI (Dansk Industri). 1997a. *Vidensamfundet – udfordinger for industrien og uddannelsessystemet*. Copenhagen: Dansk Industri.

_____. 1997b. *Vidensamfundet II – udfordinger for forskning, teknologi og produktion*. Copenhagen: Dansk Industri.

_____. 2000. *Der skal to til tango – universiteterne og industrien*. Copenhagen: Dansk Industri.

_____. 2014. *DI's 2020-Plan 'Vejen til større velstand'*. Copenhagen: Dansk Industri.

DI and CO-industri (Dansk Industri and the Central Organisation for Danish Metalworkers). 2001. *Fra forskning til faktura*. Copenhagen: Dansk Industri.

Drucker, P. 1993. *Post-Capitalist Society*. Oxford: Butterworth-Heinemann.

EC. 2005. '"The European Higher Education Area – Achieving the Goals" Communique of the Conference of European Ministers Responsible for Higher Education', Bergen, 19–20 May. Retrieved 7 February 2016 from http://media.ehea.info/file/2005_Bergen/52/0/2005_Bergen_Communique_english_580520.pdf

Ejersbo, N., and C. Greve. 2005. 'Public Management Policymaking in Denmark 1983–2005', *IIM/LSE Workshop on Theory and Methods for Studying Organisational Processes: Institutional, Narrative and Related Approaches*. London: London School of Economics.

FIVU (Ministry for Research, Innovation and Higher Education). 2012. *Danmark – Løsningernes land*. Copenhagen: FIVU.

ForskerFORUM. 2003. 'Det Frie Universitet' no. 164: 1.

Graversen, E.K., P.S. Lauridsen and P.S. Mortensen. 2003. *Danish Enterprise Managers' Perceptions of Research, Development and Innovation (in Danish)*. Århus: Danish Institute for Studies in Research and Research Policy.

Jensen, H.S. 2010. 'The organisation of the university', working papers on University Reform no. 14, April. Copenhagen: Danish School of Education, Aarhus University. Retrieved 22 January 2015 from http://edu.au.dk/filead min/www.dpu.dk/forskning/forskningsprogrammer/epoke/workingpapers/WP_14.pdf.

Krause-Jensen, J. 2010. *Flexible Firm: The Design of Culture at Bang and Olufsen*. Oxford: Berghahn.

Lundvall, B.-Å. 2006. 'The University in the Learning Economy', Working paper in the series *Danish Research Unit for Industrial Dynamics*, Aalborg: University of Aalborg.

Ministry of Education. 1997a. *Erhvervsliv og uddannelsesinstitutioner: En rapportom samspillet mellem erhvervslivet og de videregående uddannelsesinstitutioner*. Copenhagen: Undervisningsministeriet.

_____. 1997b. *National kompetenceudvikling: Erhvervsudvikling gennem kvalifikationsudvikling*. Copenhagen: Undervisningsministeriets Forlag.

_____. 1997c. *Det repræsentative demokrati i uddannelsessystemet. Undervisningsministerens redegørelse til Folketinget*. Copenhagen: Undervisningsministeriet.

Ministry of Finance. 1996. *Budgetredegørelse 96. Tillæg: Styringsformer I den offentlige sektor*. Copenhagen: Ministry of Finance.

_____. 1997. *Danmark som foregangsland: Globalisering og dansk økonomi*. Copenhagen: Ministry of Finance.
OECD. 1995. *Governance in Transition: Public Management Reforms in OECD Countries*. Paris: Organisation for Economic Cooperation and Development.
Ørberg, J.W. 2006. 'Setting Universities Free? The Background to the Self-ownership of Danish universities', Working Papers in University Reform no. 1. Copenhagen: Department of Education, Aarhus University. Retrieved 8 March 2016 from http://edu.au.dk/fileadmin/www.dpu.dk/forskning/forskningsprogrammer/epoke/workingpapers/Working_Paper_1__Setting_Universities_Free__PDF.pdf0.pdf.
_____. 2008. 'Fra ideelle studerende til ideelle medarbejdere', Working Papers in the New Work Life no. 1. Copenhagen: School of Education, Aarhus University. Retrieved 4 October 2016 from http://edu.au.dk/fileadmin/www.dpu.dk/forskning/forskningsprogrammer/epoke/forskningsprojekter/stressnyeledelsesformerogintervention/workingpapers/forskning_kompetenceprogrammet_stress-projektet_20080522115903_det-nye-arbejdsliv-nr1.pdf.
Osborne, D., and T. Gaebler. 1992. *Reinventing Government: How the Entrepreneurial Spirit is Transforming the Public Sector*. Reading, MA: Addison-Wesley.
Østergaard, H.H.H. 1998. *At tjene og forme den nye tid: Finansministeriet 1848–1998*, Copenhagen: Finansministeriet.
Pal, L. 2008. 'Inversions without End: the OECD and Global Public Management Reform', in R. Mahon and S. McBride (eds), *The OECD and Transnational Governance*. Vancouver: UBC Press, pp. 60–76.
Pedersen, O.K. 2011. *Konkurrencestaten*. Copenhagen: Hans Reitzels Forlag.
Pedersen, P.K., H.D. Sørensen and J.B. Vestergaard. 2006. 'The Contract Management Project in Denmark', in *Benchmarking, Evaluation and Strategic Management in the Public Sector*. Paris: OECD.
Pollitt, C., et al. 2001. 'Agency Fever? Analysis of an International Policy Fashion', *Journal of Comparative Policy Analysis: Research and Practice* 3: 271–90.
Porter, M. 1989. *The Competitive Advantage of Nations*. Basingstoke: Macmillan.
Produktivitetskommissionen. 2013. *Uddannelse og Innovation – Analyserapport 4*. Copenhagen: Produktivitetskommissionen.
Reich, R. 1991. *The Work of Nations*. New York: Vintage Books.
Sahlin-Andersson, K. 2000. 'National, International and Transnational Constructions of New Public Management', in T. Christensen and P. Laegreid (eds), *Transforming New Public Management*. Stockholm: Stockholm University, Center for Organisational Research.
Sarauw, L.L. 2011. 'Kompetencebegrebet og andre stileøvelser', Ph.D. thesis. Copenhagen: University of Copenhagen.
Sarauw, L.L., and G.B. Nielsen. 2012. 'Entreprenørskab: uddannelsesindustrialisering i nye klæder', *Danmarks Pædagogiske Tidsskrift* 4: 39–49.
Schmidt, E.K. 2003. *Science and Society – Building Bridges of Excellence. Perceptions on the Interaction between Public Research and Enterprises, Report no. 2003/6*. Aarhus: Analyseinstitut for Forskning.

_____. 2008. 'Research management and policy: incentives and obstacles to a better public-private interaction', *International Journal of Public Sector Management* 21(6): 623–36.
Stewart, T. 1997. *Intellectual Capital*. London: Nicholas Brealey.
Thorn, K., and M. Lyndrup. 2006. *The Quality of Public Expenditure – Challenges and Solutions in Results Focussed Management in the Public Sector in Denmark*. Paris: OECD.
VTU (Ministry of Science, Technology and Innovation), UVM and Reference Group on the New Danish Qualifications Framework. 2003. *Towards a Danish Qualifications Framework for Higher Education. Final Report*. Copenhagen: VTU.
Wright, S., and J.W. Ørberg. 2011. 'The double shuffle of university reform – the OECD/Denmark policy interface', in A. Nyhagen and T. Halvorsen (eds), *Academic Identities – Academic Challenges? American and European Experience of the Transformation of Higher Education and Research*. Newcastle upon Tyne: Cambridge Scholar Press, pp. 269–93.
_____. 2015. 'Autonomy and Control: Danish University Reform in the Context of Modern Governance', in S. Hyatt, B. Shear and S. Wright (eds), *Learning Under Neoliberalism: Ethnographies of Governance in Higher Education*. Oxford: Berghahn.

CHAPTER 4
Leadership in Higher Education
A Critical Feminist Perspective on Global Restructuring

JILL BLACKMORE

Strategic management and leadership has only recently become part of the lexicon of reform in higher education, coinciding with heightened marketization as academic capitalism 'goes global' (Degn 2015). A critical feminist perspective indicates that the sphere of decision making in higher education is increasingly distant from academics as an evermore feminized higher education field is no longer able to protect their boundaries, discourses and practices from the social fields of politics, economics, media and big business. The seemingly greater autonomy of university governance, together with reduced public funds, obliges university leaders to be strategic, innovative and entrepreneurial. The context is one in which the modern university negotiates multiple and often contradictory functions, expectations and values, particularly with regard to its private and public 'orientation' (Marginson 2011). The rapidly changing context of higher education impacts on who gets to lead and what leadership practices are valued.

This chapter draws on a critical feminist analysis that considers how the interactions of context, organizational structures, policies, discourses and practices as structural relations of power interact with national policies, institutional restructuring and leadership practice. The radical restructuring of higher education post-1987 in Australia, as elsewhere, is gendered and gendering in its practices and effects (Blackmore and Sachs 2007; Deem 2003; Knights and Kerfoot 2004; Marchand and Runyan 2000; Riegraf et al. 2010; White, Bagilhole and Riordan 2012). Considering gender as a 'structuring structure' is central to understanding the consequences of the shift from universities being publically oriented and process driven to being market oriented and proceduralist in practice. Organizational restructuring impacts on the material, cultural, spatial and temporal re/positioning of different masculinities and femininities through the re/productive processes of performing academic labour in their everyday lives. As Benschop and Brouns (2003) argue:

> The functioning of universities as social institutions, where gender is 'done' in a specific way, requiring the need to analyse how the structural, cultural and procedural arrangements of academic organising constitute gender relations ... Gender is part of organising; it is an important element in the organization and division of labour (2003: 194-95).

While a multiplicity of masculinities and feminitities at play subvert simple male/female binaries, there are also persisting structural, pedagogical and epistemological gender binaries embedded within the hierarchies of the academy, including representations of leadership (Knights and Kerfoot 2004). Martinez (2011) refers to the feminization of organizational practices – the:

> [g]ender binaries and the hierarchical appraisal they are predicated on, rather than with the distribution of sexes among the university management scale. It's the hierarchical relationship between an undervalued, soft approach to management or service ethic and a hard stance toward management that is at issue here (2011: 2).

As women move into executive leadership, how do the social relations of gender in leadership change? How is the gender division of labour reconfigured? And how does gender work through the material, virtual, cultural and epistemological practices (Leathwood and Read 2009) of higher education?

The Study

This chapter identifies processes and patterns of feminization emerging in the data of an Australian Research Council (ARC) funded three-year project on Leadership in Entrepreneurial Universities: Disengagement and Diversity. The project involved a policy analysis considering current challenges to the Australian university sector through interviews with key individuals in federal higher education policy. Three case studies of Australian universities (one was a Group of Eight ('G8') or 'Sandstone'; the second a Utech, which became a university after the Dawkins Reforms in 1989; and the third, a 1960s regional university) involved over 200 interviews. These included vice chancellors (VCs), those in formal and informal leadership positions (including line-management leaders such as deputy and pro- vice chancellors, deans and heads of school) and research leaders (professors, research institute directors, chairs of academic boards). A sample of interviews across faculties, disciplines, gender at all levels as well as post-doctoral fellows and final year Ph.D. students provided insight into how they perceived, enacted and aspired to leadership. Equal opportunity practitioners, human relation directors and union representatives were interviewed, as were heads of search firms and consultants. Interviews were unstructured and conversational in mode, but covered similar themes: challenges to the higher education sector nationally and globally and university responses; individual career pathways; and how changes in institutional priorities, policies and practices inform and are informed by the micro-politics of individual universities and understandings of leadership. Interviewees were asked whether and how gender was a factor in their careers, in university life and the policies and practices that supported or impeded a good family–work balance. Leadership was the lens through which to analyse organizational change. While not funded by the ARC, similar projects were undertaken in Europe, Taiwan, Ireland, the U.S.A. and Spain (see Blackmore, Sánchez-Moreno and Sawers 2015).

Universities in a High-Risk Global Context

Serial restructurings of Australia's education sector are indicative of the processes of globalization, fast-moving neoliberal policies and individual organizational responses that transformed the already international field of higher education (Marginson 2008). Politicians and university executives justified these structural reforms as necessary to address rapidly changing global conditions. For vice chancellors and deans, organizational restructuring has symbolic value in 'being seen to be doing something' in response to rapidly changing external environments, an overt flexing of managerial muscle, even though individual executives may not remain to see their longer-term (counter)productive effects. Since 1989, government and university executives have made similar arguments about responsiveness, flexibility, nimbleness and innovation to justify making university governance more corporate (Rowlands 2013).

Australia's university sector post-1989 has experienced three broad stages of restructuring. First, the post-1989 restructuring was imbued with a more liberal humanist focus on expansion, inclusion, comprehensiveness, massification, and efficiency balanced by equity to build research and teaching capacity. Second, the 2000s was marked by a shift from bureaucratic (Murphy 2013) to corporate managerialism through embedding practices of managerialism, marketization, increased privatization of costs, and expansion of international education (now 17.3 percent of university income) to compensate for reduced government funding, with Australia boasting one of the lowest public, and highest private, investment in the OECD (Universities Australia 2015). Executive leadership increasingly sought to differentiate universities through branding, mission statements and strategic plans, thus creating 'organizational identities' with which academics were expected to align their research and teaching (Stensaker 2014). 'Quality' and 'excellence' became the discursive drivers as the sector 'scaled up' and competition in the global field of higher education intensified. Federal centralization increased accountability in teaching and learning through the creation of the Office of Teaching and Learning, a National Qualification Framework to assure quality of courses, graduate exit surveys measuring student satisfaction (Blackmore 2009b and the quality of research, with the Excellence of Research in Australia research assessment introduced in 2012 (Blackmore, Brennan and Zipin 2010).

Third, after the global financial crisis in 2007, most commentators and the vice chancellors in this study agree, universities now exist in, and have a responded to, a context of heightened risk and uncertainty subject to rapid market and policy shifts, global financial crises, and fluxes in student demand, business confidence and the good will of philanthropic organizations, a view not well understood in various higher education reports (see, for example, Ernst and Young 2012). Since 2015, universities have operated in highly competitive globalized markets that have become more precarious for students, academics and universities. Australian universities are now transnational corporations with multiple on-shore and off-shore campuses, private arms, and business partnerships with multinational companies. Universities are strategically 'partnering up' the rankings with other universities cross-nationally in order to gain global comparative advantage in course provision, student and academic exchange and research collaborations.

Higher education has become an expanding field of commercial activity with new policy actors and providers such as Pearson and Tribal, the use of consultants such as KPMG and Ernst and Young in recruitment and policy making, and the involvement of philanthrocapitalists across all aspects. This high-risk external environment is subject to changing perceptions about the safety for students (terrorism, racism, sexual harassment) and what Brown, Lauder and Ashton

(2011) refer to as the 'global auction': graduate expectations of employment are unfulfilled for both international and domestic students as the value of university credentials falls with the rapid expansion of higher education in Asia and South America, the collapse of professional employment markets, and the entrance into the market of private providers in higher education who can offer specialist, short-term, cheaper and more profitable courses (Blackmore and Gribble 2012). Education has become the site of desire and anxiety for the global bourgeoisie.

Add to this the disruptive potential of technology. MOOCS and blended learning mean that universities are struggling to decide the extent, nature and practices of online learning, and the balance between an on-campus quality educational experience and off-campus provision (Beetham and Sharpe 2007). Significant investment in re/designing purpose-built and technologically rich real and virtual learning environments is evident as it is now critical to attract and retain students by promising graduate employability through work-integrated learning, service learning and international experience (Blackmore et al. 2014; Boden and Neveda 2010). The practices that distinguish higher education from other social formations – the credentializing of knowledge-intensive labour and basic research (Marginson 2008: 303) – are under significant threat.

Academics have thus experienced intensified labour and rising expectations to be entrepreneurial, to build partnerships, to produce more high-quality publications, to 'satisfy' a wider range of student diversity and to align themselves to faculty, university and national priorities in research (Blackmore 2009a). Academics have both resisted and internalized the new forms of surveillance and accountability of performance review, research assessment and student evaluations (Blackmore and Sachs 2007; Davies and Bansel 2010). But there is evidence of a growing disenchantment with leadership (Blackmore, Brennan and Zipin 2010; Coates et al. 2010; Scott et al. 2010) with a shift in power from intellectual to managerial leadership and the centralization of power (Blackmore and Sawers 2015; Rowlands 2013).

Greater competition in international student markets, together with massification of higher education in domestic markets, has increased cultural and academic diversity of students but not necessarily cultural diversity of academics or leadership (Blackmore and Sawers 2015). The gender equity policies of the 1990s focused on increasing the numbers of women in leadership through strategies to improve women's performance and recognition of different career opportunities; these policies were developed and then devolved to middle managers. The focus in the 2000s was to get more women into executive positions across most universities, evident in this study with the regional university appointing a female VC, and the Utech participating in an executive leadership training program and a shadowing program at the Sandstone university. But despite equal-opportunity policies, more affirmative action was required by the executive, with the male Utech Vice Chancellor appointing a woman from a head of school position as Deputy Vice Chancellor, Teaching and Learning. The Sandstone's policy was to continue to embed the notion of diversity, now supplanting that of equity, into the managerial mindset. By 2010, equity-for-women targets were part of most managers' Key Performance Indicators (KPIs), but gender had disappeared as an equity target, other than getting more female students into science, technology, engineering, maths and environment (STEME), the primary focus internationally (Morley 2013). Cameron (2012: 2), an Equal Opportunities practitioner, argued that while some universities maintained their gender equity programs, in other universities 'the equity portfolio has been downgraded or totally restructured out of the organizational structure ... programs have become limited in scope and importance'. Widening participation to increase socioeconomic diversity became the agenda after 2010.

Restructuring, Leaderism and Institutional Identity

Australia in 2015 experienced the collapse of the mining boom, which lead to a belated response to promote a knowledge-based economy, with the National Innovation and Science Agenda (Australian Government 2015)[1] focusing narrowly on industry collaboration, start-up entrepreneurship capital and improving maths, science and technology skills in schools. Innovation, as is typical of higher education policy internationally, is now equated with science, technology and commercialization. The ethos of the entrepreneurial university is now overtly instrumentalist as use value; immediate application of research and vocationalization dominate decisions about teaching, research and partnerships (Bruni, Gherardi and Poggio 2004).

In this context of radical transformation and increasing focus on institutional identity, 'leaderism' has become the solution to more effective and efficient organizational change (Morley 2013). These external forces and rapidly changing contexts produce both constraints and possibilities and encourage particular leadership sensibilities, dispositions and ways of seeing the world. Stensaker (2014: 104) argues that the notion of organizational identity is useful in the market context for understanding how external and internal dynamics interact. Change and continuity are constantly in tension. Budget constraints have forced universities to consider their core role and function while simultaneously addressing multiple exogenous factors out of their control, triggering internal change. While 'internal and external stakeholders may have very different views on the appropriate functions of universities', the state, external stakeholders and markets have an increasingly stronger pressure than internal legacies and dynamics on constructing the organizational identity of universities (Stensaker 2014: 105).

Leadership is closely tied to organizational identity which, in the literature, is understood from an essentialist and attribute-based orientation, suggesting that organizational identity could be understood as reflecting a 'true' organizational character. Another approach defines organizational identity as an organizational resource which could be applied as part of the strategic positioning and orientation of a given organization. As Stensaker argues (2014: 104), the essentialist approach implies 'organizational identity is seen as something which can be manipulated and applied as a management tool during change processes' and 'is merely an expression of cultural understandings which limits the potential for managerial influence'. The strategic approach sees identity 'as partly de-coupled from culture, and so as something which can be manipulated through the use of language, symbols and myths to fit key strategic objectives', i.e. a performative exercise (ibid.: 104). Czarniawska (2006) argues that both versions are being mobilized by management, but she attributes greater agency to leaders as organizational actors as they deconstruct and reconstruct organizational identities through narratives to imagine, communicate and enact organizational change. University leaders work at multiple levels around the notion of organizational identity: externally as a tool of designed change through marketing and image (branding), and internally as a sense-making tool to interpret for academics the rationale for change in order to build a shared culture and mobilize a discourse around managing risk (Stensaker 2014).

A deputy vice chancellor at the Utech commented about the ethos of the university:

> we're probably seen as being more corporate than many universities. We're fairly agile in terms of being able to do things and move. We're not stuck in old ways. So we will look at innovation, new ideas, and the younger universities have all got that. And so that does mean you can respond more to your environment. Now whether you'd describe

that as corporate, I don't know, but that's how others when they look at us describe it. I just think we're a bit more agile, a bit more innovative. Very collegial. ... Everyone calls the VC by name. There's no 'vice chancellor' or 'professors X or Y'. It's very egalitarian and open and the senior team doesn't fight with each other.

This narrative permeated all the interviews with leaders and academics at this university. Stensaker also argues that we need to explore 'how organizational identity affects other significant activities in organizations' and link it to different change processes.

In order to identify, communicate and retain their distinctiveness universities are also restructuring teaching and research to align with strategic national priorities and research strengths identified through Excellence in Research in Australia and move away from comprehensiveness. Each university in this study made key decisions about image, profile, organizational structure, focus and scope of provision. The Sandstone sought to improve its world ranking to being in the top ten by aligning with the European Bologna and American systems. The entire undergraduate curriculum was restructured from 120 different programs down to six liberal education undergraduate programmes, moving professional education to post-graduate fee-paying courses. The Utech developed a blueprint ten years ago (only now under revision after two iterations), which provided a consistent guideline for internal reform focusing on 'the university of the real world', campus experience and industry relationships. The regional university revisited its origins through a three-year review to reinvigorate its focus on geographical location and the tropics while positioning itself more strategically within the Pacific region through a campus in Singapore. This pattern of internal reorganization sought to differentiate each university from the others. Developing a marketable and manageable institutional identity led to greater differentiation between academics, between academics and managers, and between different knowledges that are reconstituting the social relations of gender and division of labour.

Leadership Feminization

The academic workforce is now highly casualized as well as feminized (May, Strachan and Peetz 2013; McCulloch 2013). These global trends (Maes 2013) are indicative of the 'casual and careless' treatment by universities as they seek to be nimble and agile in the quest for global ranking (Coates et al. 2009; Devine et al. 2011). In Australia, fractional and full-time staff numbers fell over the period of radical restructuring between 1997 and 2000 and only increased marginally (2–3 percent) each year until 2013, while student numbers trebled. Nonacademic staff numbers continue to rise (by 55.6 percent in 2013), a consequence of administering accountability demands, student services, e-learning infrastructure and marketing and research administration (Universities Australia 2015). Contract employment is increasing in Australia and internationally (McCulloch 2013). Contractualism has been the norm for senior management and some professors in marketable fields, both groups highly paid for taking that risk. Contractualism on the margins of academic work means casual staff, predominantly women, bear the risk (without the reward) of constant fluctuations in student demand and managerial prerogative. Internationally, the average salary of academics relative to other professions is falling, particularly relative to the senior management and vice chancellors (Altbach et al. 2012).

Since the 1990s, distinct career paths have emerged between academics in teaching and research and those in line management, as both line management and keeping up research are increasingly incompatible in terms of workload. This forces 'choice' of career path through default as much as through preference (Pike 2009).While some university senior executives are up to 50 percent women, it is increasingly difficult for women to gain research professorships due to rising expectations and time demands (Gibbs et al. 2015; Pike 2009). Women academics are largely concentrated at the senior lecturer and associate professor level in continuing teaching and research positions, which are declining due to changing policy settings, fee structures and privatization. When women do become professors, they are paid less, teach more and are invited into fewer research applications as men (Pike 2009). It is often harder to be promoted to a chair or management position for internal candidates: lack of mobility, the case for many women, reduces desirability as the candidate lacks multisectoral multinational experience. Meanwhile, more mobile 'star researchers', particularly in the male-dominated biological, material and natural sciences imbued with the potential for commercial application and funding, receive high salaries and bonuses sometimes above the very well-paid vice chancellors (Welch 2012).

Universities as multinational corporations have expanded the scale and scope of senior management and executive leadership work from teaching and research to marketing, commercialization, global engagement, international education, graduate employability and quality assurance. Universities thus compete and collaborate with commercial firms such as Pearson or Tribal to 'deliver courses' and develop commercial links and products. Feminization is occurring in how executive work is distributed and in the shifting relations of power. Women had been moving into middle and executive management as their experience as heads of school was valued. But deputy vice chancellors, executive deans and pro vice chancellors are increasingly being recruited from industry – and not due to the focus on STEME and industry partnerships, which are male-dominated fields (Scott et al. 2010). External recruitment thus foreshortens what were once vertical career paths for middle managers, increasingly women. This focus on business management and industry links is replicated in greater industry representation, declining student and academic representation on university councils and the increased presence of line managers on academic boards (Rowlands 2013), diluting or rendering irrelevant the academic voice.

Importantly, a new gender division of labour – or feminization – is emerging with the multiplication of layers of senior managers at pro vice chancellor and deputy vice chancellor levels (Scott et al. 2010). For those women accessing senior and executive management, there is a reassertion of old public/domestic binaries about the nature of the work undertaken; a vertical divide is emerging in the executive level, with men undertaking the external, public face of the university located in pro vice chancellor and deputy vice chancellor positions in marketing, research and global engagement, and the new entrants of female executives doing the domestic work of change management and the emotional labour as deputy vice chancellors in teaching and learning, access and equity and sometimes international students (Blackmore and Sawers 2015).

The ethos of change management is also being influenced externally. Increasingly, university executives are hiring marketing firms for branding, management firms such as KPMG to advise on organizational restructuring, recruitment firms to source managers and research leaders, and consultancy firms to run senior leadership development courses. This is based on the view that leading change works best by appointing outsiders as they are more committed to the executive management's agenda and bonded to organizational priorities under contractual arrangements and without internal alignments and loyalties. Rarely is the internal expertise of a university's own or other academics called upon.

Furthermore, there is greater centralization of decision making. Fashion dominates change management – with cycles of centralization and decentralization in organizations, although often for different reasons (Czarniawska 2006). As universities have become more complex multinational organizations, there has been a centralization of both academic management and general administration. The Sandstone undertook a massive restructure of professional staff, comprising 75 percent women, to centralize all the student services. This also impacted on the collegiality that had developed between professional and academic staff.

As power over allocation of resources and rewards is increasingly concentrated at the executive level, a more assertive use of executive prerogative in decision making is impacting both on academics and managers lower down the line. Decisions, such as appointing research stars to 'fit' the university research priorities, are undertaken without consultation with the head of school responsible for teaching quality. This centralization process is extenuated with the trend towards larger multidisciplinary faculties under executive deans, which changes the composition and culture of decision-making committees (Blackmore and Sawers 2015). Disciplines where women are concentrated, such as sociology, history, philosophy, gender studies, cultural studies, politics, international studies and education, are often clustered in one faculty, thus reducing the disciplinary diversity within key decision-making arenas at faculty and university levels.

Leadership in what is now the 'entrepreneurial university' rather than the enterprise university described by Marginson and Considine in 2000, is treated within this context as a generic individual capacity that is valued across all organizational contexts. Leaderism is an assertion of the self when initiating university reform rather than developing productive relational practices (Grummell, Divine and Lynch 2009). Moving into line management means academics are enculturated into a distinctive corporate ethos where they adopt the discourses and language of management by objectives, finance, KPIs, student enrolments, quality and excellence, student experience surveys, big data, learning analytics, marketing and innovation, and thus promote the corporate line.

New allegiances and alliances operate at the corporate level, with external and executive pressures requiring new ways of speaking and embodiment through dress. Within the corporate milieu, particular narratives and discourses constantly circulate, reinforcing managerial authority and the assumption that the manager's perspective represents that of their faculty or school. Yet the role requires a certain 'forgetfulness', purposeful ignorance, about what it is to be an academic. The larger the unit they manage (now the trend across Australia's universities), the more managers are able to distance themselves from the impact of their decisions – while gaining recognition (and rewards) within the upper echelons of the academy for meeting KPIs. While the power rests with executives, the managing of multiple conflicting purposes and lack of resources rests with the academics at the interface of teaching and research, where they are held responsible for both managing institutional and professional risk (Rawolle, Rowlands and Blackmore 2016).

Pedagogical Feminization and the Leadership 'Pool'

Academics confront heightened pressures over limited resources and time to produce excellence in both teaching and research on the one hand and massification to meet expected skilled-labour demands of a knowledge economy on the other. Academic work is being transformed, with the unbundling of teaching and research as the numbers of permanent lecturing positions decreases (Universities Australia 2015) and as contract positions in teaching-only and research-only increase, a trend exacerbated by the Excellent in Research in Australia (ERA) process, which counts all academics other than teaching-only in assessing a field of research. As women constitute three times as many academics on part-time contracts, they are more likely to be trapped in teaching-only positions, having to 'choose' between teaching and research.

Overload is occurring due to ever-expanding scope, scale and depth of academic work (multimodal teaching, research, university and community service, marketing, partnerships off shore/online …). Add to this the downloading of administrative and quality assurance work (online) and the ratcheting up of expectations, with research point systems and managerial capacity to wield student evaluations against teaching staff. The conjuncture of unbundling and intensification of academic work is further problematized as third-sector professionals in e-learning technologies and research administration assume aspects of the academic role. Teaching as an educative process is also being unbundled into procedurally driven packages of instructional design, content, tutoring and assessment facilitated by learning technologies. Different people design and audit courses informed by the now fashionable field of the learning sciences or data analytics that can be mobilized to measure and personalize student 'engagement'. Learning analytics claims to have 'predictive tools to improve personalized learning outcomes' (Guthrie 2013). As personalization of pedagogy intensifies, academic labour is also being directed externally through 'data', which is arguably only one aspect of what works pedagogically. Likewise, the managerial focus on student 'satisfaction' in student evaluations often devalues and even outlaws critical pedagogies (particularly feminist and anti-racist pedagogies) that trouble the sense of self, encourage questioning the norm, and makes students, particularly from dominant social groups, uncomfortable (Thornton 2008).

It is now the fashion for big data to inform executive decision making. This reconfiguration of the teaching and learning division of labour is again gendered, with male dominance of instructional design, learning sciences, data analytics and research assessment; whereas research administration and quality assurance is dominated by women (Gordon and Whitchurch 2010). All this adds to the surveillance and managerial oversight of academics by counting the everyday practices of teaching in terms of what academics and students do online (but not necessarily learn). Tightening of surveillance is possible due to workload models that, while seeking to make transparent who does what, arguably reduce professional autonomy through narrowly defining what counts. Continuous auditing for quality assurance focuses on conformity and consistency as the curriculum is 'delivered' through 'templates', while metrics have become the tool of research assessment and promotions (Besley et al. 2009. What is being contested, Unterhalter (2010) argues, is the difference between pedagogies of connection – which focus on identity formation and are 'concerned with building engaged conceptual, empirical, and professional practices that allow the valuation of different situations and guide action' (106) – and pedagogies of consequence – which typify more technicist approaches driven by procedures that require academics to mark off their teaching against particular tickbox lists of outcomes, graduate attributes or employability skills, or academic proceduralism.

At the executive level, the tension is how to balance face-to-face and online learning environments so as to be seen be in the digital space. The value of blended learning is being weighed up against the notion of the attraction of the campus-based 'real' experience (Beetham and Sharpe 2007). This is evident in the significant investment in infrastructure redesign, and pressure for pedagogical innovation such as flipped classrooms and multimodal 'delivery' in the three case studies. But this new learning architecture that intensifies time and effort is changing teaching practice. Blended learning requires constant updating of high-tech knowledge and the production of bite-size videos to fit with lock step approaches to unit guides and templates (Blackmore 2009b). While there is greater flexibility regarding when and where work is undertaken, technology has collapsed and morphed work time into home time (Gibbs et al. 2015). Male academics are also working at home more, but there is little evidence that they assume or challenge the gender division of labour in the organization and undertaking of care (Halford 2006). Additionally, recent priorities of graduate employability require academics to improvise work-integrated learning through partnerships with industry, which again takes time and effort beyond the scope of individuals (Gribble and Blackmore 2012). These fundamental shifts in academic work are largely driven from top down, rather than actively involving practitioners in redesigning the learning spaces, a key aspect of successful change management and building design literature (Blackmore et al. 2011).

Again, part-time, casual and lower-level academics bear the brunt of pedagogical innovation, for which they are held accountable in performance reviews. So at the moment, when teaching and learning has become a key aspect of management in the academy, the technology driver is reconfiguring what is valued, what knowledge counts and also who counts. Teaching is feminized at the lower levels, with increased managerial control. Whereas the emerging professions of administration, policy and data analytics, and the learning sciences, are elevated by management to be core work equivalent to teaching and research (Gordon and Whitchurch 2010), academics increasingly consider themselves to be marginal workers, servicing management, losing control over their labour and yet held individually responsible for outcomes (Blackmore and Sachs 2007). Surveys indicate that this sense of marginalization of academic labour is expressed in a generalized discontent with university leadership (Coates et al. 2009; 2010). It is evident in the disenchantment among potential leaders regarding undertaking management positions. Early career academics see little opportunity to become research leaders, with women in science leaving for more amenable climates in industry as research pathways continue to discriminate (Howe-Walsh and Turnbull 2016) and opportunities decrease with the shrinking of the humanities and the social sciences (Priess 2014). Managers are expected to gain constant improvement from a workforce that, according to this study, increasingly feel displaced, devalued, disoriented, disengaged and disenchanted with restructured academic work, their work–life balance and their workplaces. Meanwhile, students enjoy innovative learning environments, leisure/work spaces, flexibility of time and place, and high expectations regarding personalized pedagogies, but in a context of employment insecurity. In particular, those who do the most teaching – the 'feminized' workforce – have the least capacity to negotiate this pedagogical interface unless they become the self- interested, self-promoting, performing but compliant academic.

Epistemological Feminization: Innovation Rules

Universities have always privileged the 'hard' sciences and biosciences over the humanities and social sciences. Historically, in Australia, the social sciences are the 'poor relations' to the hard sciences (Macintyre 2010). Now the discourse of knowledge economies reifies science and technology as the source of both income and future solutions. Australian universities are being reprimanded for not producing innovations that can be commercialized and so the Australian Research Council, the principal funder of academic research, lists the new National Research and Innovation Priorities without mention of the HASS disciplines. The three institutions in this study illustrate this focus with the Sandstone prioritizing medical science, the Utech concentrating on science, engineering and technology, and the regional university on the tropics and marine science. Across the sector generally, research centres have prioritized research specialisms, few of them in HASS, although individual sociologists and humanities specialists are embedded in interdisciplinary strategic research centres. The humanities and social sciences are not seen to be profitable or product oriented in the short term (Thornton 2014) and therefore most vulnerable to restructuring, with HASS disappearing as structural unit in the Utech as elsewhere (Priess 2014).

Furthermore, as Thornton (2014) argues, the two-cultures model of the hard and soft sciences has returned with research assessment and excellence, with 'the distinction between the humanities and the social sciences weakening' (Macintyre 2010: 298). While the digital humanities have been able to capture the popular imagination associated with digitalization, education (a highly feminized field), was never fully legitimated as a 'discipline' (Furlong and Lawn 2011). Even philosophy, while male dominated, has had to reinvent itself to fit categories and definitions of excellence, redefining not only who one works with but how one does research (Jenkins 2015). Rankings don't just create vertical differentiation but 'obscure horizontal differences, differences of purpose and type' (Marginson and van der Wende 2007: 326). The discourse of excellence now means that any feminist claim on the basis of a critical feminist standpoint positions them as a 'special case' of excellence, rather than changing how the notion of excellence is understood (Jenkins 2015). While global rankings also demand other measures of equity (a UNESCO report identifies that only 29 percent of all researchers were female in 2010), the escalation of entrepreneurialism works against reducing the gender pay gap while positioning women as not being entrepreneurial enough (Bruni, Gherardi and Poggio 2004; Metcalfe and Slaughter 2008; Welch 2012). Wylie (2012: 67) argues that 'gender inequities can create a cascade of content effects that raise serious questions about the epistemic integrity of a field ... as the economic factors that establish the language of excellence as the horizon of judgment'. The discourses of excellence and innovation, which focus on economics and applications, exclude the social as a source of innovation and alternative knowledge in terms of critical engagement and diversity of perspectives, making innovation 'conformist' (Hassan 2015).

These discourses and new organizational division of labour also weaken the critical role of the public intellectual, more often the domain of humanities and social science disciplines and critical scholars (Thornton 2008). Australian academics are cautioned to only speak publically in their area of academic expertise and not as advocates, which limits what it is to be a public intellectual, particularly regarding issues of democratic governance or the changing nature of higher education itself. As Wylie (2012: 3) argues, this requires us 'critically unpacking the gendered modes of knowledge transmission (including factors of influence, reputation, resourcing) and production, who judges what counts, the processes by which it is judged and with what effect'.

The limiting of the intellectual voice echoes the disposition of higher education managers and their rejection of internal academic expertise and scholarly leadership that might inform organizational change. The discourse among executive managers about the professoriate in all three universities was that, except for those who aligned with management, professors were resistant, out of step, past their use-by date, or irrelevant with regard to being innovative or forward thinking. The strategy for some executive deans and deputy vice chancellors when restructuring internally, therefore, was to recruit from, as one dean commented, the 'hungry and more competitive ranks of the associate professors' who were less recalcitrant. While failure to recognize internal academic expertise is not new, change management has become more critical for university leadership to achieve certain goals as stated in their KPIs. Managing academics is considered the key to achieving the integration of strategic plans, research productivity and student outcomes. This refusal to recognize internal expertise, or to listen to feedback regarding the effects of the serial restructurings designed by external 'experts' following changes in executive leadership, produces constant organizational uncertainty for both middle managers and academics. But constant uncertainty is itself a valuable managerial mode of control as difficult, recalcitrant or 'unproductive' staff or units fear redundancy, a fear that feeds the mindset of all academics and professional staff, encouraging compliance.

Leadership Futures

In conclusion, leadership in the entrepreneurial university is increasingly about managing what managers can manage – their academic staff. Student demand, international labour markets, funding models and alternative sources are in flux. The context of heightened insecurity changes the affective economies of the university as they have become more hierarchical; individuals are held more responsible for quality of research and outcomes, raising income, getting grants, more expeditious supervision, but with fewer protections and institutional supports and no reciprocity in terms of recognition or rewards (Rawolle, Rowlands and Blackmore 2016). The risk is not shared and self-motivation is no longer enough. These factors create tensions within and between leadership units at executive and middle-management levels as well as between researchers and teachers, risk aversion and innovation, deregulation and regulation, and academic autonomy and corporate alignment. In seeking to align staff to strategic priorities and avoid risk through contracts, regulation and performance-based systems of governance, universities and governments are undermining the university's innovative and critical edge and sense of public service – what distinguishes universities from other providers. Executive management in that sense remains a masculinist environment based on whose voice dominates and what knowledge is valued (Deem 2003, Leathwood and Dear 2012).

Furthermore, internal responses to exogenous factors and policy frames around innovation and funding favour a particular logic of managerial practice – proceduralism – which, while seemingly neutral, is premised upon managing the increased contractualization of academic work. This involves layers of administrivia, reporting requirements, templated unit guides, curriculum audits, onerous travel procedures, codes of ethical conduct, doctoral supervisory agreements, performance-management systems and academic workload models (Rawolle, Rowlands and Blackmore 2016). Undertaking the performative work of proceduralism actually changes academic practice and identity (Blackmore and Sachs 2007). Paradoxically, this undermines the very things managers seek to achieve as it diverts academics' energy away from the creative teaching and research most likely to produce the twenty-first-century global worker and innovation that the university claims to do (Hassan 2015). Proceduralism also consumes middle managers' time and energy, deflecting them from more strategic thinking and planning how to develop productive workplaces through support rather than administrivia. Proceduralism implies a particular hierarchy through its logic of practice and defines relationships between academics and managers through lock-step mechanisms of decision making. Thus important issues can be sent back to subcommittees rather than debated substantively and openly in key decision-making fora.

The dominant managerialist ethos requires research leaders to learn how to speak to power through procedures rather than through dialogue, an approach encouraged by leadership development programs. Professors are defined by university managers as research leaders with a specified role as mentors, attracting students and funds, partnering collaboratively, maintaining quality, to sometimes be consulted, but actively dissuaded from informing line-management decisions. This context attracts certain academics into management with dispositions already acquired through prior experience and disposed towards proceduralism as a logic of practice best mobilized when under pressure. Managers both self-select and are selected by others as 'best fit' with the corporate mindset, as people like to work with people like themselves (Grummell, Devine and Lynch 2009; Probert 2005).

With regard to gender equity, there is significant evidence to show what works to get more women into university research and management leadership positions: frameworks, policies, procedures and so on, all set up the game plan to enable fairness to prevail by creating fairer, more equitable, accountable transparent workplaces that legimate action by leaders. Equity success in increasing numbers of women has been due largely to university policies in recruitment and promotion, having explicit equity clauses in every text triggering action, and a discourse of equity in research. One equal-opportunities practitioner said, 'over time, the consciousness of making sure that women are in leadership roles has grown'. According to a vice chancellor in this study, it is a business imperative to attract and retain women students and to access a good pool of staff, otherwise there was 'wasted talent' (Blackmore 2014). However, as in all institutions, there were also areas where women were only 'surviving not thriving' (Cameron 2012: 7).

But getting more women into leadership is not enough, as the feminization of the academy is about how power works in relation to gender and how it is distributed through institutional structures, processes and cultures. Yet gender equity policy and the more recent diversity discourse do performative work for the entrepreneurial university (Ahmed 2012). But the logic of proceduralism and its instrumentalist decision making, while claiming gender neutrality, undermines managers practising inclusive diversity. Devine, Grummell and Lynch (2011: 631) suggest:

> the rhetoric of gender equality permeates new managerial reforms. Yet our data suggest that an emphasis on performativity and an intense commitment to paid work consolidates masculinist management cultures disguised through the ideology of choice.

While the old binaries of male rationality and female emotionality are becoming blurred in terms of practices (for example, female or male styles of leadership), for those women choosing to move into executive management, the structures and culture are still masculinist in their production of leadership work along a public–domestic divide (Leathwood and Read 2010). While there is numerical feminization of the academy there continues to be a feminization of how power works, what knowledge is valued, who decides and with what effect. The issue for university management is that academics have competing loyalties and gain legitimation, credibility and rewards through means other than their university. This makes them unmanageable as their networks become more globalized and coordinated. To attract back loyalty perhaps requires a different set of managerial relationships and leadership practices and different forms of organizational innovation which engage with a diversity of ideas and knowledges that challenge rather than assert hierarchies.

◆

Jill Blackmore is Alfred Deakin Professor in the Faculty of Arts and Education, Deakin University, Director of the Centre for Research in Educational Futures and Innovation, and Fellow of the Academy of Social Sciences. Her research interests include, from a feminist perspective: globalization, education policy and governance in universities, TAFE (technical and further education), schools and communities; international and intercultural education; educational restructuring, leadership and organizational change; spatial redesign and innovative pedagogies; teachers' and academics' work and equity policy. Recent higher education research has focused on disengagement with and lack of diversity in leadership, international education and graduate employability. Recent Publications include: *Educational Leadership and Nancy Fraser*, 2016, Routledge; and *Mobile Teachers, Teacher Identity and International Schooling* (coedited with R. Arber and A. Vongalis-Macrow), 2014, Sense.

Notes

1. Australia spends just over 0.6 percent if its GDP on research and development, compared to closer to 0.9 percent in the U.S.A., Sweden and Denmark (Australian Government 2015: 2).

References

Ahmed, S. 2012. *On Being Included. Racism and Diversity in Institutional Life.* Durham, NC: Duke Press.

Altbach, P., et al. (eds). 2012. *Paying the Professoriate. A Global Comparison of Compensation and Contracts.* London: Routledge.

Australian Government. 2015. 'National Innovation and Science Agenda'. Retrieved 10 February 2016 from http://innovation.gov.au/system/files/case-study/National%20Innovation%20and%20Science%20Agenda%20-%20Report.pdf.

Beetham, H., and R. Sharpe. (eds). 2007. *Rethinking Pedagogy for a Digital Age. Designing for 21st Century Learning.* London: Routledge.

Benschop, Y., and M. Brouns. 2003. 'Crumbling Ivory Towers: Academic Organizing and its Gender Effects', *Gender, Work and Organization* 10(2): 194–212.

Besley, T. (ed.). 2009. *Assessing the Quality of Educational Research in Higher Education.* Rotterdam: Sense Publishers.

Blackmore, J. 2009a. 'Anticipating Policy and the Logics of Practice: Australian Institutional and Academic Responses to the Globalising "Quality Research" Agenda', *Access* 27(1–2): 97–113.

———. 2009b. 'Academic Pedagogies, Quality Logics and Performative Universities: Evaluating Teaching and What Students Want', *Studies in Higher Education* 34(8): 857–72.

———. 2014. '"Wasting Talent"? Rethinking the Problematic of Leadership Disengagement in Entrepreneurial Universities from a Feminist Critical Policy Perspective', *Higher Education and Research Development* 33(1): 83–96.

Blackmore, J., M. Brennan and L. Zipin. (eds). 2010. *Repositioning the University: Governance and Changing Academic Work.* Rotterdam: Sense Publishing.

Blackmore, J., and J. Sachs. 2007. *Performing and Reforming Leaders: Gender, Educational Restructuring, and Organizational Change.* New York: SUNY Press.

Blackmore, J., et al. 2011. *Innovative Learning Environments Research Study.* Melbourne: OECD/ Department of Education and Early Childhood Development. *www.learningspaces.edu.au*

Blackmore, J., and C. Gribble. 2012. 'Re-positioning Australia's international education in global knowledge economies: implications of shifts in skilled migration policies for universities', *Journal of Higher Education Policy and Management* 34(4) 341–54.

Blackmore, J., C. Gribble, M. Rahini, L, Farrell, R. Arber. R. and M. Devlin. 2014 *Australian International Graduates and the Transition to Employment,* Burwood: Deakin Centre for Research in Educational Futures and Innovation

Blackmore, J., M. Sánchez-Moreno and N. Sawers. (eds). 2015. 'Globalised re/gendering of the academy and leadership', special issue of *Gender and Education* 27(3).

Blackmore, J., and N. Sawers. 2015. 'Executive Power and Scaled Up Gender Politics in Australian Entrepreneurial Universities', *Gender and Education* 27(3): 320–37.

Boden, R., and M. Nedeva. 2010. 'Employing discourse: universities and graduate "employability"', *Journal of Education Policy* 25(1): 37–54.

Brown, P., H. Lauder and D. Ashton. 2011. *The Global Auction: The Broken Promises of Education, Jobs and Income.* Oxford: Oxford University Press.

Bruni, A., S. Gherardi and B. Poggio. 2004. 'Doing Gender, Doing Entrepreneurship: An Ethnographic Account of Intertwined Practices', *Gender, Work and Organization* 11(4): 406–29.

Cameron, H. 2012. 'Changing the Organizational Balance of Women's Representations Through a Strategic Cultural Change Approach'. Brisbane: Griffith University. Retrieved 10 February 2016 from https://www.griffith.edu.au/__data/assets/pdf_file/0006/176064/presentation-to-6th-european-conference-on-gender-equity.pdf..

Coates, H., et al. 2009. 'Australia's Casual Approach to its Academic Teaching Force', *People and Place* 17(4): 47–48.

———. 2010. 'Across the Great Divide: What do Australian Academics Think of University Leadership?', *Journal of Higher Education Policy and Management* 32(4): 379–87.

Czarniawska, B. 2006. 'Doing Gender Unto the Other: Fiction as a Mode of Studying Gender Discrimination in Organizations', *Gender, Work and Organization* 13(3): 234–53.

Davies, B., and P. Bansel. 2010. 'Through Love of What Neoliberal Universities Put at Risk', in J. Blackmore, M. Brennan and L. Zipin (eds), *Repositioning the University: Governance and Changing Academic Work.* Rotterdam: Sense Publishing.

Deem, R. 2003. 'Gender, Organizational Cultures and the Practices of Manager-Academics in UK Universities', *Gender, Work and Organization* 10(2): 239–57.

Degn, L. 2015. 'Sensemaking, Sensegiving and Strategic Management in Danish Higher Education', *Higher Education* 69: 901-13.

Devine, D., B. Grummell and K. Lynch. 2011. 'Crafting the Elastic Self? Gender and Identities in Senior Appointments in Irish Education', *Gender, Work and Organization* 18(6): 631-49.

Ernst and Young. 2012. *University of the Future: A Thousand Year Old Industry on the Cusp of Profound Change*. Retrieved 10 February 2016 from http://www.ey.dk/Publication/vwLUAssets/University_of_the_future/$FILE/University_of_the_future_2012.pdf.

Furlong, J., and M. Lawn. 2011. *Disciplines of Education. Their Role in the Future of Educational Research*. London: Routledge.

Gibbs, P., et al. (eds). 2015. *Universities in the Flux of Time. An Exploration of Time and Temporality in University Life*. London: Routledge.

Gordon, G., and C. Whitchurch. 2010. *Academic and Professional Identities in Higher Education. The Challenges of a Diversifying Workforce*. London: Routledge.

Grummell, B., D. Devine and K. Lynch. 2009. 'Appointing Senior managers in Education: Homosociability, Local Logics and Authenticity in the Selection Process', *Educational Management Administration and Leadership* 37(3): 329-49.

Guthrie, D. 2013 'The Coming Big Data Education Revolution', *U.S. News*, 15 August. Retrieved 10 February 2016 from http://www.usnews.com/opinion/articles/2013/08/15/why-big-data-not-moocs-will-revolutionize-education.

Halford, S. 2006. 'Collapsing the Boundaries? Fatherhood, Organization and Home-Working', *Gender, Work and Organization* 13(4): 383-402.

Hassan, R. 2015. 'When Innovation Becomes Conformist. Academic Research in Network Times', in P. Gibbs et al. (eds), *Universities in the Flux of Time. An Exploration of Time and Temporality in University Life*. London: Routledge.

Howe-Walsh, L., and S. Turnbull. 2016. 'Barriers to Women Leaders in Academia: Tales from Science and Technology', *Studies in Higher Education* 41(3): 415-28.

Jenkins, F. 2015. 'Gendered Hierarchies of Knowledge and the Prestige Factor: How Philosophy Survives Market Rationality', in M. Thornton (ed.), *Through a Glass Darkly: The Social Sciences Look at the Neoliberal University*. Canberra: ANU Press, pp. 49-64.

Knights, D., and D. Kerfoot. 2004. 'Between Representations and Subjectivity: Gender Binaries and the Politics of Organizational Transformation', *Gender, Work and Organization* 11(4): 389-405.

Leathwood, C., and B. Read. 2009. *Gender and the Changing Face of Higher Education: A Feminized Future?* Maidenhead: OUP.

Macintyre, S. 2010. *The Poor Relation. A history of the Social Sciences in Australia*. Melbourne: Melbourne University Press.

Maes, K. 2013. 'Women, research and universities: excellence without gender bias', LERU (League of European Research Universities). Retrieved 5 October 2015 from http://www.stages.csmcd.ro/resources/ktrien_maes_presentation.pdf.

Marchand, M, and Runyan, A. 2000. *Gender and Global Restructuring: Sightings, Sites and Resistances.* New York: Routledge.

Marginson, S. 2008. 'Global Field and Global Imagining: Bourdieu and Worldwide Higher Education', *British Journal of Sociology of Education* 29(3): 303–15.

―――. 2011. 'Higher Education and Public Good', *Higher Education Quarterly* 65(4): 411–33.

Marginson, S., and M. Considine 2000, *The Enterprise University: Power, Governance and Reinvention in Australia,* Cambridge: Cambridge University Press.

Marginson, S., and M. van der Wende. 2007. *Globalisation and Higher Education.* Paris: OECD.

Martinez, J.M. 2011. '"Feminizing" Middle Management? An Inquiry into the Gendered Subtexts in University Department Headship', *Sage Open*, 5 July 2011, DOI: 10.1177/2158244011414731. Retrieved 10 February 2016 from http://sgo.sagepub.com/content/1/2/2158244011414731.

May, R., G. Strachan and D. Peetz. 2013. 'Workforce Development and Renewal in Australian Universities and the Management of Casual Academic Staff', *Journal of University Teaching and Learning Practice.* Retrieved 10 February 2016 from http://ro.uow.edu.au/jutlp/vol10/iss3/3.

McCulloch, G. 2013. '"The dirty little secret of university expansion", union tells public parliamentary hearings into insecure employment bill', *National Tertiary Education Union.* Retrieved 14 April 2014 from http://www.aur.org.au/article/Casualisation-'the-dirty-little-secret-of-university-expansion',-union-tells-public-parliamentary-hearings-into-insecure-employment-bill-14831.

Metcalfe, A., and S. Slaughter. 2008. 'The Differential Effects of Academic Capitalism on Women in the Academy', in J. Glazer-Raymo (ed.), *Unfinished Agendas: New and Continuing Gender Challenges in Higher Education.* Baltimore: John Hopkins University Press.

Morley, L. 2013. 'The Rules of the Game: Women and the Leaderist Turn in Higher Education', *Gender and Education* 25(1): 116–31.

Murphy, P. 2013. 'The Rise and Fall of Our Bureaucratic Universities', *Quadrant* 57(5): 48–52.

Pike, J. 2009. 'Perspectives from Below the Ceiling: Academic Women and the Transition from Senior Lecturer to the Professoriate – a Case Study', Ph.D. thesis. Melbourne, Australia: University of Melbourne.

Preiss, B. 2014. 'La Trobe cuts 45 jobs in humanities', *The Age*, 20 June. Retrieved 11 February 2013 from www.theage.com.au/national/education/ la-trobe-cuts-45-jobs-in-humanities-20120620-20o5s.html.

Probert, B. 2005. '"I just didn't fit in": Gender and Unequal Outcomes in Academic Careers', *Gender, Work and Organization* 12(1): 50–72.

Rawolle, S., J. Rowlands and J. Blackmore. 2016. 'The Implications of Contractualism for the Responsibilisation of Higher Education', *Discourse*, published online. Retrieved 5 October 2016 from http://www.tandfonline.com/doi/full/10.1080/01596306.2015.1104856.

Riegraf, B., et al. (eds). 2010. *Gender Change in Academia: Re-mapping Fields of Work, Knowledge and Politics from a Gender Perspective*. Dordrecht: Springer Verlag.

Rowlands, J. 2013. 'Academic Boards: Less Intellectual and more Academic Capital in Higher Education Governance?', *Studies in Higher Education* 38(9): 1274–89.

Scott, G., et al. 2010. 'Australian Higher Education Leaders in Times of Change: The Role of Pro Vice-Chancellor and Deputy Vice-Chancellor', *Journal of Higher Education Policy and Management* 32(4): 401–18.

Stensaker, B. 2014. 'Organizational Identity as a Concept for Understanding University Dynamics', *Higher Education* 69: 103–15.

Thornton, M. 2008. 'The Retreat from the Critical: Social Science Research in the Corporatised University', *Australian Universities Review* 50(1): 5–10.

_____. (ed.). 2014. *Through a Glass Darkly: The Social Sciences Look at the Neoliberal University*. Canberra: ANU Press.

Universities Australia. 2015. 'Facts and Figures in Higher Education and Research', Canberra.

Unterhalter, E. 2010. 'Considering Equality, Equity and Higher Education Pedagogies in the Context of Globalisation', in E. Unterhalter and V. Carpentier (eds), *Global Inequalities and Higher Education. Whose Interests are we Serving?* London: Palgrave.

Waitere, H., et al. 2011. 'Choosing whether to resist or reinforce the new managerialism: the impact of performance-based research funding on academic identity', *Higher Education Research & Development* 30(2): 205–17.

Welch, A. 2012. 'Academic Salaries Massification, and the Rise of an Underclass in Australia', in P. Altbach et al. (eds), *Paying the Professoriate: A Global Comparison of Compensation and Contracts*. London: Routledge.

White, K., B. Bagilhole and S. Riordan. 2012. 'The Gendered Shaping of University Leadership in Australia, South Africa and the United Kingdom', *Higher Education Quarterly* 66(3): 293–307.

Wylie, A. 2012. 'Feminist Philosophy of Science: Standpoint Matters, APA Presidential Address', *Proceedings and Addresses of the APA* 86(2): 46–76.

PART II

Performing the New University – New Priorities, New Subjects

CHAPTER 5
Science/Industry Collaboration
Bugs, Project Barons and Managing Symbiosis

BIRGITTE GORM HANSEN

━━━ ◆◆◆

Introduction

Several decades of policy reforms have put pressure on universities to be relevant and useful to society. One of the major interventions in the Denmark has been a reform of how universities are governed and managed. In this chapter, I will trace some of the runaway effects of the policy changes taking place in Denmark through an empirical study of how research mangers manoeuvre through changes in research policy. I will put the grand visions of policymakers into perspective by looking at local empirical examples of how a particular research manager acted strategically to make his research programs survive despite changes in the way his university was funded.[1]

'From Insights to Invoice'

In the late 1990s, the Danish government launched a series of university reforms targeted at bridging a perceived gap between science and society. The core idea was to promote more interaction, especially between university and industry. At the time of the university reform in 2003, the idea of knowledge dissemination was conceived of as a market-based process. Science–industry collaboration was launched as the most important strategy for ensuring that the increased investment in knowledge production would in fact bring growth to the economy and strengthen the competitive advantage of Denmark. Under the now infamous heading 'From insight to invoice' (Fra Tanke Til Faktura) (Danish Government 2003), a series of initiatives was launched in order to strengthen science–industry collaboration and the commercialization of research from public universities. The government stressed that these changes were not made in order for the university to create its own revenue based on commercializeable innovations,[2] but rather to strengthen the dissemination and transfer of knowledge from the university sector to the world of business (Danish Government 2003).

The dominating viewpoint expressed in this period was that Danish universities still had a large proportion of 'unused potential' when it came to commercialization of research and that a much higher output should be expected. 'Output' is here conceived as 'patents, collaborations with private companies, and corporate leaders' assessment of research collaborations as a useful endeavour' (Danish Council for Research Policy 2006: 6).

One important feature of the reforms was that the state allocated increased funding to knowledge production, targeted especially at projects, proposals and research activities that had commercial potential. In 2003, the main potential was seen to lie in biotechnology and IT but these initiatives were launched as an equal opportunity across all faculties (Danish Government 2003). In order to convince the Strategic Research Council that a research proposal really did create value for society, it was beneficial to explain how industry would be directly involved in the project. So-called 'network grants' were allocated to aid the facilitation of networks and collaboration platforms, in addition to the research project. Many other initiatives were taken to facilitate industry cofunding so that public funding would be channelled to feed projects that had a direct usefulness for business. The relevance and contribution of research proposals were increasingly evaluated in terms of possible industry partnerships (Gorm Hansen 2011a).

Consumers and Producers

By changing the structure for public research funding, government attempted to encourage researchers to take the leap from their 'academic ivory tower' and begin to make themselves useful for corporate environments. Governing universities was seen as a project of steering a unidirectional flow from the production to consumption of knowledge. In the words of one of the key Danish policymakers, Hans Müller Petersen:

> I think that in the minds of many researchers this development has not really entered their [academics'] heads yet. Some still seem to think that research is simply this very ceremonial thing of finding the objective knowledge, truth; that finding objective knowledge is an activity that has legitimacy in and of itself. And to some extent

it still is. But within the recent development in how societies make use of knowledge, more dimensions have been introduced. There is a higher demand for knowledge throughout. Knowledge is not just produced today in order to find truth; it is also produced to be used. This means that, as a researcher, you have to get used to stepping out of your study chamber and entering some more dynamic relations with those who are consumers and providers of knowledge outside the university. This is a basic requirement for being a researcher today (interview with Petersen 2009, author's translation).

The changes in university management and incentive structures were guided by the goal of getting academics to 'step out of the study chamber' and enter into a new world of dynamic cross-sector collaboration. According to this particular policymaker, the role of policy is to 'create frameworks' and incentive structures. This approach to research policy, of course, did not go uncontested.

Convergence

Critical studies of the commercialization of science indicate that the above depictions of a production flow from producer to consumer are much too neat. An important point in critical accounts is that the shift towards integration is not an inevitable, self-directed or naturally occurring process but a conscious and strategic intervention whose impacts can and should be examined, questioned and, if possible, resisted (Lave, Mirowski and Randalls 2010; Mirowski 2008; Resnik 2007; Slaughter and Rhodes 2004; 2005). An overall tendency identified by critical approaches to the commercialization of science is the way academia and industry are converging in a much more systematic and pervasive way than depicted in accounts of the formal ties between academia and industry. Several studies have spotted a tendency for corporate science to mirror academic publication practices in order to gain legitimacy (Kleinman 2003; Kleinman and Vallas 2006; Sismondo 2011). Others have shown how academic training and student learning become processes of socialization into corporate norms and industrial practices (Croissant and Restivo 2001; Washburn 2005). In the critical literature on the commercialization of science, the linear flow from producer to consumer is not (necessarily) a good thing. Rather, the studies form a critique of the erosion of academic values, research freedom and the free flow of information entailed in the convergence between academia and industry.

Interestingly, both policymakers and those who criticize them seem to subscribe to the idea that academic science constitutes a separate domain that is somehow 'not society' (Strathern 2005). The idea of university research as an independent knowledge producer and industry as a different sphere of reality seems to inform both policymakers and critical accounts of how science is governed. Where the first seek to integrate the two spheres of reality, the second focuses on protecting the boundaries between them. Both accept an analytical premise that there are two well-bounded institutional entities, and are occupied with how these separate spheres of activity and institutional order should or should not converge. Where the policymaker sees university–industry collaboration as a sign of the times and a way to promote a progressive development towards integration, the critical debate sees industrial interests as a threat to the integrity of science. However, when we turn the gaze onto the study of scientific practice, a much more complex picture emerges.

'Politics by Other Means'

In the research field of science, technology and society (STS), we find decades of research following scientists through everyday work practices. An important contribution is historian Steven Shapin's account of science as vocation in the United States (Shapin 2008). He articulates in great detail how science has always been a muddled territory, where interests and practices flow into one another producing new forms of tension and fertilizing new opportunities for scientific fundability. Scientific life, Shapin argues, cannot be uniformly described in terms of coherent norms and practices, and scientists themselves do not start out with assumptions about a moral fault line between academia and industry.

Shapin's descriptions resonate with the laboratory studies of Bruno Latour (1987; 1999) and the studies of innovation processes made by Michel Callon (1986a). These studies form an important part of the foundations for what has been labelled 'the sociology of translation' or 'actor-network theory' (Callon 1980; 1986b; Latour 1996; 2005). This body of literature pays close attention to the details of scientific practice as fact making and offers an analytical vocabulary for grasping the transversal movements of scientific practice. The analyst needs to invent an analytical repertoire in response to the task at hand. When studying innovation processes Callon claims the vocabulary needs to be construed in a way that does not require the analyst to change registers when accounting for things that would otherwise be thought of as 'technical' or 'social', belonging to 'science' or belonging to 'capital interest'. In the sociology of translation these distinctions are an outcome rather than a starting point of analysis.

As argued by Latour, mixture and heterogeneity are an intrinsic property and characteristic of the construction of scientific facts:

> the very difference between the 'inside' and the 'outside', and the difference between 'micro' and 'macro' levels, is precisely what laboratories are built to destabilize and undo (Latour 1999: 258).

According to Latour, science was a mixture to begin with and we therefore need to start analysis with a vocabulary capable of detecting such mixtures rather than focusing on solid institutional boundaries, tensions between conflicting norms or separations between science and politics. The sociology of translation argues that if scientific practice is conceived a priori as an institutional enclosure, which can be integrated into or protected from outside interests, this does not do justice to the events taking place in the field. Science, Latour claims, was never a pure breed:

> Science is not politics. It is politics by other means. But people object that 'science does not reduce to power'. Precisely. It does not reduce to power. It offers *other means*. But it will be objected again that 'by their nature these means cannot be foreseen'. Precisely. If they were foreseeable, they would already be used by an opposing power. What could be better than a fresh form of power that no one knows how to use? Call up the reserves! (Latour 1988: 229)

A fresh form of power requires fresh analytical vocabularies, Latour argues. When the focus of the early studies of fact making conducted by Latour and Callon is broadened to include attempts to manage science, matters get even more complicated. Policymakers tend to view power as trickling down from the top, via management reforms, to influence academic practice. But most of the field participants in this study were not 'professional managers'; they had taken on the task of research management along with their academic work.[3] In changing the research stance from that of the policymakers to the academics that they are trying to govern, a completely new picture emerges, showing that the power dynamics of the modern university is all but a linear flow from producers to consumers where power can trickle down from the top via management reforms.

The Barons of Science

As part of eighteen months' field work, I interviewed some of the most successful research managers working in Danish universities (Gorm Hansen 2011a). The study focused on scientists from the fields of nanoscience and life sciences as these had proved to be extremely successful in adapting to the changes in Danish research policy.

One such scientist is Robert Feidenhans'l, a world-famous physicist. As a manager of multiple, large research projects and an internationally well-respected name in the world of physics, Feidenhans'l has a good overview of the most powerful actors in the Danish world of research. Unlike the policymaker, he does not see the modern university as a place where power trickles down from the top. One of the elements that he feels is completely overlooked when we are discussing the impacts of research policy is the rise of what he calls 'project barons':

> Project barons, there are many of them around the system and although, they are not heads of departments, they nevertheless have an enormous influence. They have huge networks, big grants and full professorships. And really, what does a head of department or a dean really have to do good with? The dean can't do a thing if all the project barons are going somewhere else (interview with Feidenhans'l 2009, author's translation).

Feidenhans'l goes on to name specific Danish professors that he considers to be among the barons of today's university research. These people, he says, are hugely influential. On paper, they look like ordinary professors but, in practice, the university deans cannot make a move without consulting them first. They act freely outside the formal management structures of the university and are capable of going beyond their jurisdiction. They operate by staying close to the scene of research and gain their influence by a remarkable ability to attract external funding. As Feidenhans'l puts it, 'they live by getting money all the time'.

Some field participants even say (but these are rumours) that these 'barons of science' have influence higher up in the ministries and are capable of dictating and influencing the guidelines for strategic research funding. When university professors acquire the magical status of the project baron, they muster allies such as industrialists, politicians, ministries and research councils and thereby force their dean or head of department to 'make a detour' that encompasses their research program or 'go their way' (Latour 1987).

Feidenhans'l is not the only one who has identified the rise of a new aristocracy in academic science. In a 2009 article in *Universitetsavisen* – a newspaper distributed by Copenhagen University – sociologists Heine Andersen and Inge Henningsen divided academic science up into 'the barons of science'[4] and the 'ball fetchers'. The authors evaluated the Danish research councils' distribution of public funding and criticized the idea that increased competition naturally generates better research. Andersen and Henningsen compared the distribution of funding to a tennis tournament where all players have to live exclusively by prize money. Needless to say, this system results in most of the players leaving the tournament after the early rounds and becoming ball fetchers instead, leaving only the previous winners to compete in the finals (Andersen and Henningsen 2009).

To take a closer look at how the barons of science work strategically and adapt to changes in research policy, I have followed one: plant biologist Birger Lindberg Møller, who was frequently mentioned when field participants gave examples of 'project barons'.

Toxic Policy Environments

Professor Møller is the head of a large interdisciplinary research centre called Pro-Active Plants, situated in a Danish university. The centre is based on a series of successful collaborations spanning several universities and departments as well as Møller's lifelong dedication to plant biology and genetically modified organisms (GMO). One of the major objectives for Pro-Active Plants is to find out how plants 'talk' to their environment through the exchange of chemical information (Malmberg 2007). Things have been going quite well for Pro-Active Plants; recently the institute, which houses the centre, celebrated the simultaneous appointment of six new professors – three of them situated in the centre and appointed to support its leading research programs. Things have also been going well in terms of funding, despite the fact that money has been notoriously difficult to get in the area of Danish plant GMO due to political resistance and financial risk.

Having made his career in the years when plant GMO was highly controversial, Møller was accustomed to spending a lot of time relating the research agenda of his centre to broader societal and political questions. The centre has been very successful in attracting funding, public as well as private. However, this success only came through hard work outside the confines of the laboratory, he tells me. Global resistance to GMO gave Møller a policy environment that could best be described as toxic for his research program. In addition, the fact that his research area was so new that no industry existed in his area meant he had no consumer to legitimate his production of knowledge. Establishing an academic career in a toxic environment is perhaps what has made Møller such a vivid performer and talented presenter. He never fails to make the usefulness and relevance of Pro-Active Plants visible in relation to climate problems, the quest for sustainable energy, world hunger or gender equality in developing countries. It is evident that he is extremely conscious of the importance of networking with a broad spectrum of actors and sectors.

A large part of Møller's managerial work is to mingle with people outside the university department and establish relations in order to keep a constant influx of money, staff, ideas, technologies and political goodwill. As a scientist and as a research manager he spends a considerable amount of his time travelling to conferences, going to debate meetings, giving interviews to the media, writing up patents in collaboration with biotech companies, working as an expert witness in patenting court cases, making evaluations of other university departments, being on the phone with representatives from research councils, talking to venture capitalists, and meeting with politicians who take an interest in climate and food. All of these activities are woven into his working day as he makes the seamless transition from public engagement to teaching, supervising, writing and checking up on the lab facilities.

However, Møller does not see his core activity as one of mingling and maintaining relations. On the contrary, he tells me, there is much more to plant biology than political and managerial networking. In my fourth interview with him, he began to resist:

> BLM: so there is a lot of politics in this ... (pauses, looks up) we are talking a lot of politics in this conversation! Why are we not talking about research?
> BGH: Well, from the way you seem to work the two seem to be closely related.
> BLM: Yeah, but you always ask me about the political stuff instead of asking me about the stuff I do!
> BGH: Well at some point I would actually like to hear more about the stuff you *really* do (interview with Møller 2009, author's translation).

Møller implies that I would not adequately describe his job by pointing only to his networking activities. Surely, there would be no science without these activities but, according to Møller, we would be missing the point altogether if we focused first and only on this part of his job.

Møller sees himself as a scientist, not primarily a manager, an opinion maker or an administrator. He is a plant biologist who has to take on managerial responsibility and communications work in order to do his job well. I initially questioned this account by pointing out that from a quick look at his weekly schedule Møller seems to spend more than 60 percent of his time on 'the stuff around' his research activity. For example, this plant biologist has to designate time slots twice a year in order to be sure he even makes it into the laboratory and conducts some actual experiments. If not, he will get 'rusty' and will lose touch with the lab facilities and fail to make sure that they live up to standards. Møller, however, insists that the activities we have discussed so far in the interviews constitute only 10 percent of his job.

Møller sees himself first as a plant biologist. Unless specifically asked about administrative details, policy agendas or strategic moves he will talk nonstop about plants. He will use any excuse to shift the subject of an interview to his core research interests and to get out a PowerPoint presentation, a popular science account or a journal article for me to take home. Repeatedly he will make it clear that missing his research is missing the point of what he is all about. Being a plant biologist is what matters, all the other activities are 'the stuff around it'; the things that make plant biology work.

How should we read such a plea? Møller's protest about my one-sided focus on network formations, mustering allies and enrolling actors could easily be articulated as a need for protecting boundaries between what counts as inside science and what counts as outside. We could read Møller's statements as an attempt to separate his 'real job' – pure science – from the management, mingling, entrepreneurship and politics that comes with it. Such an analysis would lead us to claim that Møller is engaged in purifying plant biology.

However, if we are to follow Latour's method, rather than his conclusions, we need a more sensitive vocabulary here; one that is able to follow Møller in the complex relationships that constitute a fresh form of power. Møller's work includes more than leaping between science, industry, government and the public. If taken seriously, Møller's protest against a one-sided focus on the 'political' part of his work may actually be read as a plea for increasing complexity, not an attempt to reduce it by stripping pure science of its strategic and political agendas. It seems we need to find an analytical vocabulary that increases complexity rather than reduces it.

During fieldwork and interviews, it became apparent that Møller uses the vocabulary of biology and evolution to make sense of his own position and room for manoeuvre in relation to changes in research policy (Gorm Hansen 2011a, 2011b). He talks about policy changes and bureaucratic structures as 'environments' in which new researchers develop their careers and he uses evolutionary metaphors when accounting for the success and failure of academic researchers and their fields. Møller seems to be suggesting an analytical route that goes in the opposite direction: that we start out in plant biology and move outwards from there. For this purpose, we will now indulge the field participant and devote some attention to his 'real job', that is plant biology.

Using Møller's biological research as a framework for analysis will give us a vocabulary for looking at the way he manages a symbiotic relationship between science and industry without having to reify the two in advance. Let us therefore proceed to the heart of the matter: plant–insect relationships.

Coevolution

Møller's main area of research is bioactive natural products that enable plants to defend themselves against insects and microbial pathogens. A plant produces a specific subset of these poisons in response to environmental challenges, in order to fend off plant-eaters and disease-producing micro-organisms. Plants are thus proactive living organisms, acting on their environment and entering complex chemical exchanges with other species in order to survive. Møller and his colleagues have done extensive research on one particular type of poisonous plant: *Lotus corniculatus*. The reason why this plant is interesting to Pro-Active Plants is that it is cyanogenic: the leaves of the plant contain cyanogenic glucosides - compounds that are able to release toxic cyanide. The presence of cyanogenic glucosides in the leaves makes the plant poisonous to anyone who tries to eat it. Møller argues that the role of the poisonous compounds they contain should be studied in a way that takes the presence of other species and their entire environment into account (Møller 2010). A plant, which is harmless to one type of insect, could be lethal when placed in a different habitat (Zagrobelny, Bak and Møller 2008). To illustrate this, Møller introduces the insect *Zygaena filipendulae* or the six-spotted burnet moth.

The six-spotted burnet is a day-flying moth, which can be found in most of Europe. Due to 430 million years of genetic attunement, it has become a highly specialized insect with some rather impressive survival mechanisms. For example, it boldly feeds on the toxic *Lotus*

Illustration 5.1: (A) *Lotus corniculatus*; (B) mature six-spotted burnet moth; (C) larva of the six spotted burnet moth. *Source*: Birger Lindberg Møller, reproduced with permission.

corniculatus and seems unaffected by the toxic cyanogenic glucosides present in the plant (Zagrobelny, Bak and Møller 2008). In fact, these insects have developed ways to survive in an ecological niche, or a 'cyanide society' as Møller calls it (Interview 2010). Cyanogenic glucosides are a vital part of the functioning of these insects, from lifecycles to mating rituals and defence strategies against predators. This has been made possible through millions of years of genetic adaptation and mutations through which the plant has tried to defend itself from the insect and the insect has adapted to the defence system of the plant. 'Coevolution' is the term Møller uses for this process through which organic life develops in mutual relationships with fine-tuned systems of mutual response to each other's presence. It is not only plants that are proactive organisms; insects have their own way of acting and responding to their environment too.

The mechanism which allows the six-spotted burnet moth to feed on *Lotus corniculatus* without being poisoned is an intelligent form of 'chemical warfare' (Møller 2010). The plant poison is supposed to harm the larvae once they start chewing on the toxic plant but the larvae of the six-spotted burnet moth have found a way to 'circumvent' the defence system of the plant (Møller 2010; Zagrobelny, Bak and Møller 2008). 'Circumvention' here means that the poison in the plant is turned around and made to work to the insect's own advantage. By feeding on the *Lotus corniculatus*, the insect itself becomes poisonous rather than being poisoned. In this way, a deterrent designed to work against the insect is incorporated into the insect's own body and given a new function: the ability to deter predators (ibid.).

Symbionts

When first presented with this plant–insect story, I questioned the complex mutuality proposed by Møller. To me, the relation he described was a rather unidirectional flow from producer to consumer. What we could call 'a parasite logic': the plant produces food; the insect consumes it, end of story. The plant suffers attacks despite its best attempts to defend itself and the clever insect reaps the benefits. In a linear process,[5] one party takes from another without giving and thereby reduces the other to a passive resource for consumption. Møller's research, however, suggests a more subtle dynamic than the unidirectional flow of parasite logic. In fact, he refuses to accept my parasite reading and claims that the plant–insect relation may actually be symbiotic:

> The knowledge we have now allows us to conclude that the larvae and the grown insect take advantage of the plant. But when we start digging deeper, I will be very surprised if we don´t find that the plant in some way also takes advantage of the presence of the insect. For example, the enzymes in the insect's saliva disrupt the plant cell walls in such a way that a signal emerges which introduces a relevant defence mechanism in the plant, for example against fungi, bacteria or virus, which the larvae are carrying. You must mean symbiont rather than parasite
> (email correspondence 2010, author's translation).

The coevolutionary framework demands that Møller studies plant poisons as part of a symbiosis between plant and insect. It is not enough to assume that plant poisons work in the same way across different relationships or ecosystems or that the order of production and consumption follows a linear parasite logic. The presence of cyanogenic glucosides in an ecosystem often has multiple complex effects in relation to other species, effects that cannot be inferred from the plant's biochemical composition alone (Møller 2010). To Møller, there is no telling what a given species may be capable of, as most of its capabilities evolve in complex relationships with other species. This is why Møller's research takes place as experiments with plants and insects in living, complex ecosystems rather than as isolated studies of plant biochemistry.

Starting with plant biology and moving outwards now seems to suggest a methodological route quite different from the study of reified and separable entities placed in a linear flow from consumption to production. Looking at coevolution means engaging in empirical experimentation with mingled bodies and symbiotic relations that pull the rug from under the distinctions by which we would otherwise make sense of the world.

Symbiosis between Science and Its Environment

Can the analytical vocabulary of the coevolution of plants and insects be used to analyse science–industry relations? In the following, I will conduct such an analytical experiment. I will be comparing the ways in which cyanogenic glucosides are incorporated in the body of the six-spotted burnet moth and the moth's enzymes activate the plant's protection against fungi and bacteria to the way Møller, as the manager of Pro-Active Plants, manages the incorporation of biotech industrial components into the practice of plant biology. In this analytical approach, science and industry are analysed in accordance with the mutual working of a symbiont relationship, rather than the unidirectional relationship of production and consumption, which characterized the logic of the parasite. Symbiosis is not about common agendas, convergence and harmonious integration of interests (Stengers 2007; 2010). According to Møller, it is rather a subtle and ongoing 'chemical warfare' where the individual organism's defence or attack against the other paradoxically becomes the very thing that binds two species together in mutual survival (Møller 2010).

Danish research policy and research funding assume science and industry to be placed in a linear and unidirectional flow: science produces knowledge as a resource for value creation, which needs to be tapped and consumed more efficiently by industry. As a consequence, at one stage, there was a requirement that scientific projects had to include an industry partner in order to receive funding. In response to this agenda, Møller and two of his colleagues split off some of the functions of their centre and started up a spin-off company, thus acquiring an industry partner for their research applications. The spin-off was later bought up by a larger international biotech company into which its activities have now been integrated. The start-up company revolved around a technology platform for 'high throughput glycosylation' – isolation of a multitude of enzymes that are able to link sugar residues to a diverse array of chemical compounds to identify possible uses in the medical industry. This could at first glance look like a unidirectional logic of making a passive resource (academic research) available for consumption by industrial interests (the company). However, when talking to Møller about the relationship between the centre and the company it becomes apparent that things are more complex:

> There were a number of reasons to establish the company. We thought it would be able to make a business because these enzymes are able to link sugars on all kinds of drugs and thereby improve the solubility or stability of the drugs or permit the use of a lower dose. So it, at one and the same time, creates a platform that enables business development and one that serves to advance our basic research. We are able to make use of it for ourselves. I mean we have people here that go down there to use the screening platform and often also take advantage of equipment they have money to buy but we can't afford. Conversely, we contribute with our research experiences in other areas that may be relevant to the company and where they lack expertise. So you shouldn't create a company just for the business. It is … it's best if you can combine it in as many ways as possible (interview with Møller 2009, author's translation).

Starting up a spin-off that develops technologies for the medical industry is a way of making academic research available as a resource for value creation. However, listening to the above description, it is clear that the relations and exchanges between Pro-Active Plants and the biotech company do not follow a linear logic. The research centre does not simply produce knowledge as a resource for consumption by the biotech industry. Rather, a different form of exchange is taking place in the mingled body of Pro-Active Plants and the biotech company. The success of Pro-Active Plants in getting technologies up and running depends on engaging the interest of actors in the environment outside the university – in this case an international biotech firm with headquarters in central Europe. In the above description of the relation, it seems the linear flow from science to industry is circumvented to work to the advantage of the scientific laboratory, not just the company. The two directions are not mutually exclusive. To Pro-Active Plants, there are many advantages of having an in-house technology platform managed and maintained by a private company. First, the company makes technologies available that would be extremely expensive for the university to acquire and maintain. Second, that kind of infrastructure would require the recruitment of specialized technical staff, which the biotech company now provides. Circumventing the science–industry food chain means that Møller and his colleagues use the biotech company to their own advantage by delegating routine tasks to professional lab technicians paid by the biotech company. The ground floor biotech company thus seems to constitute a producer as well as a consumer in the food chain of knowledge production. Møller in fact refers to the company as a resource to be utilized rather than a customer to be serviced:

> Yes, tasks which were not suited to be done by us because they are cumbersome and time-consuming repetitive experiments if performed without access to a high throughput technology platform. But a company that has technicians hired to do stuff like that, that's just beautiful. We get access to a toolbox and a platform that we would otherwise not have been able to make on our own. Also, the collaboration with the biotech company has enabled us to obtain funding that we would otherwise not have been qualified to apply for (interview 2009, author's translation).

Consumption seems to be a mutual and symbiotic affair rather than a parasite logic of one party consuming the raw material constituted by another. Pro-Active Plants feeds on the biotech industry just as much as the reverse. Without the in-house company, the trivial or routine tasks necessary to make it in the highly competitive space of plant biology could potentially form a toxic ecology for scientific practice by taking up a lot of the time and meaning routine tasks have to be done by the Ph.D. students working in the centre.

> Yeah, it is important to avoid people spending their time on the wrong things – e.g. to set up screening and platforms that may not end up being of any use for the research. For example, that industry collaboration thing there ... we had an employee who set up a huge technology platform, right? And that took him four years right, before any biological results started coming out – of course! Consequently he is being assessed as being less qualified than his colleagues when he applies for jobs because he doesn't have the biology results, even though he is actually a better researcher ... but then I tell him: 'But really, you have to take a look at the kind of environment you have around you, right? I mean why have you accepted spending so much

time doing this? Why did you and your supervisor not discuss how to set this up right?' (interview with Møller 2009, author's translation).

The fact that routine tasks like setting up a technology platform can do damage to scientific practice does not imply that science is a pure practice which should be kept free of toxic industrial influences. In fact, it means the opposite: there is no plant biology without biotech, there is no science without technology platforms. Pro-Active Plants is like a larva that needs biotech as its 'feeding plant'. Rather than trying to avoid the potentially toxic and distracting interfaces with industry partners and technology development, Møller argues that scientists have to 'take a look at the kind of environment' their practice is embedded in. Setting up a technology platform 'in the right way', as Møller suggests, means getting the biotech industry to work for your own advantage. Scientists should not separate themselves from biotech industry; they should incorporate its tools, technicians and interests into their work and the material infrastructure of the university. By having an in-house biotech company, the academic scientists will not have to go through the laborious (and boring) process of high throughput screening, enzyme production or other routine tasks. These tasks are not external to science; they are as necessary as breathing. At the same time, this incorporation gives Møller and his colleagues a competitive advantage in relation to other scientists: an expensive and smoothly running toolbox. As an extra benefit, they also get access to new types of public funding which require an industry partnership or collaboration. This constitutes a circumvention of the logic of production and consumption so that it now works both ways. The relation is symbiotic, in that this mutual flow of production and consumption takes place without disturbing or homogenizing the divergent goals of either party. Neither the university research project nor the biotech company has abandoned its own interests in favour of the interest of the other. The biotech company does not need to diverge from its goals in order to be a resource for Pro-Active Plants; nor does the collaboration with the larger biotech corporation by way of the in-house company require Møller and his colleagues to fit their research program to the interests of the biotech corporation.

Advantages of the Barons of Science: Symbiotic Relations

The power of a scientific baron like Møller seems to work according to a subtle logic of the symbiont, rather than the crude and easily identifiable game of the parasite. Møller doesn't just reap the benefits of research councils and the biotech industry: he sets up a form of subtle organizational warfare that ends up working for the benefit of both parties but without ever coming to agreement about the goal and output of academic science.

The case presented here suggests that the problem of science/industry mingling is not one of convergence between two institutional spheres. Managing symbiosis seems to be a matter of skilfully managing divergences between symbiont actors. It is worth noting that even though Møller manages to circumvent the logic of production and consumption he is in no way buying into the 'insights to invoice' agenda promoted by Danish research policy. However, Pro-Active Plants still fully manages to stand out as an academic organization in full compliance with Danish research policy. Showing off an in-house biotech company to research councils and policymakers is an efficient survival strategy that gives Pro-Active Plants access to funding that would otherwise not be available and defends it from any accusation of pursuing basic science without being of use to 'society'. Circumvention (the strategy of reversing a logic of production and consumption) is a strategy of the symbiont. It allows scientists to be divergent and pursue their own goals while at the same time being part of a habitat demonstrating the appropriate amount of entrepreneurial spirit, and a willingness to engage in solving societal problems and contribute to societal value-creation through industry collaboration.

When making sense of scientific practice in the knowledge economy, the material presented proposes a different analytical starting point than that of two separate institutional spheres. Using the biological vocabulary as a tool for analysis, Pro-Active Plants is articulated as part of a symbiotic relationship between science and biotech industry. Making symbiosis manageable is achieved by a slow, continuous process, which could be characterized as an organizational equivalent to the 'chemical warfare' taking place between Møller's plants and insects. Møller is carefully circumventing policy and corporate interests that are vital to the goals of plant biology. Without the mutual exchanges between the two, Pro-Active Plants would not be breathing for very long. Managing plant biology does *not* take place as a convergence of science with industry (for better or for worse). The particularity of mingling the divergent activities of academic science and corporate biotech is what makes the difference between toxicity and viability.

Reflecting back on Danish research policy agendas, we may be careful not to simplify the idea of symbiosis to make it sound more harmonious and stable than it is. The fact that science and industry in this case seem to engage in a symbiotic relationship should not lead us to suggest that a symbiont logic equals natural integration, science–industry synergy or adherence to common goals and knowledge-based value creation. When Danish policymakers assume an unproblematic natural process towards more convergence, they may in fact endanger the delicate balance that makes up science/industry symbiosis. Trying to find a common ground between science and industry, or trying to make one comply with the agenda of the other, may not be the most productive route to the kind of 'dynamic relationships' envisioned by policymakers like Hans Müller Petersen. Symbiotic relationships require space for blatant divergence, intelligent warfare and pragmatic demarcations in order to be productive and viable.

Construing knowledge production solely as a resource that should be utilized by 'outside' actors in order to ensure that science creates value, is inherently a 'parasite logic' of unidirectional flows, which goes against the symbiotic nature of the biology/biotech relationship depicted in this particular case. Coevolution is a delicate process and requires skilful and experimental incorporations that do not force diverging practices to assimilate to a common goal. Without this process the mingled body of science and industry becomes a dangerous and toxic habitat rather than a productive symbiosis. The strategy of circumvention is a way of making symbiotic relationships manageable and of ensuring the survival of both parties.

Let me stress that I am not highlighting the particular symbiosis between Pro-Active Plants and the biotech company as a 'best practice'. Neither do I claim that we should use this win-win example of industry collaboration as an argument to support the pressure for more convergence between science and industry. Møller's strategy only works because it manages to retain divergence while engaging in mutual flows of production and consumption. Its vitality rests on the possibility of circumventing the unidirectional logic of the parasite to make space for a productive divergence to breathe and evolve. Industry collaboration is nurturing for plant biology in this particular case and for this particular project baron, but it may be lethal if the relationship were organized slightly differently or if exported to seemingly similar disciplinary habitats without the necessary ecological sensitivity.

Not all mingled bodies form a symbiosis. Some forms of mingling are simply toxic, parasitic and predatory in a research environment like that of Pro-Active Plants. Making symbiosis manageable means that scientists have to specialize in fine-tuned processes of coevolution and symbiotic relationships involving an ongoing and ecological sensitivity to how and when to diverge. If this delicate space for divergence is not nurtured, the productivity of the symbiosis fails and one species takes over the other like a parasite. In the case of Pro-Active Plants, we may suspect that the focus on further integrating and pushing a unidirectional 'insight to invoice' agenda on such delicate processes of attunement could potentially endanger both species.

◆

Birgitte Gorm Hansen is a Postdoctoral Researcher at the University of Copenhagen, Department of Anthropology. Her current research project explores the impacts of anthropology as a practice in the field of leadership and management. Her main teaching areas are qualitative methods and science and technology studies.

Notes

1. This chapter contains some material previously published in Gorm Hansen 2011a and 2011b.
2. This strategy of university commercialization was first launched as a mission statement but was quickly abandoned as unrealistic (Danish Council for Research Policy 2006).
3. Not a lot of attention has been given to research management in the sociology of translation. Early laboratory studies seemed to concentrate mainly on scientific practice. Law (1994) is one exception. However, Law's taxonomy of four modes of ordering in research management does not take on the challenge of the mixture problem in science studies.
4. Feidenhans'l makes no explicit reference to Andersen and Henningsen and tells me he picked up the concept of the project baron from a colleague. Heine Andersen also testifies that the expression 'barons of science' was a term that had been circulating among academics in Danish universities before it was taken up by him and Henningsen in *Universitetsavisen* (Andersen, personal communication).
5. Here I am drawing on Steven D. Brown's work. Brown has written extensively on parasite logic and the philosopher Michel Serres. Serres is generally considered the philosophical ancestor of actor-network theory because of his influence on the authorship of Bruno Latour (See Serres 1982; Brown 2002; 2004; Brown and Stenner 2009).

References

Andersen, H., and I. Henningsen. 2009. 'Videnskabens Baroner og Boldhentere', *Universitetsavisen*, 16 July. Retrieved 6 October 2016 from http://universitet savisen.dk/videnskab/videnskabet-videnskabens-baroner-og-boldhentere.

Brown, S.D. 2002. 'Michel Serres, Science, Translation and the Logic of the Parasite', *Theory, Culture and Society* 19(3): 1–27.
_____. 2004. 'Parasite Logic', *Journal of Organizational Change Management* 17(4): 383–95.
Brown, S.D., and P. Stenner. 2009. *Psychology without Foundations – History, Philosophy and Psychosocial Theory*. London: Sage.
Callon, M. 1980. 'Struggles and Negotiations to Define What Is Problematic and What Is Not – The Socio-logic Transformation', in K.D. Knorr, R. Krohn and R. Whitley (eds), *The Social Process of Scientific Investigation. Sociology of the Sciences, Yearbook* 4. Dordrecht: Springer, pp. 197–219.
_____. 1986a. 'The Sociology of an Actor-Network: The Case of the Electric Vehicle', in M. Callon, J. Law and A. Rip (eds), *Mapping the Dynamics of Science and Technology*. London: Macmillan Press, pp. 19–34.
Callon, M. 1986b. 'Some Elements of a Sociology of Translation: Domestication of the Scallops and the Fishermen at St Brieuc Bay', in J. Law (ed.), *Power, Action and Belief: A New Sociology of Knowledge?* London: Routledge, pp. 196–223.
Croissant, J.L., and S. Restivo. 2001. *Degrees of Compromise: Industrial Interests and Academic Virtue*. Albany: State University of New York Press.
Danish Council for Research Policy. 2006. 'Bedre Kommercialisering af den Offentlige Forskning til Gavn for Samfundet', Copenhagen: Ministry of Science, Technology and Development.
Danish Government. 2003. 'Samspil. Nye veje mellem forskning og erhverv – fra tanke til faktura', background report from the Danish Ministry of Science, Technology and Innovation. Retrieve 10 February 2016 from http://ufm.dk/publikationer/2003/nye-veje-mellem-forskning-og-erhverv.
Gorm Hansen, B. 2011a. 'Adapting in the Knowledge Economy: Lateral Strategies for Scientists and Those Who Study Them', Ph.D. thesis. Copenhagen: Doctoral School of Management and Organization, Copenhagen Business School. Retrieved 10 February 2016 from http://openarchive.cbs.dk/handle/10398/8346.
_____. 2011b. 'Beyond the Boundary, Science, Industry and Managing Symbiosis', *Bulletin of Science, Technology and Society* 31(6): 493.
Kleinman, D.L. 2003. *Impure Cultures*. Madison, WI: University of Wisconsin Press.
Kleinman, D.L., and S.P. Vallas. 2006. 'Contradiction in Convergence: Universities and Industry in the Biotechnology Field', in S. Frickel and K. Moore (eds), *The New Political Sociology of Science – Institutions, Networks and Power*. Madison, WI: University of Wisconsin Press.
Latour, B. 1987. *Science in Action – How to Follow Scientists and Engineers through Society*. Cambridge, MA: Harvard University Press.
_____. 1988. *The Pasteurization of France*, trans. A. Sheridan and J. Law. Cambridge, MA: Harvard University Press.
_____. 1996. 'Om aktør-netværksteori. Nogle få afklaringer og mere end nogle få forviklinger', *Philosophia* 25(3–4): 47–64.
_____. 1999. 'Give Me a Laboratory and I Will Raise the World', in M. Biagoli (ed.), *The Science Studies Reader*. London: Routledge.

_____. 2005. *Reassembling the Social: An Introduction to Actor-Network-Theory*. New York: Oxford University Press.
Lave, R., P. Mirowski and S. Randalls. 2010. 'Introduction: STS and Neoliberal Science', *Social Studies of Science* 40(5): 669–75.
Law, J. 1994. *Organizing Modernity*. Oxford: Blackwell.
Malmberg, A. 2007. 'Årets Modtager af VKR Legatet: ingen forandring uden forankring', *Dansk Kemi* 88(3): 6–8.
Mirowski, P., and E.M. Sent. 2008. 'The Commercialization of Science and the Response of STS', in E.J. Hackett et al. (eds), *The Handbook of Science and Technology Studies*. Cambridge: MIT Press.
Møller, B.L. 2010. 'Functional Diversifications of Cyanogenic Glucosides', *Current Opinion in Plant Biology* 13(3): 337–46.
Resnik, D. 2007. *The Price of Truth – How Money Affects the Norms of Science*. Oxford: Oxford University Press.
Serres, M. 1982. *The Parasite*. Minneapolis: University of Minnesota Press.
Shapin, S. 2008. *The Scientific Life – A Moral History of a Late Modern Vocation*. Chicago: University of Chicago Press.
Sismondo, S. 2011. 'Corporate Disguises in Medical Science: Dodging the Interest Repertoire', *Bulletin of Science, Technology and Society* 31(6): 482–92.
Slaughter, S., and G. Rhodes. 2004. *Academic Capitalism and the New Economy – Markets, State and Higher Education*. London: John Hopkins University Press.
_____. 2005. 'From the Endless Frontier to Basic Science for Use', *Social Studies of Science* 30(4): 536–72.
Stengers, I. 2007. 'Civilizing Modern Practices', Conference of the American Anthropological Associations Conference, 28 November–2 December. Washington, DC: American Anthropological Associations.
_____. 2010. *Cosmopolitics 1. The Science Wars*. Minneapolis: University of Minnesota Press.
Strathern, M. 2005. 'Robust Knowledge and Fragile Futures', in A. Ong and S.J. Collier (eds), *Global Assemblages: Technology, Politics and Ethics as Anthropological Problems*. Oxford: Blackwell.
Washburn, J. 2005. *University Inc. – The Corporate Corruption of Higher Education*. New York: Basic Books.
Zagrobelny, M., S. Bak and B.L. Møller. 2008. 'Cyanogenisis in Plants and Anthrophods', *Phytochemistry* 69(7): 1457–68.

CHAPTER 6
On Delivering the Consumer-Citizen
New Pedagogies and Their Affective Economies

BARBARA M. GRANT

❖❖❖

> [A university] is the place to which a thousand schools make contributions; in which the intellect may safely range and speculate, sure to find its equal in some antagonist activity, and its judge in the tribunal of truth. It is a place where enquiry is pushed forward, and discoveries verified and perfected, and rashness rendered innocuous, and error exposed, by the collision of mind with mind and knowledge with knowledge. It is the place where the professor becomes eloquent, and is a missionary and a preacher, displaying his science in its most complete and most winning form, pouring it forth with the zeal of enthusiasm, and lighting up his own love of it in the breasts of his hearers. … It is a seat of wisdom, a light of the world, a minister of the faith, an Alma Mater of the rising generation. It is this and a great deal more
>
> —J.H. Newman, 'What is a university?'

For John Henry Newman, the modern university offered a rich ferment for human progress. Writing *The Idea of a University* from a mid-nineteenth century vantage point, though, he could not have imagined the future that is now our present. Just over one hundred years later, our public universities straddle a number of fault lines that threaten all aspects of academic work and presage a 'hollowed-out university' (Cribb and Gewirtz 2013). In thinking critically about our teaching mission, in particular, unsettling questions arise: is our ambition to develop intellectual independence? Or to further social equity? Or to produce ready-to-go workers for the globalized 'knowledge economy'? A look at the strategic documents published by universities in Aotearoa New Zealand (NZ) shows their ambition to be all of the above. This faintheartedness about what universities fundamentally stand for, cued by shifty government policy, leads to fractured institutional cultures that make incoherent claims on their subjects: too many demands on teaching staff and often not enough – or at least, not of the right kind – on students. In this essay, I explore the notion that changes in our teaching and learning practices are producing new kinds of collisions between teacher, students and knowledge qua curriculum. These collisions yield likely 'affects' (or emotions),[1] which – following Sara Ahmed (2004) – I understand as constitutive of both identities and social relations. The concern that prompts my path of thought is that actively cultivating the likelihood of certain student affects (which I will describe below) is in (almost) nobody's interests[2] – certainly not the student's, but also not the teacher's, the university's, nor those of a democratic society. Rather, those affects most clearly serve the affective economy of consumerism.

This chapter has the following shape. To begin, I explain my understandings of university pedagogy/pedagogies, affect and affective economies. Then I draw on experience of my own university (knowing this experience is by no means unique) to describe new pedagogies that have emerged in university education in the past three decades or so and their rationales. On the basis of nearly three decades of working as an adviser with university students and academics, I propose the affects these 'innovations' make likely for students and examine what such affects might mean for pedagogical relations and the kinds of students those relations are inviting. In closing, I argue that, in making the kinds of pedagogical changes characteristic of the recent past, our universities and the academics within them are too easily colluding with wider forces of marketization to deliver up students to the project of consumer-citizen formation. Students are turned more and more towards a preoccupation with the precarious prospects of highly paid, albeit overworked, employment than with the dream of creating an equitable society where a sense of personal entitlement is counterbalanced by a commitment to the communal good.

Pedagogy as Political and Productive

David Lusted's 1986 essay on pedagogy describes a cycle of production and exchange as well as a field of power relations between three agents: teacher, student and curriculum. In this sense, pedagogy:

> denies notions of the teacher as functionary (neutral transmitter of knowledge as well as 'state functionary'), the learner as 'empty vessel' or passive respondent, knowledge as immutable material to impart. Instead, it foregrounds exchange between and over the categories, it

recognises the productivity of the relations, and it renders the parties within them as active, changing and changeable agencies (Lusted 1986: 3).

Lusted's theorization of pedagogy proposes a productive exchange relationship (an economy) between teacher, student and curriculum: the three 'agencies' interact to produce transformations in both the student's and teacher's consciousness and knowledge. Pedagogies[3] not only teach the student knowledge and skills but also how to be someone new – a university-educated person, a person with stronger or new capacities of particular kinds, perhaps even an academic. Understood in this way, curriculum – knowledge 'chosen' by the teacher (Hagström and Lindberg 2013: 121) – is not a passive thing to be conveyed through pedagogy but a dynamic presence that, transformatively, works back over not only student and teacher but also itself.

Understanding pedagogy as Lusted does foregrounds two matters: first, it reminds us that pedagogical transformations are always political, effected through a field of power relations, which is 'a total structure of actions brought to bear upon possible actions: it incites, it induces, it seduces … [it is] a way of acting upon an acting subject or acting subjects' (Foucault 1986: 427). Second, this understanding of pedagogy foregrounds the radical openness of pedagogy's outcomes. This understanding of pedagogy sits in counterpoint to popular theorizations of university teaching, such as 'constructive alignment' or 'deep and surface learning' (Kandlbinder and Peseta 2009). The appeal of those positivist-leaning approaches lies partly in the suggestion that teachers can get pedagogy right, that they can arrange its components so that students will learn just what and how they want them to. Theorizing pedagogy as a field of power relations underscores the dynamism of pedagogy as a space of action: the power and authority of the teacher – the scope of her/his possible actions – are seen to be enmeshed with the power of the student and the curriculum, not to mention the things and spaces of pedagogy. It is a political way of thinking about pedagogy that eschews separating the possibilities of pedagogy from the cultural and institutional contexts in which it is situated and formed.

The signature pedagogies of the university have proved enduring. The core mode was – and still is – the mass lecture performed in the 'theatre'. There, students sit in serried ranks facing their lecturer who teaches from an apron of clear space at the front of the hall. The lecturer's job is primarily to convey a body of knowledge gathered from wide reading of often-disputatious sources in such a way as to assist the students to come to grips with some small fragment of a systematic study of the world. Another defining mode is the laboratory demonstration, where students are arranged singly or in small groups at the locus of a practical task: the lecturer/demonstrator shows correct practice on a raised bench at the front and then moves among the groups to observe and set right what the students do. Then there is the seminar (or tutorial), in which smaller groups of students are gathered around tables with a lecturer/tutor for discussion of what was taught in the lecture or some related activity (or, in the Oxbridge model, to read their latest essay aloud for feedback).

These distinctive pedagogies – conspicuously confined in place and time – were set up on the basis of a stretched and attenuated relationship between academic and student, alongside the expectation of an intimate, but importantly independent, relation between student and curriculum. Some have argued that the culture of the traditional academy was characterized by an 'apparent indifference' (Reimer 1998: 13) towards the students, the purpose of which was to produce a rational, autonomous individual, capable of putting affect aside and withstanding prejudice through the exercise of reasoned argument.

Affects as Constitutive Capacities

And yet affect cannot be put aside. As human capacities, affects are 'integral elements in relations of power and government' (Burkitt 2005: 679) that work, constitutively, on the actions of human subjects. Through limiting the field of possible actions, the relations of power and government characteristic of the university bring the institution's subjects to conduct themselves in particular ways for the good of the institution. In newer university pedagogies – such as 'problem-based learning', 'student-centred classrooms', 'blended learning', 'team-based projects' or 'flipped classrooms' – this coordination is increasingly engineered to achieve particular effects in the students (often framed as 'learning outcomes'), which in turn make certain affects more likely. Universities also explicitly desire to shape their students' affective capacities, as we see in the now-ubiquitous graduate profile. My university's document[4] not only describes knowledge-commanding attributes and various 'general intellectual skills and capacities' but also 'personal qualities', which include several affects. Graduates are expected to possess a *'love and enjoyment* of ideas, discovery and learning', an *'appreciation* of current issues and debates', a *'respect* for truth and for the ethics of research and scholarly activity', a *'respect* for the values of other individuals and groups, and an *appreciation* of human and cultural diversity' and an 'intellectual ... *curiosity*'. And then there is '*mastery* of a body of knowledge': mastery may not be an affect per se but it has the layered meanings of comprehensive knowledge and expertise and control and superiority over someone or something.[5] We might pause to consider the affects mobilized by fantasies of mastery (and shudder?).

Students are not the only target of power and governmentality in universities. Academic staff are targets too. At my own university, for example, academics are subject to a detailed set of behavioural specifications for leadership at every level of an academic career that count towards career progression. Internationally, there is evidence of increasing academic workload (Barcan 2013) as a result of central government and institutional leadership decisions: of particular concern to my argument here is evidence of how new '"blended", "hybrid" or "flexible"' pedagogic relationships are '24/7' (Tynan et al. 2012: 4–5). This shift reshapes academics: where before they may have sought to convey the discipline primarily through a bodily demonstration, bounded in time and space, within the materiality of the lecture theatre or the laboratory, now they are increasingly required to act like anytime-anyplace dispensers of info-bites to clamorous students.

As one example of governable human capacities, affects have been much ignored in university life – other than implicitly promoting the appropriate kinds listed above. Western science normalizes an enduring split between reason and affect, with the latter seen as a distraction from considered thought, a human frailty that reason seeks to override. Indeed, the core purpose of a university education has been to expand the powers of reason such that, as Newman argued, 'rashness [unthinking, emotive action] is rendered innocuous' (1909–1914[2001]). Yet education's productive exchange relationship between teacher, student and curriculum has always aimed to combine affects such as excitement and curiosity – in measured proportion – with reason.

Affective Economies: Contact and Circulation

Following Sara Ahmed's work (2004), I understand affects to be produced through the subject's contact with objects and others. Ahmed uses the term 'affective economies' to describe the sociality and movement of affects: 'feelings do not reside in subjects or objects, but are produced as effects of circulation' (2004: 8). For example, she says, 'hate does not *reside* in a given subject or object. Hate is economic; it circulates between signifiers in relationships of difference and displacement' (44, her italics). Affects circulate within the social, the material and the psychic in relations of exchange and, over time, the affective value of objects and others accumulates.

The contact that produces and shapes affects is not just the 'collision of mind with mind and knowledge with knowledge' that Newman describes: it is the embodied contact of subjects with objects, real (such as coursework for students) and imagined (future consequences of grades), concrete (classrooms) and abstract (new ideas), as well as with others. Some of the objects or others we collide with become 'sticky, or saturated with affect, as sites of personal and social tension' (ibid.: 11): the grade is one such object, with affective value that has accumulated over the course of a student's educational life. Since the late 1970s, university students have been graded continuously through coursework, which has increased in frequency since the modularization of courses. (And latterly, often unhappily, New Zealand academics have once again become subject to personal grades through the machinations of the national research audit.)

Ahmed's theory directs attention to how affects fashion 'the very surfaces of bodies, which take shape through the repetition of actions over time, as well as through orientations towards and away from others' (2004: 4) and thus the ways in which we make sense of ourselves and our social worlds. The 'I' and the 'we' of university pedagogies are profoundly shaped by affect, as are the social spaces – the relationships – between academic and student, between student and student. Some affects – delight or humour, for instance – may well turn us towards others. Different affects – such as anger or shame – will likely turn us away from each other, indeed perhaps even from ourselves.

Because pedagogies always put affects into circulation, and these affects reshape the selves and social spaces of higher education, academics have significant ethical responsibilities as teachers. They must think critically not only about the decisions their universities are making for teaching and learning but also carefully consider their own responses and initiatives in terms of the affective economies they may create. Faced with the requirement for pedagogical change, they might fruitfully ask questions about the kind of affective economies likely to be mobilized:

- In making this change, am I seeking to defend students from – or licensing them to feel – certain affects?
- What changes might be wrought in student-collides-with-another-student affects?

- What are the probable implications of provoking those affects for the broader pedagogical project that I am committed to? (Do I even have one?)
- What are the probable implications for the formation of graduates capable not only of thriving beyond the university in a super complex (Barnett 2004) and radically unequal world, but also of transforming that world?
- And what about my own affects as an academic who is not only a teacher but also a researcher and citizen of the university? How might these new pedagogies put undue pressure on, distort even, relations between me and my students, me and the curriculum of my course, my other work obligations and relations with my colleagues?

In considering answers to these questions, we need to remember that universities are no longer as isolated as they once were from the compulsory education sector. Quite radical changes in that sector (particularly to assessment practices) have had consequences for higher education because they have already installed a certain affective economy that structures what incoming students feel they can tolerate. For example, as a consequence of the use of standards-based assessment in the last three years of high school, many first-year university students are frightened of coursework tasks that do not have clearly specified assessment criteria. This change has already had significant effects on what is now described as the first-year experience, a new 'at-risk' category of student life that folds in a range of new interventions – new modes of governmentality – on the subjectivity of the student.

New Pedagogies in the University

In the past few decades, as a function of the shifting fault lines described above, a new set of pressures has arisen in relation to university pedagogies. The lecture in particular has come under sustained criticism in terms of whether it is fit for purpose. I have written a defence of the pedagogy of the lecture elsewhere (Grant 1999). Suffice to say here that the leading accusation, that lectures produce passivity in students, is not only overwrought but misleading, based on a simplistic cause–effect connection between observable bodily activity and learning. Gritt Nielsen's (2011) research in university science programmes provides a vivid example of this logic, where a head of department describes reforming courses to be taught in shorter blocks because 'students are forced to be active all the time' (2011: 177).

More generally, the pressures to reform our pedagogies have many different origins, including government, professions, employers and equity groups.[6] Immediate pressures also come from institutional expectations. At my university, for example, academic staff are expected to show innovation in their teaching when applying for promotion in teaching-intensive appointments, or when applying for teaching excellence awards. For promotion at any level they are also expected to show 'leadership in independent development of courses, course materials and curriculum' (University of Auckland 2014: 14); 'leadership' is repeated in that document ten times in total. Other pressures come from academic colleagues in the form of hyped-up accounts of what e-learning/new media can deliver, or the assertion that our students are now 'digital natives' with expectations/capacities that we ignore at our peril, or the shaming accusation that those who do not teach this way are 'dinosaurs'. In my experience, fear of students is prevalent among academics, and not only among those who are in their early career: how will students react if my teaching or assessment is out of line with that of my colleagues, or if I ask students to work 'too independently' or 'too much'? What student reactions will find their way into those mandatory evaluations of my teaching? And what consequences will follow in my bid for continuation or promotion? Yet further pressures come from non-academic players like the library, through the mandatory insertion of information on literacy learning outcomes or modules into course outlines or programmes, for example, or the building of new kinds of pedagogical spaces.

Finally, the most intimate pressure of all is the way in which our personal interests and desires get entangled with, or constituted by, all this. Academics today work in an atmosphere in which it is easy to feel as if our teaching is never good enough; and, in an important way, teaching never is. As a practical art, it 'can always be done differently or better' (Barcan 2013: 92). We are pressured to invest time and effort into unceasing pedagogical evaluations, improvements or innovations, in a context of increasingly unbearable academic workloads.

In engineering new pedagogies, we devise novel collisions between teacher, student and curriculum, usually in the hope of producing better student learning. Sometimes we may even deliberately target particular student affects, such as curiosity, enjoyment, or determination. Assessment is well known to be a 'sticky' object (Ahmed 2004: 11) that accumulates affects: it focuses and shapes students' responses to teachers, each other and the curriculum. I turn now to explore some of the new pedagogies that have surfaced in the past two decades or so, mostly at the insistence of institutional 'centres', and examine the collisions they engineer between teacher, student/s and curriculum and their likely affects. While I draw on what has happened in my own university, the developments are by no means unique – one of the hallmarks of the contemporary university is the transportability of 'its protocols, processes and practices' (Sturm and Turner 2011: 25): policy documents, pedagogical practices and new conditions of work flow between institutions via mechanisms like academic conferences, manager networks, national vice chancellors' committees, international university networks and so on.

Semesterized and Modularized Courses

Semesterization has accelerated pedagogical cycles such that we now have three (sometimes four) instead of one per academic year. Modularization (along with looser prerequisites) has fragmented our disciplines and fields, creating standalone courses that lack progression, meaning that students taking the same course have even more diverse knowledge backgrounds, making it difficult to build the curriculum of one course upon another. These changes have no pedagogical basis: cued by political pressure for more student enrolments, they were seen by institutions as a way to attract more students, by offering more courses and offering some (especially gateway courses) more than once in the academic year. Short summer and/or winter semesters also created the possibility of speeding up degree completion. The changes were accompanied by arguments for using institutional resources (teaching spaces, teaching bodies) more fully. In terms of affects, curriculum choice and flexibility were (and are) seen as goods for students to enjoy. Yet, if anything goes wrong for the student (health or family issues, for example), the speed of the semester significantly increases the stress they feel (Nielsen 2011: 178) – and the demands on teachers. Semesterization and modularization also communicate another message from the university itself: that you can study for a degree (especially a general degree) without making a significant time commitment.[7]

Semesterization and modularization re-engineer the collisions between teacher, student/s and curriculum to reduce the time spent in '*effective* teaching': as Ruth Barcan notes (2013: 111, her italics), relatively more time is spent getting into and out of courses. They also reduce the contact between teachers and students within courses and over the time of a degree, as students – unconstrained by prerequisites – shop around for convenient rather than personally interesting courses, blocked together to free up time for paid work or to reduce travel expenses. There are fewer collisions between student and knowledge/curriculum because of the necessary reduction in the amount of reading and writing due to the condensed length of the course. And there are shorter and fewer breaks in which students can catch up. The student–curriculum collisions that do occur are more hasty and fraught because there is less time for rereading difficult texts or for gradually building writing – or other knowledge-making – skills in a discipline or field.

In my experience, semesterization and modularization promote the dubious pleasures of curriculum choice and freedom from prerequisites and the excitement of a university degree as something students can get speedily, with as little work as possible, before their real life starts. These pedagogical changes deform the collisions between teacher, student and curriculum into a series of fast encounters, where everyone is under pressure and no one can afford to get behind.

The Emergence of Blended Courses

Blending online pedagogies into on-campus courses is now widely advocated on the grounds of efficiency and better student learning. The institution expects the routine upload of course materials – and, preferably, lecture podcasts as well – onto a learning management system (LMS). (Rarely discussed is how it moves course material printing costs over to the students – at least those who are still 'old-fashioned' enough to want to read and annotate hard-copy texts.) Lecturers are actively 'encouraged' (through, for example, funding for teaching development) to understand 'teaching innovation' as the use of electronic media to provide students with additional and/or novel learning experiences.[8] A particular attraction of this mode is that it gives students 24/7 access to a course – yet again, increasing the flexibility of the education provided to them, so that they can study anytime, anyplace. Some of the justification for this pressure is pedagogical: online environments allow learning activities difficult to support otherwise, especially in large classes. These might include practice on multiple-choice tests, review of peers' work, collective writing and so on. Moreover, despite the evidence (which is as ambiguous as any other evidence with respect to particular pedagogies), there is also a belief that students will learn better through online activities. Then there is the 'digital native' argument – usually advanced by techno-enthusiast colleagues – that says we must work with the information-technology capacities (and concentration spans) that students already possess: the first part of this argument (that students are digital natives) has been roundly challenged (see, for example, Jones et al. 2010). Further, the idea that a university education mainly, or only, works with students' extant capacities contradicts the very idea of a graduate profile as showing the 'added value' of a contemporary university education (let alone older ideas of the purpose of a university education). Lastly, there is little recognition of the additional academic labour – and specialist knowledge – required to design, implement and maintain these new pedagogies (Tynan et al. 2012) – not to mention the financial cost of maintaining state-of-the-art hardware.

Blended courses, along with online resources and lectures, offer a huge range of possibilities for re-engineering the collisions between teacher, student/s and curriculum. The affective economy they put in play is one of learning on demand, with the associated affects of impatience and frustration when those demands are not responded to quickly. The primary relation between teacher and student is now mediated by the insertion of other, more necessary, relations: between student and hardware (and help desk), and student and LMS (and help desk again). Yet watching a lecture on screen is not the same as being there: the feeling of forming a relationship with a lecturer and experiencing what excites the lecturer about the curriculum/knowledge is interrupted; the incidental student-to-student collisions that can create the feeling of being in something together are less likely. There is also a high likelihood of students multitasking while watching podcasts, which will dampen – or even remove – their collision with the curriculum. The idea that the event of a lecture itself has any pedagogical merit – that turning up can make a qualitative difference to a student's engagement with the course – is undermined.

Blended courses suggest that three-way contact between teacher, students and curriculum (in the sense of 'running the course' together) does not matter: the teacher is replaced by online materials and instructions for solo student or student–student learning activities (see Westberry and Franken 2015, for discussion of the effects of the teacher's absence), the curriculum becomes a series of pre-packaged learning activities, and the student could be a dog (as in the famous Peter Steiner cartoon in which a dog sits in front of a computer screen and says to another dog, 'on the Internet, nobody knows you're a dog').

Where, for better or worse, the shared experience of the lecture stood for the heart of a course, there is now an empty space.

Mandatory Student Evaluations of Teaching

In the late 1970s, student evaluations of teaching began to be used quite widely at my university. This growth was an outcome of the appointment of a higher education research officer (HERO) in November 1974, a position that included development activities in relation to university teaching. In an interview with the appointee, he described how the evaluations were used formatively by academic staff who were keen to improve their teaching. Although there was a standard form that could be used, it could also be modified on request to meet an individual academic's needs, and both the numerical information (Likert-scale items) and the open-ended comments were summarized in the report that went back to the academic. Sometimes, as a result, there would be a conversation between the academic and the HERO over how to make improvements to teaching. The practice wasn't widespread. As a student in the 1970s and 1980s, I don't remember ever being asked to complete an evaluation form. Because of its anonymity, the process has always been vulnerable to abuse: working next to the evaluations processing office, I was sometimes shown forms including derogatory comments about the clothing or bodies of young female lecturers, or forms that appeared to have been filled in to make a pattern on the Likert scales. As the process became more established in the 1980s, students began to complain about the fact that they filled forms in year after year and nothing ever changed.

Since the advent of the national audit system for New Zealand universities, in 1993, this practice has become mandatory and overbearingly summative. In my university, the anonymous forms have been subjected to psychometric design and become rigidly standardized. While a policy regulates the frequency of collecting student evaluations by setting a minimum, the maximum is the anxious norm. Thousands of forms are processed every year; the reports look more sophisticated and 'truth telling' than before; the open-ended comments are no longer transcribed, probably because of expense, but this also suggests they are less important. The reports are now sent to the teacher's line manager as well as to the individual academic her/himself. If overall student satisfaction with the quality of the course or teaching is less than 70 percent, the course is red-flagged, and a process of correction is put into action. Early-career staff, especially those in the continuation period, often express considerable anxiety about the outcomes of the student evaluations and are reluctant to experiment with teaching that goes against their department's norms.

What kind of affective economy do mandatory student evaluations of teaching put in play? In research I did in the 1990s, before student evaluations of teaching became mandatory, a first-year arts student described how the chance to evaluate his lecturer's teaching turned the tables, albeit briefly and in the last class: he felt schadenfreude towards the lecturer's discomfort. Nowadays, I think this routinized process contributes to evacuating the possibility of student-as-critical-citizen, for there is something deeply pointless about filling out the identical form over and over again and sending it into a void from which nothing ever returns: students' affective reactions are more likely to be boredom. Academics' fears of low results corrode the possibility that good teaching at university level might be disturbing; that learning at this high level might be uncomfortable, even frightening, or produce the affects that arise when what we know is shaken around and challenged (see Edmundson 1997 for an extended discussion of this point). Whoever that kind of imagined student might have been, s/he has been displaced by the student-as-customer who has the right, above all else, to be satisfied. This is not to argue that students will simply take up this subjectivity: they are not dupes and, moreover, affects are slippery targets for governmentality (Grant and Elizabeth 2015). Rather I seek to explore how the pedagogy of teaching evaluations entices them to do so.

But Wait, There's More

There are other new modes of teacher–student–curriculum relation that could be analysed: the mandatory use of learning outcomes or the intensified surveillance of student work via more carefully specified coursework, teamwork and learning analytics. And then there are the new 'built pedagogies' (Sturm and Turner 2011), architectonic compositions, such as massive underground lecture theatres, casual but stylish student information commons, 'interactive large class teaching' spaces (Locke 2015: 597), spaces capable of being tele-linked to other sites for synchronous, multilocation teaching. Some of these new spaces have been foisted on academic staff via 'consultation', others have just appeared and some have been produced for one academic environment and then transported into quite another, regardless of differences in pedagogical intent. Many such innovations would come under the rubric of 'templated education' (Sturm and Turner 2011: 31); many contribute, accidentally perhaps but nevertheless positively, towards the progressive commodification of knowledge and the delivering up of the student as a consumer-citizen.

In reviewing this small sample of pedagogies, and the daily collisions 'engineered' between teacher, student/s and curriculum, it seems that the gravity of their consequences lies mainly in the piling up of new practices. The affective economy they produce appears to be one in which the following responses are becoming normalized for students:

- pleasures of choice are foregrounded;
- a heightened need for instant gratification (questions answered quickly and so on);
- an unwillingness to feel uncertainty, fear or risk and a concomitant reduced capacity for wonder/curiosity;
- an impatience with, even fury towards, that which is not useful/specified;
- anger at failures of the consumer contract (fees for a degree);
- boredom with repetitive, meaningless processes of 'consumer-citizenship' (such as filling out teaching surveys) – political disaffection, annoyed subversion;
- frustration with the short time of study;
- pleasure in glamorous, cosmopolitan ('five-star') buildings as a sign of their personal value/worth, of being at the right kind of university.

Many of these student affects produce painful corollaries in teachers – irritation, impatience, frustration, fear and so on – as they find their time for other obligations (research, writing, reading, thinking) fragmented and eroded. Crucially, and problematically for the teacher–student relation, these affects are likely to be experienced as arising from their collisions with students rather than from the structures that incite such practices in the first place.

The Necessity to Think Critically about Our Pedagogies

> We must never lose sight of the classroom as a space of possibility. … For the classroom is at the heart of what most academics do and its capacity to generate dilemmas is not a sign of some contemporary decline, but a perennial feature of teaching. It is, moreover, a space where we can still unequivocally try to be a force for good (Barcan 2013: 218, 141).

Those who enter public universities may look around and see beautiful buildings and landscaped outside spaces. Yet there are not enough members of staff to allow for manageable work lives. The fault lines that those universities straddle work deeply into academic pedagogies to reform and potentially deform the relations between teacher, student/s and curriculum. One seismic shift is the normative (moralizing) refashioning of lecturers into teachers, students into learners, the carefully accumulated wisdom of our disciplines and fields into interchangeable modules of information for credit, and our disciplinary habits of mind and body into generic or transferable skills for paid employment.

Instead of working counterculturally to deliver public citizens who have concerns for the wider social good (which universities never did perfectly but at least had clearer aspirations for), academics may be too easily delivering up students to the self of consumer-citizen. By contributing to an affective economy shaped by the right to the pleasures of choice, by an intolerance of constraint or ambiguity, or of the time it takes to understand new and/or difficult things, new pedagogies risk endorsing an investment approach to higher education. Students are more and more encouraged to focus on the material rewards promised as their post-education dues in return for high debt.

That there is and should be something difficult, even painful, at the core of higher education – in the collisions between teacher, student/s and curriculum – has become almost unspeakable. Yet, in the peculiar spaces of the university, there is inevitably loneliness and uncertainty in the act of thinking towards what is not already known: this is the burdensome condition of learning and it deserves a response. At best the shock of learning may arouse wonder and inquisitiveness (as compared to acquisitiveness) but it also requires courage, resilience, humility and a determination to endure. A respectful and compassionate response on the part of teachers to students is warranted – 'I hear you and I salute you for your courage and resilience' – rather than an ameliorating, placating one. The students' painful condition is better met with the comfort of heartening presence than with the mediated absence of the virtual teacher. Moreover, students can be drawn to consider how valuable these kinds of affective capacities may be for thriving in a deeply uncertain world.

Crucially, the 'deliver' of my chapter title means not only 'give birth to' or 'hand over' but also 'save from'. In an ongoing effort to undermine the complicity of public universities in moulding their students into consumer-citizens, academics need to question their own teaching. Barcan reminds us that classrooms are always spaces of dilemmas and possibility: rather than simply appeasing managerial pressures or perceived student demands/needs, or enacting an unreflective desire to 'look after' their students, academics can act as critic and conscience of their own pedagogies. Sometimes this may mean actively resisting what seems to be required; at other times a subversive path may be the only possible one. Resistance and subversion: without doubt, we are responsible for, and capable of, both.

◆

Barbara M. Grant (Ph.D. in higher education, Auckland) is Associate Professor in the School of Critical Studies in Education at the University of Auckland. Her teaching and research interests include social theories and education (especially higher education), the politics and pedagogies of academic work, postgraduate supervision and academic development. Currently, she is working on a three-year ethnography of doctoral supervision as a form of academic work with a group of ten key informants from several universities in New Zealand. Her latest publications include 'Changing mechanisms of governmentality? Academic development in New Zealand and student evaluations of teaching' (with Mark Barrow), published in *Higher Education* (DOI: 10.1007/s10734-015-9965-8), and 'Unpredictable feelings: Academic women under research audit' (with Vivienne Elizabeth), published in *British Educational Research Journal* (DOI: 10.1002/berj.3145).

Notes

1. In this chapter, I have chosen 'affect' over 'emotion' as my primary term, even though both are interchangeable for me (as they are for Ahmed 2004).
2. Some pedagogical changes – especially those involving expensive hard- and software – are, in fact, in the interests of the industries that stand to profit from their continuous redesign.
3. My understanding of pedagogies is inclusive of any configurations of teacher–student–curriculum – for example, I think of library and academic office spaces as pedagogical.
4. 'The University of Auckland's Graduate Profile' (March 2003), available at https://www.auckland.ac.nz/en/about/learning-and-teaching/strategies-goals-and-plans/graduate-profiles.html. This document bears an uncanny resemblance to that of other universities.
5. *Collins English Dictionary: Desktop edition*, 2005, p. 995.
6. For example, New Zealand's national *Tertiary Education Strategy 2014-2019* cites the importance of 'improving culturally responsive teaching practices' (13).
7. See Barcan (2013: 110–12) for an extended discussion of the destructive effects of semesterization and modularization. Nielsen (2010) also offers a critical perspective based on empirical research with university students and staff.

8. Such funding at my university has been increasingly captured by e-learning innovations to pedagogy.

References

Ahmed, S. 2004. *The Cultural Politics of Emotion*. Edinburgh: Edinburgh University Press.
Barcan, R. 2013. *Academic Life and Labour in the New University: Hope and Other Choices*. Farnham, Surrey: Ashgate Publishing.
Barnett, R. 2004. 'Learning for an Unknown Future', *Higher Education Research & Development* 23(3): 247–60.
Burkitt, I. 2005. 'Powerful Emotions: Power, Government, and Opposition in the "War on Terror"', *Sociology* 39(4): 679–95.
Cribb, A., and S. Gewirtz. 2013. 'The hollowed-out university? A critical analysis of changing institutional and academic norms in UK higher education', *Discourse: Studies in the Cultural Politics of Education* 34(3): 338–50.
Edmundson, M. 1997. 'On the Uses of a Liberal Education', *Harper's Magazine* 295: 39–49.
Foucault, M. 1986. 'The Subject and Power', in Wallis, B. (ed.), *Art After Modernism: Rethinking Representation*. New York: New Museum of Contemporary Art, pp. 417–32.
Grant, B.M., and V. Elizabeth. 2015. 'Unpredictable feelings: academic women under research audit', *British Educational Research Journal* 41(2): 287–302.
Grant, B.M. 1999. 'Talking Back About Lectures', *Research and Development in Higher Education* 21: 145–57.
Hagström, E., and O. Lindberg. 2013. 'Three Theses on Teaching and Learning in Higher Education', *Teaching in Higher Education* 18(2): 119–28.
Jones, C., et al. 2010. 'Net generation or Digital Natives: Is there a distinct new generation entering university?', *Computers & Education* 54(3): 722–32.
Kandlbinder, P., and T. Peseta. 2009. 'Key Concepts in Postgraduate Certificates in Higher Education Teaching and Learning in Australasia and the United Kingdom', *International Journal for Academic Development* 14(1): 19–31.
Locke, K. 2015. 'Activating Built Pedagogy: A Genealogical Exploration of Educational Space at the University of Auckland Epsom Campus and Business School', *Educational Philosophy and Theory: Incorporating ACCESS* 47(6): 596–607.
Lusted, D. 1986. 'Why pedagogy?', *Screen* 27(5): 2–14.
Newman, J.H. 1909–1914[2001]. 'What is a university?' (Essay from *The idea of a university*)', in C.W. Eliot (ed.), *Essays: English and American*, vol. 28. New York: P.F. Collier & Son/Bartleby.com. Retrieved 17 July 2015 from www.bartleby.com/28/.
Nielsen, G.B. 2011. 'Timing Students' Freedom: On Paradoxes of Efficiency and Accountability', in J.E. Kristensen, M. Raffnsøe-Møller and H. Nørreklit (eds), *University Performance Management: The Silent Managerial Revolution in Danish Universities*. Copenhagen: DJØF-Forlag, pp. 175–92.

Reimer, A. 1998. *Sandstone Gothic: Confessions of an Accidental Academic*. Sydney: Allen & Unwin.

Sturm, S., and S. Turner. 2011. '"Built Pedagogy": The University of Auckland Business School as Crystal Palace', *Interstices* 12: 23–34.

Tynan, B., et al. 2012. 'Out of Hours: Final Report of the project "e-Teaching leadership: planning and implementing a benefits-oriented costs model for technology enhanced learning"', Strawberry Hills, NSW: Australian Learning & Teaching Council.

University of Auckland. 2014. 'HR policy: Academic Standards for Research Fellows, Senior Research Fellows, Lecturers, Senior Lecturers, Associate Professors and Professors'. Auckland.

Westberry, N., and M. Franken. 2015. 'Pedagogical distance: explaining misalignment in student-driven online learning activities using Activity Theory', *Teaching in Higher Education* 20(3): 300–12.

CHAPTER 7
Tuning Up and Tuning In
How the European Bologna Process Is Influencing Students' Time of Study

GRITT B. NIELSEN AND LAURA LOUISE SARAUW

Introduction

Policies that aim to speed up students' pace of studies and make them employable in a future labour market play an increasingly important role in the planning of European higher education. In this article we show how some of the main features introduced with the European Bologna process, namely the European Credit Transfer System (ECTS), modularization and a shift towards a competence-based curriculum, are far from being the neutral means to enhance student mobility across countries and study programmes that they were originally presented to be. Drawing on recent Danish university legislation, we show how these features are assembled in ways that fundamentally reframe the time in which students' education takes place. Students are increasingly incentivized to adopt a certain kind of anticipatory behaviour, redirecting their attention from the learning activities 'here and now' towards processes of piecing together and forecasting a particular future in the labour market. In order to contextualize our argument, we begin with a short account drawn from our interviews with students in Denmark:

> I want to graduate while I'm still young, so I think I will just dig in. After all, a semester isn't that long. And those ECTS, I really have to have them. You have to, you know. We have no other time to obtain them, really. Soon we have to choose our minors, and I am more and more concerned about the future, and about whether I am doing the right thing. Things would be different if you were like sixty years old when you entered university, because by then you pretty much know who you are and what you want. (Female, first-year student at the University of Copenhagen. Interview by Sarauw 2014 – our translation)

This student is only in her second semester at a Danish university. Nevertheless, she speaks with great familiarity about the necessity of accumulating enough ECTS credits within the allotted time-span and she worries about her future and about choosing the 'right courses' (for example, the minors she talks about). She thinks that young people like herself are uncertain about 'who you are and what you want'. She feels a pressure to complete her studies at a fast pace while simultaneously focusing on long-term planning and her future. The student's experiences and attitude towards her studies should be read in the light of recent political reforms related to the Bologna Process, the introduction of the European Credit Transfer System (ECTS) and of a competence-based curriculum. Bologna communiqués insist that higher education plays a pivotal role in reducing youth unemployment and getting Europe back on track after the 2008 financial crisis (EHEA 2012). At the same time, many national reform initiatives to secure students' employability go hand in hand with reforms that encourage students to complete their studies at a faster pace (Boden and Nedeva 2010; Nielsen and Sarauw 2014). Indeed, reforms in Denmark have combined a stronger standardization of students' study progression and completion time with a pressure to acquire skills that make them more employable.

In this article we explore how two central features of the European Bologna Process – the introduction of the European Credit Transfer System (ECTS) and intensified modularization combined with a competence-based curriculum – are increasingly used as technologies for hastening student completion and ensuring that they acquire certain skills and competences perceived to be central for the future labour market. Based on qualitative research into the Danish university reforms since 2003 (Nielsen 2010; 2015; Sarauw 2011),[1] we show how students in Denmark are incentivized to 'tune up' the speed of their studies and 'tune in' to align with politically defined job prospects. These initiatives seem to make certain temporalities or rhythms dominant in students' study lives. Inspired by the French philosopher and sociologist Henri Lefebvre (2004), we understand a person's life and activities as always related to, balancing and performing actions within different temporalities or rhythms. The body, in this sense, is composed of and intersected by several rhythms. Sometimes these rhythms can coexist without causing any conflict or distress for the individual. At other times, however, a dissonance between the rhythms emerges, creating what Lefebvre calls 'arrhythmia'. For the individual, such situations are often characterized by feelings of stress and inadequacy.

We show how, in the wake of a series of university reforms, many students experience a sort of arrhythmia between what we call subject-oriented time (where the student, as an acting subject, feels s/he has time to independently explore a subject) and standardized policy time (an externally defined time-frame for completion of an education). The students are encouraged to find new ways to relate to and create a coherent narrative between courses they have passed (near past), courses they plan to take (near future) and the needs of a future labour market (distant future). They have to constantly alternate between points in a near future and a near past, and simultaneously anticipate an unknown and more distant future. The new higher education system arising from the reforms, however, increasingly attempts to forestall (and thereby potentially also shape) this future through a number of forecasting techniques. These forecasts subsequently form the basis for policies that not only give direction to, but also actively reduce, students' educational possibilities and freedom of choice. In this way, we argue, students are governed to engage with their studies in a particular strategic and future-orientated way, which increasingly shifts their attention from a sense of immersion in the 'here and now' of the learning process towards tentative projections of one or more of the as-yet-unrealized futures. We therefore suggest that the university is increasingly becoming what the French anthropologist Marc Augé (1995) has described as a 'non-place', which, like an airport, a motorway or a supermarket, is designed for brief and impersonal flow of individuals. In the case of higher education, a reorchestration of students' time is taking place whereby projected futures increasingly replace presence, history and identity of the individual body.

Securing Progression and Completion: The Use of Modules and ECTS

Until the 1980s, higher education programmes in Denmark were characterized by an independent and nonstandardized process. Students designed their own curriculum to a large extent and, broadly speaking, simply signed themselves up for examination when they felt ready. From the 1990s onwards, however, Danish politicians introduced a number of new incentive-inducing measures. First the so-called 'taximeter system' from 1994 meant that universities' funding for teaching was based on the number of completed full-time equivalents, or FTEs per year (today comprising sixty ECTS). In 2009, an amendment introduced a financial bonus for institutions whenever a student completed her/his education within the prescribed time. This created new incentives to encourage fast completion (for example, by means of a linear or prestructured curriculum where students must pass their courses in a specific order).

In this development the introduction of the ECTS has played a still-more central role. ECTS is officially a neutral means of measuring the number of working hours a given course is designed to require of the student. One year of study is equivalent to sixty ECTS. ECTS is thus not a measure of academic content, level or complexity, but only of the workload related to a course. As part of the so-called Bologna Process, which aims to harmonize the higher education systems in Europe and make student mobility easier between universities in different countries, the ECTS system was originally conceived as a means to promote flexibility and mobility in students' education. Today, however, the system has also come to serve as an important tool of governance to speed up student degree completions. With the Bologna Process, education programmes are sliced up into a number of modules, each measured in terms of ECTS, and each concluded by an examination. Students therefore face frequent milestones and every single assignment is allotted a certain time-frame for completion. On top of this, the Danish Study Progress Reform (DSF 2014) recently introduced a new individualized use of ECTS in order to regulate and speed up student completion. Previously, ECTS were used to regulate the educational institutions, but with the new reform the ECTS system has become a means of rewarding and punishing the individual student. From autumn 2014 all students were automatically signed up for new exams corresponding to sixty ECTS every year, and students who fail or miss an exam are automatically signed up for a retake. If the retake is missed for any reason, students have one final try in the form of a second retake during the next term's exams, and while students were previously allowed to be up to one full year behind schedule, they are now only allowed to fall six months (or thirty ECTS) behind, before they are cut off from the Danish students' grants and loans scheme (literally called 'Public Educational Support' or 'Statens Uddannelsesstøtte' in Danish and abbreviated to 'SU').

One of the main consequences of the reform is that the post-reform curriculums offer fewer optional elements, simply because this makes it easier for the intuitions to ensure that each individual student is correctly signed up for exams corresponding to sixty new ECTS per year (Sarauw and Andersen, forthcoming). In this way the reform signals that fast completion must be considered a quality of education in line with, for instance, good grades. In fact, fast completion can now result in a financial bonus, not only to the educational institutions but also to the individual students, who are rewarded with half a month's worth of SU for each month they manage to overtake the prescribed time-frame.

Subject-Oriented Time and Standardized Policy Time

Although the ECTS framework has not been interpreted in entirely similar ways across all countries that have signed up to the Bologna Process, we see a current growth in academic discussions about the potential consequences that this logic of progression may have for the students, for their approach to their own learning as well as their attitude towards getting a university education (see, for example, Nixon, Scullion and Molesworth 2011; Naidoo and Jamieson 2006; Nielsen 2010; Sarauw 2011). In what follows, we provide an empirical contribution to these discussions by examining how fast completion and efficiency have been implemented in a specific institutional setting. The material we examine stems from fieldwork conducted by Nielsen (2010; 2015) in connection with a reform at the Faculty of Science at the University of Copenhagen (UCPH). This particular reform is telling, because it illustrates a recent and radical attempt to minimize students' time expenditure and increase the so-called study intensity. The control of time and the slicing up of study time into discrete courses is one important exemplar of a wider tendency and preoccupation with time and relevance, which has been further intensified in recent years.

Ten years ago, both science at UCPH, and the then veterinary high school (now part of 'life sciences' at the UCPH), introduced a new block structure. As a departure from a traditional organization of the academic year into two semesters, the year was now organized into four blocks of nine weeks (including examination periods). Each nine-week block usually comprises two courses of 7.5 ECTS each, while larger fifteen-ECTS courses are rare. In line with the recent Study Progress Reform, the aim was also then to speed up students' completion, to reduce dropouts and, generally, just to make students more active and efficient in their studies.

In an interview, a former head of studies argued that the shorter duration of the new blocks would automatically result in more intensive and concentrated courses, where students would be forced to take active part all the time and every day: 'They cannot slack off during the course and just cram it just before the exam', he said (Nielsen 2011: 177). Fieldwork, however, showed that many students experienced an inherent conflict between what Nielsen referred to as 'standardized policy time' (a temporality in which study time is shaped and evaluated on the basis of an externally defined measure of time), and 'subject-oriented time' (a temporality where the study time is framed by and comprises its 'own' time). In this respect, 'subject' refers to both the student as a learning subject and to the topic (the subject) of the student's studies. Subject-oriented time, in other words, refers to the student's experience of a study that can unfold in a time characterized by autonomous exploration of a subject – a time that the student used to relate to contemplation, immersion or absorption (see Nielsen 2015: 115–51).

Some students had no problem adjusting their study rhythm, and 'tuning in and up' in such a way that 'subject-oriented time' aligned with 'standardized policy time'. When asked about the intensity of the studies and the fact that they now had to pass more exams at shorter intervals, one student replied that 'you get used to it. And in terms of getting good grades, the pressure is less on each exam now because you have more of them' (Nielsen 2015: 132). However, many of the students Nielsen interviewed experienced a contradiction between the two temporalities. To paraphrase Henri Lefebvre (2004), this can be referred to as 'arrhythmia', or temporal discordance in the interaction between the various rhythms of everyday life: the students felt pressured, and found that they only had time for a superficial contact with the subject matter of their courses. They felt, in other words, that the time they spent on their studies was governed by demands on their time that were external to the actual study activities. Many of the students described the courses as highly condensed in relation to the actual objectives. Several students reported that they felt pressured to calculate exactly how much time they could and would spend on a given course in order to pass the exam. Some even described their studies as a race – a rapid journey towards a definite objective:

> Because we have these short periods, you become more exam-minded, all the time you think 'Okay, is this relevant'? … We have to know what we are supposed to do in the exam, so we know how to run this race, you know? You have to plan according to the exams and not really according to the teaching, because it is so compressed that you have to know what's necessary to know and what's not. (cited in Nielsen 2015: 137–38)

Another student said that the rapid pace meant that they constantly had to shift their attention from one thing to the next, and so they kept forgetting what they worked on before. She described her experience in the following terms: 'It's just like, "move on, move on, move on", there needs to be space on the hard disc' (ibid: 132). The students quoted show how the driver – or (cattle) prod, if you will – was often based on a sort of logic of necessity, of what seems necessary to pass the exam. This logic, many students felt, contradicted the desire for immersion and contemplation, to let curiosity lead the way and to investigate something of their own accord. Most of the students and teachers in Nielsen's study considered that a prerequisite for the kind of independent and explorative approach, which especially since the 1970s has been a prominent ideal of study and research at Danish universities, was that the students should have the opportunity to explore the roads less travelled, paths that sometimes lead to an impasse or lead the student far astray. Despite the fact that they also called for time for individual contemplation and for exploration of their various subjects, the intensified study time of the block structure meant that many students in Nielsen's study demanded unambiguous and fixed objectives for their learning, and a predefined way of reaching those objectives (ibid.). In the current reforms, the requirement for students to increase their study intensity mainly motivated them to follow the safe routes in order to pass their exams.

Employability and an Abductive Temporality

The political emphasis on fast completion and increased study intensity discussed above has gone hand in hand with a growing demand that students focus on and work towards their future employability from the day they enrol at the university. The starting point for curriculum planning has moved from broad internal criteria (such as research-based content and local ideas about good teaching and learning) to a series of fixed assumptions about the kinds of competencies students should hold in order to qualify for a particular job.In this way the reforms have profoundly redefined what students are supposed to achieve or get out of their course of education. As the Bologna Process's Framework of Qualifications (EC 2005) makes clear, the learning objective is no longer about exploring and mastering a given material (syllabus, content or input). Instead the Qualifications Framework introduced a so-called output-oriented regime that measures student learning in terms of their acquisition of a series of predefined competences that can be assessed on the basis of students' actions (learning objectives, outcome or output) (Nielsen 2015; Sarauw 2011; 2012). Ultimately, these competences should be translatable to and useful in the future job market – an obligation that is also evident in the following extract from the first national Danish Qualifications Framework, which involved a new way of thinking about the curriculum and the lecturer's and students' freedom to choose what to teach and what to study and learn:

> In the past, some curriculum board members have tended to focus too much on what academic competencies students should have. With this Qualifications Framework, they too would be forced to think in

Illustration 7.1: Posters promoting the acquisition of employment skills in the common room, Faculty of Humanities, Copenhagen University. *Source*: Sarauw 2012.

broader terms during curriculum planning to make room for other competencies in their programmes. In this way, it would be expected that certain education elements would be given higher priority (VTU 2003: 7).

The two photos above come from the coffee room at the Faculty of Humanities, University of Copenhagen. The walls are papered with posters about how to gain job experience, how to build up your CV and so on, rather than guest lectures or even music concerts. This illustrates that the changes did not only take place in the written curricula.

The European Bologna Process also addressed the students' freedom of choice and opportunities for construing their own unique course of education across national and academic borders. This aim is also evident among several of Denmark's most recent ministers of education, many of whom have been proponents of a classic liberal notion that students, when allowed to act as critical consumers in an open (education) market, will automatically gravitate towards the education programmes with the highest quality and relevance for society. As we argue below, the combination of modularization and freedom of choice with a focus on employability seems to make certain rhythms and temporalities more dominant in students' study time – temporalities which in certain cases contradict the ministers' assumptions and their attempt at promoting certain forms of student conduct.

Nielsen's (2015) fieldwork at the Faculty of Science showed an interesting correlation between the freedom of choice and the temporalities that shaped students' activities. Her interviews revealed that many students found it to be a 'time sink' if they had to constantly scout for potential courses in their own institution and in other institutions, even those abroad, in order to increase their future employability. One third-year student put it this way:

> It is very exciting that we can all end up with something different, and I think that is an advantage in relation to later job possibilities that we have different profiles. But it is incredibly time-consuming to find out which optional subjects to choose in order to get it all out and make it fit together … it can be rather confusing. The list is huge. You need to explore all modules, what pre-qualifications you need, and what each course can lead to … it's a jigsaw puzzle that takes time (cited in Nielsen 2015: 139).

If the breakdown of the curriculum into minor pieces, each revolving around a set of predefined objectives, tends to draw students' attention towards a near future and a short-term planning – defined by the end of a fixed-term period of study – then the demand that the students continuously look after their own employability seems to encourage them to focus on targets that belong in a more distant future. Indeed, the extract points to the existence of a certain study temporality which, to echo Adams et al. (2009), could be described as an 'abductive temporality'. Adams et al. use the concept of abduction to refer to:

> the processes of tacking back and forth between futures, pasts and presents, framing the life yet to come and the life that precedes the present as the unavoidable template for producing the future. Abduction names a mode of temporal politics, of moving in and mobilizing time, turning the ever-moving horizon of the future into that which determines the present (ibid: 251).

Students are constantly required to switch from a type of near past (recently passed courses) and a near future (potential courses), while at the same time relating to and anticipating a more distant future in the form of the labour market they expect to enter at some point. The present and the here-and-now of the study activities are therefore oriented towards something else – in this case particularly towards an as yet unknown, but necessarily anticipated future in the labour market. However, this orientation towards a future labour market is now no longer only or mainly for the student to create and anticipate through freedom of choice between a number of well-defined and competence-based modules. Today, as we show below, new political tools and technologies are being introduced to forecast what the future will bring and what kinds of competences future workers need to possess.

From Lifelong Learning to Foresight and Forecasting

> We aim to enhance the employability and personal and professional development of graduates throughout their careers. We will achieve this by improving cooperation between employers, students and higher education institutions, especially in the development of study programmes that help increase the innovation, entrepreneurial and research potential of graduates. Lifelong learning is one of the important factors in meeting the needs of a changing labour market, and higher education institutions play a central role in transferring knowledge and strengthening regional development, including by the continuous development of competences and reinforcement of knowledge alliances (EHEA 2012).

This extract is taken from one of the most recent communiqués in the European Bologna Process. Ministers and educational institutions from participating countries committed themselves to promoting employability, and to ensuring that students obtain knowledge, abilities and competences that they can use in the labour market. As the extract shows, the Bologna Process's notion of employability is closely connected to the notion of lifelong learning. Students must develop 'throughout their careers' (ibid.), and be capable of 'meeting the needs of a changing labour market' (ibid.).

Denmark, however, has also witnessed a trend that deviates from the Bologna Process's emphasis on 'lifelong learning, innovation, entrepreneurial and research potential' (ibid.) as the key competences in a rapidly changing labour market. The political emphasis on employability appears increasingly bound up with relatively narrow prognostics and forecasts. The Danish Ministry of Higher Education and Science, in other words, attempts to anticipate the future job market by looking at present and past employment rates. Contrary to the notion of an unpredictable future underlying the Bologna Process's emphasis on lifelong learning, current Danish higher education policy suggests a Fordist conception of a stable and foreseeable labour market, which is normally related to the industrial period where training for specific professions rather than generic and transferable skills and competences were in high demand (Sarauw 2011; 2012).

Recently the Danish government has set up an external expert committee on quality in higher education. Its terms of reference state that the objective of the committee is to create a system of high-quality education that offers the best possible opportunities and challenges for all students. According to the Ministry of Higher Education and Science's English webpage,[2] it should be 'a system, which supports highly skilled and employable graduates for the benefit of both the individual and for society as a whole – thereby contributing to growth, productivity and prosperity in Denmark'. During 2014 the committee published two reports with recommendations (respectively in March and October 2014). The recommendations are characterized by a quite narrow understanding of quality in higher education as a matter of supplying the demands of a future labour market. According to the committee, the latter can be predicted by means of a so-called 'educational foresight' which, in this case, aimed to map out quality and relevance in the professional bachelor education programmes in healthcare in relation to the job market of the future. Among other things the committee recommends: 'A central regulation of student admission within select programmes or educational streams with a substantial risk of overproduction will be conducted every three years and with a validity period of three years' (Expert Committee on Quality in Higher Education in Denmark 2014). Possibly inspired by the expert committee's recommendations, the Ministry of Higher Education and Science shortly afterwards launched a so-called 'sizing plan' – a plan which should govern and limit enrolment in certain education programmes (primarily among the humanities) based on unemployment figures from the past decade.

Anticipating an Imagined Future

The notion that future can be anticipated (and therefore shaped or changed) appears to be a dominant rationale internationally. Nowotny et al. (2001) have shown how predictions, projections, forecasts and calculations of probability, also pronounced as prognoses and trend analyses, have become ever-more popular political tools. Two Danish researchers, Niels Åkerstrøm Andersen (1996) and Maja Plum (2010), have demonstrated how this tendency has led to a significant policy change. In the 1960s, Danish educational objectives were shaped by an idealistic notion of education as a means of shaping the welfare state, social equality and equal distribution of goods, and/or as a response to undesirable issues in the present. Today, however, educational policy in Denmark and many other countries is predominantly oriented towards an imagined future, where predictions, projections, forecasts and calculations play a dominant role.

Andersen and Plum both emphasize that these predictions, projections and forecasts are often generated by comparison with other countries, institutions and individuals (for example, through OECD's PISA or PIAAC). Such comparisons are often based on liberal market-based models of discrimination between desirable and undesirable scenarios (Robertson et al. 2012). Another example is the Bologna Process's call for educational comparability and transparency (for example, as defined by the Framework of Qualifications for the European Higher Education Area from 2005, and other competence-based taxonomies). This call has not only come to influence students' learning objectives; it has also worked to promise the students that a certain professional future will be theirs if they manage to fulfil the learning objectives.

With Nowotny et al. (2001), one could argue that students in higher education increasingly deal with a condensed future that is experienced as an extended present. The idea about a condensed future has a significant parallel in the German sociologist Ulrich Beck's ideas about the 'risk society' (1992), in which policy and daily life are increasingly organized in response to projected or calculated future risks. In line with Beck, the German-American scholar Hans Ulrik Gumbrecht (1997; 2004) claims a fundamental change has occurred in the role that the 'future' plays in Western political philosophy. The period Gumbrecht refers to as Modernity (understood as a more or less univocal movement revolving around the ideas of European Enlightenment) was driven by a notion of the future as an open space that could be conquered and influenced. In contrast, current policies ,as well as student choices, which rely on predictions, projections and forecasts, suggest a notion of the future as an aggressive and invasive force coming on to the present.

To paraphrase the anthropologist Marc Augé (1995), we could also say that the university is increasingly becoming a 'non-place'. A 'non-place' is designed for a fleeting, brief and impersonal flow of individuals, like the lobby of an international hotel, the departure lounge of an airport, a highway or a supermarket. These are all characterized by a unidimensional functionality, such as consumption or transportation, whereby they transgress the specificity of time and space. As essentially timeless, identical and functional spaces, these 'non-places' are devoid of history and identity. Put differently, they are defined by a special temporality, which is characterized by a removal of the 'here and now' to one or more end goals outside of the 'non-place'.

Conclusion

Fast completion and employability stand among today's most important policy tools. In this article we have traced – and to some extend denaturalized – the status of the two concepts as neutral and necessary objectives of higher education policy. Drawing on examples from the European Bologna Process and the way it was introduced into the Danish higher education system, we have explored how the emphasis on fast completion and employability relate to, and come to influence, the temporality and rhythm characteristic of the time of study.

From the 1990s, modularization, ECTS and competence-oriented programme regulations have required students to speed up their studies and turn their attention and time to what is deemed 'necessary'– in order to pass the exams and in order to be employable in the changing job market. Both in terms of passing the next exam and landing a job after graduation, students are increasingly being exposed to the imperatives of 'necessity', where freedom of choice is no longer considered a guarantee for the relevance of their education. Ever-greater effort is placed on predicting the future by means of various politically initiated projections, forecasts and calculations of probability. In the Danish context , the so-called Study Progress Reform and the sizing plan represent two significant attempts to control the situation, where anticipations of the future are used to validate political prioritizations of different study programmes' content and structure. The research we have presented in this article does not show to what extent governments believe that they can actually anticipate the future through these policy interventions and to what extent it is mainly a question of saving money by shortening the time spent in higher education. Our research, however, shows that the future is increasingly constructed by policymakers as a threatening and intrusive force invadingthe present; labour-market prognoses, conjectures concerning global competition and a deluge of international comparisons and rankings come to define – and thereby potentially make controllable – a limited number of possible futures. These anticipated futures, however, come to profoundly restrict students' freedom, in terms of what, when and at what rate they wish to study. In this way, students' time of study at the university is increasingly governed by factors that are external to the present (in that they come before or after the present) and to the here-and-now study activity. Engaged in this abductive temporality, the student is constantly forced to orient her/himself, tacking back and forth between a near past (passed courses), a near future (potential courses) and a distant future, (the future labour market). Within the context of the contemporary university, this orientation towards, and anticipation of, a future within a competitive labour market seems to play an increasingly dominant role.

Gritt B. Nielsen (Ph.D. in educational anthropology) is Associate Professor at DPU, Aarhus University. Her research interests revolve around reforms of the welfare state – in particular, shifting notions of democracy and changing forms of student participation, politics and protest in response to austerity measures and marketized and commodified education. She has done extensive fieldwork in Denmark and New Zealand, focusing on student protests against different neoliberalizing reforms of the public university. Theoretically, she combines economic anthropology and anthropology of policy with feminist- and post-structuralist-inspired thinking. She is study coordinator of a Masters in anthropology of education and globalization and recently published the book *Figuration Work: Student Participation, Democracy and University Reform in a Global Knowledge Economy* (2015, Berghahn).

Laura Louise Sarauw received her Ph.D. in 2011 from the University of Copenhagen. She has a Masters in modern culture, also from University of Copenhagen, and a Bachelor's degree in the history of ideas from Aarhus University. She is currently a Postdoctoral Fellow in the Department of Education, Aarhus University.

Notes

1. From 2005 to 2008 Nielsen (2010; 2015) conducted a field-research project comprising three Danish Universities, during which she observed the teaching of two courses in 2005/2006 in the then newly implemented 'block structure' at the UCPH and the then Royal Veterinary and Agricultural High School. Nielsen interviewed a total of twenty-five students (some individually, others in groups), seven teachers and three managers about the (then) new reform and its impact on the education programmes and on the students' approach to their education. From 2008 to 2011, Sarauw (2011) explored how the European Bologna process (1999) and its demands for a new competence-based curriculum was negotiated and interpreted at selected study programmes in Denmark. The explorations were carried out through multisited analyses of: (1) selected international and national policy and curricula documents; and (2) interviews with heads of study boards and administrative staff at ten individual education programmes, all in the field of humanities, at five different Danish universities.
2. See http://ufm.dk/en/education-and-institutions/councils-and-commissions/the-expert-committee-on-quality-in-higher-education-in-denmark.

References

Adams, V., et al. 2009. 'Anticipation: Technoscience, Life, Affect, Temporality', *Subjectivity* (28): 246–65.
Åkerstrøm Andersen, N. 1996. *Selvskabt forvaltning – forvaltningspolitikkens og centralforvaltningens udvikling i Danmark fra 1900–1994*. Copenhagen: Nyt fra Samfundsvidenskaberne.
Augé, M. 1995. *Non-Places: Introduction to Anthropology of Supermodernity*, London and New York: Verso Books.
Beck, U. 1992. *Risk Society: Towards a New Modernity*. New Delhi: Sage.
Boden R., and M. Nedeva. 2010. 'Employing discourse: universities and graduate 'employability', in Journal of Education Policy, Vol. 25, No. 1, January 2010, 37–54.
Universities Denmark. 2013. *Høring over bekendtgørelser som opfølgning på ændring af universitetsloven (studiefremdrift)*, 11 November. Retrieved 10 February 2016

from http://www.dkuni.dk/~/media/Files/Hringssvar/HS%20111113%20uni.ashx.
DSF (Danske Studerendes Fællesråd). 2014. 'Notat om fremdriftsreformen', Retrieved 10 October 2016 from http://www.dsfnet.dk/wp-content/uploads/2016/04/Notat-om-fremdriftsreformen-1_0.pdf.
EC. 2005. 'The Framework of Qualification for the EHEA adopted at the Bergen Conference of European Ministers Responsible for Higher Education 2003–2005'. Retrieved 10 February 2016 from http://media.ehea.info/file/WG_Frameworks_qualification/85/2/Framework_qualificationsforEHEA-May2005_587852.pdf
———. 2012. 'Making the Most of Our Potential: Consolidating the European Higher Education Area, Bucharest Communiqué' (final version). Retrieved 10 February 2016 from http://www.eurashe.eu/library/ehea_2012_bucharest-communique-pdf/.
Expert Committee on Quality in Higher Education in Denmark, 2014. First set of recommendations from the expert Committee. *New Ways: A Higher Education System for the Future*. English summary. Retrived 17 November 2016 from http://ufm.dk/en/education-and-institutions/councils-and-commissions/the-expert-committee-on-quality-in-higher-education-in-denmark/the-expert-committee-on-quality-in-higher-education-in-denmark-recommendations.pdf
Gumbrecht, H.U. 1997. *In 1926 – Living at the Edge of Time*. London: Harvard University Press.
———. 2004. *Production of Presence: What Meaning Cannot Convey*. Stanford: Stanford University Press.
Lefebvre, H. 2004. *Rhythmanalysis: Space, Time and Everyday Life*. London & New York: Continuum.
Naidoo, R., and I. Jamieson. 2006. 'Empowering participants or corroding learning? Towards a research agenda on the impact of student consumerism in higher education', *Journal of Education Policy* 20(3): 267–81.
Nielsen, G.B. 2010. 'Student Figures in Friction: Explorations into Danish University Reform and Shifting Forms of Student Participation', Ph.D. thesis. Aarhus: Danish School of Education, Aarhus University.
———. 2011. 'Timing Students' Freedom: On Paradoxes of Efficiency and Accountability', in J.E. Kristensen, M. Raffnsøe-Møller and H. Nørreklit (eds), *University Performance Management – The Silent Managerial Revolution in Danish Universities*. Copenhagen: DJØF-forlag, pp. 175–92.
———. 2015. *Figuration Work: Student Participation, Democracy and University Reform in a Global Knowledge Economy*. New York and Oxford: Berghahn Books.
Nielsen, Gritt B. & Sarauw, Laura Louise. 2014. 'Fremdrift og fremsyn: kampen om de studerendes tid', *Dansk pædagogisk tidsskrift*, No. 2/2014, p. 33–42. (BFI-Level 1)
Nixon, E., R. Scullion and M. Molesworth. 2011. 'How choice in higher education can create conservative learners', in M. Molesworth, R. Scullion and E. Nixon (eds), *The Marketisation of Higher Education and the Student as Consumer*. London and New York: Routledge, pp. 196–208.

Nowotny, H., et al. 2001. *Re-thinking Science: Knowledge and the Public in an Age of Uncertainty*. Cambridge: Polity Press.
Plum, M. 2010. 'Dokumenteret faglighed. Analyser af hvordan "pædagogisk faglighed" produceres gennem lærerplanernes dokumentationsteknologi', Ph.D. thesis. Copenhagen: University of Copenhagen.
Robertson, S., et al. 2012. 'Globalisation and Regionalisation in Higher Education: Toward a New Conceptual Framework', Summative Working Paper for URGE Work Package 1. Copenhagen: Danish School of Education.
Sarauw, L.L. 2011. 'Kompetencebegrebet og andre stileøvelser. Fortællinger om uddannelsesudviklingen på de danske universiteter efter universitetsloven 2003', PhD thesis. Copenhagen: University of Copenhagen.
_____. 2012. 'Qualifications Frameworks and their Conflicting Social Imaginaries of Globalisation', *LATISS. Learning and Teaching: International Journal of Higher Education in the Social Sciences* 5(3, 2) 22–39.
_____. 2014. 'Når kvalitet bliver til ikke-teori: om kompetence- og anvendelsesorientering som ukonkret negation af teoretiske og specialiserede videregående uddannelseselementer', *Dansk pædagogisk tidsskrift* 4: 31–41.
Sarauw, L.L., and H.L. Andersen. 2016. 'Fremdrift, Målstyring og Soppe-didaktik', *Dansk Pædagogisk Tidsskrift*. Vol. 1, Nr. 2/2016, 5.
VTU (Ministeriet for Videnskab, Teknologi og Udvikling). 2003. 'Towards a Danish Qualifications Framework for Higher Education', final report approved by the Danish Bologna follow-up group 15 January (translation of the Danish version). Copenhagen.

PART III

Managing the Risk University – Research, Ranking and Reputation

CHAPTER 8
The Causes, Mechanisms and Consequences of Reputational Risk Management of Universities and the Higher Education Sector

ROGER DALE

◆◆◆

Introduction

The issues addressed by this chapter arise from asking how the wider 'societal risks' occasioned by the processes we refer to as globalization are being transferred and transformed into new and distinct 'institutional risks' for universities as institutions and higher education as a sector, both of which are now being expected to make novel and distinct contributions to economy, polity and society. The first part of the chapter attempts to set the wider scene for the changes that are typically referred to as the 'modernization of the university', asking why modernization is seen to be required, what it entails and what kinds of changes might be needed to bring it about. In the next part I focus on one relevant and significant aspect of these modernizing moves by briefly examining the shift from quality assurance to reputational risk management as a key and representative axis along which these changes may be occurring and visible. Here, the focus will be on the forms and mechanisms of individual university-reputation management as seen in the rapid development of ranking systems, usually referred to as 'university league tables'. I will seek to shed light on how they are compiled and disseminated, and in what ways they encode the conception of reputation and the risks it carries. The final section of the paper raises the wider and more profound issue of the potential threat to many of what are considered crucial characteristics of 'the university', (including academic freedom), which may be posed by the expansion of the concept of risk, and especially its association with reputation.[1]

Contextual Changes

Over the past half century, universities and higher education more generally have undergone enormous changes. However, analyses of the substance and consequences of these changes have tended to be confined and constricted by a concentration on national case studies. These are undoubtedly of great value, but there may be some space for analyses that seek to identify more clearly the global drivers of these changes, and of their nature and impact. This is not to suggest that national studies do not recognize the significance of changes on a global level, but that recognition tends to take the form of tracing the effects on domestic policy and practice of a largely unspecified conception of globalization. One aim of this chapter is to appraise the global nature, basis and consequences of changes that are now being experienced, in different ways and different places, across the world. These changes tend to carry common labels – such as 'quality' and 'modernization' – but this does not mean that we can assume that they mean the same thing everywhere, or are responded to in similar ways. Neither the labels, nor the histories that lie behind their emergence, can be taken for granted, and we cannot expect to be able to come to terms adequately with them in the absence of such an understanding. Consequently, I will attempt briefly in the first part of this chapter to situate the emergence of such terms and the problematics that generate them.

Two key features of such assumptions that we need to challenge are the tendency firstly to take a relatively abstract and fixed model of 'the university' as the fundamental if shifting object and basis of study; and, secondly, to assume the existence of a static higher education 'sector' in which universities are embedded, and which embrace a collection of activities that necessarily go together. Higher education as a field of study may be especially prone to this given that much of the literature on the topic is produced by people working in universities, writing about what they experience as well as what they observe, with clear 'interests' in the future of the institution. This not only makes 'detachment' difficult, but it makes it more difficult to 'stop seeing the things that are conventionally "there" to be seen' (Becker 1971: 10).

The intention, then, is to open up questions of the nature of the broader changes within which the university as an idea and as an institution is changing, in order to understand the nature and possible consequences of those changes more broadly, especially at the level of higher education as a distinct sector, locally, nationally and globally.

Theoretically, the argument is set at a very broad level. It begins by attempting to identify the new 'societal risks' associated with neoliberal globalization, and the kinds of 'institutional risks' they entail for universities, both in terms of their existing structures, processes and purposes, and in terms of novel and distinct expectations of their relationships with, and contributions to, society. The current state of the universities, like other institutions of modernity, is fundamentally a reflection of, and a response to, the changing nature of the relationship between capitalism and modernity. In developing the argument, I follow Boaventura de Sousa Santos (2004) in suggesting that it is crucial to the understanding of current global activities and changes to distinguish between the trajectories of capitalism (as found currently in the form of neoliberal globalization) and Western modernity and to examine the relationships between them. As he puts it:

> Western modernity and capitalism are two different and autonomous historical processes ... (that) have converged and interpenetrated each other. ... It is my contention that we are living in a time of paradigmatic transition, and, consequently, that the sociocultural paradigm of modernity ... will eventually disappear before capitalism ceases to be dominant ... partly from a process of supersession and partly from a process of obsolescence. It entails supersession to the extent that modernity has fulfilled some of its promises, in some cases even in excess. It results from obsolescence to the extent that modernity is no longer capable of fulfilling some of its other promises (Santos 2004: 1–2).

Santos goes on: '[Western] modernity is grounded on a dynamic tension between the pillar of regulation ([which] guarantees order in a society as it exists in a given moment and place) and emancipation ... the aspiration for a good order in a good society in the future' (ibid.). Modern regulation is 'the set of norms, institutions and practices that guarantee the stability of expectations' (ibid.); the pillar of regulation is constituted by the principles of the state, the market and community typically taken as the three key agents of governance. Modern emancipation is the 'set of oppositional aspirations and tendencies that aim to increase the discrepancy between experiences and expectations' and:

> what most strongly characterises the sociocultural condition at the beginning of the century is the collapse of the pillar of emancipation into the pillar of regulation, as a result of the reconstructive management of the excesses and deficits of modernity which ... were viewed

as temporary shortcomings and as problems to be solved through a better and broader use of the ever-expanding material, intellectual and institutional resources of modernity (ibid.: 7).

Further, these two pillars of regulation and emancipation have ceased to be in tension but have become almost fused, as a result of the 'reduction of modern emancipation to the cognitive-instrumental rationality of science and the reduction of modern regulation to the principle of the market' (ibid.: 9). In sum, the institutions of Western modernity may no longer represent the best possible shell, or the best possible governance model, for capitalism in its global neoliberal form.

In particular, and at a global level, the changes to the university that we are witnessing might also be seen as forms of what Santos refers to as a 'reconstitutive management' of the deficits of Western modernity. Thus, the consequences of these changes are not seen as transcending modernity, but as an intensified use of the tools of modernity, producing what might be seen as a form of ultra modernity, especially through the shifting of the scales of problem identification and solution.

A central argument of this chapter is that one particular idea of the university – or perhaps more accurately, of higher education as a sector – which differs considerably from the (already relatively 'global') conception of the university, is being globalized through the efforts of international organizations. In particular, we may see that the World Bank, OECD and EU have been involved not so much in providing responses to the new challenges of globalization, as most approaches to their work on education implicitly assume. Rather, they have been and continue to be able to frame, and define the nature of, those new challenges, through both discourse and statistics. That is, they construe and construct, specify and formulate, the nature of the problems faced by national systems, including by representing them as problems that can or should be addressed at different – local, regional or global – scales; and they adopt quantitative measures to establish the extent to which these problems have been adequately addressed.

Their reports provide the medium through which such conceptions are not merely diffused but promoted, as almost self-evident forms to be taken by higher education's response to the demands of a new 'global knowledge economy'. The response is typically announced as involving a need to modernize the university. This has been especially extensively developed at the level of the European Union, but it should not, however, be expected to be, or look, the same everywhere.

This is not to suggest that this solution, and the various forms it takes, has been in any sense directly imposed on unwilling but disempowered nation-states. Rather, I want to draw attention here to two related but underanalysed consequences of the series of projects and processes we refer to as globalization. While nation-states do not on the whole feel responsible for the problems that have befallen them, neither do they feel equipped to deal with them; there has been no 'obvious way' for states to tackle these problems, though they remain their responsibility. This has opened up a major opportunity space for 'political advice entrepreneurs', and particularly international organizations such as the OECD, World Bank, and EU, but also for commercial organizations, think tanks and international accountancy firms interested in exploiting the opportunities created by the changes in higher education as a sector.

On this basis, international organizations have been able to specify the nature of the changes addressed to education by neoliberal capitalism, largely because existing education systems interpreted them in incrementalist, or path dependent, ways. Here, loose definitions of 'globalization' provided both spaces for international organizations to specify them more closely, and justification for national governments to bow to their inexorable logic. These projects are not intended to replace existing national forms, though they may be expected to influence them, but they do also offer a distinct set of alternatives aimed at improving the contribution of education to the knowledge economy in ways that cannot be achieved through the efforts of individual nation-states alone.

Institutional Challenges to the University

Four main challenges to the university can be discussed, and they will be addressed in turn.

Massification

We get some idea of the extent of increased student enrolment in higher education from the OECD's evidence that entry rates for university-level programmes increased by an average of nearly 25 percent between 1995 and 2010 (OECD 2012: 18).

The 'logic' of massification includes greater social mobility for a growing segment of the population, new patterns of funding for higher education, increasingly diversified higher education systems, and generally a fear of an overall lowering of academic standards. Beyond this, the number of students enrolled in tertiary education outside their country of citizenship increased more than threefold, from 1.3 million in 1990 to nearly 4.3 million in 2011 (OECD 2013).

At the first stage of massification, higher education systems struggled to cope with demand, the need for expanded infrastructure and a larger teaching corps. During the past decade, systems have begun to wrestle with the implications of diversity and to consider which subgroups are still not being included and appropriately served.

Cost Sharing

While funding arrangements for universities have historically shown wide diversity, it is clear that over the course of the past twenty years, the default assumption that the state would be the funder of last resort (and often of first, or only, resort) changed fundamentally, not least as a result of massification, which meant that fewer states could afford to continue funding universities at the same level as had historically been the case. All over the world, often under the tutelage of the World Bank, universities have been 'persuaded' to alter and increase the range of their funding bases. The main form this took was in the area of students' contribution to the cost of their higher education, in the form of fees. This qualitative change in the basis of their funding presented universities with new forms of risk to manage, with far-reaching effects on the relationship between university, academics and students.

New Public Management

Universities have experienced quite extreme forms of New Public Management (NPM) as a means of controlling the public sector (see King 2011). Indeed, in the literature on higher education, NPM is often taken as the basis of the troubles that higher education faces, to the point where it is almost as if NPM only operates in higher education, rather than problematized and located as the political form of neoliberalism (sometimes known as 'constitutional neoliberalism').

The main effects of NPM have been mediated through its adoption as the basis for the framework of governance and regulation of university activities, such as quality frameworks. There, the focus has been on reducing the dangers of producer capture through putting the relationships on the basis of a range of supervisory and contractual arrangements, aimed at ensuring disinterestedness as well as efficiency. For example, prior to the introduction of NPM into the higher education sector, academics had essentially been the sole and ultimate arbiters of what was entailed in 'quality' (though the term was scarcely known before the advent of the NPM). It was taken for granted that academic expertise was both necessary and sufficient for all judgments of what is now covered by quality assurance arrangements. In a sense, this seemed convenient all round; for those who graduated it meant that graduation was in itself a guarantee of 'quality'. The press towards formalization of quality arrangements came about as a result of the combination of other forces that are discussed in this section. What has been added in the last two decades is an increasing emphasis on the need for universities to contribute, through their teaching, and especially their research, to the knowledge-based economy.

Contribution to Knowledge-Based Economy

'Promoting competitiveness' has very different implications from the human capital theory assumptions that underlay the accumulation problem twenty years ago. The same could be said about 'fostering the knowledge economy'. The state's role is no longer confined to providing an infrastructure that will underpin the productive economy; it also expands and shifts to become concerned with the promotion of nationally based industries on the world market (competition state). It is no longer confined to providing research infrastructure, but includes active involvement in the funding and direction of research. Perhaps the most frequently noted change, certainly in contexts like higher education, is that the state itself becomes directly involved in accumulation, through the development of higher education as a crucial 'export industry', that makes an increasingly important contribution to the national budget.

This is effectively linked to an expectation that universities will increase their contribution to what is perceived as a new global economy based on knowledge rather than production. Indeed, universities are seen as central to this, as is evident in the explicit formulations of the EU's three main exhortations to the universities of its member states : 'the role of universities in the Europe of knowledge', 'mobilizing the brainpower of Europe' and 'delivering on the modernisation agenda for universities' (see CEC 2003; 2005; 2006; Dale 2014). It is also made explicit in each of these publications, and in numerous other publications from international organizations, that this is a competitive game; Europe's universities (and those of the rest of the world) are assumed – and urged – to be in competition with each other. The message is clear that no country can opt out of this competition with impunity. And the chief medium and mechanism through which this is to be registered is the league tables of university success.

From Quality Assurance to Risk Management

As noted above, neither the term nor the concept of quality, as it is now understood, existed twenty years ago. 'Quality' thus both marks out a specific place in the university and defines its role and purpose, and ensures a common and commensurable place for it across institutions and jurisdictions. Fundamentally, then, we may see 'quality' – minimally in the form of quality assurance mechanisms, such as the UNESCO regional conventions – as providing an evidential basis for membership of an international higher education community. At the same time, 'indicators' are being transformed into the basis for establishing claims to individual excellence through the medium of competitive comparison on a world scale, that is enabled, advanced and above all shaped by such ranking mechanisms as league tables.

Separately and together, while quality (assurance) and indicators have added new dimensions to the programmes and operations of universities, their contributions have been very different and have had very different consequences. On the one hand, quality assurance provides elements of consumer – and other stakeholder – protection against inadequate products or service, or against cheating. On the other hand, quality assurance leads to the categorizing and reifying in various ways of the very 'tofu-like' concept of quality (by 'tofu' concept, I refer to concepts that have no intrinsic meaning in themselves, but take their meaning from the particular environment). Here, the societal requirement for a reliable and trustworthy form of protection for governments and students as two particular sets of consumers and beneficiaries of human capital at a national level – but also, with the growing emphasis on the international mobility and migration of people, at a transnational level – generates institutional responses in the form of mutually compatible quality assurance systems (of which the Bologna Process is the outstanding example). And this may be seen as the most important contribution of quality assurance to the modernization of higher education on a global scale. It brings about both a means of enhancing the mobility of labour and the possibility of the commensurability and comparability of university qualifications on a global level.

The main differences between quality and rankings is that indicators of quality are: (1) threshold concepts, not comparative; (2) in effect zero-sum – you either have them or you don't; (3) in a sense, 'nonrivalrous' – one university being quality assured does not prevent another being quality assured; (4) by intention they provide a framework for action that can be met in diverse ways; (5) subject to formal audit – how do we know that you did what you said you would do?; (6) not subject to quantification, and hence not available for ranking.

One way in which this difference emerges is that the emphasis on stakeholder protection narrows the range of possible ways that institutions might differentiate themselves from each other. In the big picture, they either are, or are not 'quality assured', and if they are not, they are likely to suffer serious consequences. They may wish to draw attention to particular elements of their quality assurance profile where they exceed minimum requirements, such as the employment rate of graduates, but the formal purpose of quality assurance is to assure stakeholders that minimum standards have been met, usually through the use of administrative mechanisms, and this leaves little room, and little incentive, for the use of quality assurance as a means of distinguishing one institution from another.

Indicators, by comparison are: (1) subject to quantification, and hence available for ranking; (2) ordinal rather than cardinal; (3) comparable; (4) 'rivalrous' – one university achieving a ranking does prevent another achieving it; and (5) providing a framework for action that can be met in a limited range of externally defined ways.

The fundamental change signalled by the shift from quality assurance to indicators and benchmarks is the change from national (and increasingly inter-national) consumer protection to global competitive comparison. This is an instance of the growing gap between the institutions of a fundamentally nationally based version of capitalism to a neoliberal form with the ambition of minimizing the influence of borders both between and within countries.

This is not to play down the importance of international agreements on quality assurance (see Hartmann 2010). Comparability itself represents a very important tool of governance of the sector internationally. This has been pointed out by Novoa and Yariv-Mashal (2003) in the case of work in the field of comparative education, and is especially apparent in the case of the Bologna Process in Europe. So, the point is not to ignore, or downplay the importance of, the 'quality in higher education' discourse but to try to locate those debates in a wider, if less deep, context.

Reputational Risk

We can see this changed significance of indicators as signalling shifting conceptions of risk, within and for universities. The use of indicators also shows the different salience of risk, nationally and internationally, and the way that these require new forms of 'risk management', which may be defined as 'a system of regulatory measures intended to shape who can take what risks and how' (Hood et al. 1992: 136). The implications of this are clear:

> Whereas trust, on the one hand, deals with the inherent unknowableness of the future (Keynes 1921) by assuming away aspects of uncertainty ... risk management seeks to bring a certain degree of measurability to expectations, even though certainty about the future is impossible. In this way, risk reflects how 'the nature of modern culture, especially its technical and economic substructure, requires precisely such "calculability" of consequences' (Weber 1978: 351 quoted in Brown and Calnan 2009: 14).

The significance of 'risk' for universities became most apparent when, in 2000, the Higher Education Funding Council for England (HEFCE) required all universities to introduce risk management as a governance tool. Significantly in this context, HEFCE guidance 'direct(ed) the governing body towards a high level, risk-based approach to establishing a sound system of internal control, covering all types of risk' (HEFCE 2001: 1). Among other things, this in itself creates a new kind of risk for higher education institutions in the form of their reputation with HEFCE. The broader assumptions and implications of such a shift are well captured by Power et al.:

> Risk management is part of a broader set of transformations of universities from being ungovernable and idiosyncratic collections of individuals to being accountable organizations with clear missions, formal structures, professional management and an 'appetite' for risk (Power et al. 2009: 306-7).

However, and more directly relevant in this context, Huber points out that:

> something only becomes a risk if it is socially considered to be one. A disadvantageous ranking is therefore just an unfavourable position in an arbitrary data sheet, but as soon as it is defined as a risk, it needs to be avoided, registered, anticipated, dealt with, recorded, audited, and

so forth. Thus the power of definition becomes an important one as it shapes the organisation's future scope of actions and self-perception (Huber 2009: 85).

As we have just seen, quality assurance neither creates significant comparative risks, nor would be sufficient in itself to manage the risks of being in a global knowledge economy. This becomes particularly crucial when, as Huber goes on:

> mandatory risk management makes HEIs become strategic entrepreneurial actors ... universities become organisational actors (Krücken and Meier 2006) which must engage in practices like competition and strategy development formerly exclusive to the private sector. So the rationale behind risk management becomes a dominant one as it is reproduced through internalisation (Power, Scheytt, Soin and Sahlin 2009). The organisation has no other means to see itself but through the lens of risk management (Huber 2009: 85).

What is crucial here is that 'reputation' has emerged as the key and dominant currency of risk to universities worldwide. This has occurred through a process where agencies external to the organization, and initially possibly peripheral to, and even parasitic on, the field, not only collect information from institutions within the field, but combine, produce and publicize it in new forms, typically as aggregate rankings.

Power et al. suggest that 'these dense, often single-figure, calculative representations of reputation constitute a new kind of performance metric and are a growing source of man-made, institutionalized risk to organizations as they acquire increased recognition in fields' (2009: 311). And they go on to suggest that:

> organizations have incentives to support legitimated evaluators by supplying the component information and, in so doing, they can come to internalize ... elements of the metric as performance variables. Reputational metrics and rankings are 'reactive' or performative by generating self-reinforcing behaviours and shifting cognitive frames and values over time (ibid.: 312).

In this way, seemingly innocuous internal management indicators come to have 'the potential to shift motivations and missions by constructing self-reinforcing circuits of performance' (ibid.).

The key point for this chapter is that in this process, 'organizational performance indicators for internal purposes come to be reactively aligned with those which inform an evaluation or ranking system' (ibid.). Power et al. go on to suggest that:

> Reputation, as a perceptual construct may be one component of a ranking metric in the first instance, but the rank itself comes to influence the perceptions of key constituencies, such as clients. In this way, reputation is produced by the very systems which measure it (Schultz et al. 2001) ... which are then re-imported by organizations for internal use. They perpetuate the internal organizational importance of externally constructed reputation and give it a new governing and disciplinary power within organizations (Power et al. 2009: 312).

University Ranking Systems

One fundamental set of institutions propelling this shift towards reputational risk management are transnational organizations – which include not just OECD, the World Bank and the EU, but major commercial organizations, such as the Times Higher Education World University Rankings, and the QS World Education Rankings. These organizations are essentially seeking to instantiate a competitive basis for a global knowledge economy through the operation of league tables and rating agencies in an enterprise that has become as lucrative as it is stratifying. The central feature of both of these from the present perspective is that they are indeed 'transnational' rather than 'international' (Moutsios 2012). While the chief objective of international quality assurance mechanisms is to facilitate comparability of national systems for the purpose of enabling greater mobility, the chief objective of the international organizations, and the ends towards which the efforts of the rankings agencies are bent, is essentially the creation of 'competitive comparison' by means of a supranational set of criteria for ranking the performance of individual universities in a burgeoning global knowledge economy. A crucial element of this, as Olds (2012) points out, is that these rankings directly concern only a very small percentage of all universities in the world, but their influence – and that of other forms of inter-university comparison, such as the National Student Survey in the U.K. – is much more pervasive.

It will be useful at this point to make a brief detour to clarify a little how university ranking systems work. Robertson and Olds (2010) point to three prominent explanations of them, each of which sheds some light on the argument being developed here:

1. Rankings can be seen as a discrete project that aims at accountability and transparency, is a response to stakeholders' demands for greater accountability, transparency and efficiency, and gives rise to new incentives for 'quantifying quality' (Salmi and Saroyan 2007: 35).
2. Rankings can be part of a programme of strategies aimed at generating competitiveness within the higher education sector at multiple scales (national, regional and global), where rankings act as mechanisms and instruments for deep social change within the higher education sector. Hazelkorn (2009) identifies six ways in which rankings influence and reshape higher education institutions: (i) student choice – competitive post graduates in particular seek highly ranked universities; (ii) strategic thinking and planning – particularly the selective choice of indicators for management purposes; (iii) the reorganization and restructuring of higher education institutions to enable them to respond to, or take advantage of rankings; (iv) reshaping priorities – such as focusing on research, changing the curriculum, attracting international students, harmonizing programmes; (v) academic profession – used to identify (and recruit) the best performers; and (vi) stakeholders – such as alumni, who view rankings as a proxy for the return on their investment in the institution (Robertson and Olds 2010: 111).
3. Rankings are a manifestation of wider processes of globalization taking place within the higher education sector, which reflect, and are also constitutive of, transformations in wider social formations (ibid.: 106). Here, rankings are seen as social and political projects that are also key features of the emerging knowledge economy, where 'the means of knowledge creation are pulled gravitationally into strong centres that secure a superior capacity for creation and dissemination, and are able to claim formal authority in the K[knowledge]-economy' (Marginson 2008: 7).

Conclusion

I have identified some key features of the global macro-political economic condition of the world today, and suggested some ways in which the societal challenges it generates have been transformed into challenges to the university as an institution. I have suggested that one useful perspective on this is to see the issues as involving 'reputational risk management' at the level of the institution. I have suggested that indicators and ratings, when quantified, produce reputational rankings, which not only measure, but effectively define the nature of universities' reputations; and it is this which underpins the broader potential (or, of course, threat) of the extensive use of any indicators that involve more than the ticking of boxes.

I want to conclude by pointing to some potentially significant consequences of the main argument of this chapter, that 'reputation', mediated through rankings as the best known but not the only 'calculative representations of reputation', has emerged as the key and dominant currency of risk to universities worldwide. As noted above, the significance of rankings has increased as they 'generat(e) self-reinforcing behaviours and shift cognitive frames and values over time' (Power et al. 2009: 312; Espeland and Sauder 2007). Rankings not only order, but also determine the basis of ordering, and thereby construct reputation, which is produced by the forms that measure it.

The consequences of this for universities are profound, since it makes externally constructed reputation central to their whole organization. This takes at least two crucial forms, direct and indirect. First, the direct impact of rankings and ratings of universities is not confined to their research output, though that may be the most prominent example. Their teaching, too, is similarly rated comparatively (for instance via the annual National Student Survey in the U.K.), as is their success in placing their graduates in employment, or even in how they welcome overseas students to their campuses. For example, see the publications of the 'i-graduate' organization, which announces itself as:

> the world leader in customer insight for the education sector, tracking and benchmarking student and stakeholder opinion across the globe. Our purpose is to help education providers to enhance competitive advantage and quality (www.i-graduate.org).

Indirectly, all the various forms and areas of reputational risk may come to fuse together, as interconnected elements of a reputational whole. The consequence of this is that 'if everything may depend on organizational reputation, then reputational risk management demands the risk management of everything' (Power 2004: 36).

The 'indirect' effect of rankings emerges when we see that while they are formally designed to enable external/public accountability, they also have significant consequences for the internal operations of institutions, as 'organizational performance indicators for internal purposes come to be reactively aligned with those which inform an evaluation or ranking system' (Espeland and Sauder 2007: 312). We should also notice that a common response to the problems caused by reputational risk has been the introduction, across the board, into universities of a wide series of performance metrics.

This brings us to what is possibly the most important point of this argument – that as reputation becomes the key nexus linking together all aspects of the organization's work, it becomes extremely difficult to maintain the levels of 'loose coupling' on which universities have historically been thought to depend for their effective operation in their own terms, and especially in respect of academic freedom.[2] Weick's (1976) concept of loose coupling refers, roughly, to the degree of flexibility and independence of subsystems within a system like a university; thus, does a problem for teaching (automatically) become a problem for research, or administration? As Sauder and Espeland put it, rankings are less 'decouple-able' than other forms of institutional control; 'rankings, as commensurate, relative, and broadly circulating measures, are more difficult to buffer (de/loose-couple) than are ... other types of institutional pressures' (Sauder and Espeland 2009: 65).

This is the crucial point to be made about the reach and significance of reputational risk in the management of universities. While we have become accustomed to the nature and consequences of the threats to the freedom of the university posed by New Public Management, academic audit and changing power relations between academics and administrators, the university has struggled to isolate them from each other, and keep them loosely rather than tightly coupled. The difference, and the source of the danger to academic freedom represented by reputational risk, is that it is not confined to particular domains, or even the relationships between them, but pervades the institution, since it is difficult, if not impossible, to insulate shortcomings in one area from all other areas of activity. This represents a particular threat to the 'traditional' conception of the university, which is based on the idea, and even the necessity of loose coupling, or the mutual insulation of its different elements in order for it to flourish in the ways and in the directions which it has been able to do. The most significant consequence of these is that some degree of loose coupling is essential for the ability to practice academic freedom; the insulation of academic activities from other demands on the university is what above all enables and acts as the basis for academic freedom.

Roger Dale is Professor of Sociology of Education at the University of Bristol. Previous appointments include Professor and Head of School of Education at the University of Auckland (1989–2002), and Lecturer and Senior Lecturer at the U.K. Open University (1970–1989). He was a founding member of the editorial board of the *British Journal of Sociology of Education*, and is cofounder and editor, with Susan Robertson, of *Globalisation, Societies and Education*. In 2014 he was President of the British Association for Comparative and International Education. He has published numerous articles on sociology of education, and most recently was coeditor of *Shaping the Futures of Young Europeans* (2015, Symposium).

Notes

1. This chapter draws on work carried out under the U.K.'s ESRC project, LLAKES (Learning and Life Chances in Knowledge Economies and Societies), project number RES-594-28-0001.
2. As Larry Gerber (2001: 23) put it: 'Because of the uncertainty of their technologies, universities have evolved so that their core activities are only loosely coupled to both their formal structure and their environment. One consequence is that they are less responsive to both administrative and political influence; the trade-off is that their core technologies can continue without disruption'.

References

Becker, H. 1971. 'Footnote', in M. Wax, S. Diamond and F. Gearing (eds), *Anthropological Perspectives on Education*. New York: Basic Books, pp. 3–27.

Brown, P., and M. Calnan. 2009. 'The Risks of Managing Uncertainty: The Limitations of Governance and Choice, and the Potential for Trust', *Social Policy and Society* 9(1): 13–24.

CEC (Commission of the European Communities). 2003. 'Communication from the Commission: The role of universities in the Europe of knowledge', COM (2003) 58, 5 February. Brussels.

———. 2005. 'Communication from the Commission: Mobilising the brainpower of Europe: enabling universities to make their full contribution to the Lisbon Strategy', COM (2005) 152, 14 April. Brussels.

———. 2006. 'Communication from the Commission to the Council and the European Parliament: Delivering on the modernisation agenda for universities: education, research, innovation', COM (2006) 208, 10 May. Brussels.

Dale, R. 2014. 'European Coordination and Globalisation', Working Papers on University Reform no. 22. Copenhagen: Danish School of Education, Aarhus University. Retrieved 10 February 2016 from http://edu.au.dk/fileadmin/edu/Forskning/Working_papers/wp_22_-_final.pdf.

Espeland W., and M. Sauder. 2007. 'Rankings and Reactivity: How Public Measures Recreate Social Worlds', *American Journal of Sociology* 113(1): 1–40.

Gerber, L. 2001. '"Inextricably linked": Shared governance and academic freedom", *Academe* 87(3): 22–24.

Hartmann, E. 2010. 'The United Nations Educational, Scientific and Cultural Organisation: Pawn or Global Player?', *Globalisation, Societies and Education* 8(2): 307–18.

Hazelkorn, E. 2009. 'Rankings and the Battle for World-Class Excellence: Institutional Strategies and Policy Choices', *Higher Education Management and Policy* 21(1): 1–22. Retrieved 12 January 2016 from http://arrow.dit.ie/cgi/viewcontent.cgi?article = 1001&context = cserart.

HEFCE. 2001. 'Risk management: A briefing for governors and senior managers', 24 January. London.

Hood, C., et al.1992. 'Risk Management', in Royal Society Study Groups (ed), *Risk Analysis, Perception and Management*. London: The Royal Society, pp. 135–201.

Huber, C. 2009. 'Risks and Risk-Based Regulation in Higher Education Institutions', *Tertiary Education and Management* 15(2): 83–95.

King, R. 2011.'Governing Knowledge Globally: Science, Structuration and the Open Society', in R. King, S. Marginson and R. Naidoo (eds), *Handbook on Global Higher Education*. Cheltenham: Edward Elgar, pp. 415–37.

Marginson, S. 2008. 'A funny thing happened on the way to the K-economy: The new world order in higher education: research rankings, outcomes measures and institutional classifications', IMHE General Conference, Paris 8–10 September. Paris: OECD.

Moutsios, S. 2012. 'Academic Autonomy and the Bologna Process', Working Papers on University Reform no. 19. Copenhagen: Danish School of Education, Aarhus University. Retrieved 10 February 2016 from http://edu.au.dk/fileadmin/www.dpu.dk/forskningsprogrammer/epoke/WP_19.pdf.

Novoa, A and Yariv-Mashal, T. 2003 'Comparative Research in Education: A mode of governance or a historical journey? *Comparative Education* 39 (4): 423–38.

OECD. 2012. 'Education at a Glance 2012: Highlights'. Paris.

———. 2013. 'Education Indicators in Focus'. Paris.

Olds, K. 2012. 'World University Rankings: Time for a Name Change?', *Global Higher Ed* 8 November. Retrieved 10 February 2016 from https://globalhighered.wordpress.com/2012/11/16/world-university-rankings-time-for-a-name-change/.

Power, M. 2004. *The Risk Management of Everything*. London: Demos.

Power, M., et al. 2009. 'Reputational Risk as a Logic of Organizing in Late Modernity', *Organization Studies* 30(2–3): 301–24.

Robertson, S.L., and K. Olds. 2010. 'Explaining the Globalisation of University World Rankings: Projects, Programmes and Social Transformations', *Revue internationale de Sevres* (Special Issue on 'League Tables and Rankings in Education') 54: 105–16.

Salmi, J., and A. Saroyan. 2007. 'League Tables as Policy Instruments: Uses and Misuses', *Higher Education Management and Policy* 19(2): 31–68.

Santos, B. de Sousa. 2004. *Towards a New Legal Common Sense*. London: Butterworth.
Sauder, M., and W. Espeland. 2009. 'The Discipline of Rankings: Tight Coupling and Organizational Change', *American Sociological Review* 74(1): 63–82.
Weber, M. 1978. 'The Development of Bureaucracy and its Relation to the Law', in W. Runciman (ed.) *Weber: Selections in Translation*. Cambridge: Cambridge University Press, pp. 341–56.
Weick, K.E. 1976. 'Educational Organizations as Loosely Coupled Systems', *Administrative Science Quarterly*, 1–19.

CHAPTER 9
The Rise and Rise of the Performance-Based Research Fund?

BRUCE CURTIS

◆◆◆

Introduction

In 2003 the New Zealand Government introduced a metric for assessing and grading the research outputs of individual academics, and of their departments and institutions. This metric is part of the Performance-Based Research Fund (PBRF). The PBRF is one of a family of such assessment systems used globally. The PBRF is an approximation of the Research Assessment Exercise (RAE) from the United Kingdom (Robertson 2010: 194; Wright et al. 2014). Furthermore, it is not alone in sharing this family resemblance to neoliberal drivers of change in higher education, all of which prioritize global research outputs; the RAE of Hong Kong (Chan 2007), the Australia's Research Quality Framework (RQF) and Excellence in Research for Australia (ERA), and the Netherlands' Research Embedment and Performance Profile (REPP) are also related, and all use mixed methods to evaluate research quality (Grant et al. 2010). In common with other such systems, the PBRF is used by Government to allocate funding between universities and other institutions of higher education (although the universities secure the vast bulk) and this is a major reason why it is taken so seriously by university managers and academics. PBRF research evaluations were undertaken in 2003, 2006 and 2012 (Tertiary Education Commission 2004; 2007; 2013a) and discussions are underway between the Tertiary Education Commission (TEC) and the higher education sector for a fourth round in 2018 (Tertiary Education Commission 2014b). This chapter explores the intended and unintended consequences that the PBRF has generated for academics, university managers, and policymakers.

The PBRF research evaluation involves three components, which are combined to determine funding to participating tertiary education organizations (TEOs): the Quality Evaluation, resulting in institutional or average quality scores (AQS); Research Degree Completions; and External Research Income. The Quality Evaluations involve very significant peer reviews to produce a quality score for each individual academic and a Quality Evaluation that is the average of all the individual quality scores achieved by eligible staff at each tertiary education organization. The research outputs and activities of individual staff were rated by multidisciplinary peer review panels (twelve panels) which gave ratings across forty-two subject areas. Research-active staff were rated A, B, C or R (A = 5; B = 3; C = 1; research-inactive staff were rated R, or 0). The numerical values associated with the ratings form the numerator in calculations of average quality scores for institutions. As a result, research-inactive staff accrue no funding for their tertiary education organization (TEO). The denominator for the institutional scores is the number of qualified staff at each organization considered eligible by the Tertiary Education Commission. The Quality Evaluation was compulsory for all eligible staff employed at universities (and other tertiary education organizations of higher education) that sought funding under the PBRF. The other two components of the PBRF are Research Degree Completions (RDC); and External Research Income (ERI). These are updated annually by institutional reporting to the Tertiary Education Commission. In 2003, 2006 and 2012 the Quality Evaluation contributed 60 percent of total funding to tertiary education organizations, Research Degree Completions contributed 25 percent of total funding, and External Research income gained 15 percent of total funding. In 2013, Cabinet announced a rejigging for the 2018 evaluation wherein the Quality Evaluation would be reduced to 55 percent of total funding and External Research Income would rise to 20 percent of total funding (Office of the Minister for Tertiary Education, Skills and Employment, Cabinet Social Policy Committee 2013).

The PBRF has stimulated a range of responses from the higher education sector and, in turn, counter-responses from the Tertiary Education Commission, which was established by Government to administer the fund. My focus is the universities. Thus, the PBRF has been understood from the outset as a driver for change in higher education, which extended neoliberal policies that favoured market-like solutions (Curtis and Matthewman 2005; Roberts 2007; 2009; Smith and Jesson 2005). It undoubtedly remains a neoliberal driver for change, although as discussed below, the goals and means of desired transformation have slipped somewhat (see Duncan 2007; Shore and Taitz 2013). If nothing else, there is a clear change in language of the respective Ministers for Tertiary Education between the first and the most recent evaluations. Their framing of the research evaluation moves from the arms-length, technocratic (Roberts 2013) and knowledge-focused to the blunt and purportedly business-like:

> A dynamic, knowledge society requires the active creation, application and dissemination of new knowledge, together with a constant quest for greater understanding – in all areas of human endeavour. New Zealand's tertiary education organisations play a vital role in this process. Not only do they contain within their ranks a high proportion of the country's leading researchers and scholars, but they also serve as the primary vehicles for advanced learning and research training. It is crucial that their research activities are properly funded and that the research they produce is of the highest possible quality (Hon Steve Maharey, in Tertiary Education Commission 2004: vii).

> Innovation and skills are at the forefront of the Government's Business Growth Agenda. The Government is working to ensure New Zealand has the infrastructure, skills, and system to support faster economic growth – and research and innovation are key to this (Hon Steven Joyce, in Tertiary Education Commission 2013a: 4).

Steven Joyce, Minister for Business, Innovation and Employment as we all as Higher Education, conveys an entrenched anti-intellectualism in New Zealand life, which has been associated with the National Party (Simmons 2007) and expresses a functional view of higher education as a private good. He has signalled a realignment of Government funding so that STEM subjects (science, technology, engineering and mathematics) are likely to receive additional funding.[1] The problem of the PBRF for policymakers, at least, was that in 2003 and 2006 its published results demonstrated the quality of non-STEM subjects. This was corrected by a 'fix' to the published results of the PBRF, which will be discussed below. Regardless, the PBRF has endured (will be repeated in 2018) and seems likely to remain important to universities and academics. The fund provides approximately one fifth of direct and indirect Government funding to universities, and the lead up to and the aftermath of each evaluation round is of central importance to the majority of academics and university managers. What is less clear is how the PBRF will be administered by policymakers with their monomania for STEM subjects and with their dislike of technocratic, arms-length polices like the somewhat contestable PBRF.

Cultural Cringe and Marginalization

This section explores the ways the PBRF metric reifies and quantifies a cultural cringe within academia in New Zealand and in doing so marginalizes local work. Pickles (2011) discusses the common historical cringe of Australia, Canada and New Zealand in terms of a shared inferiority complex in the face of British 'cultural hegemony' (Hume 1991). The term was coined by Phillips in his analysis of the inferiority complex ingrained in Australian literature. It is the belief that 'intellectual standards are set and innovations occur elsewhere' (Head and Walter 1988: viii). Arguably, the critique or acceptance of cultural cringe is related in some way to the ebb and flow of national self-confidence (Curtis 2015).

This cringe is most evident in the Quality Evaluation of the PBRF, which is the most significant component in terms of funding and which is based on a form of peer review. As Adams noted in his analysis of the peer review process in the Quality Evaluations of 2003 and 2006: 'A number of interviewees suggested that a lack of confidence in assuming a judgmental role was attributable to a "colonial cringe factor"' (Adams 2008: 65). I suggest that there is more at play than any individualized hesitancy. Previously I have worked with a number of colleagues on the gendered impacts of the PBRF, by which female academics are disadvantaged (Curtis 2007; 2008; 2015; Curtis and Matthewman 2005; Phibbs and Curtis 2006). In short, female academics are rated significantly lower than male academics under the Quality Evaluation. Here, I also suggest that a broad, structural operationalization of a cultural cringe is inscribed in the PBRF metric.

The most obvious consequence of the PBRF is manifest in the published data of the Tertiary Education Commission (2004; 2007; 2013a) and centres on the comparatively low-quality scores of peer review panels and subject areas in which New Zealand academics and themes predominate (Curtis 2008; 2015). The comparison is with panels and subjects dominated by foreign academics and dealing with international themes. This is at base a product of the PBRF metric for the Quality Evaluation of individual academics' research outputs, in which a very considerable premium is given to those which are considered 'world-class'. In other words, Australasian, national and local research outputs and activities are somewhat discounted in the evaluation (Tertiary Education Commission 2004; 2007; 2013a).

Although contextual and definitional issues around neocolonialism have not, yet, coalesced as a local (New Zealand) body of writing, much of the literature about the reform of higher education in New Zealand points to cringe-worthy anxieties about the sector being world-class: 'It is taken as given that all New Zealanders will embrace the goal of creating an internationally competitive knowledge-based economy' (Roberts 2009: 7). In part this reflects that higher education is now inextricably linked with the export sector, and the need to recruit foreign students is pressing (Lewis 2005). The PBRF is indicative of a nuanced but market-oriented framing of education as an export sector. What is at play in the metric of the PBRF is a 'neoliberalized' cultural cringe wherein research about New Zealand and by New Zealand-trained academics is undervalued in comparison to what is considered international. This fascination with being world-class and its definition aligns with government policy and rhetoric. The Quality Evaluation quantification of cringe was reified and implemented by the New Zealand professoriate who designed the metric, and who are predominantly foreign-trained, internationally focussed and, it must be noted, male (Phibbs and Curtis 2006).

The bias in the metric can be seen by calculating the percentages of New Zealand-trained and foreign-trained academics (determined by origin of their highest degree, drawn from the relevant university calendars) for each of the twelve peer review panels in the Quality Evaluation of 2006. The relationship between quality score and origin of highest degree is shown in Table 9.1. It demonstrates a negative (Pearson's) correlation of minus 0.774, between the quality score for PBRF peer review panels and the percentage of New Zealand-trained academics assessed by those panels.[2] This correlation is significant at the 0.01 level (2-tailed test).

In the main the high scoring subjects have lowest number of New Zealand-trained activities, confirming a cultural cringe. At least two panels somewhat buck the correlation. The first panel is Medicine and Public Health (a panel consisting of Biomedical, Clinical Medicine, and Public Health). This panel has a high quality score despite a high percentage of New Zealand-trained academics. Given this mix of staff it might be considered to be overperforming in comparison to other panels but there are both professional and hierarchy-of-knowledge aspects to consider. The panel incorporates academics primarily qualified as medical practitioners, and doctors in New Zealand remain the most effective grouping in securing traditional forms of professional closure: they fiercely restrict training, certification and practice within their jurisdiction. A likely consequence of this is that New Zealand degrees and training also suffice in local academic contexts, most significantly

Table 9.1. Quality scores of PBRF review panels and the percentage of New Zealand-trained academics from the 2006 Quality Evaluation.

PBRF Review Panel	Quality Score	New Zealand-Trained Academics
Physical Sciences	4.63	35%
Engineering, Technology and Architecture	4.30	37%
Medicine and Public Health	4.07	53%
Biological Sciences	4.05	38%
Humanities and Law	4.02	29%
Mathematical and Information Sciences and Technology	4.01	26%
Social Sciences and Other Cultural/Social Studies	3.82	40%
Creative and Performing Arts	3.45	40%
Business and Economics	3.29	34%
Maori Knowledge and Development	2.67	80%
Health	2.60	54%
Education	2.03	68%

Source: Tertiary Education Commission 2007: 101–84; Haines, pers. com. (recalculated for university-based staff only, by the author).

when it comes to research and publishing in terms of the PBRF. The second panel is Business and Economics and here the dynamic of the labour market is worked through differently. The panel (consisting of Accounting and Finance, Economics, Management, and Marketing and Tourism) seems to be underperforming, given its relatively low percentage of New Zealand-trained academics. This might be the result of faculties or schools of business historically emphasizing high staff / student ratios (bums-on-seats) and externally funded research in the form of consultancies, which generate little by way of peer reviewed research outputs measured in the Quality Evaluations of the PBRF.

The cringe aspect of the Quality Evaluation, insofar as it relates to panels, is probably best regarded as an intended aspect of the PBRF. Certainly it has generated no great outcry from policymakers, Tertiary Education Commission officials or even the professoriate that played a central role in peer review and the awarding of quality scores. In other words, being world-class must have winners and losers and it would be unsurprising, *ceteris paribus*, if foreign-trained (and perhaps better globally connected) academics fared better than their local rivals/colleagues.

A discussion of the quality scores for different subject areas also provides an insight into the PBRF and cringe (see Table 9.2).

Table 9.2. Subject area by quality score (QS) from the 2006 Quality Evaluation.

Subject Area	Quality Score
Philosophy	5.80
Religious Studies and Theology	5.41
Biomedical	4.89
Earth Sciences	4.88
Physics	4.77
Ecology, Evolution and Behaviour	4.62
Pure and Applied Mathematics	4.58
Engineering and Technology	4.56
Anthropology and Archaeology	4.42
Psychology	4.40
Human Geography	4.38
Chemistry	4.35
Music, Literary Arts and Other Arts	4.27
History, History of Art, Classics and Curatorial Studies	4.26
Political Science, International Relations and Public Policy	4.24
English Language and Literature	4.03
Law	4.01
Pharmacy	3.98
Economics	3.93
Molecular, Cellular and Whole Organism Biology	3.92
Computer Science, Information Technology, Information Sciences	3.83
Dentistry	3.81
Statistics	3.81
Public Health	3.66
Clinical Medicine	3.63
Agriculture and Other Applied Biological Sciences	3.62
Marketing and Tourism	3.52
Architecture, Design, Planning, Surveying	3.48
Visual Arts and Crafts	3.44
Veterinary Studies and Large Animal Science	3.40
Management, Human Resources, Industrial Relations & Other Businesses	3.24
Sociology, Social Policy, Social Work, Criminology & Gender Studies	3.16
Foreign Languages and Linguistics	3.03
Accounting and Finance	2.69
Maori Knowledge and Development	2.67
Communications, Journalism and Media Studies	2.49
Theatre and Dance, Film, Television and Multimedia	2.48
Other Health Studies (including Rehabilitation Therapies)	2.43
Sport and Exercise Science	2.21
Design	2.04
Education	2.03
Nursing	1.58

Source: Tertiary Education Commission 2007: 101–84 (recalculated for university-based staff only, by the author).

Table 9.2 shows the distribution of quality scores across the forty-two subject areas to which academics were assigned in the Quality Evaluation. The distribution suggests an inverse relationship between quality score and engagement with local/national issues. Such an inverse relation is most obvious for the extreme results – highest and lowest ranked subject areas. The two top-scoring subject areas from the 2006 Quality Evaluation, philosophy, and religious studies and theology are probably the subject areas least engaged with local/national themes, and certainly among the least contextualized by location. For example, there are no local philosophy journals, nor local philosophizing. Philosophy also benefits from other factors, including relatively high rates of professors, foreign-trained academics, and men in its ranks (Curtis 2008; 2015). While religious studies and theology includes bible studies and training for some local Christian ministries, it excludes the analysis of Maori spirituality (this activity is incorporated into the subject area of Maori knowledge and development). This combination of high scores, low local involvement and high numbers of foreign-trained academics is further confirmation of New Zealand's inferiority cringe.

The other end of the table confirms the pattern. Education (Smith and Jesson 2005) and nursing (Phibbs and Curtis 2006) performed very poorly. Yet these disciplines are putatively among the leaders in addressing and responding to local and New Zealand issues. Similarly, the amalgams management, human resources, industrial relations and other businesses, and sociology, social policy, social work, criminology and gender studies, alongside communications, journalism and media studies, and especially Maori knowledge and development, have an ostensible engagement with New Zealand issues and communities, which seems to be to their detriment in the PBRF. It seems logical that New Zealand would be world-class in the subject area of Maori knowledge and development, if only because indigenous researchers/researchers of indigeneity in New Zealand enjoy something of a global monopoly in this subject. However, the subject area did poorly in all three Quality Evaluations, providing yet more confirmation of an inverse relationship between quality score and engagement with local/national issues.

Gaming Around 'Eligibility' and Its Resolution Post-2012

The research evaluations stimulated forms of gaming by universities in order to maximize their average quality scores and reputational values. Much of this gaming centred on the eligibility of academic staff for the Quality Evaluation. This aspect of the PBRF metric provided opportunities for university gaming while it simultaneously marginalized non-university tertiary education organizations (for example, polytechnics) as valid sites of research.

The PBRF evaluations are voluntary exercises for tertiary education organizations, but any institutions that choose not to participate are excluded from all related funding. For those tertiary education organizations that do participate – including the entire university sector in every round so far – participation across all three aspects of the PBRF (measures of Quality Evaluation, Research Degree Completion and External Research Income) is compulsory. It is compulsory for all 'eligible' staff at participating tertiary education organizations to participate, by preparing an evidence portfolio (EP) that may or may not be submitted by the tertiary education organization to peer review panels. Tertiary education organizations may decide not to submit the evidence portfolio of those they deem research-inactive staff and who would receive a quality score of 'R' (0) in the metric of the Quality Evaluation (and hence attract no PBRF funding).

The number of research-inactive staff at any tertiary education organization has no impact on the amount of funding received by the institution, but in the wake of the 2003 and 2006 rounds it did have a significant impact on the average quality scores of universities, nominated academic units (for example, schools and/or departments) and disciplines. This reflected the fact that average quality scores for any of the above, quite reasonably, reported the average for all eligible staff where all ratings of research activity were included: A(5), B(3), C(1) and R (0). However, when the average quality scores for organizations, or academic units or disciplines were calculated and reported, the denominator became 10 rather than 5. Regardless of the denominator (5 or 10, used for <u>reporting</u>), research-inactive staff scored 0 and reduced averaged quality scores and, arguably, had a negative impact on their tertiary education organization's reputational value.

It is sufficient to say that there was an incentive to game staff eligibility, if only for reasons of reputation and average quality scores. The somewhat convoluted genesis of the PBRF as a contested fund created this possibility (Curtis 2007; 2008). The Performance-Based Research Fund was created by diverting funding to tertiary education organizations that was previously allocated on the basis of graduate teaching. That is, tertiary education organizations were funded by Government for teaching students (on the basis of equivalent full-time students

(EFTS)) and received a top-up for graduate students. The PBRF was created by recategorizing this teaching-based funding and it reflected efforts by the Government of the day to modify a bums-on-seats or EFTS-based model of funding that was arguably undermining research (Curtis 2007). It is moot if the PBRF has actually increased funding to tertiary education organizations overall, although it has probably played a reallocative role.

The eligibility of academic staff for Quality Evaluation remains marked by the teaching basis of Government funding, which in turn reflects longstanding assumptions about the roles of academic staff and higher education. For example, the Education Act (1989) [section 254] included the requirement that a degree 'is taught mainly by people engaged in research'. As a result, the staff eligibility criteria for the initial rounds of the PBRF entailed the assessment of the research activities of staff employed to teach at participating tertiary education organizations. This criterion meant that staff employed on teaching-only contracts, the norm for academic staff at non-university tertiary education organizations, were evaluated for their non-existent, or unpaid, research activities. This definition of eligibility meant that the forty-six non-university tertiary education organizations in the first round of the PBRF averaged a ludicrous AQS (average quality score) of 0.42/10 (the universities' scores ranged from 0.77/10 at a former polytechnic to 3.96/10 at the University of Auckland). Unsurprisingly the eight universities gained 98.38 percent of total PBRF funding and the forty-six non-universities a paltry 1.62 percent (Tertiary Education Commission 2004: 74–81). This pattern of funding and marginalization remained in place in 2006 and 2012 (Tertiary Education Commission 2007; 2013a).

In response to the 2003 Quality Evaluation it now appears obvious that considerable institutional effort went into removing existing R-rated (research-inactive) staff prior to the Quality Evaluation of 2006 (See Table 9.3).

Vance, Alexander and Sandhu (2007) demonstrated the extent to which four of the eight universities (Massey, Otago, Waikato and AUT) gamed the PBRF by removing research-inactive staff from eligibility (it would appear by rewriting their employment contracts). For these universities the benefits accruing from hiring new, research-active staff or through improvements in the quality score of existing staff were swamped by several magnitudes by the benefits of making research-inactive staff ineligible for Quality Evaluation. Indeed, this gaming around eligible academic staff accounted for all the changes in the

Table 9.3. Changes to average quality scores and percentage of eligible staff between the 2003 and 2006 Quality Evaluations.

	Percentage Change to Average Quality Scores	Change to Percentage of Eligible Staff (FTE) (2003% – 2006%)
Auckland University of Technology	241.5%	8 – 5 = 3%
Massey University	40.3%	16 – 14 = 2%
University of Otago	30.9%	16 – 14 = 2%
University of Waikato	25.1%	7 – 6 = 1%
Non-university TEOs	21.1%	15 – 24 = – 9% (increase)
Lincoln University	19.5%	3 – 3 = 0%
Victoria University of Wellington	12.9%	8 – 9 = – 1% (increase)
University of Auckland	5.7%	19 – 18 = 1%
University of Canterbury	7%	8 – 8 = 0%

Source: Tertiary Education Commission 2004: 71–74; 2007: 73.

ranking of average quality scores when the 2006 results are compared to the 2003 results (Curtis 2007). An initial response on the part of the Chief Executive Officer of the Tertiary Education Commission (TEC) to the effect that this simply represented a correction to the census of staff undertaken in the 2003 Quality Evaluation probably only throws doubt on the validity of the initial staff census approved by Tertiary Education Commission (Curtis 2008; Curtis and Matthewman 2005; Web Research 2004).

The changes in the average quality scores between 2003 and 2006 showed that the first movers around gaming accrued significant gains. Anecdotal evidence suggests that the other universities made similar moves to control eligibility after 2006. This sort of gaming resulted in an elaboration by the Tertiary Education Commission of the criteria for eligibility, including, most significantly, the introduction of a 'substantiveness test':

> There are two key principles underpinning the eligibility of a TEO's staff member to participate in the 2012 Quality Evaluation:
> • The individual is expected to contribute to the learning environment at the degree level
> AND/OR
> • The individual is expected to make a sufficiently substantive contribution to research activity (Tertiary Education Commission 2013b: 37).

The Tertiary Education Commission's document went on to stay that it expected ALL academic and research staff who are substantially involved in teaching and/or research to be included in the PBRF research quality assessment, and tertiary education organizations had to justify any exclusions. The document summed it up as follows:

> The audit will look to ensure consistency and fairness, and conformity with the principle that the Quality Evaluation should be inclusive of all those contributing to degree-level teaching and/or research (Tertiary Education Commission 2013b: 37).

With, seemingly, all the university tertiary education organizations gaming eligibility in the lead up to the 2012 round, the Tertiary Education Commission faced something of a conundrum in terms of resourcing the appropriate census of eligible staff. No significant increase in the resourcing of the census was manifested in 2011 and 2012. That is, the reports provided by tertiary education organizations did not appear to be subjected to a more thorough checking by Tertiary Education Commission than in 2003 and 2006. However, following the research evaluation, including of course the Quality Evaluation component, the Tertiary Education Commission announced changes to the reporting of average quality scores:

> The release of the audit report on TEO preparedness to participate in the 2012 Quality Evaluation raised concerns that different human resource practices at TEOs had the potential to impact on the average quality score (AQS) measure. The TEC consulted on potential changes to the calculation of the AQS. The outcome of this consultation was the exclusion of staff whose EP received an unfunded Quality Category ('R' or 'R(NE)') from the calculation of the AQS and the reporting of results. To support this decision, the TEC did not collect information on staff who TEOs identified as PBRF eligible, but who did not submit EPs. For the 2003 and 2006 Quality Evaluations, the Quality Categories assigned to the EPs of these staff were identified as 'R' or 'R(NE)' and these Quality Categories were included in the AQS measures (Tertiary Education Commission 2013a: 20).

The Tertiary Education Commission's solution of excluding research-inactive but eligible academic staff from the calculation of 'institutional' quality scores effectively ended any benefits to tertiary education organizations from gaming eligibility. On the one hand, in 2012, tertiary education organizations did not benefit from rendering research-inactive staff ineligible in order to enhance their average quality score, reputational value, media profile or multiplier effect. On the other hand, tertiary education organizations still have an incentive to include all research-active staff because they are the source of 60 percent (in 2012, and 55 percent in 2018) of funding from the PBRF. At the same time, the Tertiary Education Commission replaced the average quality scores with other measures, which attracted little media attention and frankly provide little analytical worth. The Tertiary Education Commission's decision to discontinue reporting practices that allowed time-series analysis based on published data can be understood as a response to gaming, wherein a lack of transparency on the part of tertiary education organizations has resulted in the ending of transparency in terms of reporting AQS (Curtis 2015).

Some Unintended Results: Mixed Messages and Empowered Academics, Undermining STEM

The metric of the PBRF is primarily the result of discussions between the New Zealand Vice Chancellors' Committee and the Tertiary Education Commission. These discussions are ongoing for the 2018 evaluation round, and include calls for limited input from academics in line with neoliberal understandings of consultation. Widespread dissension from academics seems very unlikely. While the rationale for the PBRF attracted considerable criticism, its practices, especially the peer review associated with the Quality Evaluation, are relatively unproblematic and not substantially different from practices around appointments and promotion in university contexts. Further, peer review provides academics, or the professoriate who are involved, with a sanctioned metric that demonstrates their excellence in determining excellence (and, as noted, operationalizing a cultural cringe).

Correspondingly, the PBRF sends mixed messages to academic management, a consequence of the mixed model of assessment, including peer review (Curtis 2007; 2008; 2015). The results in terms of employment and its conditions have been relatively conservative: this is because of the diversity of the metric and the resulting diversity of dimensions across which staff performance might be managed. It is also because of the conflicting aspects of these dimensions over and above a simple intensification of labour (for example, should academics do more publishing, applying for research grants, supervising and lecturing?). Indeed, the Quality Evaluation has arguably reified academics as professionals who balance contesting demands, and are essentially the best arbiters of quality. In this sense, the PBRF has not directly fostered a neoliberal agenda in restructuring academic life, or at least not without unforeseen limits.

These limits to the PBRF as a neoliberal driver have not gone unnoticed by both policymakers and university management. Further, the published results of the PBRF rounds in 2003 and 2006 stand at odds with present political claims that increased funding of STEM subjects can and should be justified in terms of excellence. The success of the subject areas of philosophy, and religious studies and theology, are obviously spoilers to this discourse (see Table 9.2).

The response of (Labour) Cabinet ministers to the first research evaluation (2003) was decidedly mixed. On the one hand, the Honourable Steve Maharey was enthusiastic about the world-class character of tertiary education organizations (Hon Steve Maharey, in Tertiary Education Commission 2004: vii–viii). On the other hand, Michael Cullen, the Minister of Finance in 2003 (and subsequent Minister of Education) was forced to admit that the wrong subject areas had done well in the Quality Evaluation. Cullen's statement can be seen as an early signal of a policy preference for STEM subjects:

> The recent analysis for the Performance-Based Research Fund showed that New Zealand academics are world-class in areas such as philosophy and criminology [sic]; but we need to ensure that we are world-class in biotechnology and the other disciplines that, in the medium to long-term, will pay the bills. It is time to shift the balance of our tertiary system towards more of an explicit industry-led approach (Cullen 2004).[3]

The decision by the Tertiary Education Commission not to publish the average quality scores that included research-inactive staff, to prevent gaming around eligibility, had the very beneficial result for policymakers and champions of STEM of reordering the quality scores for the forty-two subject areas. Most significantly, philosophy dropped from first ranked to fourth, and religious studies and theology fell from second ranked to twenty-first. Pure and applied mathematics (when shed of its research-inactive staff) rose to first place. Table 9.4 shows the effect of excluding research-inactive staff from the calculations by comparing the ten top-ranked subject areas from 2006 and 2012.

The decision by the Tertiary Education Commission to change this reporting of average quality scores highlights the unchallenged power of the administrative fix and the resulting longevity of the PBRF. The move ended gaming by tertiary education organizations and removed philosophy, and religious studies and theology from the top-two ranked

Table 9.4. Ten top subject areas from the 2006 and 2012 Quality Evaluations.

From the 2006 Quality Evaluation	From the 2012 Quality Evaluation
Philosophy	Pure and Applied Mathematics
Religious Studies and Theology	Human Geography
Biomedical	Physics
Earth Sciences	Philosophy
Physics	Psychology
Ecology, Evolution and Behaviour	Ecology, Evolution and Behaviour
Pure and Applied Mathematics	Law
Engineering and Technology	Anthropology and Archaeology
Anthropology and Archaeology	Pharmacy
Psychology	Clinical Medicine

Source: Tertiary Education Commission 2007; 2013a.

subject areas. The idea that the wrong subject areas topped the rankings, reflected the increasing centrality of STEM subjects and is likely to be more fully resolved in a similar manner in future. That is, the PBRF metric already involves a 'subject-area weighting' that somewhat limits the wrong subject areas from being funded on the basis of research quality. This somewhat obscures the origins of 'subject-area weightings' as rough measures of the cost of teaching in different subject areas. As a result, not all quality scores (rated A, B, C(NE) or C) are equal in terms of funding to tertiary education organizations, because the scores achieved by individual staff (5, 3, 2 and 1) are multiplied by the subject-area weighting (of which there are three bands or ratios of funding: 1, 2 and 2.5) (see Table 9.5).

The funding accruing to an individual staff member is calculated by multiplying the individual quality score by the subject-area weighting. An almost unacknowledged aspect of the PBRF is therefore that an assessment based on the Quality Evaluation of the research of individual staff is modified by an estimate of the cost of teaching in the individual staff member's subject area. Staff are assigned to subject areas by their tertiary education organizations and supposedly verified/ audited by the Tertiary Education Commission (another fascinating realm of gaming could be explored in this respect). Table 9.5 shows that the STEM subject areas (with the exception of mathematics and statistics) are located in the higher weighted categories. In this respect the PBRF is already channelling funding towards STEM subject areas and away from those which raised the ire of the Minister of Finance more than a decade ago (Cullen 2004). Shifting the subject-area weightings to further attenuate funding to low-banded subjects seems an obvious

Table 9.5. Subject-area weightings.

Subject area	Weighting
Māori knowledge and development; law; history, history of art, classics and curatorial studies; English language and literature; foreign languages and linguistics; philosophy; religious studies and theology; political science, international relations and public policy; human geography; sociology, social policy, social work, criminology and gender studies; anthropology and archaeology; communications, journalism and media studies; education; pure and applied mathematics; statistics; management, human resources, industrial relations, international business and other business; accounting and finance; marketing and tourism; and economics.	1
Psychology; chemistry; physics; earth sciences; molecular, cellular and whole organism biology; ecology, evolution and behaviour; computer science, information technology, information sciences; nursing; sport and exercise science; other health studies (including rehabilitation therapies); music, literary arts and other arts; visual arts and crafts; theatre and dance, film and television and multimedia; and design.	2
Engineering and technology; agriculture and other applied biological sciences; architecture, planning, surveying; biomedical; clinical medicine; pharmacy; public health; veterinary studies and large animal science; and dentistry.	2.5

Source: Tertiary Education Commission 2014a: 8

administrative fix for the protagonists of STEM (because STEM subjects tend to have higher teaching costs). Such a shift in funding based on the costs of teaching might even involve a recategorization of favoured subjects. To speculate just a little; if the costs of teaching mathematics/statistics were decided to be less like those associated with teaching philosophy (as is currently the case) and more like those associated with teaching information sciences, then the STEM subject would gain a 50 percent fillip in funding. Such refinements of the subject-area weightings would certainly align the PBRF metric more closely with the intended outcomes of higher education policies and in that respect at least would make the fund an even more effective neoliberal driver.

Conclusion

Between research evaluations, the Tertiary Education Commission has commissioned a substantial number of reports into the rigour of the PBRF (a small minority of which are referenced below). These reports and other forms of consultation have all tended to confirm, and even celebrate, the rigour of the metric and its implementation. There have been a number of incremental changes in the form of administrative fixes since the first round in 2003, including the creation in 2006 of categories for new staff otherwise rated as C or R(R(NE)) and C(NE)) and, from 2006, increasing the funding accruing to newly employed C(NE)-rated staff. In addition, funding and oversight for the Maori Knowledge and Development panel was enhanced in 2012 and the weighting of the three components for funding were rejigged for the 2018 round. These fixes have gone unchallenged by academics.

The PBRF creates categories of academics, subject areas and institutions in the very process of rigorous measurement (Middleton 2009). This fundamental insight, about discourse and performativity, is implicated in much of scholarly, as opposed to any popular, response. Indeed something of an academic cottage industry has developed around the PBRF, and reifies its 'rise and rise' and its persistence as a neoliberal driver. These are typically accounts of loss. For example, critiquing the discourse of the PBRF for marginalizing aspects of academic life has proliferated in the subject areas of accounting research (Mathews and Sangster 2009), computing (Clear 2011), education (Smith and Jesson 2005), Maori research (Roa et al. 2009), nursing (Phibbs and Curtis 2006), physical education (Pope 2014). Only the top-ten rated subject area of human geography (see Table 9.4) has generated an account of the PBRF that stresses success (Cupples and Pawson 2012).

◆

Bruce Curtis (Ph.D. in sociology, University of Canterbury) teaches sociology at the University of Auckland. He is interested in the study of New Zealand as a neocolony, and of the developments in Late Capitalism that are reworking the international order. He is interested in Marxism as a materialist methodology and the problems this poses for researchers confronted with bourgeois/nominal datasets.

Notes

1. Joyce, S. 2012. 'National Party Conference Speech – Tertiary Education', 29 April 2012. Retrieved 31 December 2014 from http://stevenjoyce.co.nz/index.php?/archives/30-National-Party-Conference-Speech-Tertiary-Education.html.
2. The tables presented in the balance of this chapter are drawn from the Quality Evaluations of 2006 and in some cases 2003. This reflects very significant

changes in the reporting of average quality scores in the wake of the 2012 research evaluation; most notably the difference between AQS (2003 and 2006) and AQS(N) (2012).
3. Cullen, M. 2004. Speech to Hamilton Club ABN AMRO Craig's Economic Breakfast Briefing: NZ's Path to Growth, Hamilton Club, Hamilton, 15 July.

References

Adams, J. 2008. *Strategic Review of the Performance-Based Research Fund: The Assessment Process*. Leeds: Evidence Limited.

Chan, D.K.K. 2007. 'Global Agenda, Local Responses: Changing Education Governance in Hong Kong's Higher Education', *Globalisation, Societies and Education* 5(1): 109–24.

Clear, A. 2011. 'The Fate of Computing in Research Performance Evaluations: ERA vs PBRF', in S. Mann and S. Verhaart (eds), *2nd Annual Conference of Computing and Information Technology Research and Education New Zealand (CITRENZ2011) Incorporating the 24th Annual Conference of the National Advisory Committee on Computing Qualifications*, 6 July 2011. Retrieved 31 December 2014 from http://aut.researchgateway.ac.nz/bitstream/handle/10292/3520/51-62.pdf?sequence=2.

Cupples, J., and E. Pawson. 2012. 'Giving an Account of Oneself: The PBRF and the Neoliberal University', *New Zealand Geographer* 68: 14–23.

Curtis, B. 2007. 'Academic Life: Commodification, Continuity, Collegiality, Confusion and the Performance-Based Research Fund', *New Zealand Journal of Employment Relations* 33(2): 1–16.

_____. 2008. 'The Performance-Based Research Fund: Research Assessment and Funding in New Zealand', *Globalisation, Societies and Education* 6(2): 179–94.

_____. 2015. 'The Performance-Based Research Fund, Gender and a Cultural Cringe', *Globalisation, Societies and Education*, 14(1): DOI: 10.1080/14767724.2014.996856.

Curtis, B., and S. Matthewman. 2005. 'The Managed University: The PBRF, its Impacts and Staff Attitudes (in the Humanities and Social Sciences)', *New Zealand Journal of Employment Relations* 30(2): 1–18.

Education Act, New Zealand Statutes. 1989.

Duncan, G. 2007. *What's Wrong with the PBRF?* Retrieved 31 December 2014 from http://grantduncan.blogspot.co.nz/2007/08/whats-wrong-with-pbrf.html.

Grant, J., et al. 2010. *Capturing Research Impacts: A Review of International Practice*. Santa Monica: RAND Corporation.

Head, B., and J. Walter (eds). 1988. *Intellectual Movements and Australian Society*. Melbourne: Oxford University Press.

Hume, L.J. 1991. 'Another Look at Cultural Cringe', *Political Theory Newsletter* 3: 1–36.

Lewis, N. 2005. 'Code of Practice for the Pastoral Care of International Students: Making a Global Industry in New Zealand', *Globalisation, Societies and Education* 3(1): 5–47.

Mathews, M., and A. Sangster. 2009. 'Exporting the RAE: Adoption of Similar Practices in Australia and New Zealand', *Asian Review of Accounting* 17(2): 115–35.

Middleton, S. 2009. 'Becoming PBRF-able: Research Assessment and Education in New Zealand', in T. Besley, (ed.). *Assessing the Quality of Educational Research in Higher Education – International Perspectives*. Rotterdam: Sense Publishers, pp. 193–208.

Office of the Minister for Tertiary Education, Skills and Employment, Cabinet Social Policy Committee. 2013. 'Improving the Efficiency and Effectiveness of the Performance-Based Research Fund'. Retrieved 12 October 2016 from http://www.education.govt.nz/assets/Documents/Further-education/Policies-and-strategies/Performance-based-research-fund/PBRFCabinetPaper.pdf .

Phibbs, S., and B. Curtis. 2006. 'Gender, Nursing and the PBRF', *Nursing Praxis* 22(2): 4–12.

Pickles, K. 2011. 'Transnational History and Cultural Cringe: Some Issues for Consideration in New Zealand, Australia and Canada', *History Compass* 9(9): 657–73.

Pope, C.C. 2014. 'The Jagged Edge and the Changing Shape of Health and Physical Education in Aotearoa New Zealand', *Physical Education and Sport Pedagogy* 19(5): 500–11.

Roa, T., et al. 2009. 'New Zealand's Performance Based Research Funding (PBRF) model undermines Maori research', *Journal of the Royal Society of New Zealand* 39(4): 233–38.

Roberts, P. 2007. 'Neoliberalism, Performativity and Research', *Review of Education* 53(4): 349–65.

_____. 2009. 'A New Patriotism? Neoliberalism, Citizenship and Tertiary Education in New Zealand', *Educational Philosophy and Theory* 41(4): 410–23.

_____. 2013. 'Academic Dystopia: Knowledge, Performativity and Tertiary Education', *Review of Education, Pedagogy, and Cultural Studies* 35(1): 27–43.

Robertson, S.L. 2010. 'Corporatisation, competitiveness, commercialisation: new logics in the globalising of UK higher education', *Globalisation, Societies and Education* 8(2): 191–203.

Shore, C., and M. Taitz. 2013. 'Who "Owns" the University? Institutional Autonomy and Academic Freedom in an Age of Knowledge Capitalism', *Globalisation, Societies and Education* 10(2): 201–19.

Simmons, L. (ed.). 2007. *Speaking Truth to Power: Public Intellectuals Rethink New Zealand*. Auckland: Auckland University Press.

Smith, R., and J. Jesson (eds). 2005. *Punishing the Discipline – The PBRF Regime: Evaluating the Position of Education – Where to From Here?* Auckland: Auckland University of Technology.

Tertiary Education Commission. 2004. 'Performance-Based Research Fund, Evaluating Excellence: The 2003 Assessment'. Wellington.

_____. 2007. 'Performance-Based Research Fund, Evaluating Excellence: The 2006 Assessment', Wellington.

_____. 2013a. 'Performance-Based Research Fund, Evaluating Excellence: The 2012 Assessment', Wellington.
_____. 2013b. 'Performance-Based Research Fund Quality Evaluation Guidelines 2012', Wellington.
_____. 2014a. 'Performance-Based Research Fund User Manual Version 3', Wellington.
_____. 2014b. 'Sector Reference Group – Consultation Paper #1: Approach to the Design of the 2018 Quality Evaluation', Wellington.
Vance, P., S. Alexander and A. Sandhu. 2007. 'Phase Two PBRF Evaluation – Context for the Analysis of Data in Evidence Portfolios', Wellington.
Web Research. 2004. 'Phase I Evaluation of the Implementation of the PBRF and the Conduct of the 2003 Quality Evaluation', Wellington: Centre for Research on Work, Education and Business Ltd.
Wright, S., et al. 2014. 'Research Assessment Systems and their Impacts on Academic Work in New Zealand, the UK and Denmark', Summative Working Paper for URGE Work Package 5, Working Papers in University Reform no 24. Retrieved 10 February 2016 from http://edu.au.dk/fileadmin/edu/Forskning/URGE/WP_24.pdf.

CHAPTER 10
Evaluating Academic Research
Ambivalence, Anxiety and Audit in the Risk University

LISA LUCAS

♦♦♦

Introduction

Risk is an increasingly important idea in contemporary societies and is often associated with increasing individualization, ambivalence and anxiety as individuals try to make sense of ever-more complex and risky environments (Beck 1993; 2009; Lash, Giddens and Beck 1994). According to Beck (2009), we live in a 'risk society' and this also creates risk organizations, including the 'risk university' (Huber and Rothstein 2013). The 'risk university' can be framed predominantly around the idea of 'reputational risk', which is an all-encompassing idea that creates the need for complex systems of auditing and control to protect an institution's reputation (Power et al. 2009). Universities struggle to protect their 'reputational risk' amidst a plethora of national and global rankings (see Dale this volume) and this tension influences both the organizations' structures and the auditing mechanisms they use to evaluate the work of academics. This has resulted in what could be seen as a frenzy of audit practices. In the U.K., the Research Assessment Exercise (RAE), now Research Excellence Framework (REF), has been particularly important as a mechanism for auditing and evaluating research at a national level. While there are multiple influences on structuring and decision making within academic work, in the U.K. the RAE/REF have acquired particular prominence.

In their research on audit and ranking systems in countries in Northern Europe, Berg, Huijbens and Larsen argue that, 'neoliberalism in the academy is part of a wider system of anxiety production arising as part of the so-called "soft governance" of everything, including life itself' (forthcoming: 1). Furthermore, Gill and Donaghue (2015) argue that there has been a psychosocial and somatic catastrophe amongst academics that manifests in chronic stress and anxiety representing the 'hidden injuries of the neoliberal university' (Gill 2010).

This analysis chimes with my own work looking at the effects and influences of the various U.K. research assessment exercises since the 1980s (Lucas 2006; 2009; 2014) and the kinds of anxieties talked about by academics in their concerns to be included and considered successful in successive RAE/REF exercises. As the ubiquitous nature of these forms of national performance-based research evaluations becomes clearer, it is important to look at how these systems of evaluation are influencing academic knowledge production and academic work. The anxiety reported in studies of academics' experiences, may relate to their positioning within this complex, uncertain and risky environment, where they struggle to reflexively mediate a meaningful and successful career.

The Normalizing Practice of Research Evaluation and Its Impacts

The U.K. research assessment exercise (RAE, now Research Excellence Framework, or REF) was established in 1986 and has gone through many changes, with successive exercises conducted in 1992, 1996, 2001, 2008 and 2014. It is a national system of university research evaluation that is conducted through a process of peer review with specialist panels evaluating the research work of all universities in the U.K. In the REF2014, grading is awarded from the lowest ranking of one-star through to two-star, three-star and the highest ranking of four-star. A four-star grading corresponds to research work which is seen as 'world leading'. The result of each successive RAE/REF determines the amount of research funding that is distributed to U.K. universities via the Higher Education Funding Councils (for England, Scotland, Wales and Northern Ireland). The U.K. was an early adopter of this type of national system, though several countries with historical ties to the U.K. have also introduced such exercises though with some significant differences in terms of content, process and outcome, including Hong Kong, New Zealand and Australia. Such systems have also been expanding across Europe including, Spain, Italy, Denmark, Portugal and Finland (Lucas 2006; 2016).

In my earlier work (Lucas 2006) I found there had been an intensification of the management and organization of research activities within universities in response to successive RAEs. This empirical analysis of U.K. universities showed how all aspects of the research environment, research leadership, research strategy and research culture, including the socialization of academic staff, were formed in order to meet the mission of departments to increase research activities, and predominantly research that would be highly ranked in the RAE (Lucas 2009). These forms of 'new managerialism' involved manipulating staff workloads and also auditing staff outputs and achievements to determine whether they were eligible for submission to the RAE and hence considered 'research active' or 'research inactive'. Being ineligible for submission to the RAE – and hence potentially being labelled as 'research inactive' – can have extremely negative consequences for academic staff and their careers, either in terms of redundancy or being moved to a 'teaching only' contract (Lucas 2006).

Nonsubmission of staff was an important issue in the last REF2014 as the number of staff submitted apparently dropped. This was seen to be partly influenced by the decision to further concentrate resources and remove funding for two-star (classified as nationally excellent) and fund only three-star and four-star research (classified as internationally excellent and world leading). Despite encouraging an inclusive approach, the rules set down by the Higher Education Funding Council for England (HEFCE) in relation to (1) not funding two-star outputs and (2) linking the number of impact case studies required to the number of staff submitted, served to encourage institutions to be more strategic in their selectivity of staff. Figures from HEFCE show that there was a small drop in submission numbers, with 52,077 academic staff submitted to REF2014 compared to 52,401 submitted to RAE2008. The largest drop in submission numbers (5 per cent) was found in the humanities (Jump 2014). However, there are significant differences in the number of staff submitted to the REF2014 as a percentage of those eligible to be submitted. So, for example, the percentage of staff submitted ranges from the lowest at 27 percent (education) and 33 percent (allied health) to the highest at 94 percent (history) and 89 percent (philosophy) and a mixed range of 51 percent (law), 67 percent (biological sciences) and 73 percent (political studies). In looking at the education unit of assessment in more detail, there were fifteen fewer institutional submissions for education to REF2014 compared with REF2008 (though there were also nine new submissions). There were twenty-three out of seventy-six (almost one third of submissions) with less than 20 percent of eligible staff submitted (Lucas 2015). However, this data does need to be interpreted with some caution, as the means of calculating 'eligible staff' using available HESA data is not without complications and potential errors (Jump 2015a). It is a complex picture overall but there is certainly concern about the approach taken by universities in the REF2014 submissions and the potential human costs in terms of career and professional esteem for those not submitted in universities where a less inclusive approach was taken (Lucas 2006). Although the potential negative impact on academic career is dismissed by some university leaders (Jump 2015b), this concern with the costs to academics' careers and professional identity is at the heart of Sayer's (2015) insistence that the REF is a flawed and damaging system for judging and rewarding research excellence.

Much of the research evidence produced has been scathing of the impact on academic work and the sense of identity in the new managerialist and audit cultures engendered by the RAE and REF2014 (Harley 2002; Loftus 2006; Shore and Wright 1999; Sparkes 2007). Loftus (2006) has argued that there has been a process of 'RAE-ification' and that the consciousness of the academic has been changed such that 'we have built ourselves into the body-walls of the system that now encloses us' (Loftus 2006: 111). What this means is that academic researchers and the production of research knowledge have been moulded in order to fit the demands of audit regimes such as the RAE/REF. One concern is that researchers, in their endeavour to meet the requirements of the evaluation exercise, might change their research areas or approach to those they perceive to be valued by an assessment panel. Some argue that researchers may be more likely to work within mainstream areas of research as these are perceived to be safer options than working at the margins, which may not be viewed positively by a panel and/or may result in them being unable to publish in the most prestigious journals (Lee 2007). Others argue that there is a potential rush to mediocrity as a result of researchers choosing to do less risky research, which they hope will guarantee them timely results that can be published in prestigious outlets. There is also an argument that applied research is less valued than 'blue skies' or basic research and this is particularly important in professional subjects such as education (McNay 2003). In short, the potential for distortion of research is high.

Other distorting factors include the intensification of academic working environments and the valuing of research activities over all other forms of academic work (Sikes 2006). Leathwood and Read's study (2013) found that gender differences of workload pressures and time constraints were still evident, with women participants reporting less time for research due to increased workloads in relation to teaching and administration (see also Blackmore this volume). Some respondents were considering leaving academia or considering volunteering for teaching-only contracts. However, not all saw the RAE/REF as wholly negative. Some reported that they could now have their research efforts taken seriously within their departments and that the RAE/REF allowed them to have a more successful research career (Leathwood and Read 2013; Lucas 2006; 2009). This could perhaps reflect the different experiences of those who are considered 'research active', whose research is valued, and those who are not. This is also supported by more recent literature highlighting the potential positive influence as individual academics who-appropriate these processes as a way of reinvigorating academic subjectivities (Cupples and Pawson 2012). However, the overwhelming conclusion from Leathwood and Read's (2013) study is that despite gains for some, there remains substantial inequity in the system. Furthermore, there is significant evidence that the neoliberal process of auditing and control creates risk and anxiety for academics (Berg, Huijbens and Larsen forthcoming; Gill and Donaghue 2015). In what follows, I explore this idea of risk more thoroughly and then use it to explore the experiences of academics in U.K. universities in what has been described as the rise of the 'schizophrenic university' (Shore 2010).

Theorizing Risk in the Academy

A key premise underpinning the theories of risk is the 'disintegration of certainties' in modern societies and the compulsion to makes one's own life and construct a biography that is 'self rather than socially produced' (Lupton 1999: 73). Increased individualization within society is emphasized and greater importance is placed on individual agency and responsibility. Theorists recognize that such agency may be differentially distributed in a very unequal social world and that the ability to play a role in creating one's biography is more likely a preserve of the privileged. However, far from being necessarily a greater freedom, this potential for increased agency can result in heightened forms of anxiety:

> Risk society is thus characterized by the contradiction that the privileged have greater access to knowledge, but not enough, so that they become anxious without being able to reconcile or act upon that anxiety (Lupton 1999: 71).

Reflexivity is central to how individuals are considered to act upon and exert their agency in weighing up courses of action to construct their life course and, crucially, to ameliorate the possibilities of risk:

> Because the self is seen as a reflexive project in late modernity, as a problematic rather than a given, there is far more emphasis on the malleability of the self and the responsibility that one takes for one's life trajectory ... As knowledge is being constantly revised in late modernity, the process of reflexivity is more complicated and uncertain. There are choices to be made: the self, like the broader institutional contexts in which it exists, has to be reflexively made. Yet this task has to be accomplished amid a puzzling diversity of options and possibilities (ibid.: 79).

While individuals may be compelled to make decisions in constructing their life course, they do not do so in conditions of their own choosing. Many critiques argue for the continuing significance of structural determinants like class, gender and race in determining life chances. However, where the need for the reflexive project is accepted, this is arguably enacted amidst complex, ambivalent and often contradictory conditions. The work of Lash (1993) in particular emphasizes the contradictions, uncertainty and ambivalence that the reflexive self has to navigate. This uncertainty and precarity is also highlighted by Lupton (1999);

> People often feel, however, that knowledge about risks, including their own, are so precarious and contingent that they simply do not know what course of action to take. As a result they may move between different risk positions at different times, sometimes attempting to control risk, at other times preferring a fatalistic approach that simply accepts the possibility of risk without attempting to avoid it (Lupton 1999: 122).

The idea of compulsive self-reflexivity and attempts to monitor actions can be at odds with the contingencies, ambivalences and contradictions of social life. This can make calculating risk impossible or encourage what Giddens, Beck and Lash (1994) call a 'pragmatic acceptance' of circumstances in order to avoid potentially debilitating anxiety'.

All areas of social life are potentially constructed around the idea of the 'risk society' and this can be analysed at the global, national, regional, organizational and individual level. My interest in this chapter is in the university and academics working within it. In recent years, the discourse around risk in universities has increased and governing bodies such as HEFCE have encouraged – and in some instances even mandated – universities to introduce processes of risk management (HEFCE 2001; 2002; 2006). The use of risk management strategies has arguably been embraced and it has been seen as a 'key component in university reform, refashioning universities as rational and efficient entrepreneurial actors' (Huber and Rothstein 2013: 659). The potentially all-encompassing term 'reputational risk' is therefore utilized to increase the forms of audit and accountability across all areas of universities and, not least, to increase the attention paid to league tables and all forms of evaluation of research and teaching (Hardy 2015; Power et al. 2009). As Huber and Rothstein (2013) emphasise;

> In the risk organisation, those rationalisations reach deep down into organisational life, reframing both the negative externalities and internalities of ever fine-grained levels of organisational decision-making activities and practices in terms of calculated gambles across ever more diverse areas of organisational practice. As such, risk management represents a new organisational ideology that provides a formal methodological means of rationalizing the idea of failure in institutional environments of heightened accountability (Huber and Rothstein 2013: 671).

This idea of the 'risk organization', or 'risk university', demonstrates how individuals at all levels can be held accountable for institutional failure through new systems of external scrutiny and internal control. The individualization of risk management is spread throughout the organization. In universities, for example, individuals are held accountable by their success or failure to contribute to the REF. But what of academic subjective experiences of engaging in the REF process and how might this be understood in relation to conceptualizations of risk? These questions are explored in the next section through the experiences of a sample of academics working in U.K. universities.

Methodology

This chapter utilizes interviews with U.K. academics, following a survey of academics in research-intensive environments in six Australian and six English universities (Brew and Boud 2009; Brew, Boud and Namgung 2011; Brew et al. 2015). The study explored how academics make sense of the competing pressures of teaching, research and administration and their experiences of academic work. Semi-structured interviews with twenty-seven mid-career academics were conducted. Purposive sampling from those who indicated on the survey a willingness to be interviewed was used to select thosewith five to ten years' experience

Table 10.1. Profile of Interviewees.

Pseudonym	Higher Education Institution	Discipline	Discipline cluster	Gender	Job title
Antonio	De	Chemical engineering	S&E	Male	Lecturer
Arjen	Be	Physics	S&E	Male	Senior Lecturer
Brett	De	International security	SS	Male	Professor
Carlos	Ge	Computer science	S&E	Male	Senior Lecturer
Emily	Be	Law	A&H	Female	Senior Lecturer
Geert	Ge	Economics	SS	Male	Reader
Gregorio	Ce	Analytical chemistry	S&E	Male	Reader
Jane	Fe	Criminology	SS	Female	Senior Lecturer
Katie	Fe	Law	A&H	Female	Senior Lecturer
Natalie	Ce	Life sciences	S&E	Female	Senior Lecturer
Rosemary	Ce	Health and social care	Health Sciences	Female	Senior Lecturer
Sophie	Be	Education	SS	Female	Reader
Stephen	Be	Computer science	S&E	Male	Lecturer

beyond their doctorate in three broad disciplines – sciences and engineering (S&E); social sciences and humanities (SSH); and health sciences (HS) – from three Australian and five English universities. The focus here is on the thirteen interviews conducted with academics in five U.K. universities. These individuals were self-selecting and chose to take part in the interview study by indicating their willingness on the survey questionnaire. This sample is therefore not representative of all academics in terms of experience and positioning, although there is a good mix of male and female mid-career academics from a range of institutions and disciplines.

Interview questions focused: on how participants saw themselves as an academic; critical career incidents; perceived personal and structural influences in their current role; what constrains and what enables teaching and research decisions; and their future aspirations. No direct questions were asked about REF2014 but interviewees did spontaneously bring up the subject and wanted to talk about their experiences. All interviewees were informed of the purpose of the research and signed an informed consent form. Participants and their universities have been given pseudonyms to protect confidentiality.

Academic Risk in the University

The accounts of interviewees show that there is much contingency and ambivalence that academics must navigate and this uncertainty can increase anxiety. The rather fraught ambivalence around the risks of research engagement and how this might affect the interviewees' ability for inclusion in the REF is palpably clear. The need to understand competing systems of value in their research work is something that these academics must mediate and attempt to balance in different ways. There are three key areas of perceived risks that will be considered: (1) academics' awareness (and critique) of the 'risk university' and the auditing mechanisms and bureaucracy that this imposes; (2) academics' experiences of risk in relation to their own research work and potential inclusion (or not) in the REF; and (3) academics' concerns with the risk of having their contracts changed or experiencing redundancy if they are not contributing to the research efforts and REF requirements demanded by the university.

Huber and Rubenstein (2013) argue that the risk university is concerned to avoid unnecessary failure and to utilize mechanisms and controls to ensure this does not happen. Some academics, particularly those with experience in other systems, spoke of the 'iron cage' of bureaucracy that they saw operating in U.K. higher education. They perceived the university as tightly governed and overly concerned with risk aversion:

> What I personally don't like is the – what I see if you want as a philosophical attitude of the system which is working on the assumption that there is something wrong to find out. In the U.S. system, the system is you trust (people) and if (they) do something wrong (they) get punished quite harshly I would say. Whereas in the U.K. – and I would say, this is very, from my point of view, a European attitude – we try to prevent as much as possible, anything wrong from happening. And that entails a tight web of controls and restrictions that applies to government and applies to university (Antonio, Lecturer in Chemical Engineering).

For many academics, this means restrictions in what they are doing and difficulties with processes and procedures. There is also a process of trying to ensure performance by processes of auditing and setting targets for performance, particularly in relation to individual's getting research funding. Such practices are increasing in U.K. institutions and Jump (2015c) suggests that one in six U.K. universities have grant income targets for staff. This kind of practice was blamed for the death of a professor at Imperial College London and the stress that this can impose on individuals is well documented in numerous cases (ibid.).

In order to try to understand expected outcomes (and hence ameliorate risk of failure), universities may categorize individuals around expectations and, failure to meet these expectations can have consequences as participants testify:

> Study leave isn't without its pressures. And I feel – I mean there's always the pressure to publish and there's the pressure to publish well, and at the end – for REF, for yourself, for your own career progression. So yes, I don't think study leave is without its problems or difficulties because you've always got this oh gosh I've really got to publish at the end and it's got to be a worthy publication or X number of worthy publications and be REF-able, you know, and be all those elements. So I don't think it's an easy year. It's quite a stressful year but an enjoyable year nonetheless (Emily, Senior Lecturer in Law).

The issue of a 'worthy' publication indicates that not all publications are valued, and in relation to the REF it is vitally important to achieve a three-star or four-star ranking. This can result in decisions being taken based on the perception of what can be classified as a three-star or four-star publication, leading to a shift towards the mainstream and away from more risky research (Lee 2007):

> I think it's again creating incentives, a set of incentives that basically say, 'As long as you produce your four, three-star or four-star papers …' Then you see where it completely distorts where people send their work. These days you don't send your work to a journal that you think is most appropriate. You send it to a journal that you think, the panel might think, is going to be three-star, four-star (Geert, Reader in Economics).

There is a risk, therefore, that your research outputs will not be considered sufficiently worthy of a three-star or four-star rating. The procedures for judging this can be opaque, not just within the REF process itself, but also within internal evaluation processes run by institutions to determine likely ratings of academic research output. These internal evaluations can then determine whether or not someone is submitted to REF. Sayer (2015) has written extensively, criticizing these internal institutional evaluations and he attempted to protest these unfair judgements being made by refusing to allow himself to be included in the REF for his institution. These evaluations and the lack of transparency in the process can produce anxiety and stress for individual academics. However, some are also determined to ensure that they are not completely governed by evaluations like the REF and that their research work continues to be meaningful to them, even if this risks it not being valued by the institution:

> I feel slightly frustrated about the process because the type of work I do now with the empirical work that I'm doing, it's very focused on end reports. And end reports depend to a large extent on the funding that you've got and the organization that you're writing for. Some are very open-ended, as I was saying. Some have to be very constrained. And unfortunately – the difficulty is what you perceive and what the research committee here perceive REF to want compared with what you can deliver based on the work you're doing at the time. And it's that balance, isn't it? It's balancing it as best as possible. And I think you can only be true to yourself and do the work that you think is appropriate for you and what you think is ultimately – ultimately as an academic you want – I think ultimately I want to make a difference and I want to feel that the work I'm doing is assisting in some way. And if that means that it's reports that are potentially not REF-able and therefore I get hauled over the coals for not being REF-able but they have an impact in another sense, I'd much rather that. But that's my notion of being an academic. And if it prevents me from having some career progression or it delays it, then okay, that may be the case and I think I've probably reconciled myself to that. I could write a nice theoretical black letter article if I wanted to, and it could be a three-star or a four-star. It might also be a two-star. But you – I don't think I would be enjoying that work as much as I'm enjoying the work that I'm doing at the moment and feel that I'm making an impact outside of academic theory (Emily, Senior Lecturer in Law).

This chimes with my research on resistance in academic work (Lucas 2014), and academics, despite the risks, are determined to uphold their own values of academic research work. At the same time, Emily is adopting a fatalistic approach as a way of dealing with the potential anxiety of not being included in the REF. She also highlights, however, the potentially conflicting deadlines and the contradictory messages from funders and the university (with REF considerations), who want the research packaged and delivered in different formats and to different timeframes:

> But – so we've managed to negotiate that. But that was hard work to negotiate that, to get that level. So I think in terms of REF, whether

> that will be suitable is a question mark. It'll be – I mean the data is great data. I mean it's such new data. There isn't data like it. But whether it's in a REF format is difficult to know, whereas I think the (other) project we can – because we haven't got those same constraints on an outside agency, we can make it into the format that we want it to be (Emily, Senior Lecturer in Law).

> Well I think it was driving my things but it's a little bit like now. So I suppose I feel a little bit frustrated by the REF because for me, personally, my ESRC project, having finished in January, there's just no way my publications are going to be out in time for that. So it's great for the next REF round but it's not great now. And whilst I have enough publications for the REF, I just have to, you know, wait for the final scoring or whatever in terms of whether I'm going to be submitted or not (Jane, Senior Lecturer in Criminology)

Emily, therefore, the differing demands of the outputs needed on her research project means that she is uncertain whether this can be produced in a way that is suitable for REF. Whereas, Jane is concerned with the timeframe within which she is working and whether publications can be produced to fit with REF deadlines. Even when she has publications that can be submitted, there is the ongoing concern as to whether these will be judged to be good enough for REF submission.

The extent of anxiety experienced can also relate to whether the immediate environment is supportive of academic research work beyond the constraints of what is demanded for REF:

> I was never put into pressure or I was never told if you're not submitted to REF things are going to get very ugly for you; it was never like this. We're – we are positively motivated or stimulated to have a good – select the best publications and during the process ... Given the latest discussions I think I will be in, I think the whole of my research group will be in and we were given a lot of advice on how to prepare, we were given a lot of motivation: look, this is what we are looking for, we want quality not quantity and so on and so forth. So I was given instructions, I was given advice ... I didn't feel under pressure; perhaps I should have but I didn't. I thought that, okay, that should be a consequence of my acts and not necessarily the reason why I'm doing research. And I think that's what my – the senior professor within my group – that's what he said: REF is one way to evaluate what we do but it's not the (only way) ... our target; we are not doing research for them, we are doing research because we are good researchers and we want to do what's best (Carlos, Senior Lecturer in Computer Science).

It is clear from Carlos's experience that within some departments there is a lot of support and advice given that can enable researchers to plan their research strategies and activities. This can also help to ameliorate the sense of risk and anxiety as there is a support and a shared responsibility, as well as a sense of purposeful research endeavour beyond the REF. This is a very different approach from the more punitive target-setting approach:

> But from a personal point of view (REF) hasn't really affected me in a specific way. I think the message we've got from the dean and from the department is continue to publish, continue to win money, continue to graduate students. So I think it hasn't specifically changed what I do (Antonio, Lecturer in Chemical Engineering).

What seems to be crucial is for individuals to be positioned in a way that allows them to meet the university's goals and this usually amounts to publications, funding and successful (usually graduate) students and for them to feel supported in doing so. Oftentimes, however, academics are given targets and demands are made for specific outcomes, which can be difficult to achieve. The experiences of academics like Emily, Katie, Jane and Geert, demonstrate the risk entailed and the potential for increased anxiety when the immediate environment is less supportive and more inclined to classify, constrain and punish individuals. Those who are unable to balance competing and ambivalent demands are often put under extreme pressures of performance monitoring and face risks of having their contracts changed to teaching-only, or redundancy. There is evidence of much anxiety from the academics' interviewed, particularly where jobs and careers are seen as potentially under threat:

> So we've obviously got the REF coming up. We don't know yet who is in, who is not in. We've got a good idea, but the university has basically said that there is an expectation that we will be producing at least one three-star piece per year. And there is a long, long process that you will go down if you do not produce that. And when I mean long, I'm talking three, four A4 pages of procedures that the bottom line is transfer to a teaching-only contract. Whether that will happen, I have no idea (Katie, Senior Lecturer in Law).

> Yes, but at the same time I'm ignoring possibly the most critical and almost loss of my job which was, you need to do research and if you don't do research, well I wasn't going to be in trouble because I'm

not on probation, it was, we're going to keep you on but you have to do this and you have to do this within twelve months. Well I haven't done it (Natalie, Senior Lecturer in Life Sciences).

Whilst this sample of academics is small, self-selected and cannot represent the diversity of positions and experiences of U.K. academics, it is nevertheless possible to consider how their experiences of, and positioning within, REF2014 impacts on their research and on their identities as researchers. The structuring conditions of the institution are crucial to academic decision making around research and the levels of anxiety and stress provoked. The concern for the 'reputational risk' of the university can result in tighter forms of auditing and control that are potentially detrimental to academic careers and ultimately research work undertaken, as academics struggle to ameliorate the risks faced.

Academics struggle to balance the different demands within which they are operating and live with the constant risk of threats to their research identity and even their employment. In terms of the overall experiences of these academics, it would seem that there is evidence of a RAE-ification (Loftus 2006) and also much evidence of anxiety and stress around research work and the potential or inclusion and success in REF submission. However, this is balanced by an unflinching sense of what it is to be an academic and what is meaningful in the research work that they are undertaking. Overall, there is a continuing resistance to the constraints of evaluation exercises such as REF, but also a kind of sanguine acceptance of their inevitability.

Acknowledgements

Thanks are due to my colleagues Angela Brew, David Boud and Karin Crawford for permission to quote from our joint study of academics in Australia and the U.K.

Lisa Lucas is Senior Lecturer in the Graduate School of Education, University of Bristol. She is a sociologist of higher education and is a Co-Director of the Centre for Knowledge, Culture and Society. Her research focuses on policy issues in higher education, primarily the funding and evaluation of university research, and has looked at the impact on university management as well as academic work in different European and Australasian countries. She has also been researching academic work and identity. She is author of *The Research Game in Academic Life* (2006, SRHE/McGraw-Hill) and *Academic Research* and Researchers (coedited with Angela Brew) (2009, SRHE/McGraw-Hill). Recent publications include: 'Academic Resistance in the UK: challenging quality assurance processes in higher education' Policy and Society (2015); and a review of 'Performance-based Research Assessment in Higher Education' for Oxford Bibliographies (2016).

References

Beck, U. 1993. *Risk Society: Towards a New Modernity*. London: Sage.
_____. 2009. *World at Risk*. Cambridge: Polity Press.
Berg, L.D., E.H. Huijbens and H.G. Larsen. Forthcoming. 'Producing anxiety in the neoliberal university', *The Canadian Geographer*.
Brew, A., and D. Boud. 2009. 'Understanding academics' engagement with research', in A. Brew and L. Lucas, (eds), *Academic Research and Researchers*. London: Open University Press and Society for Research into Higher Education, pp. 189–203.
Brew, A., D. Boud and S.U. Namgung. 2011. 'Influences on the formation of academics: perspectives of Australian academics', *Studies in Continuing Education* 33(1): 51–66.
Brew, A., et al. 2015. 'Research productivity, researcher identity and views of research in two countries', *Higher Education* 71(5): 689–97, DOI: 10.1007/s10734-015-9930-6.
Cupples, J., and E. Pawson. 2012. 'Giving an account of oneself: The PBRF and the neoliberal university', *New Zealand Geographer* 68: 14–23.
Giddens A., U. Beck and S. Lash. 1994. *Risk, Trust, Reflexivity: Reflexive Modernization*. Cambridge: Polity Press.
Gill, R. 2010. 'Breaking the Silence: The Hidden Injuries of the Neoliberal University', in R. Flood and R. Gill (eds), *Secrecy and Silence in the Research Process: Feminist Reflections*. London: Routledge.
Gill, R., and N. Donaghue. 2015. 'Resilience, apps and reluctant individualism: Technologies of self in the neoliberal academy', *Women's Studies International Forum*, online first.
Hardy, I. 2015. 'Education as a "risky business": Theorising student and teacher learning in complex times', *British Journal of Sociology of Education* 3(3): 375–94.
Harley, S. 2002. 'The Impact of Research Selectivity on Academic Work and Identity in UK Universities', *Studies in Higher Education* 27(2): 187–205.
Huber, M., and H. Rothstein. 2013. 'The risk organisation: Or how organisations reconcile themselves to failure', *Journal of Risk Research* 16(6): 651–75.
Jump, P. 2014. 'Early career academics make mark on REF', *Times Higher Education*, 13 February.
Jump, P. 2015a. 'REF 2014 Rerun: Who are the "Game Players"?', *Times Higher Education*, 1 January.
_____. 2015b. 'Careers at risk after case studies "game playing", REF study suggests', *Times Higher Education*, 22 January.

———. 2015c. 'Grant income targets set at one in six universities, THE Poll Suggests', *Times Higher Education*, 11 June.
Lash, S., A. Giddens and U. Beck. 1994. *Reflexive Modernization: Politics, Tradition and Aesthetics in the Modern Social Order*. Cambridge: Polity Press.
Leathwood, C., and B. Read. 2013. 'Final Report: Assessing the Impact of Developments in Research Policy for Research on Higher Education: An Exploratory Study'. London: Society for Research in Higher Education.
Lee, F.S. 2007. 'The Research Assessment Exercise, the State and the Dominance of Mainstream Economics in British Universities', *Cambridge Journal of Economics* 31: 309–25.
Loftus, A. 2006. 'RAE-ification and the Consciousness of the Academic', *Area* 38(1): 110–12.
Lucas, L. 2006. *The Research Game in Academic Life*. Maidenhead: McGraw-Hill/Open University Press.
———. 2009. 'Research Management and Research Cultures: Power and Productivity', in A. Brew and L. Lucas (eds), *Academic Research and Researchers*. Buckingham: SRHE/Open University Press.
———. 2014. 'Academic resistance in the UK: challenging quality assurance processes in higher education', Special issue: 'Regulating Higher Education: Quality Assurance and Neo-Liberal Managerialism in Higher Education – A Global Perspective', *Policy and Society* 33: 215–24.
———. 2016. 'Performance-based Research Assessment in Higher Education', in L.H. Meyer (ed.), *Oxford Bibliographies in Education*. Oxford: Oxford University Press.
Lupton, D. 1999. *Risk*. London: Routledge.
McNay, I. 2003. 'Assessing the Assessment: An Analysis of the UK Research Assessment Exercise, 2001, and its Outcomes, with Special Reference to Research in Education', *Science and Public Policy* 30(1): 1–8.
Power, M., et al. 2009. 'Reputational Risk as a Logic of Organizing in Late Modernity', *Organization Studies* 30(2–3): 301–24.
Sayer, D. 2015. *Rank Hypocrisies: The Insult of the REF*. London: Sage.
Shore, C. 2010. 'Beyond the multiversity: neoliberalism and the rise of the schizophrenic university', *Social Anthropology* 18(1): 15–29.
Shore, C., and S. Wright. 1999. 'Audit Culture and Anthropology: Neo-Liberalism in British Higher Education', *The Journal of the Royal Anthropological Institute* 5(4): 557–75.
Sikes, P. 2006. 'Working in a 'New' University: In the shadow of the Research Assessment Exercise?', *Studies in Higher Education*, 31(5), 555–568.
Sparkes, A. 2007. 'Embodiment, academics and the audit culture: a story seeking consideration', *Qualitative Researcher* 7: 521–50.

CHAPTER 11
The Ethics of University Ethics Committees
Risk Management and the Research Imagination

TAMARA KOHN AND CRIS SHORE

◆◆◆

Introduction: The Proliferation of Ethics Bureaucracy and Its Effects

The past decade has witnessed a dramatic increase in the number and scope of university 'research ethics committees' (RECs), as they are called in the U.K., New Zealand and Australia, or 'institutional review boards' (IRBs), as they are called in North America. The aim of these bodies is to promote rigorous independent review processes and ensure the highest ethical standards, particularly for research involving human participants or personal data. They also aim to provide assurance that researchers treat participants with respect and dignity, protect privacy and safety, and safeguard personal and cultural sensitivities. Yet, despite these laudable intentions, there is a growing chorus of complaint within universities about these ethics committees and their proliferating regulatory regimes. Social scientists, particularly those who do ethnographic fieldwork, find themselves increasingly at odds with the assumptions that underpin these committees' judgements about what constitutes research ethics (Wynn 2011) or indeed what constitutes viable 'research'. Indeed, some argue that the current model is so fundamentally misconceived (and its implementation so often misguided) that efforts to foster ethical research conduct are actually undermined (Schneider 2015). If so, then why is this the case? Critics frequently highlight institutional bias towards the hard sciences and biomedical models of research, arguing that the individuals who staff these boards often fail to understand qualitative approaches or the participatory methods that ethnographers commonly use. But often such committees are staffed by a predominance of social sciences and humanities scholars who certainly do appreciate qualitative methods (even if that appreciation is often limited in scope). We suggest, therefore, that beyond any bias for scientifically structured research, other key factors are involved, including the spread of new managerial systems of accountability and risk management, or what has been termed the rise of 'audit culture' within universities (Shore and Wright 1999; Strathern 2000). One result of this has been an increased concern with legal liability, and protecting the university's reputation (or 'brand') rather than ensuring the ethical conduct of researchers or the wellbeing of research participants. As Roger Dale shows (this volume), reputational risk has become a major issue for universities as a result of the increase in competitive research assessment exercises and university ranking systems. If this is so, then how should we explain and analyse these developments? Are they symptoms of the rise of 'risk society' (Beck 1999) and the political economy of insecurity – i.e. the proliferation of risks leading to a proliferation of anxieties about ethics? Or is it the other way around – are they reflective of a growing anxiety, awareness and mainstreaming of ethics that is leading universities to become more risk averse and thus more controlling?

Issues of risk, management and compliance raise a number of important questions that this chapter seeks to address: what is driving the expansion of university ethics committees and what assumptions guide these committees' actions? How is the growth of institutionalized ethics reshaping policy and practice, and how is it impacting on knowledge production? More fundamentally, given the obstacles and strictures these committees create for ethnographic and participatory research, how ethical are these research ethics committees?

To explore these questions we draw on examples of university regulatory practice collated from the United States, Canada, the U.K., New Zealand and Australia, as well as our own personal experiences as academics and anthropologists who have witnessed first-hand the extraordinary growth of university ethics committees over the course of our academic careers in both the northern and southern hemispheres. These examples highlight issues that (together with the other contributions to this volume) cry out for change and urge us forward into a far less regulated but surprisingly more ethical and rich research future.

The scene is set by reading the following excerpts of emails received at approximately the same time by anthropology Ph.D. students in different universities and continents:

> Dear Matthew
> The University Human Participants Ethics Committee has reviewed your proposal for your Ph.D. research entitled 'Nationalism and Interculturalism in Quebecoise Politics and Society'. The Committee has agreed to grant conditional approval for your fieldwork, subject to a few changes. One of these concerns the use of the word 'nationalism' in the consent form. The Committee is of the view that this term could be seen as offensive and may cause distress for some participants. We therefore suggest you remove it from your Consent Forms.

The second email was received by a student after passing a rigorous confirmation process with a panel of experts in his department and in advance of embarking on a year-long field study on fatherhood and disability in the United States:

> The Faculty's Human Ethics Advisory Group (HEAG) was concerned that the student researcher plans to take along his wife and two children, one of whom has multiple disabilities, to the social events organised by the fathers' group. Is it disingenuous to argue that this is common practice?
> The HEAG is also concerned that the student researcher has insufficiently addressed the need to manage the possible emotional risks both for participants and himself. They would also like some clarification as to how the people who are not being interviewed, but will be part of the participant observation, will be made aware of the research being conducted and be given the option to decline. We suggest a PLS [Plain Language Statement] for observation participants.

These short excerpts above highlight a problem at the heart of this chapter; namely, what happens when ethics committees expand their remit to the point where entire project topics approved within disciplines or by external funding bodies are rendered inadmissible, or where researchers are required to respond to near-impossible demands to guarantee that participants are protected from assumed emotional 'harm' arising from any interpersonal encounters? What is striking in these particular stories are the paternalistic, distrustful and ethnocentric assumptions reflected in the committees' verdicts ('nationalism' is an offensive term for Canadians; fathers of disabled children may be upset by the presence of the researcher's own disabled child). Other emails received by the authors and their students included the following statements: 'committees must apply a standard formula to protect the vulnerable'; 'researchers always occupy a position of power vis-a-vis their informants'; and 'third party intervention is necessary to ensure participants (even judges and government ministers) do not feel coerced'. We will return to unpack these issues later, but first we offer a brief overview of how the institutional structures have developed.

Mission Creep: A Brief History of Ethical Review Committees and Their Proliferation

Since the 1990s, the scope of university RECs and IRBs has grown dramatically. From being peripheral to the research process (and in some countries, non-existent), institutional ethics committees have proliferated and become increasingly prominent features of the university research process (Boden, Epstein and Latimer 2009; Caplan 2003; Haggerty 2004; Heimer and Petty 2010; Lederman 2006b; Sieber and Tolich 2012; Van den Hoonaard 2011). They increasingly monitor the planning of any institutionally affiliated research on 'human subjects', their aim being to protect the university and also research participants from both actual and potential harm. Many now insist that all research involving 'human subjects' – and not just funded research projects – must be reviewed, including research to be conducted by university students at any level. Much time is devoted to discussing ever-shifting ethical codes (cf. Pels 1999) and obtaining institutional ethics approval has today become a major milestone in any grant application no matter how small or innocuous, and a major source of anxiety for researchers.

Looking at our own institutions in New Zealand and Australia respectively we see why such anxiety prevails. At Auckland University, for example, the standard Human Participant Ethics Committee form now typically runs to twenty-seven pages and usually requires between four and six annexes, from concept notes and participant information sheets, to official consent forms that must be signed and stored for a period of six years, under lock and key. Faculty guidelines typically recommend that staff members set aside half a day to upload the form onto the research office portal. Melbourne University's online forms are similarly extensive, requiring numerous attachments including interview questions, plain language statements, consent forms and suggested lists of psychiatric counsellors and local services to allow informants to attend to any distress that the committee imagines might develop due to what is seen to be the intrinsic precariousness of many human encounters. Further anxiety is produced by the many weeks, if not many months, of communications over the processing and reworking of the application until all issues are addressed to the satisfaction of the panel.

If this is the state of play today in some parts of the world, it was not always so. The present scenario evolved out of a system in which researchers' values and disciplinary knowledge guided research practice. In the late 1990s, Chalmers and Pettit (1998) usefully identified three stages in the historical development of RECs across various disciplines. The first stage related to the call that we all have to be fair and treat others properly – to a lived 'ethics in practice' and ethics as a general sensibility to the other. The second stage was when professional research bodies, such as the ASA (Association of Social Anthropologists of the U.K. and Commonwealth), produced discipline-specific guidelines to their members for general codes of conduct. The third stage was when independent authorities (universities, hospitals, governments) took control of the processes of ethical review – when loose 'guidelines' were replaced by less nuanced directives (ibid.). To these we predict a fourth stage that is likely to emerge if current trends persist, when the institutions are no longer deemed sufficiently capable – or independent – to oversee their own research practices so that the task of ensuring ethical compliance must be handed over to an external regulatory body. Indeed, several universities in the United States (including Michigan, Colorado, West Virginia and Phoenix) have now created new professional positions in the ethics review process called 'quality assurance analysts'.

Pettit's early study of institutional review (1992) documented how 'terrible tales' of dangerous practice led to public scandals that provided the initial catalyst for more surveillance and regulatory action. Some of these ethical horror stories included the injection of cancer cells, without informed consent, into elderly patients in New York; and the withholding of treatments that led to people dying, as in the famous Tuskegee study of syphilis in Alabama in 1972. The researchers in the Tuskegee study had decided that black subjects were too 'uneducated' to offer informed consent (ibid.). Significantly, most of these notorious (and historical) cases involved medical procedures and health threats. However, the movement from the earlier disciplinary guideline stage to the larger external review stage came to affect all researchers working in any way with human subjects. The same demands were placed on researchers conducting interviews about lifestyle and belief, or watching public ritual ceremonies, as there were on researchers using patients' bodies as medical guinea pigs.

Pettit's study also noted how committee members often felt the need to legitimate their presence and time spent in long meetings by finding things to correct or object to, in order to demonstrate their rigorous contribution to the process. This is what Rena Lederman has usefully termed 'regulatory hypervigilance' (2006a: 489). Pettit additionally highlighted the fact that there are few penalties for a 'false negative' (1992: 101). This means that a panel's decision to delay or halt a worthy research project will only ever upset a few people or produce complaining emails from a handful of individual researchers or supervisors. If, however, a decision is too easily approved – too 'adventurously liberal' – and this results in any problematic issues later on, then there is the risk of a loud public outcry with serious consequences (1992: 103). This implicit line of reasoning, Pettit has suggested, has driven ethics committees towards increasingly conservative and restrictive decision making, ostensibly to protect themselves.

In North America, Europe and Australasia, critics complain about 'mission creep', arguing that ethics committees have become so intrusive that they now exercise a stranglehold over the design and implementation of field research (Lederman 2006b; Schrag 2010). Indeed, the policing of IRB compliance is now extending to the realm of journal publication, such that some journals refuse to accept manuscripts for review – let alone publication – without evidence of IRB approval (Yanow and Schwartz-Shea 2008: 483). According to Yanow and Schwartz-Shea (2008) (and as we illustrate below), universities are being pressured to adopt a biomedically oriented model of ethics review without fully understanding the contexts in which the IRB model emerged, or, indeed, how it is currently changing – what Schrag (2010) has termed 'ethical imperialism' (see also Van den Hoonaard 2011).

We list here some criticisms that have frequently been directed towards university ethics committees, alongside illustrative examples and reflective considerations that could inform future changes and improvements.

1. Structures of Science: Predetermined Research Parameters

Ethics committees operate largely within a biomedical and scientific framework even when they are assessing largely qualitative research projects. Their approach to ethics tends to be normative and 'deontological' (based on abstract rules rather than on considerations of the effects of those rules). This partly explains why many university committees have problems dealing with disciplines (such as anthropology) that require fieldwork and open-ended qualitative research methods: biomedical approaches do not sit comfortably with research in the social sciences or education (see Tolich and Fitzgerald 2006). As the chair of one university ethics committee put it:

> The primary goal for the committee is to protect participants against harm, but that goal is much less clear in the social sciences. The problem is deciding what is needed to ensure 'informed consent'. This is not clear in participatory research. The committee needs to understand what exactly the information is that you are after. It also wants to ensure that information obtained for one purpose is not used for another. So the inductive approach of ethnographers is hard to deal with. Research that involves looking for problems poses challenges for the committee. With participatory research, the committee needs to know what things will not be studied. It wants reassurance that information gained through participant-observation will not be used outside the parameters of the research (Shore – fieldwork transcript 31 October 2014).

This statement is revealing. What some ethics committees seem to be looking for is absolute certainty that research will be risk free. Such certainty is, of course, impossible to attain. Any human research encounter, just like any other human encounter, will involve at least some small degree of risk (Pettit 1992). But the everydayness of human encounters and the emergent nature of knowledge are not in any way represented in the forms that guide university ethics regulation. Committees worry about imagined risks and somehow extraordinary human encounters that experts in those fields have not considered risky (or extraordinary). Committees also worry about the dangers of 'wandering off topic' – of researchers asking and doing things that were not planned in the original research design (and therefore were not approved in advance). In short, research that involves serendipity and informality is seen as problematic as well as 'un-scientific' (see Lederman 2006a). The concern with the use of information outside of the designated research parameters assumes as well that the data must not have an afterlife – that it cannot be revisited by a fieldworker who, for example, might have resided in a particular site over many years and returns in future with a new angle and new project that necessarily looks back at previous experience. The notion that 'parameters of research'(topics, questions to ask, timeframes and so on) are entirely determined in advance of entering a field – even one you have never been to before – cannot sit comfortably with experienced fieldworkers for whom 'parameters' and key questions emerge out of the field encounters themselves; that is, inductively.

2. Imagined Dangers

A key problem identified by critics of university ethics regimes is that many committee members tend to view social science research as intrinsically risky and potentially unethical. Given the biomedical backgrounds of some and the disciplinary biases of most committee members, there is a profound lack of understanding of what fieldwork actually entails. Even talking with people is seen as problematic and fraught with danger, as the second of the above vignettes illustrates. Committee members often seek to find ways to prevent researchers from getting too close to the people they work with, on the assumption that this would mitigate harm and allay power imbalances.

For example, a research project led by one of the authors on 'Constitutional Reform in New Zealand and Other Commonwealth Countries' entailed in-depth interviews with various categories of experts, including senior civil servants, government ministers, journalists, high court judges and constitutional experts. However, the ethics committee refused to grant approval for a number of reasons. One of these was summed up in the panel's comments:

> **Recruitment and coercion**: Given the status of the PIs [Principal Investigators] and the acknowledged presence of possible special relationships (Section C7) it might be that invited participants would find it difficult to decline. It would be desirable if a recruitment methodology were devised in which (a) a direct approach from the PI was omitted and/or (b) a process in which the PI was unable to ascertain who participated and who did not was put in place (e.g., this information was compartmentalised within the research team). In a design employing purposive sampling this is not a simple matter but the Committee would like to know if this could be considered to minimise any likelihood of coercion (Letter from the University of Auckland Human Participants Ethics Committee, 2013).

To minimize potential 'harm' to participants, the committee proposed that an intermediary (rather than the researcher) contact participants, and perhaps also conduct the interviews, in order to minimize the 'likelihood of coercion'. A subsequent letter of objection sent to the university's ethics committee produced only a defensive response from its chair, who defended her committee by saying it had an 'obligation to protect' participants, but acknowledging that 'sometimes we get it wrong'. However, in this case 'getting it wrong' effectively meant telling a team of anthropologists to abandon their technique of ethnographic fieldwork based on participant-observation – a methodology that, since the early twentieth century, has largely defined anthropology as a discipline. Making face-to-face contact with participants, it seems, is something that ethics committees find deeply problematic and risky.

One effect of such a high level of intervention is that the length of the review process often threatens the start or completion of projects, or students' coursework and degree programmes. Many of the problems raised by committees are outside the remit of the ethical. As political scientist Robert Hauck has noted, university ethics committees pass judgement on their (usually disciplinarily uninformed) ideas about the general quality of a proposal and the methodologies to be used, rather than the actual risks involved (2008: 475–76). One senior anthropologist, in describing a year-long email 'battle' with her Australian university's human ethics committee over a student's long-delayed project, clearly demonstrated that most of the objections made either ran counter to, or took huge liberties in interpreting, the National Statement on Ethical Conduct in Human Research. As she noted, 'these committees are increasingly adversarial and heavy handed – they always begin with "what can go wrong?" rather than with asking "is this ethical research?"' (email communication with Tamara Kohn).

As the examples above illustrate, the behaviour of university ethics committees is often based on a set of assumptions framed within a discourse of 'risk' that tends to position the researcher as the powerful agent against whom research participants need 'protection'. It is implicitly assumed that the ideal condition for ethical research is a relationship of social detachment between researchers and the researched – that proper research should be conducted in clinical situations where, as far as possible, interaction is limited and prescribed and where 'leakage' of information can be contained and minimized. Yet informality and relations of trust are often central to ethical social research. Lesley Conn (2008) provides a vivid illustration of the problems that can arise from IRB insistence on formalized and standardized ethical practices. In her case, which involved ethnographic research in a Canadian teaching and research hospital, she was required to obtain IRB approval from four different university and hospital boards. These also insisted she obtain signed consent forms from her research subjects, mostly senior doctors, with whom she had initially established a good rapport. But her relationship with the doctors changed dramatically for the worse after they received her written consent form, which almost put an end to her study. As she explains, they wanted their relationship with the ethnographer to be based on informality and trust, not formalized audit protocols. For these doctors, the consent was imbued with particular significance and represented a type of legal contract that, in her words:

> signified a waiving of control over one's involvement in the study, over one's representation in the study, and especially over the collaborative production and ownership of knowledge that results from the study. These meanings inevitably became the new terms under which I was asking my informants for consent; participation in my research was herein translated into a dissociated, passive objectification (Conn 2008: 506).

For qualitative researchers, particularly those who do fieldwork, this raises an obvious question: how can one produce a proposal for an REC/IRB that satisfies the inevitably reductive worldview of 'clinical' research, when disciplinary best practice tells us how critical the building of personal relationships is to long-term processes of intersubjective understanding and trust? In addition, how can one design a project that caters to a committee's assumptions about researcher/subject power relations that one knows do not actually apply in 'the field'?

3. Ethics Committee Decisions Are Often Nonsensical

While in some instances university RECs make decisions that are regrettable yet understandable, in other cases the reasoning offered is just plain silly. Take, for example, the case reported by Will van den Hoonaard (2002: 11): 'A member of a departmental ethics committee told a graduate student to turn her face the other way when she was doing participant-observation in a group that had any human subjects who did not explicitly consent to the research' (cited in Schrag 2011: 123). In another example, Irena Grugulis reacted to a university ethics committee's response to her proposed ethnographic study of a how skills were learned in a computer games company, by reporting that the ethics committee 'insisted on full written consent from every worker in the offices (about 250), every delivery person and – on the occasions I went off for a chat with informants – every barista who served us coffee and waitress who brought us pizzas (no, seriously)' (ibid.).

If Irena and Will's examples illustrate the 'silliness' of regulatory hypervigilance applied to benign qualitative research projects, another example that Schrag offers alongside them demonstrates how the same craziness applies at the other end of the spectrum – for research with people who are indeed considered 'dangerous' to the public.

He documents the case of Scott Atran, whose research project was designed to explore the causes of terrorism through interviews with failed suicide bombers in jail. The committee determined that prisoners cannot give free, informed consent and, at the same time, felt that any interviews would potentially endanger any other not-yet-captured terrorists (ibid.). Consideration of how these perceived potential dangers weigh up against the dangers of not conducting this research (such as the danger of stifling research that aims to find ways to avoid future suicide bombing) is avoided by a committee that is attendant to rules, rather than a more subjective but humanistic consideration of ethical research practice.

What is interesting about these divergent examples, in our view, is that the committees' decisions appeared to have been made without the larger contextual and cultural – and indeed moral – understandings that allowed the projects to be designed in the first place. Within that procedural rule-focused vacuum, human subjects must all be treated equally at risk, in the reasoning of the committee, regardless of what you actually plan to 'do' with them – if researchers should not inject members of the public or prisoners for experimental medical research, then they also cannot observe individuals in public spaces or even speak to prisoners about their experiences without encountering risks that should be avoided.

The reality, however, is that ethical rules and attendant forms designed around biomedical experimentation research should not comprise the initial template for determining the ethics of all human-subject research. Rules that prohibit research that aims to give a voice to people who should be heard and are often unjustly silenced, should also be rebuked, or at least rewritten. Often the silenced (such as patients, prisoners, young offenders, refugees, asylum seekers and other kinds of detainee or inmate) reside behind a nearly impenetrable screen of Kafkaesque institutional bureaucracy in their own environs, which cannot even be touched if approached the wrong way. In these cases, an individual researcher navigating a range of often entirely conflicting institutional desires and notions of 'best practice' needs to be creative and flexible – to make decisions when the decisions are required, in situ (and not before). It is not, however, in the nature of current university ethics reviews to allow for full flexibility in method, in practice, in design or in the shaping of the research question after research starts, so that other institutional barriers may be averted. Indeed, the conditions of some 'fields' require a soft humanistic approach – one that entirely avoids the attention of those in power who would not wish for subjects to speak. If RECs cannot accommodate this, then paradoxically they too need to be avoided in order to engage ethically in the world.

4: Committee Decisions Are Inconsistent

Within universities, ethics committees often fail to explain the bases for their decisions, leaving researchers guessing about what to do to rectify the problems, particularly when the same apparently problematic aspects of a project have been shaped and condoned by other expert committee decisions (for example, from supervisory panels to funding bodies). It understandably worries researchers when the official nature of the ethics clearance hurdle trumps and often (inadvertently, perhaps) upturns the previous expert counsel provided by supervisors, expert reviewers of national grant proposals and so on. To add to that cognitive dissonance, researchers in Australia, for example, have reported idiosyncratic decisions made by ethics panels at particular universities – James Cook University has reportedly banned 'snowball sampling', a nonprobability sampling technique through known acquaintances that is widely used by sociologists and other social scientists working at other Australian universities and abroad. Meanwhile the University of Newcastle in Australia decided, idiosyncratically, that all research participants should have the chance to edit or erase any audio recordings they are involved in. These cases demonstrate the effects of what Van den Hoonaard (2002) calls 'ethical norming'. Such lack of consistency, he argues, proves that risks and benefits are not being 'objectively' assessed, but rather the committees are, in effect, randomly 'throwing darts at a board' (Van den Hoonaard 2011: 124).

5. Ethics Committees Claim but Often Lack Appropriate Expertise

The problems of inconsistency mentioned above are directly related to an assumption that any intelligent person should be able to recognize what is ethical and what is not in a research proposal. Unfortunately, this is not the case. There is a tremendous variation in disciplinary histories and methods within the modern social sciences, and detailed knowledge of those disciplinary variances is critical to any reasonable ethical review. However, ethics committees are not necessarily representative of the disciplines they govern. While most members are nominated by their faculties, disciplinary representation is rarely achieved. The University of Auckland's Human Participants Ethics Committee, for example, finds it increasingly hard to recruit members because of the sheer scale of the work involved (committee members typically have to deal with over eighty applications per month). Similarly, at the University of Melbourne structural changes have resulted in the elimination of school-level committees in favour of faculty-level committees, and this has inevitably resulted in reduced disciplinary contact. The higher-level university-wide ethics committees (one for medical research, the other for social research) include academics and administrators, as well as members of the public – ex-headmasters, clergy, retired public servants and so on. These people are often welcomed and valued on the committees for their interest and enthusiasm, but they are also known to baulk at projects that do not readily fit into their ideas about what 'research' is – views largely informed by the requirements flagged on the forms. The answer for dealing with a lack of disciplinary understanding is education. Institutional committee memories, however, are short – as a shifting composite of people with partial knowledge, committees don't learn well. Kohn, for example, gave a series of short lectures at Melbourne University to explain to committee members how empirically-driven anthropological research is often badly serviced by current institutional ethics forms and processes. After finishing her presentation to the HAPS (humanities and applied sciences) HESC (a committee she had served on for several years), one long-serving member came up to say how much he enjoyed it, and added: 'Another anthropologist gave us a talk about five or six years ago and your talk reminded me of all the points he raised'! Clearly action points and shifts in process and understanding are not being implemented. People listen, nod and then move on; and the committee is ever reformulated as tenures lapse.

6. Ethics Committees' Deontological Approach Is Flawed

Deontological (duty-based) ethics are concerned with what people do, not with the consequences of their actions. Someone who follows duty-based ethics should do the right thing, should follow the rules, even if that produces more harm (or less good) than doing the wrong thing vis-a-vis rules: in this view, people have a duty to do the 'right thing', even if it produces a bad result. A case that illustrates the danger of following institutional duty involves an Australian Ph.D. student who was studying indigenous leaders' experiences. The ethics board required her to present 'plain language statements' and a list of trauma counsellors to each interviewee. When she did this, her first interviewee, a highly educated Aboriginal elder, became extremely angry, throwing the forms back into the young researcher's face and insisting that those forms and the messages within them were not only patronizing but racist. This came at the beginning of a Ph.D. project from a key informant – hardly the right way to start. The actions prescribed did more damage than good for the researcher.

Sometimes ethics committee regulations and prescribed actions that appear to protect vulnerable groups may actually adversely affect vulnerable groups in terms of their safety and future relations within their larger community. For example, Schrag cites a report about Canada's 1998 Tri-Council Policy Statement: Ethical Conduct for Research Involving Humans. Apparently the statement 'required researchers to get approval from Band Councils before interviewing Aboriginal peoples. But that meant that dissidents within Aboriginal communities would need their opponents' permission to speak with an outside researcher' (Schrag 2011: 8).

Clearly, if a culturally sensitive field researcher can sense or predict these negative outcomes that would result from the application of deontologically oriented ethics procedures, then the obvious answer is to disobey – to subvert the system for a greater good. This is a choice that one can make, but it is more likely that only people in established academic posts with a high degree of confidence and field experience will be in a safe enough position to do so. A student or early career researcher would be less inclined to disobey.

7. Ethics Review Can Harm or Obstruct 'Good' and Innovative Research

Experience of dealing with these kinds of institutionally mandated restrictions often leads researchers into a defensive minimal-information mode in an effort to achieve clearance and save time and effort. For example, at the University of Melbourne, Honours students, who only have one year to design, execute and write up a field-based research project, are encouraged to plan projects that will not set off alarm bells. They therefore avoid not only certain sensitive topics but also whole vocabularies that might trigger a 'high risk' categorization (and thus elicit delays) from the online system. These words include 'ethnicity', 'nationalism', 'trauma', 'stress', 'conflict', 'indigenous' and 'minority'. Fears about bureaucratic obstruction – or simply not wanting to get on the 'wrong side' of the committee – leads to a constriction in the pre-field research imagination and consequently in the field experience and ethnographic understanding that can be produced through it.

In anthropology one can already see the effects of such conservative and defensive advising on new projects and on the teaching of research methods. The sad irony is that while the anthropological community is increasing in numbers and the discipline is growing in popularity, the research gaze is shrinking (Kohn 2017). In short, university ethics committees are producing a narrowing and standardizing generation of social science research. This also occurs – and is amplified – when researchers internalize these ethical regulations and bureaucratic norms to pre-emptively self-censor their own research (Kohn 2014). As Boden, Epstein and Latimer argue:

> These regimes institute 'technologies of the self' that require researchers to become 'docile bodies' within the research process, self-regulating and self-disciplining their own actions against particular ideas of what is standard and good. This reduces the researchers' autonomy and capacity for exercising their imagination and doing innovative work. For example, they may begin to change what they feel they can research, or the way they design studies, developing projects in ways that fit the procedures and have a chance of getting past the apparatus of approval (Boden, Epstein and Latimer 2009: 743).

The growth of ethics committees is part of a series of technologies of accountability and control that have been introduced since the 1990s to elicit conformity and render academics more responsive to management. Ethics committees have 'flourished in the wake of the increasing scale and pervasiveness of "audit culture"' in universities (Cowlishaw 2014: 377), which has helped to introduce new forms of illiberal, coercive and 'authoritarian governmentality' (Shore and Wright 1999: 557; Shore 2008). Hence, to answer the question posed at the outset, 'risk society'(Beck 1999) has indeed generated a proliferation of anxieties about ethics, yet those anxieties – and the institutionalization of ethics committees they result in – have made universities increasingly more risk averse and controlling. The bureaucratization of university risk management, it seems, is both cause and effect of itself: a process that feeds on the fears and uncertainties that the system itself produces. Ultimately, however, these ethics regimes are destructive of critical social science, as their aim is to elicit the 'pursuit of correctness rather than truth' (Boden, Epstein and Latimer 2009: 746). Submission to ethics committee protocols often serves as a vehicle to silence critical voices in the academy. For example, in 2014, New Zealand's Chief Scientific Advisor to the government, Sir Peter Gluckman, caused controversy when he proposed that the Royal Society of New Zealand revise its code of ethics so that in future academics may only speak out on issues where they have 'recognized scientific expertise' (Allison 2014). This proposal, which was aimed at protecting New Zealand's commercial interests, followed comments by outspoken environmentalist Dr Mike Joy, who had publicly criticized the Prime Minister John Key for his boasts about '100% Pure New Zealand', pointing out that 80 percent of New Zealand's rivers are polluted. The idea that an academic must be an 'expert' on a subject before they are allowed to comment publically sets a dangerous precedent that would be wide open to abuse (for example in decisions over who should be granted permission to speak out as an 'expert'), and could seriously undermine academic freedom.

With few exceptions (see Hedgecoe 2008), the social science and humanities literature on research ethics committees is overwhelmingly critical. Committees stand accused of strangling legitimate research, curtailing academic freedom, substituting professional for bureaucratic ethics, and being less concerned with protecting research subjects from harm than with protecting their own universities and research centres (Heimer and Petty 2010; Baloy, Sabati and Glass 2016). Even former optimists like Will van den Hoonaard (2011) now see that the imposition of medical ethics represents a serious threat to the future of the social sciences.

How Can Ethics Reviews Be Done Differently?

> Ethical practice—in research or any other domain—has an improvisational subtlety that exceeds what can be managed by bureaucratized processes (Lederman 2007: 301).

Evidently, much needs to change if we value academic freedom and wish to preserve ethnographic research and critical social science. Even the U.S. Department of Health and Human Services has acknowledged the intolerable administrative burdens and ambiguities created by the current system of ethics review and has embarked on a major overhaul of the entire IRB process, although to date even this effort falls short in its inability to account for participant-observation (see American Anthropological Association 2016). If the primary concern of university ethics committees is about protecting the institution and preventing lawyers' bills, then they should be honest and upfront about this and limit the ethics approval forms to those concerns accordingly. But it is also important to reflect on the wider context in which ethical review occurs so that we acknowledge and are sensitized to the way new managerial practices have intruded upon and colonized the research imagination. As Boden, Epstein and Latimer (2009: 746) conclude: '[w]e need to recover the idea that ethics are relational and ultimately and inherently personal'. For anthropologists, reflexive social scientists and ethnographic researchers, that idea would seem to be fundamental and axiomatic.

Given the detrimental effects of the current processes on the design and implementation of much qualitative research – particularly ethnographic – there needs to be a much more focused and discipline-friendly process that would only assess those projects that truly are deemed to pose a risk (see Foster 2015). Better options than the current biomedical model of ethics review undoubtedly exist. Ethics is not about imposing a uniform set of rules about the conduct of research; it is about inculcating an ethical awareness or sensibility on the part of the researcher. The core of ethicality in field-based research is inevitably embedded in the practice itself, in feeling responsible to do the right thing, in working towards protecting others from harm, in altering one's expectations about what is needed or right, based on what the field itself teaches us (Kohn 2017). More responsibility should be returned to disciplinary panels, and supervisors, who are more likely to possess the appropriate expertise and research sensibility.

There also needs to be stronger communication between social scientists, funding agencies and university managers so that lessons learned about best practice can be fed back into the process of ethical review. That includes not only taking note of lessons from the field, but also from the numerous publications and presentations that have addressed the flaws in the current system. The existing literature is not short on solutions. Some authors have argued that levels of institutional oversight should be commensurate with the level of risk (Plattner 2006). Others argue for more ethical self-evaluation and greater delegation of more responsibility for ethical oversight to professional organizations (Chalmers and Pettit 1998). Most agree that ethics review bodies and researchers should put an end to their obstructive, defensive posing, which tends to cast each party into the unhelpful roles of police enforcer and offender, respectively. Such positioning is extremely detrimental to the research process. Another solution is to construct an ongoing process of self-evaluation in order to create more reflexivity in the design and implementation of ethically informed research, or what Chenhall, Senior and Belton (2011) term an 'ethics of practice'. As Bob Simpson argues, 'ethics begins with a responsibility not just for the physical bodies of others, but for the social life by which they are connected' (Simpson 2011: 386). These social considerations are often absent in the current ethics review process, which tends to focus primarily on the individual.

The operation of ethics committees themselves should also be subject to greater scrutiny so that we can better understand their social composition, modus operandi – and how to make them more fit for purpose (Van den Hoonaard 2002: 5). As Lederman (2006) has reminded us, if institutional review boards were not reviewing ethnographic proposals, other organizations would need to do so to satisfy the requirements of the research-funding agencies. However, even if we accept the necessity of some form of ethics monitoring, the oppositional framing described above could be changed so that it is more flexible, reflexive and collaborative and less driven by concerns about institutional risk management. Deciding pre-fieldwork on what researchers are permitted to do or not do in human-subject research may be necessary to protect individuals and institutions in some cases, but in most instances it is wholly inappropriate and only narrows researchers' imaginations and ability to be flexible and open to the lessons the field itself will produce (Kohn 2017).

Being an ethical researcher in the field should primarily be understood as a learning experience that requires cultural competence and skill in navigating one's way through complex ethnographic encounters and often deeply personal relationships which cannot be predicted beforehand. A critical understanding of 'ethics in practice' (Chenhall, Senior and Belton 2011) should lie at the core of any teaching on field ethics and for all institutional ethics committee training. Clearly, institutional attempts to rule out uncertainty – through a demand that researchers adhere to ever-more restrictive codes of conduct – is not working. Institutional ethics committees might therefore do better to rethink their purpose, reconsider where ethical oversight is and is not required, rework their forms (which may involve different strokes for different folks), and focus less on tick-box compliance and more on the deeper challenge of how to nurture ethical sensibility and awareness among university researchers.

◆

Tamara Kohn (D.Phil., Oxford; MA, University of Pennsylvania; BA, Berkeley) is Associate Professor of Anthropology in the School of Social and Political Sciences, University of Melbourne. Her research interests include death studies, digital commemoration, research ethics and methods in anthropology, identities in communities of practice, and the anthropology of the body and senses. Relevant publications include: 'Appropriating an Authentic Bodily Practice from Japan: on "being there", "having been there" and "virtually being there"', in V. Strang and M. Busse, M. (eds), *Ownership and Appropriation*, (2011, Berg); 'Crafting Selves on Death Row', in D. Davies and C. Park (eds), *Emotion, Identity and Death: Mortality across Disciplines*, (2012, Ashgate); and 'Posthumous personhood and the affordances of digital media' (cowritten with J. Meese, J. Nansen, M. Arnold and M. Gibbs), *Mortality* 20(4): 408–20 (2015).

Cris Shore (D.Phil. in social anthropology, Sussex) is Professor of Social Anthropology at the University of Auckland, having previously worked at Goldsmiths College, London. His research interests include political anthropology, the study of organizations, power and corruption, higher education, and the European Union and the anthropology of policy. Cris was founding Editor of *Anthropology in Action*, founding Director of Auckland University's Europe Institute and, with Sue Wright, is Editor of Stanford University Press's book series, *Anthropology of Policy*. Current research includes a study of the 'Crown' in post-colonial settler societies and a book exploring how indicators and ranking are reassembling society.

References

Allison, O. 2014. 'Fears proposed code could gag science', *Radio New Zealand National*, 2 October. Retrieved 8 January 2016 from http://www.radionz.co.nz/news/national/255991/fears-proposed-code-could-gag-science.

American Anthropological Association. 2016. 'Commentary on Notice of Proposed Rulemaking (80 FR 53933 published 09-08-2015; docket ID HHS–OPHS–2015-0008): Proposals for Modernizing the Common Rule'. Retrieved 31 January 2016 from http://www.americananthro.org/ParticipateAndAdvocate/AdvocacyDetail.aspx?ItemNumber = 13302, accessed on 31.01.2016.

Baloy, N., S. Sabati and R. Glass (eds). 2016. *Unsettling Research Ethics: Collaborative Conference Report*, Santa Cruz: UC Center for Collaborative Research for an Equitable California (CCREC).

Beck, U. 1999. *World Risk Society*. London: Polity Press.

Boden, R., D. Epstein and J. Latimer. 2009. 'Accounting for ethos or programmes for conduct? The brave new world of research ethics committees', *The Sociological Review* 57(4): 727–49.

Bosk, C.L., and R.G. de Vries. 2004. 'Bureaucracies of Mass Deception: Institutional Review Boards and the Ethics of Ethnographic Research', *The Annals of the Academy of Political and Social Science* 595: 249–63.

Caplan, P. (ed.). 2003. *The Ethics of Anthropology: Debates and Dilemmas*. London: Routledge.

Chalmers, D.R.C., and P. Pettit. 1998. 'Towards a Consensual Culture in the Ethical Review of Research', *Medical Journal of Australia* 168(2): 79–82.

Chenhall, R., K. Senior and S. Belton. 2011. 'Negotiating Human Research Ethics: Case Notes from Anthropologists in the Field', *Anthropology Today* 27(5): 13–17.

Conn, L.G. 2008. 'Ethics policy as audit in Canadian clinical settings: exiling the ethnographic method', *Qualitative Research* 8(4): 499–514.

Cowlishaw, G. 2014. 'Auditing ethics committees', *The Australian Journal of Anthropology* 25(3): 377–79.

Foster, G. 2015. 'Universities are misguided to evade controversy with "ethics"', *The Conversation*, 3 March. Retrieved 12 January 2016 from http://theconversation.com/universities-are-misguided-to-evade-controversy-with-ethics-38092.

Haggerty, K.D. 2004. 'Ethics Creep: Governing Social Science Research in the Name of Ethics', *Qualitative Sociology* 27(4): 391–414.

Hauck, R. J-P. 2008. 'Protecting Human Research Participants, IRBs, and Political Science Redux: Editor's Introduction', *Political Science and Politics* 41(3): 475–76. DOI: 10.1017/S1049096508080839.

Hedgecoe, A. 2008. 'Research Ethics Review and the Sociological Research Relationship', *Sociology* 42(5): 873–86.

Heimer, C., and J. Petty. 2010. 'Bureaucratic Ethics: IRB and the Legal Regulation of Human Subjects', *Annual Review of Law and Social Science* 6: 601–26.

Hoonaard, W.C. van den. 2002. 'Introduction: Ethical Norming and Qualitative Research', in W.C. van den Hoonaard (ed.), *Walking the Tightrope: Ethical Issues for Qualitative Researchers*. Toronto: University of Toronto Press.

_____. 2011. *The Seduction of Ethics: Transforming the Social Sciences*. Toronto: University of Toronto Press.

Kohn, T. 2014. 'Ethics review and the limited gaze: a plea for an intervention', *The Australian Journal of Anthropology* 25(3): 379–81.

_____. 2017. 'On the Shifting Ethics and Contexts of Knowledge Creation', in L. Josephides and S. Grønseth (eds), *The Ethics of Knowledge Creation: Transactions, Relations and Persons*, Oxford: Berghahn.

Lederman, R. 2006a. 'Introduction: Anxious borders between work and life in a time of bureaucratic ethics regulation', *American Ethnologist* 3(4): 477–81.

_____. 2006b. 'The perils of working at home: IRB "mission creep" as context and content for an ethnography of disciplinary knowledges', *American Ethnologist* 33(4): 482–91.

_____. 2007. 'Educate Your IRB: An Experiment in Cross Disciplinary Communication', *Anthropology News* 48(6): 33–34.

Pels, P. 1999. 'Professions of Duplexity: A Prehistory of Ethical Codes in Anthropology', *Current Anthropology* 40(2):101–36.

Pettit, P. 1992. 'Instituting a Research Ethic: Chilling and Cautionary Tales', *Bioethics* 6(2): 89–112.

Plattner, S. 2006. 'Comment on IRB Regulation of Ethnographic Research', *American Ethnologist* 33: 525–28.

Schneider, C.E. 2015. *The Censor's Hand: The Misregulation of Human-Subject Research*. Cambridge, MA: MIT Press.

Schrag, Z.M. 2010. *Ethical Imperialism*. Baltimore: John Hopkins University Press.
_____. 2011 'The Case against Ethics Review in the Social Sciences', *Research Ethics* 7(4): 120–31.
Shore, C. 2008. 'Audit Culture and Illiberal Governance: Universities and the Politics of Accountability', *Anthropological Theory* 8(3): 278–99.
Shore, C., and S. Wright. 1999. 'Audit Culture and Anthropology: Neoliberalism in British Higher Education', *Journal of the Royal Anthropological Institute* 7(4): 557–75.
Sieber, J., and M. Tolich. 2012. *Planning Ethically Responsible Research*, vol. 31. London: Sage Publications.
Simpson, B. 2011. 'Ethical moments: future directions for ethical review and ethnography', *Journal of the Royal Anthropological Institute* 17(2): 377–93.
Strathern, M. (ed.). 2000. *Audit Cultures: Anthropological Studies in Accountability, Ethics, and the Academy*. London: Routledge.
Tolich, M., and M.H. Fitzgerald. 2006. 'If Ethics Committees were Designed for Ethnography', *Journal of Empirical Research on Human Research Ethics* 1(2): 71–78.
Wynn, L.L. 2011. 'Ethnographers' Experiences of Institutional Ethics Oversight: Results from a Quantitative and Qualitative Survey', *Journal of Policy History* 23(1): 94–114.
_____. 2014. 'Ethics Review Regimes and Australian Anthropology', *The Australian Journal of Anthropology* 25(3): 373–75.
Yanow, D., and P. Schwartz-Shea. 2008. 'Reforming Institutional Review Board Policy: Issues in Implementation and Field Research', *Political Science and Politics* 41(3): 483–94. DOI:10.1017/S1049096508080864.

PART IV

Reviving the Public University – Alternative Visions

CHAPTER 12
Who Will Win the Global Hunger Games?
The Emerging Significance of Research Universities in the International Relations of States

CHRISTOPHER TREMEWAN

◆◆◆

Dystopian futures figure large in the imagination of the new generation. The popular film series *The Hunger Games* exemplifies this morose realism: a generation feeling manipulated in a deadly game, where a privileged elite rules over a repressed majority that is physically separated in environmental dead zones, deprived of basic freedoms, forced into hard labour for bare subsistence and subjected to saturation electronic propaganda and surveillance backed by merciless state violence. Since all these social realities already exist in large measure today, the young cannot be accused of wild fantasy when considering their own futures, or of unreasoned selfishness in their frenetic attempts to join the elite.

A report from a citadel of global capitalism, the recent Bank of America Merrill Lynch's 300-page analysis of the business of robots and artificial intelligence, can only add to their anxiety. It surmises that robots will cut the cost of doing business while displacing up to 47 percent of all workers in the United States, and 34 percent in the U.K., without creating a significant number of new jobs. The less educated will bear the brunt but even doctors may find themselves at risk (Stewart 2015). If you want to make serious money quickly, invest in killer robots (Vigna 2015).

This mix of hope and despair infuses many informed views of the future. On 13 November 2012, a few months before his death, and on the sixtieth anniversary of his matriculation from Oxford, James Martin, widely acknowledged as one of the most influential figures in computer science over the past fifty years, delivered a lecture on 'The Transformation of Humankind' at the Oxford Martin School, which he had endowed with U.S.$150 million to 'formulate new concepts, policies and technologies that will make the future a better place to be'.[1]

His big picture of the probable scenarios for the rest of the twenty-first century inevitably had much that was familiar: pollution of the atmosphere, the need for alternatives to carbon-based energy, the loss of topsoil, the end of traditional agriculture in worst-affected areas, fresh-water depletion, death of the oceans, degradation of other ecosystems, reaching a peak population of ten billion around 2070 and, much sooner than that, getting to the tipping point of climate change when runaway transformations become irreversible.

He balanced these negative trends with the promise of rapid technological developments, many already well under way: hydroponics farming, water conservation, solar energy, fusion research, nanotechnology, 'climate change cities', stem cell and other biomedical advances, huge increases in computing capability, increased life expectancy, the ability to modify human beings, the compounding importance of the humanities and ethics, and the use of high technology for avoiding or prosecuting war. In his view, the technological advances over recent decades are as nothing compared to those currently in the pipeline at Oxford and other research institutions.

He saw a twenty-first century of revolutionary technological paradigm shifts in the midst of social collapse or extreme chaos, possibly followed by a global renaissance in the twenty-second century. The truth of the latter is less important than his accompanying observation that there will continue to be winners and losers, especially with respect to climate change, with some climactic zones benefitting and others, currently densely populated, becoming unproductive and perhaps uninhabitable, some countries pulling through (he puts his money on the United States, China, India and Russia – largely because of size, the capabilities of state power and, one assumes from his use of 'Darwinian', the ability to absorb massive shocks), and the biggest winners of all being global corporations with their ability to operate and spread risk across borders. He saw the possibility of 'giga-famines' and the death of a billion people alongside the emergence of 'eco-affluence' – an extension of current global inequalities but with an adjusted set of beneficiaries and victims and even higher stakes. He concluded with what must be the justification for his generosity: that 'interdisciplinary research is a powerhouse for tackling these massive issues' (Martin 2012). This scenario-building therefore highlighted not only the role of research universities in solving future challenges; it also, unintentionally perhaps, placed them in the crosshairs of the many dilemmas of the international relations of states, as governments confront global crises which none can solve alone.

Research universities are not marginal institutions in this human and ecological drama. Their huge intellectual resources already address global challenges and find solutions. But they will confront more sharply their moral responsibility to ensure that education and research serve the many not just the few; to do this, they need to rise to the challenge of cross-border issues by acting collectively, in a manner commensurate with the scale and seriousness of the issues.

I recognize that universities already contribute much to society through fundamental and applied research, that much research has always been international through the cooperation amongst scholars in different countries and that many research universities have institutes and partnerships that focus on global concerns. My argument here goes beyond that. It is that research universities have yet to use the full potential of strategic collaborations between international networks of universities and the building of coalitions with other sectors on key issues from climate change and global health to population ageing and sustainability. This will involve far more intentional use of the institutional strengths of public leadership, research capability and social influence to relate research and education to international public policy. I hold also that, not only will such a strategy contribute more directly to urgent imperatives of human wellbeing, but they will also give universities far greater leverage in resolving many of the dilemmas they currently face in terms of public funding, political legitimacy and the attraction of original, fearless thinkers as academics and students.

As I have argued elsewhere, international consortia can be a transformative space where institutions can shape a more effective kind of internationalization: they provide the opportunity to 'develop an internationalization "governmentality" that operates in the service of communities – local, regional, global ... [and thus] reposition narrowly competitive futures as much less predetermined, and alternate ones much more possible' (Tadaki and Tremewan 2013: 384).

This means being clear about the ethical choices involved. How can research universities better act in the interest of humanity as a whole – in accordance with the humanitarianism of traditional academic values – rather than being constrained by their relationships to nation-states and the ties of ideology and money to business and industry? How can they develop a sufficient degree of autonomy from national jurisdictions so that their research will contribute to solutions for the common good, not just for their nation or for the interconnected global elite who can afford it? How can we best reform the existing structures of global science, and its relationships with government and corporations, to deliver timely and equitable benefits from discoveries overcoming, step by step, the inequalities in political and economic power and the luck of geographical location in the biosphere?

The closeness to government and business of many university policy institutes has tended to dampen the traditional role of intellectual critique, embedding universities as servants rather than as independent actors. This is not a neutral position. Intellectual leadership has been given away. The resulting intellectual vacuum has assisted a default to neoliberal forms and processes that conform to an unsustainable paradigm of economic exploitation of the world's natural resources and undemocratic control of its populations. Instead, research universities need to reclaim their role as global engines of critical thinking and basic research working in an equal partnership with other sectors, including multilateral organizations and NGOs, to build alternative forms of social, political and economic life attuned to rescuing a threatened ecosystem and creating more equitable societies.

In addition, research universities routinely use their role of social reproduction, of sorting people into their social places (mostly according to their ability to pay), for revenue generation and elite influence through highlighting the pathways they provide to membership of a tiny moneyed elite. This has intensified as global elites have been constituted through the business of 'knowledge and innovation' as they once were through education for government and the professions and, before that, through aristocratic lineages spanning borders. Now is the time to build cohorts of students and academics more explicitly committed to the future of the planet through a variety of cross-disciplinary initiatives and external collaborations. Existing models, of which there are many, need to be scaled up, the social commitment of universities used as a far more dynamic part of attracting students and faculty, and international connectivity reoriented to this purpose. In short, the scale of the challenges the planet now faces requires responses from universities of similar scale and reach, far beyond anything attempted to date. I do not wish to diminish the difficulties currently faced by research universities, and expect that some will see my analysis as marginal to the role of a university or simply impossible to encompass among a plethora of demands. In order to illustrate the possibilities of my approach, I consider the opportunities that could arise from research universities contesting ideological assumptions in three areas where the neoliberal consensus is considered normative even though failing to deliver on its promises. These are: inequality and risk; innovation and techno-nationalism; and internationalization and techno-globalism.

In this manner I intend to draw out some of the positive steps that could and should be taken in order for research universities to position themselves for a socially responsible and academically productive role in a turbulent century. Prior to examining the three dimensions, it is necessary to address, if briefly, the scepticism in some policy circles (and often within the institutions themselves) that universities have anything to contribute to global deliberations.

Global Impact of Research Universities

The specific role of research universities was highlighted by Castells more than twenty years ago, when investigating how university systems function as 'the engine of development in the new world economy' or 'fundamental tools of development'. Furthermore, '[i]f knowledge is the electricity of the new informational economy, then institutions of higher education are the power sources on which the new development process must rely' (Castells 1993: 66). He went on to propose an analytical framework of universities as 'dynamic systems of contradictory functions', some of which predominate at particular times and in specific contexts, namely:

1. ideological apparatuses expressing the ideological struggles present in all societies;
2. mechanisms of selection of dominant elites;
3. the generation of new knowledge (the most obvious function today but in reality the exception globally);
4. the training of the bureaucracy (Castells 1993: 70–72).

Research universities have all these functions but focus on the generation of new knowledge (although how this is defined, and by whom is increasingly problematic). Research universities are seen as an elite – and certainly see themselves as such.

In 2009, Marginson and Van der Wende provided a conceptual framework for higher education in the context of globalization, which noted that 'higher education institutions are more important than ever as mediums for a wide range of cross-border relationships and continuous global flows of people, information, knowledge, technologies, products and financial capital' (Marginson and Van der Wende 2009: 18). Furthermore:

> The concentration of research, resources and prestige in major universities constitutes institutions of key importance in their nations

and powerful engines of globalization on a world scale. The research performance of universities signifies their capacity to produce global knowledge goods and their status in the eyes of other institutions, prospective students and financial capital (ibid.: 34).

Observing the effects of new public management in weakening professional regulation and strengthening institutional control (ibid.: 20) and the heightened competitiveness and exclusionary nature of international ranking tables (ibid.: 35), their definition of globalization aims to be 'neutral' and 'free of ideological baggage' (ibid.: 19). Problematic though this is (more on this later), they are nevertheless probably correct in their judgment that:

> For the first time in history every research university is part of a single worldwide network and the world leaders in the field have an unprecedented global visibility and power (ibid.: 54).

The aggregate research power of these universities is best measured, not by the ubiquitous and highly questionable international rankings, but through the mining of the huge databases which now contain immense amounts of detail on the productivity and quality of output of every institution down to the individual researcher. Searches can reveal the quality and quantity of research by country, by institution, by discipline or research focus through monitoring citations, funding and other measures of 'impact', especially in the STEM disciplines. Elsevier, the world's largest publisher and dominant in the publication of academic journals in science and medicine, is now the world's fourth-largest data company. It can track capabilities globally and also see, through monitoring downloads in real time, whether, and which, research is being used in government and industry.

This big data development enables the measurement of the aggregate research power (productivity and quality) of, for example, the network of forty-five research universities which are members of the Association of Pacific Rim Universities (APRU). This is shown at a high level in the graph below, which places APRU in relation to countries with major research profiles, and two other university networks (both national not international: the Association of American Universities, or AAU, and fifteen Canadian universities – U15). The vertical axis is a proxy for quality, the horizontal axis for quantity of output.

On the vertical axis, the research output of APRU universities is greater in quality than all countries (not counting research networks) except the United States, and the U.K., and on the horizontal access

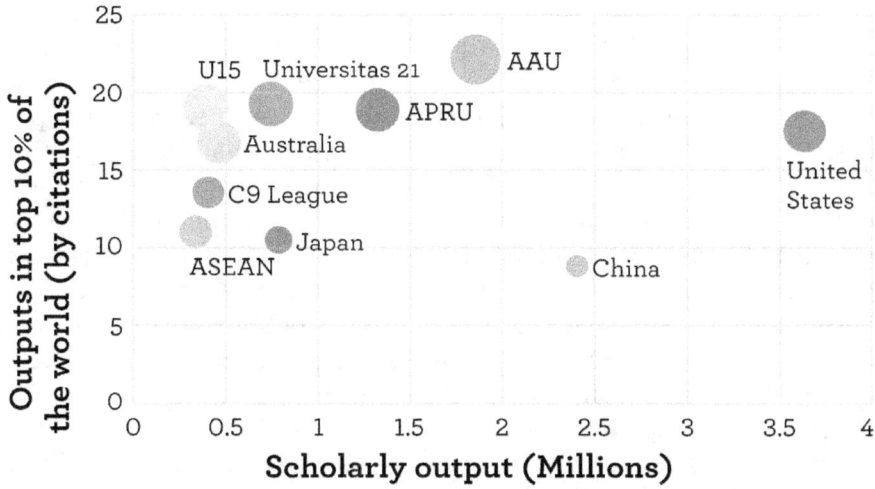

Figure 12.1. Scholarly output (2015) and field-weighted citation impact (2015). AAU = Association of American Universities, the sixty-two most research-intensive U.S. universities; C9 League = top nine Chinese universities; U15 = group of Canadian research universities; ASEAN = Association of Southeast Asian Nations. *Source*: 'The APRU Impact Report', June 2016, (Hong Kong: APRU).

APRU's research is greater in quantity than all countries except the United States and China. The APRU network contains a significant percentage of the research and innovation capabilities of the APEC economies.

As APRU progressively mines the data at levels of finer granularity to show the network's capability in major research themes of immediate relevance to governments in the Asia-Pacific region (for example, global health, disaster science and risk reduction, population ageing, climate change and sustainability), it becomes even more evident both that there is a role for a collective presence in international public policy formation and that universities need to organize themselves as a collective voice at the international level on specific issues in which they have leading expertise. They are increasingly being invited to do so by multilateral agencies seeking their input.

Inequality and Risk

In 2011, the Occupy Wall Street movement galvanized popular opinion and spread across the globe, drawing a picture of the predatory one percent thriving at the expense of the 99 percent (see also Oxfam 2015). Soon after, Thomas Piketty's *Capital in the Twenty-First Century* (2014) brought a long-standing debate on wealth and inequality into focus within mainstream economics. At the same time, neoliberal policies continued to be proposed by governments that lacked political autonomy owing to decades of dominance of an ideology which subordinated human wellbeing to financial power. This political force has permeated many social democratic institutions, including universities, establishing the norm of running education and research as a business under the enforced disciplines of new public management and its accountability regimes. These render universities politically docile and alienate them from the societies they serve, under the rubric of international competitiveness.

The laggardly, reluctant response by business to inequality and ecological depletion has also shifted into more positive gear. The World Economic Forum's annual report on global risks in 2015 laid out, as would be expected, a comprehensive global-risks landscape ranging from terrorist attacks and the spread of infectious diseases to the failure of critical infrastructure and man-made environmental catastrophes (World Economic Forum 2015: 2, Table B). However, the report's graphic representation of the connections between trends and risks highlights 'profound social instability' as the strongest risk and connects it to rising income disparity (ibid.: 3, Figure 3). It is interesting to note the input to the report by research universities including James Martin's beneficiary at Oxford (ibid.: 4).

There are many similar reports from other international agencies and think tanks, such as the World Bank's *World Development Report* which, in 2014, was entitled 'Risk and Opportunity: Managing Risk for Development', and several reports from the OECD (OECD 2011; 2014). The International Monetary Fund's Managing Director, Christine Lagarde, speaking at the World Economic Forum on 23 January 2015, expressed her wish to 'move the IMF in the direction of looking at inequality as mainstream and core business' (Nunn 2015: 2).

Does this acknowledgement of social dislocation attest to a change of heart from global economic institutions, the harbinger of a new effort to counter inequality and other threats to human society? Will we see the encouragement of policies which quickly redistribute wealth and fund remedial measures for the environment? As these insights permeate public policy, will research universities find themselves better funded to bring holistic solutions from the full range of their research portfolios, with the humanities/

social sciences and STEM disciplines both integrated into research on current global challenges?

Alex Nunn sees an underlying consistency, but it is not this. 'The ultimate purpose of this exercise', he says, 'is to defend world market integration from its own integral tensions which might undermine it' (Nunn 2015: 10). Analysing the 'new global politics of inequality', Nunn observes that the global institutions, which, for decades, promoted policies that produced inequality, are now concerned that emerging challenges to social cohesion and political legitimacy from large-scale social and political unrest will undermine economic growth and the reproduction of working populations with adequate competitive capacity (ibid.: 13–16). He sees global economic integration as now requiring the management of risks, inequality foremost among them, 'to save world market society from itself' (ibid.: 20).

In this process, even the muted democratic accountability and the specific political interests of states are seen as problematic. Global risk management by international economic institutions and global business (such as the OECD, World Bank, World Economic Forum) simultaneously becomes a bid for autonomy from member states by shifting policy formation onto the terrain of global business from national politics (ibid.: 20–21). A recent example is the secrecy surrounding the Trans-Pacific Partnership negotiations involving states and global corporations but not legislatures, and the erection of supranational organs through which companies can sue governments for taking measures that protect their own citizens but affect profitability (Schwartz and Thomas 2015).

Research universities are implicated in the new politics of inequality and its regime of risk management in many ways. As Castells observed, 'technology has become a development tool of paramount importance, but is one of the most unevenly distributed capacities in the world' (Castells 1993: 68). Research universities are also unevenly distributed and this matters because they are the deep structure of discovery behind much of this technology and their existence is determined by national wealth, public investment, integration with the global economy, the use of English, and other historical factors. In this structural way, inequalities are perpetuated.

Universities are also increasingly implicated through the ethical choices they make and their failure to bring to bear the full range of their research on policy debates which appear primarily technological but have deep social consequences in unequal societies. Risks to people and their societies must take precedence over risks to profit.

I recently attended an international conference organized by the Japanese government on 'Crafting Cyber Security in a Less Secure World'. The conference was notable for the high level of business (CEOs of major IT firms and other major industries), government representatives (security intelligence officials, military) and academic specialists.[2] Their impressive knowledge and their corporate interests steered them primarily to technical fixes for threats to profitability and state security. A 'less secure world' and the implications of hyperconnectivity for unequal societies, though apparently part of the brief, received little attention. This is symptomatic of exclusion by default, sometimes by design, which relegates researchers and their institutions to that of technical advisers to those who have steerage of the larger policy picture and may desire to keep policy deliberations away from democratic accountability and the public eye.

It is time for research universities collectively to exercise much stronger leadership in such debates, in a manner which does not shy away from the critical evaluation of the strategies of business and government while, at the same time, seeking a positive partnership for the common good.

Some existing forums may have potential for this. For example, the World Economic Forum has established 'a community of the presidents of the top twenty-five universities in the world' called the Global University Leaders Forum focusing on the future of higher education and the role of science in society, as well as various sustainability and entrepreneurship initiatives.[3] Some might argue that university presidents attend the annual meetings of the World Economic Forum mostly for confirmation of their membership of the global elite and that they are playing into the inequality agenda of amelioration for the rich rather than real solutions for the poor. In contrast, there is an argument that this is exactly where the leaders of research universities should be present to bring critical insights, alternative worldviews and the latest international research to solving global issues. APRU now sits alongside governments as a member of APEC's Policy Partnership on Science, Technology and Innovation and as a member of APEC's Human Resources Development Working Group. However, in both these instances, to be effective over the long term, involvement needs to be based on a commitment to social equity and on a process of collective policy formation amongst research universities on the basis of their research and of their collaboration with NGOs, cities and local communities, as well as with national governments and business. They are ideally positioned for this, but have yet to fully realize a collective and effective independent role at the international level. This means taking the next step beyond marginal membership of an international forum to creating new platforms for international intervention and cooperation. Universities must emancipate themselves from the tendency merely to resuscitate an unsustainable global economic model and its elite. Instead, as mentioned above, they must collectively 'formulate new concepts, policies and technologies that will make the future a better place to be' (Oxford Martin School 2015).

Innovation and Techno-nationalism

The 'knowledge society' ideology of developed economies emphasizes the need for international competitiveness and the essential role of research universities in technological innovation for national and social benefit. These produce constant pressure for improved performance on research productivity metrics. The propagation of the notion of a 'world-class' university has intensified efforts by developing countries to mould their leading institutions on the singular model of a U.S. research university. This is despite the risk that the quest for 'world-class' may well minimize their own strengths and endowments, not to mention the broader objectives of education.

The pursuit of international competitiveness is also based on a premise of techno-nationalism, which is seriously contested. Edgerton, in a historical analysis of technological innovation and economic growth, refutes the claim 'that *national* economic and technological performance is determined by *national* rates of innovation'. He disputes that the purpose of national research funding is 'to overtake rich countries and that to do so a nation needs to innovate more, and that if it doesn't innovate it will descend to the depths of the poorest countries' (Edgerton 2007: 5). He continues:

> It was known in the 1960s that national rates of economic growth did not correlate positively with *national* investments in invention, research and development, and innovation. It has *not* been the case that countries innovate and grow a lot (ibid.: 6).

He later concludes that:

> Global innovation *may* be the main determinant of global economic growth, but it does not follow that this is the case for particular nation states. ... Global technological sharing, between rich countries, and between rich and poor, has been the norm (ibid.: 10).

Edgerton's corrective is important for locating research universities more accurately in the techno-nationalist rivalries between states. While universities may use instrumentalist arguments about their impact on national economic growth (or national security) to bolster their chances of more public funding, the fact is that the sharing of technology between countries has had more impact than purely national innovation (even for the U.S.). Such sharing has resulted in a convergence of the technological level of the richest nations and improved levels for developing nations. These facts pose questions about the way institutional collaborations across national borders have been salient and could be more so. There is clearly potential for even greater international collaboration between research universities.

Yet current tendencies appear to militate against deepening such collaborations. The politics of inequality allied with Hiromi Mizuno's analysis of science and nationalism in East Asia, and Shigeru Nakayama's observations on the new phase of techno-nationalism shading into a techno-globalism embraced by both the United States and China, do not augur well (Mizuno 2012; Nakayama 2012). The crackdown on dissent by president Xi Jinping's Administration in China has included strong political pressure on leading universities and scientific academies to conform more closely to the Communist Party's political line and to intensify their efforts to support the nation's economic agenda.[4] The Party's direction of education and research in pursuit of international leadership in the life sciences, technology, space and defence research has become more explicit and heavy handed.[5]

In January 2006, during the last Bush Administration, the Association of American Universities – the elite group of U.S. research universities – produced a report entitled 'National Defense Education and Innovation Initiative: Meeting America's Economic and Security Challenges in the 21st Century'. It began:

> The United States has exercised global leadership in economic and security matters for more than 50 years, and the American people have experienced extraordinary security and economic progress as a result.
>
> But in this still-young century, the nation faces new challenges to both our security and our prosperity: the danger to our national and homeland security posed by terrorism, the increasing competitive pressure from the growing economies of Asia and elsewhere, and the threat to our economic and national security posed by dependence on Middle East oil. These challenges demand a dramatic, creative response.

Yet they come at a time when the continuous innovation that has been the hallmark of America's economic success and military prowess is threatened at its very foundation. Serious problems in our educational system and a weakening federal commitment to research in the physical sciences and engineering are eroding the nation's innovative edge, with increasingly evident and alarming results.

Nearly 50 years ago, faced with similar challenges following the launch of Sputnik by the Soviet Union, America responded by enacting the National Defense Education Act and by multiplying the nation's investment in university-based research. The Association of American Universities (AAU) believes that today's challenges demand a comparable response (Association of American Universities 2006: 2).

Such an appeal to the Bush Administration may have been partly a marketing tactic aimed at a conservative government. Nevertheless, the framing of the role of research universities within the national interest of winning the global technological competition is a ubiquitous and long-standing rationale promoted by U.S. institutions despite evidence that they remain far ahead (see Hacker 2015; Teitelbaum 2015).

More generally, research universities face increasing constraints from governments. For example, the annual meeting of the Global Research Council, in Tokyo in May 2015, pondered over the common trend that research funding bodies were increasingly constrained by national governments both in terms of more limited funding and the political steering of research agendas according to short-term economic growth objectives. This financial steering funnels through to research universities, which are increasingly expected to be the publicly funded and student-funded research and development arms of private businesses delivering profits to private shareholders. This pressure disenfranchises traditions of public service and international solidarity which now, in the face of so many urgent cross-border issues, need to be reclaimed as core to the academic mission.

Cooperation between researchers across borders regardless of nation-state agendas has deep historical roots but has always required nurture and protection against the imposition of narrowly political imperatives. Edgerton's finding that 'sharing across borders' has been the norm for global innovation is another spur to reach beyond national agendas and embed the traditions of collaboration amongst not only an international community of individual scholars but also of whole institutions and networks of institutions. The potential of this latter step remains to be developed.

The internal homework implied for research universities includes a redefinition of research impact in order to realign academic incentives for researchers. As a recent APRU meeting of university vice presidents for research noted, a professor might change international policy and practice in a key area (in this case, the treatment of AIDS) yet not be promoted because he did not publish in a high-impact journal. International collaborations that may shift whole health systems or upgrade the disaster preparedness of developing nations may not be recognized in current internal promotion policies. The same meeting proposed that such internal policy issues could be taken up by APRU in order to propose shifts at the international level, which may assist in overcoming institutional inertia.

Internationalization and Techno-globalism

A more complex task is to build the external interfaces and international sites for partnerships. This requires a fundamental rethinking of the way research universities understand internationalization.

Universities draw on the conventional narratives of internationalization and techno-globalism both as self-understanding and as institutional positioning. The results have been a mix of dynamic international outreach, greater global connectivity, new models of collaboration, increased revenues or the substitution of public funding with fees from international students, as well as inauthenticity, avoidance of social and cultural criticism, and strategic confusion.

This ambiguous result emerges from the post-Second-World-War cosmopolitan idealism of internationalism, and the extension of democracy existing alongside the Cold War competition for the global dominance of capital. Or, as Nunn would put it, the contradictory elements of the post-war liberal project to 'extend emancipatory rights to individuals alongside democratization' and 'the project to expand capitalist social relations and the world market to the scale of all human organization' could be held in check until the end of the Cold War. Now, 'competitiveness – rather than cosmopolitanism – is the principal objective shaping and rescaling political authority in support of the WMS [World Market System]' (Nunn 2015: 3):

> The implication of this is that the world society and supra-national constitutionalization of political authority that we currently have are dependent on, subordinate to, and a pale shadow of, the world market (ibid.: 3).

Nunn observes that a focus on national competitiveness has permeated not only the level of states but that this political culture has driven 'these pressures down to sub-state scales' while global economic institutions, appearing to take on a progressive agenda of poverty reduction have, in reality, worked to ensure that 'the extension of social and political rights was consistent [with] and supportive of world market integration', hence adopting 'a dual role, adding systemic crisis and risk management to their prior role of promoting world market integration' (ibid.: 5).

Caught in this ambiguous discourse, universities propagate an ideology of internationalization which promotes cross-border interaction but is curiously shorn of the realities of its global political context. The critique of the causes of inequality, or of the political and social roots of current crises, is often muted. The questioning of social attitudes, and cultural and religious outlooks, is shied away from instead of being understood as fundamental to education. The international role of research universities is generally viewed through an apolitical 'internationalization' focus on foreign partnerships, the global positioning of a 'brand' through elite partnerships, the replication of courses or campuses in some form in other countries, the attraction of foreign students or giving them a short-term international cultural experience, and, to a more limited extent, joint research with international partners.

University leaders are often caught up in a populist techno-globalism as they faithfully seek to expound the achievements of their institutions. The dangers of this are exposed by Edgerton's critique of an 'innovation-centric techno-globalism focused on technologies of *communication* [that] has been at the heart of any number of histories of the world, the musings of information society gurus and many a portentous address about science and technology' (Edgerton 2007: 10). He reviews the nineteenth-century's globalization through the steamship, railway and telegraph, which was then ignored in the 1920s when commentators, Henry Ford among them, praised the aeroplane, the wireless and the motion picture for eliminating national boundaries and ushering in a world of peace and understanding. He notes George Orwell's weariness in 1944 with the clichés about 'abolition of distance' and 'disappearance of frontiers' at a time in the mid twentieth century when science and technology were 'key tools of autarchy'. Furthermore, '[t]he very technologies that were at the heart of the naïve techno-globalism vision of an interconnected world were the tools of a new national despotism' (Edgerton 2007: 13). Edgerton shows that the radio and the aeroplane were closely tied to the military and the latter 'was primarily a weapon of war, even in peacetime'. Such a reminder is timely today, as China gets a vice-grip on the Internet, the U.S. National Security Agency trawls cyberspace globally, and aerial bombing appears to be as far as international cooperation can go to address the deep causes of crisis.

While it can be readily understood that presidents of universities have the task of boosting their achievements through appropriating popular views of scientific developments and that they avoid overtly political stances which would put their institutions at odds with governments or donors, it is less easy to understand why the academic literature on internationalization still focuses mainly on building 'world-class', high-ranking universities, cross-cultural understanding, the educational benefits of international experience for the individual student or faculty member, and the various models for international cooperation in teaching, research and, sometimes, community service.

Positive though these activities are, why do both theorists and university practitioners of 'internationalization' not go further and see the necessity and urgency of honing collective institutional capabilities and collaborations to face the big challenges of the age? Why do they not generate more pressure on their institutions to provide this kind of leadership? Why are they not insistent on the university's role of social critique to get at fundamental causes rather than just create a soft internationalist aura of intercultural sharing?

A familiar and partial explanation is the rejection of class analysis and the shift towards cultural explanations for political behaviour that was embraced by both left and right towards the end of the Cold War and since. Analyses of the internationalization of higher education in East Asia are often overlaid with the terminology of cultural exceptionalism through allusion to Confucianism or Confucian ethics (Marginson 2011). Alternatively, 'Anglo-Saxon standards or ideologies' were thought to lead to 'traps of recolonization, resulting in learning experiences that may not really fit the specific cultural and political environments of the East' (Mok 2007: 438). Yet mentioned only tangentially is the association of nation building and global competitiveness with political legitimacy and the authoritarianism of party-states, as in Singapore and China or the Gulf states, where the exercise of civil rights is severely circumscribed.

The use of higher education in the political project of constructing a national identity and containing the democratic expectations and the revolutionary social effects of the shift to globally integrated market societies constrains the value of much 'internationalization'. These constraints are rarely subjected to critique in the academic literature. The use of higher education for political objectives and the calibrated pretence of academic autonomy are therefore hidden from view, disguised as a cultural imperative. Throughout Asia, students and scholars have constituted radical political forces for national independence and democracy for more than a century. This history too is buried and political conformity posited as culturally normative and accepted as politically expedient. This is a higher education sector characterized by fear rather than intellectual creativity.

The stance that fundamental research has to be curiosity-driven by the researcher, a key value in a research university, can also be a kind of camouflage. University administrations make decisions daily on where to invest resources, what grant applications to support, or what to define as research excellence. This is not a value-free exercise and is heavily influenced by governments and by perceptions that research in STEM disciplines is more productive of economic outcomes and high international rankings. As Boden and Epstein observe, the logic of the public accountability surrounding research funding 'avoids discussion of the hidden operation of power: who determines resources and objectives, what knowledge is valued, how is 'well-spent' defined and to whom or how should public bodies such as universities be accountable and why?' (Boden and Epstein 2006: 233).

The most important question to arise from this analysis is the way in which agency can be exercised in the coming decades. It has to be done in the tension between an idealistic post-war internationalism and the extension of Nunn's world market system of constant competition. It has to organize universities internationally to focus on issues of common importance rather than to acquiesce to a general convergence towards institutional uniformity in the service of economic imperatives.

Appadurai has written on the possibilities of the democratization of knowledge and 'grassroots globalization', by which he means to link different social realities and to:

> create partnerships in teaching and research so that our picture of areas does not stay confined to our own first-order, necessarily parochial, world pictures. The potential payoff is a critical dialogue between world pictures, a sort of dialectic of areas and regions, built on the axiom that areas are not facts but artefacts of our interests and our fantasies as well as of our needs to know, to remember, and to forget (Appadurai 2000: 8).

He holds that this globalization must be associated with seeing research as a democratized practice of imagination. While it is 'in and through the imagination that modern citizens are disciplined and controlled', it is also 'the faculty through which collective patterns of dissent and new designs for collective life emerge' and therefore have emancipatory potential:

> As the imagination as a social force itself works across national lines to produce locality as a spatial fact and as a sensibility ..., we see the beginnings of social forms without either the predatory mobility of unregulated capital or the predatory stability of many states (Appadurai 2000: 6).

Boden and Epstein see merit in this approach, while being sceptical of the possibility because 'what marks the contemporary idea of research is its capture and control by the dominant ideology of neo-liberalism' and that 'the aspects of discipline and control within university research have come to predominate with potentially catastrophic consequences' (Boden and Epstein 2006: 233). Yet even they concede that after incorporation into the neoliberal regime of practice and governmentality and the constriction of research imagination, 'knowledge producing institutions and people remain a potential destabilizing force by virtue of their capacity to imagine different worlds and different futures' (ibid.: 234).

It is this capacity to imagine different futures, and Appadurai's 'collective patterns of dissent and new designs for collective life', that is the core promise of a new level of international collaboration. Appadurai holds that the:

> democratization of knowledge and globalization from below rely on two factors: first, the capability of transnational advocacy networks and non-Government organization to participate in such a process. And second, there must be a willingness and capacity amongst academics to re-form themselves and engage in 'collaborative research on globalization ... that could level the theoretical playing field for grassroots activists in international fora' (Appadurai 2001, cited in Boden and Epstein 2006: 236).

One of the strong concepts to emerge from APRU's work on sustainability and climate change has been the idea of 'knowledge action networks' by Charles Kennel at the University of California at San Diego, former director of the Scripps Institution of Oceanography and chair of the NASA Advisory Council. By this he means establishing the relationships which connect the latest international research to detailed understanding of local contexts (cities, regions, nations) so that civic leaders, NGOs, private-sector organizations and researchers have the benefit of each other's knowledge:

> Knowledge action networks that focus on specific regions and impacts can link the global science, technology and policy communities to local initiatives, and local knowledge to the global science community (Kennel and Daultrey 2010: 6).

Kennel's strategy is also a useful prophylactic against the wilder ideas of scientists about their own omniscience. In 2006, James Martin advocated 'an upper house for the globe' consisting of scientists.[6]

Such an international community of different sectors that imagines alternative futures while being fully informed by both the latest research and the details of local contexts as well as connected to policy processes, has the possibility of being a form of political independence, even resistance, which exists in a neutral space not dominated by elite economic or political imperatives. Such ideas rely on an imperative of mobilization on a multisectoral basis. What we need now is for universities to work together at scale, building on their myriad smaller initiatives in education and research, and to create the autonomous international sites and high-level external collaborations for the independent advancement of solutions to international relations and cross-border issues. Only then will universities play their proper role in the international relations of states through exercising an ethical and intellectual influence that is commensurate with their research and education capabilities. In the process, they will secure their own futures.

Whether or not research universities decide to take up this challenge in a serious manner, invest in it on the scale required and direct their international strategies towards it, they will inevitably be judged by their own societies regarding the contribution they make to solving the challenges of an increasingly turbulent century. This will mean championing intellectual excellence and equity against social elitism and the singular focus on economic growth, if dystopian visions of a global hunger games are to be prevented their full realization.

◆

Christopher Tremewan is Secretary General of the Association of Pacific Rim Universities (www.apru.org) and previously Pro Vice-Chancellor International at the University of Auckland. He holds degrees in social anthropology (Auckland), political science (Canterbury, New Zealand) and public administration (Harvard). Chris's main interests include Southeast Asian politics, identity politics, the politicization of ethnicity and the internationalization of higher education. He was founding Director of the New Zealand Asia Institute and has held visiting positions at Peking University, Georgetown University and St Antony's College, Oxford. His published work includes *The Political Economy of Social Control in Singapore* (1994, Macmillan) – a book banned from distribution in Singapore and reprinted in 1996.

Notes

1. http://www.nasscom.in/Dr-James-Martin-Headstrong-s-founder-pledges-50-million-to-research-The-Independent-UK-59426.
2. See http://www8.cao.go.jp/okinawa/3/cyber3/program.pdf.
3. See http://www.weforum.org/academic-networks.
4. See http://www.theguardian.com/world/2014/dec/30/chinese-president-signals-tightening-of-control-over-universities.
5. See http://www.chinadaily.com.cn/china/2014-12/14/content_19083596.htm.
6. See http://www.socialaffairsunit.org.uk/blog/archives/001150.php.

References

Appadurai, A. 2000. 'Grassroots Globalization and the Research Imagination', *Public Culture* 12(1): 1–19.

_____. 2001. 'Grassroots Globalization and the Research Imagination', in: A. Appadurai (ed.), *Globalization*. Durham, NC: Duke University Press.

Association of American Universities. 2006. 'National Defense Education and Innovation Initiative'. Washington, DC. Retrieved 10 February 2016 from https://www.aau.edu/WorkArea/DownloadAsset.aspx?id = 6424.

Association of Pacific Rim Universities. 2016. 'The APRU Impact Report'. http://apru.org/press/publications

Boden, R., and D. Epstein. 2006. 'Managing the Research Imagination? Globalisation and Research in Higher Education', *Globalisation, Societies and Education* 4(2): 223–36.

Castells, M. 1993. 'The University System: Engine of Development in the New World Economy', in A. Ransom, S.-M. Khoo and V. Selvaratnam (eds), *Improving Higher Education in Developing Countries*. Washington, DC: World Bank, pp. 65–80.

Edgerton, D.E.H. 2007. 'The Contradictions of Techno-Nationalism and Techno-Globalism: A Historical Perspective', *New Global Studies* 1(1): 1–32.

Hacker, A. 2015. 'The Frenzy About High-Tech Talent', *New York Review of Books*, 9 July. Retrieved 10 February 2016 from http://Www.Nybooks.Com/Articles/2015/07/09/Frenzy-About-High-Tech-Talent/.

Kennel, C.F., and S. Daultrey. 2010. 'Knowledge Action Networks – Connecting Regional Climate Change Assessments to Local Action', UCSD Sustainability Solutions Institute. Retrieved 10 February 2016 from http://escholarship.org/uc/item/8gd6j0k5.

Marginson, S. 2011. 'Higher Education in East Asia and Singapore: Rise of the Confucian Model', *Higher Education* 61: 597–611.

Marginson, S., and M. van der Wende. 2009. 'The New Global Landscape of Nations and Institutions', in Centre for Education Research and Innovation, *Higher Education to 2030*. Paris: OECD, pp. 17–62.

Martin, J. 2012. 'The Transformation of Humankind', lecture delivered at Oxford University, Clarendon Laboratory, 13 November. Retrieved 10 February 2016 from https://www.youtube.com/watch?v = rmRk887rBwA.

Mizuno, H. 2012. 'Science and Nationalism', *East Asian Science, Technology and Society* 6(1): 1–8.

Mok, K.H. 2007. 'Questing for Internationalization of Universities in Asia: Critical Reflections', *Journal of Studies in International Education* 11: 433–54.

Nakayama, S. 2012. 'Techno-Nationalism versus Techno-Globalism', *East Asian Science, Technology and Society* 6(1): 9–15.

Nunn, A. 2015. 'Saving "World Market Society" from Itself? Risk, the new politics of inequality and the guardians of global capitalism', *International Studies Association Annual Convention, February 2015*. New Orleans. Retrieved 10 February 2016 from https://www.Academia.Edu/10430338/Saving_World_Market_Society_From_Itself_Risk_The_New_Global_Politics_Of_Inequality_And_The_Guardians_Of_Global_Capitalism_Paper_To_The_International_Studies_Association_Annual_Convention_2015.

OECD. 2011. 'Divided We Stand: Why Inequality Keeps Rising'. Paris. Retrieved 10 February 2016 from http://www.Oecd.Org/Els/Soc/Dividedwestandwhyinequalitykeepsrising.htm.

———. 2014. 'Policy Challenges for the Next 50 Years', Economic Policy Paper 9. Paris. Retrieved 10 February 2016 from http://www.Oecd.Org/Economy/Policy-Challenges-For-The-Next-Fifty-Years.pdf.

Oxfam. 2015. 'Wealth: Having It All and Wanting More'. Oxford. Retrieved 15 October 2016 from https://www.oxfam.org/en/research/wealth-having-it-all-and-wanting-more.

Piketty, Thomas. 2014. *Capital in the Twenty-First Century* (London: Belknap)

Schwartz, N.D., and K. Thomas. 2015. 'Business Leaders React With Dismay to Defeat of Trade Bill', *New York Times*, 12 June. Retrieved 15 October 2016 from http://www.nytimes.com/2015/06/13/business/business-leaders-react-with-dismay-to-defeat-of-trade-bill.html.

Stewart, H. 2015. 'Robot Revolution: Rise of "Thinking" Machines Could Exacerbate Inequality', *The Guardian*, 5 November. Retrieved 5 November 2015 from https://www.theguardian.com/technology/2015/nov/05/robot-revolution-rise-machines-could-displace-third-of-uk-jobs.

Tadaki, M., and C. Tremewan. 2013. 'Reimagining Internationalization in Higher Education: International Consortia as a Transformative Space?', *Studies in Higher Education* 38(3): 367–87.
Teitelbaum, M.S. 2015. *Falling Behind? Boom, Bust, and the Global Race for Scientific Talent*. Princeton, NJ: Princeton University Press.
Vigna, P. 2015. 'Merrill Lynch Warns of Robot Apocalypse', *Wall Street Journal*, 5 November. Retrieved 9 November 2016 from http://blogs.wsj.com/moneybeat/2015/11/05/merrill-lynch-warns-of-robot-apocalypse/.
World Bank. 2014. *World Development Report*. Washington DC.
World Economic Forum. 2015. 'Global Risks 2015'. Geneva. Retrieved 10 February 2016 from http://www3.Weforum.Org/Docs/Wef_Global_Risks_2015_Report 15.pdf.

CHAPTER 13
Resistance in the Neoliberal University
SANDRA GREY

◆◆◆

Introduction

At the beginning of the twenty-first century, New Zealand's universities are dominated by auditing and accountability measures which serve to discipline academic staff and students. Government-funding levers and policy directives are being used to ensure that universities support economic and labour market growth. This economic focus is constraining attempts to fulfil the socially progressive goals of universities at the very time when such projects are sorely needed. The picture is one of institutions and their academics being robbed of the space to be engaged in projects which are not countable, auditable, measurable or commercializable. Called by Winter (1991) the 'new higher education' environment, these symptoms are found in universities across the OECD most commonly under the banner of managerialism (Fredman and Doughney 2012; Lorenz 2012; Trowler 2001). The difficulty faced by academic staff and students alike is how to resist the myriad of managerial and auditing techniques infusing daily life in universities and narrowing the purpose of tertiary education.

To find a possible route for emancipation from the purely economic destination currently set out for New Zealand's universities, I draw on Eric Olin Wright's development of 'real utopias'. This concept allows us to consider an alternative to current neoliberal and capitalistic approaches to further and higher education (and other spheres) in a way that can be practically implemented. Wright notes that:

> The exploration of real utopias is an integral part of a broad agenda of an emancipatory social science that includes four basic tasks:
> 1. Specifying the *moral principles* for judging social institutions.

2. Using these moral principles as the standards for *diagnosis and critique* of existing institutions.
3. Developing an account of the *viable alternatives* in response to the critique.
4. Proposing a *theory of transformation* for realizing those alternatives.
(Wright 2012: 3, emphasis in original)

I use the three moral principles advanced by Wright – equality, democracy, and sustainability – as benchmarks against which to evaluate the way tertiary education institutions in New Zealand operate, and, as the basis for transformation to a 'higher education real utopia'. But those of us working in further and higher education must extend Wright's approach, as proposing a theory of transformation is no longer enough. Over the last decade as an activist in the New Zealand Tertiary Education Union (TEU), I have been frequently told by university staff that 'the union' just needs to show the government evidence of the harm being caused by the 'new higher education' (NHE) environment and the government will change course. This fundamentally ignores the political and economic power defending the institutions of capitalism, including the NHE universities. The diagnosis and prognosis which come so easily to social scientists are not enough to change the direction of our universities. Academics and students in NHE universities are going to have to fight for transformation:

> All of us working on these issues in research universities ... have been waiting for someone else to take the lead in moving civic engagement work but it hasn't happened. What we have now discovered is that *we are the ones we've been waiting for* (Gibson 2012: 238).

This chapter sits in the tradition of engaged scholarship, drawing on discursive analysis of three decades of government-policy documentation and on six years working in the executive of the TEU (three of those as the full-time National President). The TEU represents around 10,000 academic and general staff working in further and higher education in Aotearoa New Zealand. While writing from the position of an academic and unionist, the views in this chapter are those of the author, not the TEU. The focus of this chapter is on a diagnosis and critique of the state of universities in New Zealand (all of which are publicly owned), though many of the effects have also been felt by colleagues in institutes of technology and polytechnics. Added to this, many of the trends, conditions and approaches found in New Zealand will be familiar to academic staff and students across the globe, particularly in

English-speaking advanced democracies. New Zealand provides useful insights because the unicameral political system, the small size of our tertiary education sector, and the reliance of the tertiary education sector on state funding have worked together to enable successive governments to implement the rules of the NHE environment effectively and deeply.

The Moral Principles for Judging Higher Education Institutions

In order to judge the social institutions that advance and stabilize late capitalism, Wright's 'real utopias' project sets out three moral principles for the basis of a better society: equality (material and social goods necessary to flourish); democracy (self-determination); and sustainability (justice principles for future generations). Each will be examined in turn to establish their relevance for tertiary education.

The TEU asserts that tertiary education is a public good which means the material and social goods 'produced' by universities need to be shared equally (Grey, Sedgwick and Scott 2013: 7). This view centres on an understanding of universities as having a moral function through 'combining an intellectual purpose of free and open inquiry and a social purpose as a source of social criticism independent of political authority and economic power' (M. Tasker and D. Packham in Bridgman 2007: 3). The TEU is not alone in making this claim about tertiary education as a public good. For example, Shamsh Kassim-Lakha notes (in Hoyt and Hollister 2014: 1695): 'Universities have an obligation to share their intellectual material resources with their immediate community and not simply to co-exist with them'. This role is recognized in the New Zealand Education Act of 1989 (Ministry of Education 1989: 160), which sets out that universities and other tertiary education interests will operate in 'the national interest'.

The sharing of intellectual resources involves the dissemination of research beyond universities, but is also tied to the very nature of the institutions and the learning experienced within them. As Christopherson, Gertler and Gray (2014: 214) note, the collective and civic role of universities 'is manifested in diverse scholarly research agendas. But this civic role is also enacted because universities are the place where young people from diverse backgrounds come together to learn from and about one another and craft routes to new social and political values and identities'. If these are the moral purposes of tertiary education and the modes of operation of universities, then it is crucial that there is equality of access to the social and material goods produced within universities.

Equality of access is closely linked to the second moral principle advanced by Wright – democracy in the form of self-determination. If we agree that universities are sites where new social and political values are created, where social and political critiques are developed and where new knowledge is produced, then we will be concerned to ensure there is autonomy (for institutions) and freedom (for scholars and students). Academic freedom is recognized in the New Zealand Education Act of 1989 (Ministry of Education 1989: 161), which sets out the freedom of academics to 'question and test received wisdom', to 'state controversial or unpopular opinions' and to regulate what is taught and how achievement is to be assessed. What is reflected here is that the development of sound critiques of 'received wisdom' can only come if scholars are separated from the political, social and economic elite of the day. Autonomy and academic freedom are not just crucial for academic staff; they are important for students as, ironically, while they are learning the rules and regulations of a discipline and are being prepared for a productive life in their society, they are also learning resistance. It is the fourth 'R', so to speak, the one that universities don't like to address, and it makes an unruly subject (Edelman Boren 2001: 7).

The final moral principle, advanced by Wright for challenging the institutions of capitalism, is sustainability. In New Zealand, government and institutional publications alike note that universities are training students for jobs yet to be invented and generating knowledge for problems yet unseen. Behind this rhetoric is an important moral principle – future generations must have access to institutions which can help them develop the critical skills needed to engage with the social, scientific, economic and environmental problems of their age. To do this we need to sustain institutions that are able to maintain, in the long term, their separation from the social, political and economic elite of the nation. This means universities that are autonomous and are able to advance academic freedom and fulfil the role of critic and conscience set out for them.

For those who see universities as crucial to social, economic, scientific and environmental progress, Wright's three moral principles are a sound base for higher education reforms and will be used in the next section as 'standards for *diagnosis and critique* of existing institutions'. The problems in NHE have been well diagnosed internationally but we must continue to articulate them publicly so as to disrupt the power of

NHE being taken for granted (Trowler 2001: 197). In New Zealand, for example, the Ministry of Education (MoE) states that the government's approach, which links the 'outputs' of the tertiary education sector to goals of economic advancement and labour market productivity, is 'accepted by the sector as the necessary way forward' (Ministry of Education 2006: 17–18). This might not be the case.

Equality and New Zealand Universities

Equality of access to teaching and research in New Zealand has been undermined by the narrow focus of current tertiary education policy and the administrative processes being adopted by tertiary education leaders. New Zealand governments, like those of many other 'Westminster' countries, have long had a hand in steering the direction of education at all levels. This role is set out in the1989 Education Act:

> The object of the provisions of this Act relating to institutions is to give them as much independence and freedom to make academic, operational, and management decisions as is consistent with the nature of the services they provide, the efficient use of national resources, the national interest, and the demands of accountability (Ministry of Education 1989: 160).

But over the last three decades successive New Zealand governments have sought to achieve a much closer alignment between the actions of tertiary education institutions and the goals of government (see, as an example, Ministry of Education 2008). Institutions must deliver material goods which generate a return for 'NZ Inc' (Jesson 2012; McLaughlin 2003; Zepke 2012).

The 'steering' over the last three decades has privileged commercialization and corporatization in New Zealand's tertiary education sector, turning universities into tools for economic growth. This is reflected in the government strategy documents:

> There are three particular priorities that should shape the agenda for the sector: First is the drive to enhance New Zealand's economic growth performance and raise labour productivity (Ministry of Education 2011: 3).

> [The goals are] ... ensuring that the tertiary education system performs well, not just as its own system, but also as a part of the wider New Zealand economy ... ensuring the system can adapt more quickly ...

addressing changing skill needs (Ministry of Business Innovation and Employment (MBIE) and Ministry of Education 2014: 7).

Tertiary education is seen as a private economic good, rather than a public good and, as Roberts (1999: 80) notes, goals such as promoting a love of learning, fostering public debate, and enhancing democratic citizenship disappear from the agenda. If the economic focus continues to dominate, what little remains of the social and civic ideals buried deep inside the audited and risk adverse New Zealand university system will not just go underground: they will disappear altogether.

The 'economic focus' of government policy leads to a narrowing of who gets to study, where and when – a clear attack on the principle of equality. In an environment of fiscal constraint, New Zealand's National-Party-led government has decided to 'target' its investment on learners aged between eighteen and twenty-five (New Zealand Treasury 2011: 21) to drive higher economic returns for the taxpayers' investment in education (Ministry of Education 2008: 11). Steering ensures the 'right' students are admitted to tertiary study: 'There is little value for anyone if learners enrol in tertiary provision that they are unlikely to complete, or which lacks a clear progression to higher-level study' (Ministry of Education 2011: 30). Mature students and those studying part-time have been increasingly excluded from tertiary studies through changes to student financing policies. The impact is dramatic. In 2008, before the government narrowed student financial support rules, there were 33,009 students over fifty-five years old in New Zealand's tertiary education system; by 2014 the number had almost halved, to 18,927 (Joyce 2015).

The focus on 'economic outputs' from the tertiary education sector has also led to a drive towards higher-level qualifications in New Zealand. This has involved 'redirecting government expenditure away from low-value spending, such as adult and community education courses for personal interest, towards higher-value spending, such as degree level study' (Ministry of Education 2011: 11). This steering based on rules around student and course financing means that 'higher education no longer plays its historical role as a social leveller' (Christopherson, Gertler and Gray 2014: 209).

The changes with regard to who gets to study, what they study and where they study, has been accompanied by a narrowing of the research vision for New Zealand universities. A significant level of noncommercial research is carried out in universities in New Zealand but the government has made clear that it will 'increase the incentives for research and tertiary education institutes to undertake more firm-relevant research and to transfer knowledge to firms' (New Zealand Treasury 2011: 5). This narrow approach to research has been criticized by academics, including the Prime Minister's Chief Science Advisor, Peter Gluckman:

> I think New Zealand has ended up with too much end user involvement in the contestable funding system, in the way it's set forward, which has led to much more short-termism in some of our research (Gluckman 2015).

Self-Determination and New Zealand Universities

The heightened steering of universities by successive New Zealand governments has cut across institutional autonomy and academic freedom, despite the protections set out in legislation. The continuous stream of auditing and measurement tools used to ensure university activity is aligned to government goals constrain the rights of institutions and their academic staff to make decisions about teaching and research. As the OECD notes (2003: 75), governments internationally have generally been withdrawing from direct management of institutions, yet at the same time they have been introducing new forms of control and influence, based largely on holding institutions accountable for performance, via powerful enforcement mechanisms including funding and quality recognition. In New Zealand, the government sets out its overarching goals in the Tertiary Education Strategy and then requires institutions to reflect the aims in their strategic plans, which are sent to the Tertiary Education Commission (a government regulatory and funding agency) for approval. The strategic plans of universities set out clearly how the institution will meet government 'output' targets around student completions, research outputs and fiscal prudency. (The details of the system are set out on the website of the Tertiary Education Commission[1]). Achievement of the government targets are measured and reported annually.

From time to time the ongoing attacks on the autonomy of universities have erupted publicly. For example, when the University of Auckland's vice chancellor questioned the targeting of funding to engineering places, following the 2102 budget, and suggested that the institution would not strictly follow the rules set out, the response from the government was swift. The Minister for Tertiary Education Steven Joyce retorted: 'If they want us to be more directive, I'm more than willing' (see Collins 2012). This type of response has meant any challenge to the Minister's approach for targeting in the sector has been short-lived.

The auditing, counting and measuring of 'outputs' used to steer the direction of tertiary education have required the imposition of a suite of managerial techniques within universities. From the 1990s there has been an increase in line management within institutions and a 'drift upwards' in decision making from faculty to professional administrators (Gumport 2001 in Stewart 2010: 57). The 'professionals' interested in education are being dethroned in favour of 'managers' interested in 'balanced books' and 'KPIs'(Karran 2007; Jones et al. 2012), though in New Zealand these are labelled educational performance indicators (EPIs) to make them appear more palatable. This is about reregulation, with tools such as performance development plans, staff satisfaction surveys, and research portfolios, creating a culture of performativity where the performance is measured against external benchmarks (Jesson 2012: 6).

New Zealand's university staff are acutely aware of this reregulation and its disempowering effect. This was evident in a 2013 survey on the state of the tertiary education sector in New Zealand, completed by 2,931 academic and general staff working in the sector. A clear majority of respondents (88 percent) agreed with the statement that there was a top-down style of management at their institutions, with only 36.4 percent agreeing that there was a climate of collegiality in decision-making processes (Bentley, McLeod and Teo 2014: 14). Participants noted that: 'Top-down hierarchical management is increasingly autocratic in its decision making process' and '[s]enior staff and divisional heads actively clamp down on staff initiative, and do not let us lower creatures do anything without checking with them a million times' (ibid.: 14).

The 2013 survey also illustrated the impact of the managerial processes on 'self-determination': 39 percent of academic staff reported that their level of academic freedom was worse to some degree than when they joined the sector, and 41.9 percent said their opportunity to act as critic and conscience had declined (Bentley, McLeod and Teo 2014: 13). The 'conformism' and 'constraint' expressed in these survey results are evidence of how self-determination (democracy) is under strain due to both government policy approaches and managerial directives. As Marilyn Strathern noted: 'The auditing of research and teaching outputs of universities promotes a standardization and normalization of practices fostering conformity which has direct consequences, and for many dire ones, for intellectual production' (quoted in Dew 2004: 188).

The government's approach to strategic planning and alignment of university outputs with government goals has also impacted upon another element of democracy – direct lobbying of the state with regard to the moral principles that should guide tertiary education policy and practice. Documentation from Universities New Zealand (the Vice Chancellors Committee) shows that the leaders of New Zealand's universities are shying away from publicly 'biting the hand that feeds them'. For example, the 'Universities New Zealand Briefing: Contributing to Government Goals' (Universities New Zealand 2011: 2) notes that universities are 'uniquely well placed to partner with government in pursuit of these objectives [four government goals for the next four years]'. The focus on partnering with government to achieve economic outputs has become the dominant narrative in publicity releases of Universities New Zealand since 2008.[2] Partnering with government, without setting clear moral principles for that partnership, is problematic for Universities New Zealand, as the NHE environment they are signing up to rules out of court any discussion about advancing the non-economic objectives of university activity.

The 'self-determination' of universities is not predicated solely on the protection and advancement of institutional autonomy and academic freedom; it also requires workplace democracy. Wright (2012) speaks about the tyranny of existing in a system where wage labourers never have the power to negotiate on equal terms because of a lack of workplace democracy. Academics need to participate in the governance of the institutions in which they work in order to protect academic freedom (Karran 2007). Through academic freedom, and the creation of a community of scholars bound by its principles, the institution is separated from the current political, economic and social elite. In New Zealand, the spaces for academic staff involvement in decision making have come under attack over the last three decades. Academics and students, and their representative unions, are seen as 'vested' interests, seeking special advantages or 'privileges' for themselves that are contrary to the public interest and to the long-term prospects of the country (Mulgan 2004; Olson 1982). Purging tertiary institutions of their 'vested interests' has meant dismantling collegiality and academic staff participation in decision making (see Russell 2007: 113). The most significant acts to purge the 'vested interest' from New Zealand's tertiary education sector have been made under the current conservative National-Party-led government. The first was the move to make student association membership voluntary in 2011. After decades of compulsory student association membership, students now had to 'opt in' to the student association but they still had to pay the student services levy to their institutions, which was then 'redistributed' to service providers (often the student association). This move has decimated student activism on university campuses. It was followed, in 2015, with a government decision to remove the legislated right of academics and students to sit at the highest level of decision making – university councils.

Another trend cutting across workplace democracy in the tertiary education sector is the rise of insecure work. In New Zealand, like other English-speaking tertiary systems, there has been a rising casualization of the workforce. The number of part-time academic staff grew 48 percent between 2001 and 2011, while the full-time academic workforce grew by only 9.5 percent (Ministry of Education 2013: 13) (the Ministry notes that these trends in the part-time academic staff suggest both a casualization of the academic workforce as well as an increase in the number of joint appointments which provide academics the opportunity to job-share). The link between tenure and the ability to carry out the responsibility to engage in academic critique (even of one's own sector) has long been written about, yet the number of non-tenured, insecure and casualized roles continues to rise in New Zealand, and internationally.

Sustainability and New Zealand Universities

The trends and approaches to funding and reregulating New Zealand universities that have been outlined above do little to defend quality public education for future generations. The policies and processes now in place are fundamentally shifting the nature of universities, and often without any open debate about the underlying principles.

In New Zealand, the NHE agenda is based on short-term goals: 'The focus [of the Tertiary Education Strategy] is much more explicitly on what the government expects the tertiary education system to contribute and the priority outcomes for the immediate future' (Ministry of Education 2008: 4). Any future-oriented goals are inhibited by 'austerity measures' which have meant that financial resources in higher education are 'more stringent and more contingent' (Sharrock 2012: 324). In particular, the focus on mechanical efficiency (the ratio of a system's work output to its work input) (Lorenz 2012: 604) is undermining the sustainability of quality public tertiary education. For example, to cope with the cost of hiring additional senior staff to meet the mechanical efficiency demands for more peer-reviewed publications, the Ministry of Education (2013) notes that New Zealand institutions have turned to using temporary and casualized contracts for low-level teaching academics in order to meet the rising student numbers that make up another mechanical efficiency. This means that the university workforce profile in New Zealand is ageing and there are reduced opportunities for the quality mentoring and training of the next generation of academics.

So how do we transform our universities and defend equality, democracy and sustainability, all of which are under threat because of the more market-based NHE approach to education?

Developing a Viable Alternative and a Theory of Transformation

Wright's real utopia project involves scholars moving from diagnosis and prognosis into the development of viable alternatives. Given the moral principles used to evaluate the current system, the viable alternatives for tertiary education in New Zealand must be ones which defend equality, self-determination and sustainability. From the perspective of both TEU members and the New Zealand Union of Student Associations (NZUSA), the only viable alternative is one which is publicly funded and controlled. It does not take long to find this within the core claims of both student and academic staff associations. For example, the TEU document 'Te Kaupapa Whairoanga', sets out a clear vision for tertiary education:

> We assert that tertiary education is a public good – the system belongs to all of us, we all contribute to it, and we are all responsible for it.
>
> Access to life-long learning in publicly funded tertiary education institutions is a basic right for all New Zealanders (Grey, Sedgwick and Scott 2013).

NZUSA has similar claims in its vision documentation:

> We believe every New Zealand child should have the opportunity to be anything they want to be. That means building a universal, accessible tertiary education system ready to support their dreams whether they choose university, polytechnic or trades training.
>
> We believe education is empowering, enlightening and liberating for individuals and our society. Education is inherently good for New Zealand and crucial to the strength, cohesion and advancement of

our communities and democracy (New Zealand Union of Student Associations 2015).

These claims are not just those made by academic staff and student unions, but are embedded in the New Zealand Education Act of 1989, giving scope and room for them to be enacted across the sector. The Act includes as objects of tertiary education the provision of 'high quality learning and research outcomes, equity of access, and innovation' that contribute to 'the development of cultural and intellectual life in New Zealand' and 'to the sustainable economic and social development of the nation' (Ministry of Education 1989: Section 159AAA). However, as has been illustrated in this chapter, these objectives are far from being met under the current regulatory and financial model. The analysis of the current New Zealand NHE environment shows we are a long way from accessible, free tertiary education, and it is therefore crucial for academics and students to set out a theory of transformation and to act upon it. While the NHE environment at times feels like it is a brick wall, like all neoliberal projects it is neither singular nor impenetrable.

Any transformation of the institutions of capitalism requires an 'agent-centred notion of power' (Wright 2012: 12) and certainly this is true in the NHE environment. Despite the current constraints of the NHE environment, university staff – particularly academics – and students do have considerable resources and power, and their institutions have considerable possibilities for influence. As noted by Cynthia Gibson (2012: 237) for Campus Compact:

> because of research universities' significant academic and society influence, world-class faculty, outstanding students, state-of-the-art research facilities, and considerable financial resources, they are well-positioned to drive institutional and field-wide change relatively quickly and in ways that ensure deeper and longer-lasting commitment to civic engagement among colleges and universities for centuries to come.

So how can this happen? For Wright (2012: 20) challenging the institutions of capitalism takes a range of forms – it can involve ruptural, interstitial or symbiotic transformations. Ruptural transformations are revolutionary in nature; interstitial transformations involve finding the cracks in the system and building small-scale changes which can add weight to its transformation; and symbiotic transformations centre on entering existing institutions to try to expand their potential for empowerment (Wright 2012).

Within the context of tertiary education in New Zealand, there is little desire or political will for ruptural (revolutionary) action. Academic staff and students are inside the institutions which are to be transformed – universities – so are already working in a symbiotic way when trying to bring change. But I would argue that the foundations of the NHE environment, based in casting education as an individualized private good, have been so internalized that it is difficult to bring fundamental and lasting change from within universities without looking to Wright's third method of transformation – interstitial transformation. The NHE environment exploits the professional drive of academics, keeping them focused on production of 'research outputs' and meeting 'EPIs' (Educational Performance Indicators), and away from moral goals such as equality, democracy and sustainability. As Kreber (2014: 127) notes, 'what happens is that professionals' commitment to achieving targets is, thus, controlled indirectly; by believing that their deeply held values are being honoured, they actually collude in our own oppression'. Staff will have to make a commitment to spending time on transforming their workplaces and pushing back against the counting and measuring which is used to judge their professional worth. 'As academics we have a commitment not only to scholarship, but also to the communities in which we profess our craft' (Fiztgerald 2014: 215). Similarly, students who pay fees have been recast and have largely internalized the idea that they are 'buying a credential', as consumers of education.

Given the insider setting and difficulties this raises, any transformation of higher education institutions away from being agents of capitalism, requires academics and students to find the cracks within universities and collectively exploit these to change the system itself. By using the cracks in the system to illustrate the impacts and perverse outcomes of the NHE environment, it is possible that an increasing number of academics and students could move into a space where they feel collectively empowered to assert their rightful roles in knowledge development and dissemination, founded on the principles of equality of access, sustainability for generations to come and self-determination. So where do the cracks exist and what is currently found in these interstitial spaces?

One major area which is, and can be further, used to challenge the NHE environment centres on the very rationale for universities – their role to act as the 'critic and conscience of society' (a term used in the New Zealand Education Act of 1989). This role involves not only critiquing the approach of the current political, social and economic elite

– including their own institutions or universities – but also setting out the 'moral foundations' for such claims in the conscience role.

New Zealand academics can use their teaching spaces for generating agency for students. For example, debating with students about the collective rights and responsibilities encompassed in the critic and conscience function is a way of challenging the NHE environment and the economic focus imposed by government policy. This conversation can have surprising effects. In 2014, after discussing the importance of acting as the critic and conscience of society, students in a third-year social movement course at Victoria University of Wellington set up a new activist group – 'Reclaim Vic' – and organized 'illegal' demonstrations in the university's student hub. The university required any group using the hub to seek the permission of the institution and to pay a bond, something the students rejected as evidence of how education had been commercialized and privatized.

Similarly, while government measures affect the operations of universities, academic members of staff have the agency to resist some of the trends. One is the commodification of our students and the transformation of them from students to 'consumers'. Classrooms are still a domain in which academics and other teaching staff have considerable agency. It is a space that can be used to highlight to students that the public in New Zealand still pays for nearly three quarters of the cost of their education. A space in which academic staff can talk through and negotiate the social contract between student and teacher, student and the that fund them, and so on. A space in which we can acknowledge the crippling student debt generated by NHE policies, but also ensure that students see their role in higher education as being one of learning, not merely gaining a credential.

Academics in tertiary institutions can also use the spaces created in the auditing of the quality of teaching in institutions to reclaim some self-determination. Even though the government is steering the New Zealand tertiary education system more tightly than ever before, the auditing of the quality of education and research still sits with the academic community. As such, academics can choose to use their legislated critic and conscience role to challenge within institutions, and publicly, any rules or processes within the higher education system that are failing students and the broader public that universities serve.

The critic and conscience function afforded New Zealand university academics and students also opens space to bring the impact of NHE techniques out of the shadows, which is an important act for, as Lorenz (2012: 607) notes: 'the colonization of higher education by management has never been openly discussed'. The New Zealand Education Act (1989) gives academics the right to challenge their own institution's actions and policies. That same legislation also means that academic staff can reject the privatization of research by reclaiming and defending their place in public debate. The importance of the role of academics and students in public debate has led to the creation of Academic Freedom Aotearoa in 2013.[3] Academics at the University of Auckland have set up a group to educate and train colleagues in their fundamental role of acting as the critic and conscience of society.

Academics are able to use their position as a community of scholars to challenge the NHE and all its processes. The critic and conscience function set out in New Zealand law has already been used to create some spaces for transformation. Academics within the New Zealand university system have successfully used that role to write public critiques of the system itself. There have been conferences held on the state of tertiary education, such as the 'University Reform, Globalisation and Europeanisation' and 'Universities in the Knowledge Economy' conferences held in Auckland (from which this book emerged). Journal articles and book chapters have been written on the harm caused by the NHE environment and the marketization of education (Bridgman 2007; Codd 1999; Grey 2013; Middleton 2009; Shore 2008; 2010); and new journals such as ARGOS have been established, which published a first edition called 'The university beside itself' and focussed on the challenges facing academics and students in New Zealand NHE universities (*Argos Aotearoa* 2014).

One of the interstitial spaces that must be used to transform higher education is in redefining who the university is. Over the last few decades, when speaking of 'the university', academics, students, politicians and the public are often referring to the brand of an institution. What are needed are actions which highlight that it is academics, staff and students who are the institutions (this is set out in New Zealand's Education Act). Certainly this was at the heart of actions carried out in 2011 and 2012 by students at the University of Auckland. The students' multiple actions included a blockading a road (to protest at the government's budget and its lack of attention to the issue of student support) and occupying the university library to try to make real the catchphrase 'we are the university' (Carlos and Cohn 2014). These actions by groups of students, with the support of a handful of academics, reclaim for a moment the civic focus of the university and the democratic ideals underpinning this.

What is crucial is that any actions aimed at illustrating the damaging outcomes of the NHE environment must be carried out collectively. In the last decade, however, academics who have spoken out against free market orthodoxy or been involved in controversial debates which challenge the nation's political and economic elite have been attacked by government ministers in the media (Grey 2013) and, as noted by Shore: 'there are huge costs and penalties if individuals, or individual institutions, try to challenge or opt out of the auditing process' (2008: 293). This hostile environment was also revealed by 40 percent of 384 scientists who responded to a survey by the New Zealand Association of Scientists by stating they felt gagged (Radio New Zealand 2014). The attacks on academic staff carrying out their legislated critic and conscience role illustrates the importance of collective action to challenge both the NHE environment and the political and economic elite who defend the 'more market' approach to tertiary education.

As well as publicly supporting each other, academics must support students who challenge the marketization of education. In New Zealand, small numbers of academic staff have supported student activism such as the groups 'We Are the University' in Auckland and 'Reclaim Vic' in Wellington. What is needed is much broader public support of student activism which challenges the commodification of education, something students know only too well (Carlos and Cohn 2014).

Any collective action must also work to bring senior academic staff on board: 'Fundamentally, the university remains the critic and conscience of society and intellectual leadership by the professoriate remains essential to speak back and contest orthodoxy and dogma' (Edward Said quoted in Tanya Fitzgerald 2014: 214). Academics must work to turn around the NHE structures which have managers and academic leaders looking ever upward to please a government that will never be satisfied. Instead, academic leaders must be persuaded to work with their staff in a collaborative fashion, fully embracing workplace democracy. The United States' 'Campus Compact' exemplifies the type of project that can be undertaken. 'Campus Compact is a national coalition of college and university presidents – representing more than five million students – who are committed to fulfilling the civic purposes of higher education' (Gibson 2012: 235). This is their by-line: 'A Collective Initiative of Representatives of Research Universities and Campus Compact to Renew the Civic Mission of Higher Education'.

With only eight universities in New Zealand, there could be coordinated and collective responses to NHE rules. For example, all eight universities could choose to admit 'risky' students (those studying part-time, or mature students) in order to challenge Educational Performance Indicators (EPIs), which are arbitrarily set by government. Similarly, a much stronger response to the government changes that removed the legislated protection for academic staff and student representation on university councils would have been for all university senior managers and council members to stand firmly with academics and students and ensure the places were retained under their new constitutions. Such collectivism from the universities of New Zealand would cut across the competitive NHE agenda, which has contributed to the narrowing of the vision and role of universities.

Collective action is necessary to protect individual academics who find themselves on the wrong side of the political and economic elite, who promote a marketized education system focused on economic outputs. Similarly, in an audited and risk-averse tertiary education sector, individual institutions can be picked off if they deviate from the set path. However, working collectively as academic staff and students, provides a way to resist the NHE environment. Collective action also challenges the very nature of the NHE environment. Individualism is central to the structures of NHE environment, and our activities and words must critique the process of structuration (see Trowler 2001: 195) and disrupt the rigid hierarchies which are used to structure NHE universities (Lorenz 2012: 615). Reinvigorating collegial forums and collective action will break down this hierarchy and lead to the reclamation of self-determination as the core moral principle of democracy.

Conclusion

Moving from diagnosis to action is not simple in the tertiary education system. In part, the structure of the NHE environment predicates against the fundamentals needed to transform the system – time, energy and collectivism. The NHE environment in New Zealand atomizes academics, general staff, and students and imposes external measures of 'efficiency', which keep these actors so busy that they often have no time to stop and consider the conditions of their own oppression. As noted, this is not the case for everyone working and studying in New Zealand universities: there are small collectives of academic staff and students who do find the time, energy and collectivism needed to publicly challenge the more market approach to education. This is about political will. The simple fact now is that academics and students who do see universities as important to democracy and to ensuring equality must find that political will. There is no option – if we want sustainable tertiary education, then we are going to have to fight for it.

◆

Sandra Grey (Ph.D. in political science and international relations, Australian National University), is Honorary Research Fellow at Victoria University of Wellington and is serving her second term as the President of the Tertiary Education Union, Te Hautū Kahurangi o Aotearoa. Sandra is a political scientist and has published on a range of topics centred on civil society and citizen engagement in democracy, including the role of academics in public debate. Sandra's most recent work includes: 'Activist academics: What future?' in *Policy Futures in Education* (2013); 'Interest Groups and Policy' in *New Zealand Government and Politics* (Oxford University Press, 2015); and 'Outcomes Plus' (with Brent Neilson and Charles Sedgwick), a research report commissioned by the New Zealand Council of Christian Social Services (2015).

Notes

1. See http://www.tec.govt.nz.
2. Fifty-five press releases and publications from Universities New Zealand, between 2008 and 2013, are available from www.universitiesnz.ac.nz.
3. See www.academicfreedom.nz.

References

Argos Aotearoa. 2014. 'The University Beside Itself'. Auckland: The University of Auckland. Retrieved 10 February 2016 from http://argosaotearoa.org/wp-content/uploads/issues/1-university/argos-aotearoa_issue-1_the-university-beside-itself.pdf.
Bentley, T., L. McLeod and S. Teo. 2014. 'The State of the Tertiary Education Sector in New Zealand – 2013: Final Report of Findings from the Survey of Work and Wellbeing in the Tertiary Education Sector', May 2014. Auckland: New Zealand Work Research Institute, AUT University.
Bridgman, T. 2007. 'Assassins in Academia? New Zealand Academics as "Critic and Conscience of Society?"', *New Zealand Sociology* 22(1): 126–44.
Carlos, H., and G. Cohn. 2014. 'The Subject of Chance and Decision', in *Argos Aotearoa*, 'The University Beside Itself'. Auckland: The University of Auckland, pp. 54–61. Retrieved 10 February 2016 from http://argosaotearoa.org/issue/the-university-beside-itself.
Christopherson, S., M. Gertler and M. Gray. 2014. 'Universities in Crisis', *Cambridge Journal of Regions, Economy and Society* 7(2): 209–15.
Codd, J. 1999. 'Educational Reform, Accountability and the Culture of Distrust', *New Zealand Journal of Educational Studies* 34(1): 45–54.

Collins, S. 2012. 'Skills Crisis: Engineering students get 1000 extra places after Joyce cracks whip', *New Zealand Herald*, 19 November 2012. Retrieved 10 February 2016 from http://www.nzherald.co.nz/business/news/article.cfm?c_id = 3& objectid = 10849355.

Dew, K. 2004. 'Academic Freedom and its Limits', in K. Dew and R. Fitzgerald (eds), *Challenging Science: Issues for New Zealand Society in the 21st Century*. Palmerston North: Dunmore Press, pp. 187–204.

Edelman Boren, M. 2001. *Student Resistance: A History of the Unruly Subject*. New York: Routledge.

Fitzgerald, T. 2014. 'Scholarly Traditions and the Role of the Professoriate in Uncertain Times', *Journal of Educational Administration and History* 46(2): 207–19.

Fredman, N., and J. Doughney. 2012. 'Academic Dissatisfaction, Managerial Change and Neo-liberalism', *Higher Education* 64(1): 41–58.

Gibson, C.M. 2012. 'New Times Demand New Scholarship I: Research Universities and Civic Engagement: A Leadership Agenda', *Journal of Higher Education Outreach and Engagement* 15(4): 235–69.

Gluckman, P. 2015. 'Questions over Industry Research Funding', Radio New Zealand, 27 May. Retrieved 10 February 2016 from http://www.radionz.co.nz/news/national/274702/questions-over-industry-research-funding..

Grey, S. 2013. 'Activist Academics: What future?', *Policy Futures in Education* 11(6): 701–11.

Grey, S., C. Sedgwick and J. Scott. 2013. 'Te Kaupapa Whaioranga: The Blueprint for Tertiary Education'. Wellington: Tertiary Education Union. Retrieved 10 February 2016 from http://teu.ac.nz/wp-content/uploads/2013/11/TKW.pdf.

Hoyt, L.M., and R.M. Hollister. 2014. 'Strategies for Advancing Global Trends in University Civic Engagement – The Talloires Network, a Global Coalition of Engaged Universities', *All Ireland Journal of Teaching and Learning in Higher Education (AISHE-J)* 6(1): 1691–710.

Jesson, J. 2012. 'The Effects of Globalisation on University Academics: The Political Economy of Academic Churn', *Creative University Conference, August 2012*. Waikato, New Zealand: University of Waikato.

Jones, S., et al. 2012. 'Distributed Leadership: A Collaborative Framework for Academics, Executives and Professionals in Higher Education', *Journal of Higher Education Policy and Management* 34(1): 67–78.

Joyce, S. 2015. 'Hon David Cunliffe to the Minister for Tertiary Education Skills and Employment', written questions, 5416. Retrieved 10 February 2016 from http://www.parliament.nz/en-nz/pb/business/qwa/QWA_05416_2015/5416-2015-hon-david-cunliffe-to-the-minister-for-tertiary.

Karran, T. 2007. 'Academic Freedom in Europe: A Preliminary Comparative Analysis', *Higher Education Policy* (20): 289–313.

Kreber, C. 2014. 'The "Civic-minded" Professional? An Exploration through Hannah Arendt's "Viva Activa"', *Educational Philosophy and Theory* 48(2): 123–37, DOI: 10.1080/00131857.2014.963492.

Lorenz, C. 2012. 'If You're So Smart, Why Are You Under Surveillance? Universities, Neoliberalism and New Public Management', *Critical Inquiry*, 2012 (spring): 599–630.
McLaughlin, M. 2003. 'Tertiary Education Policy in New Zealand', Ian Axford Fellowship Report.
Middleton, S. 2009. 'Becoming PBRF-able: Research Assessment and Education in New Zealand', in T. Besley (ed.), *Assessing the Quality of Educational Research in Higher Education – International Perspectives*. Rotterdam: Sense Publishers, pp. 193–208.
Ministry of Business, Innovation and Employment and Ministry of Education. 2014. 'Draft Tertiary Education Strategy 2014–2019'. Wellington. Retrieved 10 February 2016 from
http://www.minedu.govt.nz/ ~ /media/MinEdu/Files/TheMinistry/Consultation/DraftTertiaryEducationStrategy2013/MOE23TES2014_2019_finalV1.pdf.
Ministry of Education. 1989. 'New Zealand Education Act' (reprinted 2015). Retrieved10 February 2016 from http://www.legislation.
_____. 2006. 'OECD Thematic Review of Tertiary Education: NZ country background report', Wellington.
_____. 2008. 'Tertiary Education Strategy 2007–12: A Framework for Monitoring', Tertiary Sector Performance Analysis and Reporting Strategy and System Performance. Wellington.
_____. 2011. 'Briefing for the Incoming Minister for Tertiary Education, Skills and Employment', prepared by the Tertiary Education Group Ministry of Education, 13 December. Retrieved 10 February 2016 from http://s3.documentcloud.org/documents/723166/tertiaryeducationbim2011.pdf.
_____. 2013. 'The Changing Structure of the Public Tertiary Education Workforce', Wellington. Retrieved 10 February 2016 from http://www.educationcounts.govt.nz/publications/tertiary_education/the-changing-structure-of-the-public-tertiary-education-workforce.
Mulgan, R. 2004. *Politics in New Zealand*, 3rd edn. Auckland: Auckland University Press.
Retrieved 10 February 2016 from http://www.legislation.govt.nz/act/public/1989/0080/latest/DLM175959.html.
New Zealand Treasury. 2011. 'Briefing to the Incoming Minister of Finance: Increasing Economic Growth and Resilience'. Wellington.
New Zealand Union of Student Associations. 2015. 'Our Vision'. Retrieved December 2015 from http://www.students.org.nz/vision.
OECD. 2003. 'Changing Patterns of Higher Education Governance', in OECD, *Education Policy Analysis*. Paris, pp. 59–78. Retrieved 10 February 2016 from http://www.oecd.org/edu/innovation-education/17861703.pdf.
Olson, M. 1982. *The Rise and Decline of Nations: Economic Growth, Stagflation and Social Rigidities*. New Haven and London: Yale University Press.
Radio New Zealand. 2014. 'Forty Percent of Scientists Feel Gagged', 4 November 2014. Retrieved 10 February 2016 from http://www.radionz.co.nz/news/national/258512/forty-percent-of-scientists-feel-gaggedostile.

Roberts, P. 1999. The Future of the University: Reflections from New Zealand, *International Review of Education* 45(1): 65-85.
Russell, M. 2007. '"Slicing up the Funding Pie" Tertiary Funding in New Zealand: Where It's Been, and Where It's Going', *New Zealand Journal of Teachers' Work* 4(2): 111-16.
Sharrock, G. 2012. 'Four Management Agendas for Australian Universities', *Journal of Higher Education Policy and Management* 34(3): 323-37.
Shore, C. 2008. 'Audit Culture and Illiberal Governance: Universities and the Politics of Accountability', *Anthropological Theory* 8: 278-98.
_____. 2010. 'Beyond the Multiversity: Neoliberalism and the Rise of the Schizophrenic University', *Social Anthropology* 18(1): 15-29.
Stewart, P. 2010. 'Academic Freedom in These Times: Three Lessons from York University', *Cultural and Pedagogical Inquiry* 2(2): 48-61.
Trowler, P. 2001. 'Captured by the Discourse? The Socially Constitutive Power of New Higher Education Discourse in the UK', *Organization* 8(2): 183-201.
Universities New Zealand. 2011. 'Universities New Zealand Briefing: Contributing to Government Goals', Wellington.
Winter, R. 1991. 'Looking Out on a Bolder Landscape', *Times Higher Education*, 17-18 October.
Wright, E.O. 2012. 'Transforming Capitalism through Real Utopias', *American Sociological* Review 78(1): 1-25.
Zepke, N. 2012. 'What of the Future for Academic Freedom in Higher Education in Aotearoa New Zealand?', *Policy Futures in Education* 10(2): 155-64.

CHAPTER 14
The University as a Place of Possibilities
Scholarship as Dissensus

SEAN STURM AND STEPHEN TURNER

The university today makes increasingly visible its design in its strategic plans and policies, built spaces and pedagogy, and knowledge management. Yet there is much that remains invisible: affect, error, invention, idleness, sharing – even just thinking, talking and walking (thankfully, perhaps, given the tendency of that which is visible to become subject to measure in the university today). This unseen critical-creative surplus suggests to us *skholè* (Greek: 'leisure' or 'play'; 'study' or 'learned discussion'), or scholarship, as the raison d'être for higher education. *Skholè* is not the scholasticism of the drive to systematize knowledge that characterized the scholarly teaching of medieval academics (Le Goff 1993). Nor is it the scholarship of the drive to demonstrate 'pedagogical content knowledge' (Shulman 1987) that characterizes that of academics today, namely, the 'scholarship of teaching' (Boyer 1990). Instead, it is the scholarship that Plato (see Ferrari 2000: 246, 536d–537a)[1] calls the *spoudaiôs paidia* (Greek: 'serious play') that informs *paideia* ('education'). For us, the idea of *skholè*/scholarship as serious play can serve to ground the university as a place given over to the free play of possibilities, a place of 'dissensus' (Rancière 2010). To speak of the university this way is to conjoin the medieval idea of the university as a *universitas magistrorum et scholarium* – a 'community of teachers and scholars' (Denifle and Chatelain 1887: 77) – and the 'community of dissensus' that was Bill Readings' hopeful prognosis for the university in *The University in Ruins* (Readings 1996: 190). Nonetheless, the university today often seems far from a place for the free play of possibilities – or perhaps its possibilities are just invisible to eyes accustomed to measure. How did it come to be seen this way?

The University Today

It was a ruinous critique of the university today by a collective of students and staff of higher education institutions in Leeds, called the Really Open University, which occasioned this reflection.

Here are the Really Open University's (ROU) 'Four Theses on the Invisible University':

1. The University is a Machine in the Network of Capitalism & Empire.
   ...
2. There is No Crisis. It is all Business as Usual.
   ...
3. The University Cannot be Saved.
   ...
4. Defect to the Invisible University! (Really Open University 2010a)

For us, these theses suggest four (rhetorical) questions. The first: is not the university of a piece with the global economy? Denizens of universities everywhere reckon daily with the commodification of knowledge and the vocationalization of education, supposedly to repay the debt that they owe to the state – or, increasingly, to the banks that own states – for their survival. As a result, universities are increasingly beholden to transnational capital, as they once were to national capital. The second question is implied by the first: has not the university always served outside interests? The idea of the university as once having been a law unto itself is mostly fantasy. Before the university served transnational capital (as the neoliberal 'university of excellence'), it served the nation-state (as the Kantian 'university of reason' and the Humboldtian 'university of culture') and, before that, monarchs or the church (the terms are from Readings 1996). For it to serve some master is just business as usual – a measure of the indebtedness, we would say, that marks the university as a 'parasitic' institution (see Serres 1982), one hosted by its master grudgingly because it is disruptive, or, in the language of the university of excellence, 'critical' and 'innovative'. As for the third question: rather than conceding that the university cannot be taken back or transformed, as the ROU would have it, can we not occupy the visible university in the name of an invisible one? To do so is for us dependent on the following, final question: can we not return to the idea of scholarship as the principle of an invisible university? Like the ROU, we would argue that a new community must be built (albeit on a venerable model): a *universitas scholarium*, or community of scholars. As the ROU's 'Charter' (2010b) contends, the university should be

Illustration 14.1 What is a Really Open University? *Source*: Really Open University, 2010c. Used under Creative Commons Attribution-ShareAlike 2.0 Generic License.

- 'communitarian'– because 'the university is the people in it, not the buildings or even the institution';
- 'autonomous', or disruptive – insofar as its indebtedness allows, we would note;
- 'open', or offering free access for students and to information; and
- 'invisible', or not identified with the institution or its buildings.

The first three conditions seem clear, but how can a university be invisible?

Invisibility

Between 2010 and 2013, in the wake of the Arab Spring and 'Occupy' movements worldwide, a number of collectives looked to create 'para-universities' independent of or parallel to existing universities – no doubt influenced by the anarchism of The Invisible Committee's *The Coming Insurrection*, in which it was declared that 'organizations are obstacles to organizing ourselves' (The Invisible Committee 2009: 15). Those we followed most closely included the ROU in Leeds (see Really Open University 2010a; 2010b), the University for Strategic Optimism in London (USO; see University of Strategic Optimism 2012) and WATU (We Are the University) in New Zealand (see WATU 2011), with which we were affiliated. (There has been a long tradition of para-universities in Britain since the Renaissance, one being the 'Invisible College' of Robert Boyle and others, which evolved into the Royal Society of London.)

All argued for a university not identified with an institution or its buildings, invisible to the strategic plans and policies, built spaces, pedagogy and knowledge management that characterize the University of Excellence. Thus, the ROU (2010b) conceived of its invisible university as insurgent: it is '[i]nvisible the way a guerrilla movement melts back into, and is part of, the landscape'. Similarly, Stefano Harney and Fred Moten (2013) describe their invisible university as illicit. It involves a class of subversive intellectuals drawn from the

> [m]aroon communities of composition teachers, mentorless graduate students, adjunct Marxist historians, out or queer management professors, state college ethnic studies departments, closed-down film programs, visa-expired Yemeni student newspaper editors, historically black college sociologists, and feminist engineers (Harney and Moten 2013: 30).

Illustration 14.2 *The Invisible College of the Rosy Cross Fraternity*, by Theophilus Schweighardt, 1604. *Source*: Wikimedia Commons. Used under Creative Commons Attribution 2.0 Generic License.

These 'maroons' (fugitive slaves), some 'tenured' and some not, work in the university and partake of 'the outcast mass intellectuality of the undercommons' (Harney and Moten 2013: 33). They are tasked 'to sneak into the university and steal what [they] can. To abuse its hospitality, to spite its mission ... to be *in* but not *of*' (Harney and Moten 2013: 26; our emphases). They can be neither for the university, which is to endorse the universalist Enlightenment project of the 'State', nor against it, which is to be co-opted by the existing state's project to replace it with teaching institutions (Harney and Moten 2013: 33). For this reason, Harney and Moten abjure critique and advocate 'study', a kind of scholarship that involves 'talking and walking around with other people, working, dancing, suffering, some irreducible convergence of all three', a 'common intellectual practice' that can take place anywhere (Shukaitis 2012). Their university is invisible to the university of excellence and, like those of the para-universities, not identified with it because its class of subversive intellectuals identifies with a tradition of 'black study' that is independent of the university and identified with 'the surround', that is, 'the common beyond and beneath – before and before – enclosure' (Harney and Moten 2013: 17).

How do such ideas of the invisible university fit with more familiar ideas of scholarship – and how do the latter fit with our idea of *skholè/*scholarship as serious play? In *Scholarship Reconsidered* (1990: 15), Ernest Boyer defines – and calls for the rehabilitation of – scholarship, which he argues 'in earlier times referred to a variety of creative work carried on in a variety of places, and its integrity was measured by the ability to think, communicate, and learn'. Nowadays, he has it: 'Basic research has come to be viewed as the first and most essential form of scholarly activity, with other functions flowing from it' (Boyer 1990: 15). Better to capture the scope of academic work, Boyer offers a descriptive typology of scholarship as practised: the scholarships of discovery ('original research'), integration ('looking for connections'), application ('building bridges between theory and practice'; in Boyer 1996, it is called 'the scholarship of engagement') and, most importantly for him, teaching ('communicating one's knowledge effectively to students'). Boyer's call for the rehabilitation of scholarship has resonated in universities in three unexpected ways. First, scholarly teaching, in the work of teaching fellows and other adjunct teaching roles, has been devalued to teaching informed by current research in the discipline of the teacher and in how to teach in that discipline (for the 'demise' of scholarship, see Rolfe 2013). Secondly, 'truly' scholarly teaching has been reframed as teaching that takes itself as an object of research (Andresen 2000). Boyer's text has thus become the reference point for 'Scholarship of Teaching and Learning', or SoTL, in the United States and elsewhere (see Glassick, Huber and Maeroff 1997) – somewhat oddly, given that is doesn't say anything about what such research into teaching might look like. In our institution, teaching fellows are increasingly advised (despite their positions being explicitly not research-required) to research their teaching and others' as a way to exhibit leadership in their discipline. Thirdly, and as a result of scholarly activity being reframed as research, research has come to dominate talk about scholarship: the four scholarships have been reconceived as research proper ('discovery'), synthesizing research ('integration'), applying or sharing research ('application' or 'engagement') and researching teaching ('teaching'). (Research dominates scholarship even in the case of Lewis Elton's (2005) argument for scholarship as the bridge between research and teaching.) This is a long way from scholarship as 'creative work' (Boyer 1990: 15).

To think more 'creatively', or constructively, about scholarship, it is necessary to consider Michael Oakeshott's scholarly institution in 'The Idea of a University' (2003, originally published in 1950) and Pierre Bourdieu's idea of scholarship in 'The Scholastic Point of View' (1998, originally published in 1989; see also Bourdieu 2000a; 2002b). Both conceive of scholarship as immune from worldly concerns. Oakeshott describes the university as 'a corporate body of scholars [who] live in permanent proximity to one another' – and, thus, 'a home of learning' (2003: 24) that is marked by a 'conversation' about 'how to pursue learning' (ibid.: 26). For him, '[t]he characteristic gift of a university is the gift of an interval' (ibid.: 28):

> Here is a break in the tyrannical course of irreparable events; a period in which to look round upon the world and upon oneself without the sense of an enemy at one's back or the insistent pressure to make up one's mind; a moment in which to taste the mystery without the necessity of at once seeking a solution (ibid.: 28).

Though we like Oakeshott's evocation of a sense of possibility for the university here, we would contend that his 'doctrine of [an] interim' granted to students supposedly without regard to 'pre-existing privilege' or 'the necessity of earning [a] living' cannot hold up in the era of student debt (2003: 29). Others would assert (we would not) that his injunctions to universities to 'beware of the patronage of [the "real"] world' and of the 'ulterior purpose' of 'training [students] to fill some niche in society' (ibid.: 30) sound predictably unworldly. In his view of the university, Oakeshott silently evokes the discussion of *skholè* in Plato's *Theaetetus* (Plato 2014: 50–55, 172c–176a). Here Socrates distinguishes unworldly philosophers 'brought up [or "educated"] in freedom and leisure' (ibid.: 54, 175d–e) from those more worldly citizens – lawyers are his prime example – who are made 'boorish and uneducated' by a 'lack of leisure' (ibid.: 53; 174d–e). The latter frequent the *agora* (Greek: 'marketplace') and might as well be slaves. (Plato was in the habit of disparaging the Sophists for peddling their litigious brand of philosophy in the *agora*.) This passage is the locus classicus for the pun in Greek on *skholè* as both 'leisure' or 'play' and 'study' or 'learned discussion' to which most definitions of scholarship are indebted. For Plato, as for his student Aristotle (see Everson 1996: 178, 1329a1),[2] *skholè* came to mean freedom from a less important activity, namely, work (Greek: *askholia*, or 'being not at leisure') in order to pursue a more important activity, namely, philosophy, which requires leisure (Greek: *skholè*). Those who must live by their labour to provide their daily needs – as many students (law students included) do today – can have no *skholè*.

Because of his view of scholarship, Oakeshott assumes that the university cannot be worldly. Bourdieu similarly sees the 'scholastic point of view' as 'a prolongation of [the] originary (bourgeois) experience of distance from the world and from the urgency of necessity'. He asks after the 'social conditions of possibility' (Bourdieu 1998: 129) of such a point of view – and of the 'unconscious dispositions [and] unconscious theses' that it conditions. He concludes that 'the condition of possibility of everything that is produced in fields of cultural production is [the] bracketing of temporal emergency and of economic necessity'. But because of the dominance of this unworldly precondition of 'the fields of cultural production' from law to philosophy, he argues, scholarship has a 'monopoly of the universal ... promoting the advancement of truths and values that are held, at each moment, to be universal, indeed eternal' (Bourdieu 1998: 135), which has conditioned all the works – and the world – such fields have generated. The 'unconscious universalizing' (Bourdieu 2000b: 49) that marks these works and this world produces the three forms of what he calls 'scholastic fallacy': the epistemological, moral and aesthetic universalism that ignores that these modes of reasoning are socially conditioned. For Bourdieu, then, *skholè* is 'the condition for the academic exercise as a gratuitous game' (Bourdieu 1998: 128) and, writ large, for '[t]he history of reason' (ibid.: 138).

What might Bourdieu mean by saying that *skholè* is 'the condition for the academic exercise as a gratuitous game' (ibid.)? To answer this question demands that we quote at length his description of the 'serious play' that he takes to inform the scholarly situation:

> The scholastic point of view is inseparable from the scholastic situation, a socially instituted situation in which one can defy or ignore the common alternative between playing (*paizein*), joking, and being serious (*spoudazein*) by playing seriously ... busying oneself with problems that serious, and truly busy, people ignore – actively or passively. *Homo scholasticus* or *homo academicus* is someone who can play seriously because his or her state (or State) assures her the means to do so, that is, free time, outside the urgency of a practical situation, the necessary competence assured by a specific apprenticeship based on *skholè*, and, finally but most importantly, the disposition ... to invest oneself in the futile stakes, at least in the eyes of serious people, which are generated in scholastic worlds (1998: 128).

For Bourdieu, in short, *skholè* conditions the 'disposition to play gratuitous games', namely, 'the inclination and the ability to raise speculative problems for the sole pleasure of resolving them, and not because they are posed, often quite urgently, by the necessities of life' (ibid.: 128). Again, there is an echo of Plato's leisurely *skholè*.

What, we would ask, is there of politics – of the serious – in such an idea of *skholè*? And what is to be made of the fact, as Bourdieu argues, that '*skholè* [is] being monopolized by some today' (1998: 135), such that it is 'unevenly distributed across civilizations ... and within our own societies, across social classes or ethnic groups' (ibid.: 137)? Does this limit *skholè*/scholarship to a (white, upper-class) scholarly elite in the ('Western') university? How might it be seen as, firstly, neither independent of the institution and insurgent (the ROU) or illicit (Harney and Moten), nor dependent on the institution and immune from society (Oakeshott and Bourdieu); and, secondly, not the privilege of a scholarly elite (ditto)?

Possibility

For us, *skholè* must be grounded in the university as it is today, albeit in that part of it that is invisible. A university must remain a learning community and place, as Oakeshott argues (though he can imagine it only as a geographical place):

> What distinguishes a university is ... the pursuit of learning as a co-operative enterprise. ... A university, moreover, is a home of learning, a place where a tradition of learning is preserved and extended, and where the necessary apparatus for the pursuit of learning has been gathered together (1989: 97).

This is why we would argue for the return of a medieval idea of the university as a *universitas magistrorum et scholarium*, a 'community of teachers and scholars' (Denifle and Chatelain 1887: 77). But it must be a university (from Latin: *universitas*, 'whole, aggregate') that is less a whole than an aggregate, a non-universalizing university that gives rise to what Readings calls a 'community of dissensus', of differences:

> Such a community, the community of dissensus that presupposes nothing in common, would not be dedicated either to the project of a full self-understanding (autonomy) or to a communicational consensus as to the nature of its unity. Rather, it would seek to make its heteronomy, its differences, more complex (Readings 1996: 190).

A university that 's[ought] to make its heteronomy, its differences, more complex', rather than seeking to play down differences through central planning, design and management, would be a more political – and more open – university, a place of dissensus rather than consensus.

Bourdieu goes some way towards an idea of the university as a place of dissensus. He maintains that the university status quo of *skholè* being monopolized by a scholarly elite can be overcome only by 'working to universalize the conditions of access to universality' (1998: 137). By this, he means not that entry to the scholarly elite must be opened to all in society, but that the university must be defended as the 'social condition' of a 'struggle ... for the legitimate monopoly over the universal' (ibid.: 139): the university is that place that guarantees that consensus is contested. This, for us, is a disappointingly commonplace 'realpolitik' solution, to use Bourdieu's term (1998: 139). Rancière goes further. To extrapolate from his discussion of the democratic school as 'the paradoxical heir of the aristocratic *skholè*' in *On the Shores of Politics* (Rancière 1995: 55), the university status quo can be disrupted only by making it 'the site of a permanent negotiation of equality'. The university would neither reproduce nor reduce inequality, whether that be 'by virtue of the universality of the knowledge it imparts or ... social levelling' (ibid.: 55). Instead, 'by virtue of ... a separation from productive life', that is, by virtue of *skholè*, it allows for equality by opening to negotiation a multiplicity of political possibilities:

> for some it is the realization of equal citizenship, for others a means to social mobility and for yet others a right, independent of its actual use, be it successful or otherwise – a right which democracy owes to itself and to the wishes of its members, however indeterminate these may be (Rancière 1995: 55).

The university is a place of political possibilities – or, as Rancière might say, a place of many worlds. Rancière makes explicit the link between political possibilities and worlds. He grounds his politics in what he calls 'aesthetics' (after the Greek *aisthesis*, 'perception'), namely, 'the system of *a priori* forms determining what presents itself to sense experience' (Rancière 2006: 13). He argues that people perceive the world according to a certain 'distribution [French: *partage*] of the sensible': 'the system of self-evident facts of sense perception that simultaneously discloses the existence of something in common and the delimitations that define the respective parts and positions within it' (ibid.: 12). This 'distribution of the sensible' thus determines both how the world is ordered and how it is partitioned. To take a straightforward example, the design of university buildings mirrors power relationships in the university: in the case of the University of Auckland Business School's iconic Owen G Glenn Building, faculty managers inhabit the top floor; academics, the middle floors; reception and retail outlets (the ASB Atrium), the ground floor; teaching spaces (and most students), the basement. For Rancière, such a 'distribution' divides the world into that which 'counts' (and those who count, or take part) in society and that which doesn't (and those who don't). That which doesn't count, an 'uncounted' supplement, makes up what he calls the 'part of those who have no part' (Rancière 2010: 35). In the University of Auckland example, it could be argued that students are the 'part of no part', consigned to the basement for the most part, except as retail customers or when 'swiped into' academics' offices (or perhaps the real part of no part is the contracted workforce of cleaners and other support staff ... or those denied entry to the Business School as students or visitors). Rancière argues that politics makes itself felt through dissensus, which is 'not a confrontation between interests or opinions', but 'the demonstration of a gap [an opening] in the sensible itself' or 'of a possible world' (ibid.: 38–39) – or, when he speaks more loosely, 'a clash between two distributions of the sensible', or possible worlds (ibid.: 39; translation amended). He gives the example of a factory being revealed to be a public rather than a private space when a worker speaks up about a public issue at work, which reveals another world. Taking the Owen G Glenn Building as an example, when we took a group of students into the reception area to sit under the portrait of Owen G. Glenn and map the movement of people around us, we were moved on within minutes by security guards, apparently at the request of the Dean. We were told that the reception area was not for studying or, indeed, for sitting: our class had become an occupation. When a corporate space (the ASB Atrium) became a learning space, not only did the clash immediately reveal the 'distribution' of the space, but it also 'redistributed' it – if only for a short while. Thus, real politics is 'the manifestation of dissensus as the presence of two [or more, we would argue] worlds in one' (ibid.: 37) by the revelation of 'conflicting ways of doing things with the "places" that [a distribution] allocates: of relocating, reshaping or redoubling them' (Rancière 2011: 6).

The University as a Place of Possibilities

This brings us full circle to the idea with which we first began: that *skholè*/scholarship as serious play can serve to ground the university as a place given over to the free play of possibilities, a place of dissensus. The university is that (part of the) world that allows for the free play of political – and thus serious – possibilities, and thereby for the 'worlding' of many worlds (Heidegger 2010: 99). It is not a heterotopia, a place 'outside of all places' (Foucault 1986: 24), but a polytopia, and it is not just a university but a polyversity, a place of many possibilities. Further, it is, in a sense, both of and not of the world, both worldly and unworldly. In what does its unworldliness consist? It is unworldly because its condition of possibility, its ground, is its problematization of conditions of possibility. There is a clue to how this works in Bourdieu's 'Critique of Scholastic Reason', in which he evokes Vaihinger's (1924) philosophy of 'as if' to explain *skholè* as possibilizing: 'the "as if" posture – very close to the "let's pretend" mode of play which enables children to open imaginary worlds – is what makes possible all ... possible worlds' (Bourdieu 2000a: 12–13). However, Bourdieu's 'play-worlds' are not unworldly – or un-serious (ibid.: 13). The 'as if' of *skholè* is not fictive, as Derrida (2002: 212) argues in 'The University without Condition', where he takes the 'as if' to characterize the 'fictions, simulacra, or works of art' that define the humanities. Rather, it is conditional – but not unconditionally so. *Skholè* marks the university as a place of possibilities, but one where conditions of possibility – grounds and rules, or 'ground rules' (Sturm and Turner 2013: 55) – are asked after as a matter of course. (What marks Derrida's 'university without condition' is the 'unconditional freedom to question' – but also to 'profess the truth' (Derrida 2002: 212). Professing the truth strikes us as a universalist Enlightenment project not in keeping with the university as a place of possibilities.)

One way in which we as scholars ask after the ground rules of our university – or perhaps of any university in an indigenous place – is to ask about the ground on which it sits. Ours is sited on a former colonial fort, Albert Barracks, on the site of a former indigenous fort, the Māori *pā* of Horotiu. The wall of the Barracks conspicuously bisects the campus; the stream that sustained the *pā*, and gave it its name, issues inconspicuously via a tap in the carpark of the School of Law. But seeing the university, as it were, in view of the place in which it sits and of everything that has happened there means more than reading the place as a historical palimpsest; it means seeing the correspondences between its military history and the paramilitary nature of management in the university of excellence (see Hoskin, Macve and Stone 2006). And it is to see it as an uncommon commons, an eruption of place in the 'non-place' (Augé 1995) of the globally convergent university of excellence. That commons might even presage an Oceanic undercommons (Hau'ofa 1993), of indigenous peoples across the Pacific, which they share with each other, but not necessarily with non-indigenous peoples – though they might otherwise 'share' the same place.

We also attend to people and place in the university setting as models for worlds and ways of being other than neoliberal ones, to generate possibilities and explore their grounds. To this end, in our classes we explore a range of 'playful' tactics such as productive idleness, critical creativity and post-pedagogy. To do this, we use games, digital artefacts and Situationist *dérives* (French: 'drifts'), which allow the surrounding architecture and geography to subconsciously direct the traveller in an exploration of a space/landscape. We also use tactics already in play in the university such as invention, idleness and sharing ... and just talking and walking, as Harney and Moten rightly say (Shukaitis 2012). Such tactics echo the techniques of 'ontological reframing (to produce the ground of possibility), rereading (to uncover or excavate the possible) and creativity (to generate actual possibilities where none formerly existed)' that inform J.K. Gibson-Graham's 'politics of possibility' (2006: xiv, xxix–xxx). Through such tactics, *skholè*/scholarship as serious play marks the university as a place given over to the free play of possibilities. In fact, we would go one step further: the university is that part of the world that is open to, that awaits, the worlding of possible worlds. Before *skholè* meant 'play' or 'study', it meant 'a holding back, a keeping clear' (Harper 2015), a kind of watchful waiting that has been misread from Plato onwards as a withdrawal from the world. *Skholè* is an openness to the world, to new worlds. As Heidegger writes in *Country Path Conversations* (2010: 75): 'In waiting we leave open that upon which we wait. ... Because waiting lets itself be involved in the open itself'.

◆

Sean Sturm (Ph.D. in English, University of Auckland, 2009) works at the Centre for Learning and Research in Higher Education (CLeaR), University of Auckland. As well as coordinating the University of Auckland's tertiary teaching programmes, Sean researches the university as a place of teaching and learning. Often in collaboration with Stephen Turner (University of Auckland), he has written about the 'entrepreneurial' university, learning spaces, critical-creative pedagogy, and digital and academic writing. His current project explores how students learn with spaces to reveal the university as a place of possibilities.

Stephen Turner is a Senior Lecturer in English, Drama and Writing Studies at the University of Auckland. He completed his Ph.D. at Cornell University, in Eighteenth-century and Postcolonial studies. His research interests include settler colonial, Indigenous and environment studies, pedagogy, literacy and cultural transmission. He is currently working on a book about post-settlement in Aotearoa New Zealand and, with Sean Sturm, a book about the place-based university and social futures. His latest publication, with Tim Neale, is a coedited special issue of *Settler Colonial Studies* in 2015 ('Other People's Country: Law, Water and Entitlement in Settler Colonial Sites'), 5(4): 387–97.

Notes

1. Plato includes Stephanus pagination.
2. Citations from Everson's *Aristotle* include Becker pagination.

References

Andresen, L.W. 2000. 'A Useable, Trans-disciplinary Conception of Scholarship', *Higher Education Research and Development* 19(2): 137–53.
Augé, M. 1995. *Non-places: Introduction to an Anthropology of Supermodernity*. New York, NY: Verso.
Bourdieu, P. 1998. 'The Scholastic Point of View', *Practical Reason: On the Theory of Action*, trans. R. Johnson et al. Stanford, CA: Stanford University Press, pp. 127–40.
Bourdieu, P. 2000a. 'Critique of Scholastic Reason', in *Pascalian Meditations*, trans. R. Nice. Stanford, CA: Stanford University Press, pp. 9–32.
Bourdieu, P. 2000b. 'The Three Forms of Scholastic Fallacy', in P. Bourdieu, *Pascalian Meditations*, trans. R. Nice. Stanford, CA: Stanford University Press, pp. 49–84.
Boyer, E.L. 1990. *Scholarship Reconsidered: Priorities of the Professoriate*. Princeton, NJ: The Carnegie Foundation.
_____. 1996. 'From Scholarship Reconsidered to Scholarship Assessed', *Quest* 48(2): 129–39.

Denifle, H., and A. Chatelain. 1887. *Chartularium Universitatis Parisiensis*, vol. 1. Paris: Delalain.
Derrida, J. 2002. 'The University without Condition', in P. Kamuf (ed. and trans.), *Without Alibi*. Stanford, CA: Stanford University Press, pp. 202–37.
Elton, L. 2005. 'Scholarship and the Research and Teaching Nexus', in R. Barnett (ed.), *Reshaping the University*. Maidenhead: Open University Press, pp. 108–18.
Everson, S. (ed.). 1996. *Aristotle: The Politics and the Constitution of Athens*. Cambridge: Cambridge University Press.
Ferrari, G.R. (ed.). 2000. *Plato: The Republic*, trans. T. Griffith. Cambridge: Cambridge University Press.
Foucault, M. 1986. 'Of other Spaces', *Diacritics* 16(1): 22–27.
Gibson-Graham, J.K. 2006. *A Postcapitalist Politics*. Minneapolis, MN: University of Minnesota Press.
Glassick C., M. Huber and G. Maeroff. 1997. *Scholarship Assessed: Evaluation of the Professoriate*. San Francisco, CA: Jossey-Bass.
Harney, S., and F. Moten (eds). 2013. *The Undercommons: Fugitive Planning and Black Study*. Brooklyn, NY: Autonomedia.
Harper, D. 2015. 'School', in *Online Etymology Dictionary*. Retrieved 10 February 2016 from http://www.etymonline.com/index.php?term=school.
Hau'ofa, E. 1993. 'Our Sea of Islands', in V. Naidu, E. Waddell and E. Hau'ofa (eds), *A New Oceania: Rediscovering our Sea of Islands*. Suva: The University of the South Pacific, pp. 2–16.
Heidegger, M. 2010. *Country Path Conversations*, trans. B.W. Davis. Bloomington, IN: Indiana University Press.
Hoskin, K., R. Macve and J. Stone. 2006. 'Accounting and Strategy: Towards Understanding the Historical Genesis of Modern Business and Military Strategy', in A. Bhimani (ed.), *Contemporary Issues in Management Accounting*. Oxford: Oxford University Press, pp. 166–97.
Invisible Committee, The. 2009. *The Coming Insurrection*. New York, NY: Semiotext(e).
Le Goff, J. 1993. *Intellectuals in the Middle Ages*, trans. T.L. Fagan. Oxford: Blackwell.
Oakeshott, M. 2003. 'The Idea of a University', *Academic Questions* 17(1): 23–30.
Plato. 2014. *Theaetetus*, trans. J. McDowell. Oxford: Oxford University Press.
Rancière, J. 1995. *On the Shores of Politics*, trans. L. Heron. London: Verso.
_____. 2006. *The Politics of Aesthetics: The Distribution of the Sensible*, trans. G. Rockhill. New York, NY: Continuum.
_____. 2010. *Dissensus: On Politics and Aesthetics*, trans. S. Corcoran. London: Continuum.
_____. 2011. 'The Thinking of Dissensus: Politics and Aesthetics', in P. Bowman and R. Stamp (eds), *Reading Rancière*. New York, NY: Continuum, pp. 1–17.
Readings, B. 1996. *The University in Ruins*. Cambridge, MA: Harvard University Press.

Really Open University. 2010a. 'Four Theses on the Invisible University'. Retrieved 10 February 2016 from https://reallyopenuniversity.wordpress.com/2010/12/11/four-theses-on-the-invisible-university/.

_____. 2010b. 'Preliminary Notes on the Charter of the Invisible University'. Retrieved 10 February 2016 from https://reallyopenuniversity.wordpress.com/2010/12/12/preliminary-notes-on-the-charter-of-the-invisible-university/.

_____. 2010c. 'Launch of the Really Open University: What is a Really Open University?' Retrieved 10 February 2016 from https://reallyopenuniversity.wordpress.com/2010/02/22/event-what-is-a-really-open-university/.

Rolfe, G. 2013. *The University in Dissent: Scholarship in the Corporate University*. London: Routledge.

Serres, M. 1982. *The Parasite*, trans. L.R. Schehr. Baltimore, MD: Johns Hopkins University Press.

Shukaitis, S. 2012. 'Studying Through the Undercommons: Stefano Harney and Fred Moten Interviewed by Stevphen Shukaitis', *Class War University* [blog]. Retrieved 10 February 2016 from http://classwaru.org/2012/11/12/studying-through-the-undercommons-stefano-harney-fred-moten-interviewed-by-stevphen-shukaitis/.

Shulman, L. 1987. 'Knowledge and Teaching: Foundations of the New Reform', *Harvard Educational Review* 57(1): 1–23.

Sturm, S.R., and S.F. Turner. 2013. 'The University Beside Itself', in T. Besley and M.A. Peters (eds), *Re-imagining the Creative University*. Rotterdam: Sense, pp. 49–59.

University for Strategic Optimism. 2012. *Undressing the Academy, or the Student Handjob*. Brooklyn, NY: Minor Compositions.

Vaihinger, H. 1924. *The Philosophy of "As if": A System of the Theoretical, Practical and Religious Fictions of Mankind*, trans. C.K. Ogden. London: Kegan Paul, Trench, Trubner.

WATU. 2011. 'We Are the University', 2 vols. Auckland: WATU.

CHAPTER 15
Crisis, Critique and the Contemporary University
Reinventing the Future

SUSAN L. ROBERTSON

Introduction

The title of this final chapter – 'Crisis, Critique and the Contemporary University: Reinventing the Future' – could be viewed as an invitation to imagine a series of alternative, indeed competing, future worlds, shaped by a set of anticipations about social and political orders and their geopolitics. So how might we go about that task, and with what purpose? One approach favoured by the OECD is through the development of discrete scenarios for higher education (Lancrin 2006) which provide a reading of the trends and issues facing the sector and, from there, the necessary skills for rowing forward to arrive victorious. A second might be to kick away the weight of the past, and the leg iron of critique, and perform a very different kind of post-capitalist economy – and thus post-entrepreneurial university – along the lines proposed by Gibson-Graham (2008). In this response, we are challenged to change our worlds through changing our understandings of the world, much like Haruki Murakami's protagonists in the epic novel *1Q84*, or Miéville's *The City and the City*. This means stepping out of one world into another; a parallel world of a new present, not hampered by the thoughts, practices and institutions of the past.

Yet such sharp cleavages – that break with the structuring of the present/past – are almost impossible, short of a radical revolution and all that is implied with it. A third approach might be to take the past seriously, not as an impetus to rush towards a false promise, or to sidestep the burden of our own responsibilities for past and present making, but as a means for questioning, or 'cracking open', our present/past, as John Holloway (2010) proposes in his book *Crack Capitalism* (2010), so as to quarrel with, and quarry out, a new grammar of social change. Such a grammar would imagine, and set in motion, processes that seek to understand, and recover, moments of struggle, human action and possibilities for changing future trajectories and the role the university might play in these processes. In this new world, the university and its members (academics, administrators, students) might metaphorically act as compass and engine; and create arenas and spaces for critique and experimentation. What kinds of quarrelling, quarrying and remaking is possible regarding the contemporary university? What alternative realities can be produced from the current crisis in higher education? What categories might we bring to the fore and split open to reveal other, alternative, possibilities for our actions? In short, how might we 'do' university life in ways that reshape its purposes and outcomes towards more societal rather than economic ones?

Crisis, Critique and the Contemporary University

The underpinning political project for the transformation of the higher education sector throughout much of the world – and the basis of its current crisis – has been guided by neoliberal ideas about the relationship between the state and market, competition to generate efficiencies, notions of individualism, free choice, the rights of consumers – the list goes on (Docherty 2011; Holmwood 2011). Equally important is the ongoing transformation in capitalist production itself, and the role of the national (competition) state in searching for the basis for a new long wave of accumulation (Cerny 1990). As many of the chapters in this book have shown, around the world higher education is now expected to play a key role, not only in human capital formation but also in producing the ideas, innovations and entrepreneurs which might stimulate, if not emulate, the flowering of a thousand Silicon Valleys. This in turn would form the basis for a new wave of wealth generation in the developed and developing world and the materialization and realization of a knowledge-based economy.

How might we view these tendencies and what they mean for the changing structure of social relations of the sector, as well as outcomes for individuals and institutions? I will proceed with three lines of argument around what is an emerging political economy and geography of higher education; one that is now increasingly visible through: (1) processes of territorializing; (2) the increased financialization of higher education as a value-producing sector in its own right; and (3) the resectoralizing of higher education as the boundaries around the sector are being reworked to include new actors, activities and outcomes. I will then turn to an agenda for change that moves beyond critique to take account of current struggles, experiments and novel arrangements.

Cracking Open 'Territorializing' – and the Production of a New Geography of Higher Education

As Elden (2010) argues, territory tends to lack a political theory, in part because it is assumed to be obvious; a bounded space, or fixed power container (Giddens 1987) equated with the nation-state. In this case, the territorial space of higher education is viewed as national, governed by the nation-state. Yet even when viewed as a bounded space, this requires conceptual work to understand both boundaries and space as the outcomes of historically-produced and contested strategies, rather than stable, enduring practices that give rise to categories – like 'the nation', 'the national' and, in this case, 'the university' (Elden 2010).

However, I suggest that territory is best understood in relation to space, as a dynamic process of governing both space and its subjects and is dependent upon the mobilizing of cultural and political rationalities (such as the relationship between the lord/serf) and range of governing techniques (made possible by (new) modes of calculation, such as geometry and, later, statistics). Many of these calculative practices, argues Elden, paralleled and enabled the rise of the modern state, and acted as an important basis of state power. Such calculations include measuring and controlling land, terrain, and populations (cf. Scott 1998). Applied to the higher education sector, this has variously included which actors could operate within national (or indeed a sub-national) boundaries and under what conditions; who might receive state subsidies (institutions and students); what kinds of reporting are required from which kind of institution and in which time frame, and so on. We might view these higher spaces and their constituent practices as the outcome of governing processes – for instance, systems of degree recognition, quality assurance frameworks, reputational tables and national audits.

If territorializing is a process of making governable spaces and subjects, then it follows that making anew depends upon moments of unmaking. Whilst this seems an obvious point, this dialectic of moments is not reflected in the seminal work that inspired a shift towards flow thinking, by writers such as Appadurai (1996), later, Castells (1999) and then Bauman's 'liquid modernity' (2000). Appadurai (1996) used the term 'deterritorialization' to signal that territory has lost significance and power in everyday social life; whilst Bauman's modernity is represented as being in a state of movement and flux.

In the education policy reform literature, Steve Carney (2009; 2011 also uses the idea of deterritorialization to describe the education policy terrain; as one characterized by flows, motion, instability and uncertainty: or, in other words, a world of global unmakings and deterritorialized flows. At one level this is true, as Heyman and Campbell (2009: 136) note, when; 'the global exists as a space that is neither here nor there; it has no distributed patterns, and it has no internal relations reproducing convergence or differentiation. It is simply a space that is everywhere'. The problem here is that we are not then directed to the moments of necessary 'reterritorializing' that are fundamental to social reproduction and the material conditions of life. Indeed many of the chapters in this volume show the new ways in which higher education borders, spaces and social relations are being fixed, ordered and governed (Robertson 2011).

So what does this mean for how we understand the nature of the transformations taking place in universities? We can begin by noting that universities have historically been located in, and governed by, national or subnational territorial states. This is not to suggest that higher education institutions have been contained entirely within the national. Far from it. Universities have a long history of formal and informal inter-institutional and international cooperation, collaboration and competition, involving students and staff as well as resources of various kinds.

From the 1990s onwards, however, the spatial organization of national higher education sectors and institutions had begun to take a visibly different shape as a result of the shifting borders around institutions and the sector, and the nature of the governing tools deployed both on and in it (Sassen 2006). Institutions located in countries such as the United States, the U.K., Australia, France and Germany began to stretch out into global space through the establishment of branch campuses in other national spaces, such as Hong Kong, Malaysia, Singapore, China and the Middle East – all in search of new opportunities, sources of funds, and pipelines to students. From 2000 onwards, new patterns began to emerge, with Malaysia and India engaged in creating branch campuses, whilst China has used Confucius Institutes to promote China as a cultural and political presence in the world, as a form of soft power (Yang 2010).

This transformation in the spatial organization of the contemporary university has also run into other nationally-located governing projects, around where to draw the boundary and what this means for governing. Who governs U.S. academics in Singapore, when Yale University sets up its liberal arts college? Who governs U.K. academics' work when they engage in their work in Malaysia or China, for example regarding the University of Nottingham? Who governs the work of a Chinese academic whose research investigations generate findings that come to be codified as intellectual property on a U.S. campus?

One notable form of territorializing has been the emergence of new regionalizing projects around the world – from Europe, to Asia, and Latin America. The most prominent of these is the European Union. However, other regionalizing projects are underway, taking different spatial forms, all being advanced to address accumulation, regulatory, and governing challenges for the economy more broadly, and to bring the higher education sector more closely into line with political and economic development projects. Older regional projects, like Mercosur in Latin America, are being reinvigorated (Gomes, Robertson and Dale 2013); newer, more fully formed ones are being launched, such as the ASEAN free trade community in the Asian region (Sirat, Axman and Abu Bakar 2016), whilst more radical regional projects have also been initiated, that include higher education as a means for building an anti-neoliberal economic agenda, which in this case includes the provision of social welfare across national boundaries (Muhr 2010).

Within Europe, bypassing institutionalized interests at the national scale through strategizing space has created a dynamic which has resulted in the changing division of labour around who does what in education and at what scales. We might call this the politics of scale jumping; a highly strategic move for those actors advancing change when confronted with fixed institutionalized interests (Collinge 1999). In 1998, the French state, with the support of Italy, Germany and the United Kingdom, announced the Sorbonne Declaration: the platform from which the Bologna Process was created in 1999 (Ravinet 2008). This was a radical spatial move for, in that moment, a new scale of higher education governing was launched, aimed at transforming the institutional architectures, as well as teaching and learning practices, of many universities across Europe and beyond.

The purpose of the Bologna Process was to rupture the glacial pace of much nationally-directed reform in higher education by manoeuvring in an alternative political project (Keeling 2006). For its own part, the European Commission, a long-time champion and thus beneficiary of a European Higher Education Area that was to emerge as the umbrella for the Bologna Process, was also at pains to point to the European Universities Association as a member-driven organization, which represented national and not supranational interests. Yet, over time, the European Commission has become a major funder of the Bologna Process through the Bologna Follow-Up Group, and the various activities that occur through Ministerial and Bologna Policy Forum meetings.

These political slipways have thus lubricated the channels for the Bologna Process. It is a framework for restructuring and governing higher education institutions in national territorial spaces with goals of competitiveness, increasing the stock of human capital, and promoting increased institutional efficiency and the expansion of higher education as a value-producing global market (Robertson 2008). Within ten years, boosted by funding from the European Commission, the Bologna Process had expanded to forty-seven countries, taking in countries well beyond the borders of official 'Europe'.

Along the way, the complexity of the regulatory architecture, and thus governing capacity, has been thickened to include a myriad of institutions, registers and peer-learning activities – from the European Research Council (ERC) to the European Association for Quality Assurance in Higher Education (EAQAHE), student mobility schemes, funding programmes and new statistical representations (such as the Eurostat annual figures on the level of embeddedness of the Bologna Process and activities that support the European Research Area). Many of these regulatory initiatives are carried out under the aegis of a highly innovative 'open method of coordination' (OMC) rather than a top-down set of regulations, so as to manage legitimacy concerns for nation-states regarding subsidiarity (Dale 2004; de la Porte and Pochet 2012).

Yet oppositional higher education projects have also emerged – from student protests within Europe and Latin America (notably Chile), to alternative regional projects, such as the Bolivarian Alliance for the Peoples of Our America (ALBA),[1] which are critical of the dominance of competition in the organization of social and economic life (Muhr 2010). ALBA is an international cooperation organization based on the idea of the social, political and economic integration of the countries of Latin America and the Caribbean. It is associated with socialist and social democratic governments and is an attempt at regional economic integration based on a vision of social welfare, bartering and mutual economic aid. Contrasting the European EHEA project with ALBA makes visible the possibility of imagining other kinds of outcomes and practices in higher education, and not only those associated with neo-liberalism and market marking.

So what kinds of processes are at work in the example I have outlined above? Is this simply a case of a national scale being trumped by a supranational scale? What does this mean for how we think about the relationship between the state and education? What kinds of problems are being solved through processes of territorializing? Following writers like Hameiri (2013), I argue that strategizing, materializing and institutionalizing a new politics and spatial geography of higher education is itself 'a unique kind territorial politics' (Hameiri 2013: 315) emerging out of wider social and political processes. The precise location of the boundary between the domestic and regional politics and agency is neither fixed nor pre-given; rather it is what is at stake and the object of contestation. Regional territorializing thus involves contestation over at which scale the labour of higher education is to be distributed and governed so as to advance political projects, such as a new long wave of capitalist development (economic competitiveness, efficiency, innovation). To secure this future requires key populations to be positively committed to making this new polity. In the case of constructing a European political territory, this also involves the creation of new spatial or territorial constructs and boundaries, rather than simply a defence of them.

Hameiri and Jayasuriya (2011) argue that what we are witnessing is the transformation of the state itself, so that parts of its domestic governance are now being regionalized. They term this 'regulatory regionalism', or 'regulatory statehood', where; 'state agencies and actors increasingly act as regulators bringing to bear regional disciplines on domestic social and political structures' (Hameiri 2013: 321). Hameiri cites regulatory mechanisms such as meta-governance, new forms of functional specialization, and 'de-bounded' risk management, as the new forms of governing regional territories (ibid.: 329). We see many of these regulatory aspects at play in higher education, including the open method of coordination, the Bologna Process, Tuning, the European Credit Transfer System (ECTS), European Research Council, Eurydice and Eurodoc.

If the reterritorializing of higher education is part of the transformation of state space with a new regional frontier, what does this mean for the kind of scholarship needed to understand these processes, and for how to organize acts of resistance? Clearly we need new ways of thinking about these processes. We also need research projects that examine these processes to explore how we might challenge governing practices that tend to present themselves as neutral, apolitical processes, and thereby limit contestation over their politics.

One problem with work on Europe is that academic research is often supported through European Commission funding – and potentially scrutinized by European officials for their criticality towards Europe, though I acknowledge my personal experience of this as an evaluator cannot be generalized. A second problem is accessing the sites and spaces of decision making in the various EU institutions in ways that reveal the processes at work. When units are small, this poses major problems of research ethics. A third problem to counter and overcome is precisely what scale jumping is meant to avoid; the nosy, noisy, quarrelling and quarrying academics whose questions about what is going on have been troublesome for nationally located sites of power. Rescaling power means academics have to rescale their research gaze to look beyond what they have tended to focus on, and to keep all scales in view and in relation to each other. Fourthly, we might look at other spatial geographies of higher education, including regionally and globally based consortia, such as the World Universities Network, Universitas 21, or the Asia Pacific Rim Universities network, to see if counter-geographies of organization might take on those higher education sector transformations that place limits on criticality, on a broad base of knowledge creation, and on knowledge as a common and a collective good.

Cracking Open Financialization – Value Chains and the Circuit of Capital

Financialization is a term used to describe a process that attempts to reduce all value that is exchanged (whether tangible or intangible, future or present) either to a financial instrument or a derivative of a financial instrument (cf. Erturk et al. 2008). A key feature of the contemporary higher education sector is the extent to which it is being financialized, with more and more complex ways of extracting value from within the sector as a result of new value chains being created, new 'services' to be sold, new players to be given recognition and new products to be imagined and sold (McGettigan 2013). Education has become a service sector, contributing to GDP via: student loans for fees; living costs of students returned as value to a city; and organized mobility programmes and placements as a new revenue-generating activity. Value is also extracted through philanthropic donations, money raised on capital markets, and bonds that are issued to investors. These elements are interlinked and are part and parcel of unbundling the sector and making education activities tradeable commodities whose value can be calculated in the economy.

Education as Trade

The shift to viewing education as a tradeable service rather than a public good began in the 1980s, with the United Kingdom, Australia, Canada and New Zealand. Each of these countries began to pursue a different policy towards internationalization, one that included establishing overseas branch campuses and recruiting full-fee-paying undergraduate and graduate students. These developments of course required negotiations around the commercial presence of foreign providers, including around issues of quality, recognition, the definition of who or what is a university, what access to student loans might look like, and so on.

Viewing education as a tradeable service was given impetus by a growing view within government departments and amongst influential lobby groups, that 'selling' education as a service (of which they had a comparative advantage) would go some way to compensating for the developed economies' declining share in the production of goods (Harvey 2005; Marginson and Considine 2000). This, of course, has meant a thriving business in English language courses in preparation for entry into universities, in marketing and recruitment specialists who deliver a particular configuration of students to meet institutional policy, and in newer kinds of providers – such as INTO, Navitas and StudyGroup – who enrol students in foundation or preparation courses that act as a pipeline into a course in an accredited institution (Robertson and Komljenovic 2016). In this way, the value chain is also extended to include a myriad of new means for drawing funds from students, from visas to language courses, foundation courses to undergraduate and graduate courses, and so on.

By 2010, Australia, Austria, Luxembourg, New Zealand, Switzerland and the United Kingdom had the highest numbers of international students amongst their tertiary students, though not all of these countries charge full fees and hence generate the same level of revenues (OECD 2012). What such density of international students does, however, is transform the nature of the student body and, as a result, the learning experiences of those within the classroom. In Australia, for example, close to 22 percent of the student body is made up of foreign students, whilst in New Zealand this is close to 15 percent. What such national figures disguise, however, are the uneven distributions of students across the higher education sector, so that some institutions, and indeed some subjects, will have significantly higher concentrations that the national average. In New Zealand, for instance, 61.5 percent of the international students are concentrated in the largest city, Auckland. The OECD's 'Education at a Glance' reported a five-fold increase in the number of students studying abroad; from 0.8 million in 1975 to a phenomenal 4.1 million in 2010 (OECD 2012: 46). Of this percentage, 52 percent of the students studying abroad were from Asia and, in absolute terms, the largest numbers came from India, China and Korea, whilst the destination countries for 77 percent of the students, studied in OECD countries – or, as some say, the 'rich countries club'.

What this means to the economy of Australia is captured in the following statement:

> Australia's education services exports have continued to grow in importance this decade. Since 1982, education services exports have grown at an average annual rate of around 14 percent in volume terms, with their share in the value of total exports increasingly from less than 1 per cent to almost 6 per cent in 2007. ... Indeed, education exports are now Australia's largest export, behind only coal and iron ore (Reserve Bank of Australia 2008).

The estimated value of education to the Australian economy has been calculated to be in the order of AUS$19.7 billion in 2014/2015.

The effect of policies aimed at increasing the flow of international students has invigorated particular local and national economies, whilst the composition and character of parts of institutions and cities have changed. Cities like Vancouver, Sydney, London and Auckland, and more recently Singapore and Hong Kong, have seen their institutional profiles and their built environments and cultural milieus transformed.

There are also governance concerns regarding trade in education services; this includes universities' financial overdependence on flows of international students that are in turn particularly sensitive to price changes (increases in fees, the strength of currencies), security issues, demographic shifts, geostrategic rebalancing, and new providers in the sector. Flows are also affected by concerns over safety and racism (Marginson et al. 2010) and, most recently, the labour market absorptive capacity in the sending countries of graduate and undergraduate students in ways that return the cost of the investment.

Viewing education as a services sector regulated through global trading rules has paralleled the rise of transnational education flows. Yet to date, there has been considerable resistance by public service unions and other activist groups to bring education into these agreements. However, since 2011, trade negotiations amongst different bilateral partners and regional blocs have reconvened following the challenges facing the World Trade Organization's General Agreement on Trade in Services aimed at locking in the interests of capital, especially in sectors like higher education.

From 2005 there had emerged a proliferation of trade agreements involving Europe and education as a services sector in a game of cat and mouse with actors/institutions seeking to advance trade rules strategically (Robertson and Komljenovic 2015). This occurred in two waves: a first wave shaped by national strategies, and regional and bilateral negotiations; and a second, which now includes the Trade in Services Agreement (still underway), the Trans-Pacific Partnership (concluded), and the Transatlantic Trade and Investment Partnership (still to be concluded). Higher education is included in these negotiations, yet quite what its form is, and what this means for the sector, is as yet unclear. That said, the rules of the trade negotiation games are all aimed at constraining the regulatory autonomy of the state and its citizens, by entrenching competition as the dynamic shaping the sector (with no concessions as to whether it is for car making, chemical production or providing learning), and by putting downward pressure on those non-tariff barriers (such as standards) that chews into and erodes both profit margins and flexibility.

What is at stake for education is its incorporation into binding trade rules; it ceases to be an arena for national or local contestation, on the one hand, and a space of democratic possibility, on the other hand. Given the (sub)nation-state's role in the provision of welfare and other public services, and in the area of education an obligation under the Universal Declaration of Human Rights (United Nations 1948) to provide free public education, it is of the utmost importance that any trade agreement and its regulatory apparatus does not privilege the rights of capital to make claims about future returns by placing serious limits on the sovereignty of (sub)nation-states to deliver on this. Equally as important is the expectation that citizens have the possibility to imagine a different world, and to implement these policies so as to bring this about.

Student Fees and Student Loans

Student fees are related to student loans. Increases in fees mean increases in the overall cost of student loans. In England, where the Student Loan

Company lends money to students to cover the cost of fees and study, underwritten by the state, this is referred to as the student loan book. Increases in student fees and loans, however, generate both affordability and equity issues. How much is too much? What does this mean for student calculations about whether or not a degree is worth it? What might this do to subject areas where there is no close link between the area of study and labour market entry to ensure the capacity to pay it back? Again, I will focus on the U.K. case, as it highlights many of the issues that governments more generally have to be concerned about.

In the U.K., the recent round of fee increases to £9,000 per year for undergraduate students was justified with the following observation: that in 2006 the ceiling of the graduate student contribution had been raised to £3,000 but, contrary to popular opinion, this had not discouraged students from seeking places. Instead, demand for student places had actually increased (Browne 2010: 20). The justification for the increased burden on students was that having a degree generated a significant increase in salary of well over £100,000 over a lifetime. However, as I have argued elsewhere (Robertson 2010), reporting an average in this way makes invisible the fact that some professions (such as medicine, law, dentistry and business studies), generate significant returns, which distorts the average. Students enrolled in areas such as the arts will earn significantly less than this over a lifetime.

However, the effect of setting an upper limit has meant that most universities in the sector, irrespective of their mission, status or social class intake, now charge students at or close to the ceiling of £9,000 and not the recommended £6,000. This has not only created new problems for the state in terms of the overall costs of underwriting the student loan book until students pay back the loan, but it has emerged that around 5 percent of middle class students have decided not to attend universities in the U.K. The significance of this shift is that these students are more likely to get a job with an income over £21,000, and indeed would cover the expected 40 percent shortfall repayments by students to the student loan book. The key issue now facing government is the size of the shortfall between the total value of the student loan book and what students ultimately repay.

Despite the inequalities that are built into this new system, and the financial disaster that seems to be looming for governments down the line, there are now significant pressures to stay on course with this form of financialization of the higher education sector. Many of the elite universities (known as the Russell Group) are well placed to take middle- and upper-class students, who are seen to be financially solvent and whose risks around completion are considerably less. It is this group of students, their loans and their future prospects, which have also attracted private sector financiers, such as Banco Santander, when the pressure to sell off parts of the student loan book have materialized.

Yet as Beckert (2013: 331) points out, what makes credit and money so interesting from a sociological point of view is that though there is an expectation that the debtor (for example the student, a university, other edu-business actors or the state) will live up to their promise to repay the loan, this cannot be rationally calculated because the future cannot be known or foreseen. Here creditors must act as if they can anticipate the future. New companies, like Lumni and Upstart, operating in the United States and Latin America, have put into place and normalized new kinds of opportunities for investors to enter into the higher education sector, offering innovative credit arrangements to students and institutions. Human capital financing, or income sharing agreements, are examples here. They mostly use a web presence to bring an investor into a contractual relationship with a debtor/student. In this case, the investor lends the money to cover the costs of higher education with a view to taking a share of the debtor's employment income over a fixed period into the future. Online intermediaries, like Lumni and Upstart, map the risk of the investment to the investor using statistical models that assess plans, country of residence, academic performance and the job market. These risks are then used to determine repayment requirements and loan amounts. Lumni has been a pioneer in this field, and has financed nearly 7,000 students in Chile, Colombia, Mexico, Peru and the United States since its launch in 2001.

The risk to the investor is clearly what happens if the student does not pass, or secure well-paid future employment. What the 'risk calculation' tools suggest, however, is a class bias in that it is seeking to determine who is likely to do well at university; and the proxy for this is family background and the reputation of the university. More importantly, it also points to the normalization of indebtedness as part of the making and expansion of higher education markets, on the one hand, and the ways in which expectations around repaying might need to be generated, also through global institutions in the face of more global working populations.

Philanthropy

Philanthropic contributions are a further form of financialization and universities face growing pressure to look to alumni and foundations to augment declining funding. Universities now fund a significantly higher proportion of capital expenditure from their own internal cash reserves following reductions in public capital funding since 2010/2011. Yet it is only possible for some institutions to acquire significant endowments because of the nature of their alumni and their status in the global league table of universities. For instance, in the U.K., total endowments across the sector stand at roughly £10.3 billion, with Oxford and Cambridge holding £8.3 billion of that.

Nor is philanthropic funding neutral either in its preferences, politics or potential outcomes. The benefactor normally has a say in how the funding is used, which gives rise to uneven development within the university. More than this, we have seen political scandals that have rocked institutions, such as the LSE and funding from the Gaddafi family, at the time that Libya was engaged in a blood-letting civil war. Finally, the long-term health of philanthropic contributions is dependent upon securing investments that will have a financial return, as well as ideological alignments between the philanthropists and the university. In the current financial climate, the low levels of interest have encouraged universities to be less than careful in their search for better returns on investments as well as more willing to turn a blind eye to ideological and other differences.

In cracking open the financialization of the sector, we see that it is legitimated by the view that this will make the sector more efficient and lean because of market disciplines. Policymakers and politicians point to increases in student fees as well as consequent growth in student numbers. However, as Carpentier (2012) and Douglass (2010) argue, there is a persistent myth on both sides of the Atlantic that public money can be replaced with private money (whether through fees, funds raised on capital markets or donations) without any detriment to the overall system. This is not the case. The decline in funding has meant increased casualization of academic labour; an overall reduction in salaries through furloughs for tenured staff in the United States; burdensome student debt in countries that run student loan schemes; more precarious financial circumstances when investments and other financial decisions made by universities either go wrong or are undermined by wider political events; and growing technologization of the sector – such as through outsourcing of marking, recruiting and so on, and the uneven development of infrastructures.

More recently, universities have been developing a range of partnerships with global publishing firms such as McGraw Hill and Pearson Education. The model works in this way: knowledge about students' reading and learning practices enables these firms to make assumptions about which parts of the text seem to generate what kinds of learning successes. This in turn provides the firm with a sales pitch: use of the companies texts will lead to better learning outcomes.

So what does this mean for our own human actions and struggle? The first thing is to recognize the complex nature of financialization within higher education and what this does for the learning relationship. The second is to begin the political work of limiting these intrusions, not least because they are not necessarily cheaper, as we have learnt from public–private partnerships, or with the student loan system that has been set up in the U.K., and the recent excesses in the United States. It means organizing (dare I say, unionizing), scrutinizing, advancing alternatives and considering new initiatives. When students who are heavily indebted say 'We are the 99 percent', what are they saying? When Occupy advance their agenda, what do we make of it? How do we support it? What actions do we take? When alternatives are proposed, such as a cooperative economic model of organizing teacher training, what ways might we work to ensure that we help to realize these initiatives?

Cracking Open Resectoralization – New Actors and Logics

Resectoralization implies a sector undergoing change. A sector refers to a set of institutions and actors whose activities are bundled together and given coherence at the level of representation (such as who can practise as a university academic; what defines being a student), and at the level of practice (such as norm setting, for instance, academic autonomy) (see Olds and Thrift 2005; Robertson 2011). And it is the boundaries, or boundary settings and their management, that define what is inside and what is outside that which comes to call itself 'the sector'. Bordering, boundary management, internal norm-setting, and the reproduction of norms, help to make visible who can be counted as a legitimate actor and who is to be excluded.

Ongoing projects aimed at reworking the boundaries around the sector, and meanings within, can be described as 'resectoralization' (see also Robertson 2011). Sectors, like higher education, are dynamic, and their shape and content at any one point in time are both the object and outcome of political and governance projects and struggles over meaning. Mapping the sector at different points in time will enable us to move away from the idea of 'the university' as a fixed set of social relations, towards one where universities and other related actors are placed into a relationship with a range of other actors and their projects – some of whom are located at other scales (such as the global and regional).

An important challenge facing both traditional higher education providers and governments is: what to do about a burgeoning number of for-profit providers who have sought access to the sector rather than operating along the sectors boundaries. Here we might take the case of the U.K. government, which has used the financial crisis as a means for opening up higher education to for-profit providers. The U.K. government, under pressure from large conglomerates like Pearson Education, Laureate, Kaplan and others, has sought to open up the sector as a 'free market' arguing that this means letting the for-profits operate under similar conditions to existing universities (the right to call themselves a university, with degree-awarding powers) and rights to the student loan system. Currently these providers operate under different rules and thus outside the sector. This has an impact on both marketing and profitability.

There has been growing pressure on the U.K. government to rethink its position. This has paralleled the steady expansion of private providers in the U.K. higher education sector (Fielden, Middlehurst and Woodfield 2010; Middlehurst and Fielden 2011), though the scale and scope of their activity have not been officially monitored. Many private providers are the branch campuses of foreign universities, whose degrees are awarded by their home institution. Others are firms who specialize in joint ventures with existing public HE providers, largely in the area of foundation and language courses for international students, in preparation for entry into university programmes. Many of these firms have intentions of expanding, and it is possible to see significant mission creep as they learn how to work with, and around, the existing regulations. However, new for-profit providers wanting to enter British higher education have to make their claims for entrance and recognition to national regulatory bodies on a case-by-case, rather than multilateral or bilateral, basis as hoped for through the WTO and Regional Trade Agreements (RTAs). This has irritated the new providers, as well as slowed down their capacity to enter the sector under conditions that might be more profitable.

In the U.K. higher education sector, up until the beginning of 2012, only five organizations had been granted degree-awarding powers (DAPs). Amongst the five is BPP Ltd, a high profile, for-profit, provider (of undergraduate and graduate law, accounting and health studies) which was acquired in 2009 by private equity firm, Apollo Global; a subsidiary of the Apollo Group based in the United States. In April 2012, Montagu Private Equity acquired the College of Law for £200 million and, in doing so, also acquired the college's degree-awarding powers.

The U.K. situation can be contrasted with that of the United States, where, until recently, there has been remarkable year-on-year growth over the past decade of for-profit higher education providers, much of it driven by the rise of degree-granting institutions by publicly traded corporations (cf. Breneman, Pusser and Turner 2006; Hentschke, Lechuga and Tierney 2010; Kinser 2006). However, confronted with more demanding regulation by the U.S. Department of Education, and seeking economies of scale and scope through transnational expansion, the for-profit providers have looked to entering new markets, including the U.K. This has meant pressuring governments to 'level the playing field' to enable their entry – a phrase that has meant allowing for-profit providers access to student loans. But it has also meant pressuring government to lift the ceiling on student loans so that it was able to work out a range of fee niches. In cracking open resectoralizing processes at work, we need to ask questions about where decisions get made with regard to these new actors in the sector, what this means for knowledge creation, and which knowledges are to be valued.

Inventing the Future University: From Critique to Action

Drawing this chapter to a conclusion, I hope it is now possible to outline an agenda for critical enquiry that might lead to the reimagining and reinvention of the contemporary university. This must be based on a critical and close reading of the current state of play so as to best understand the interests involved and their stakes. Investors in education as a service sector are not going to give up easily. Nor will governments, used to viewing higher education as a golden goose that will fill their national income coffers with ever-greater returns. Yet I have also shown that national governments are not always fully in control of their higher education sectors, as a result of new regional governing strategies and spaces, and where innovative financial instruments now tie institutions and students to debt and credit in new ways.

These are deep, divisive and sometimes devastating developments for an activity that lies at the root of how we might imagine and remake a different kind of future. That we make a better and different world through the kinds of higher education institutions we imagine, make and remake, has to be the responsibility of all of us.

Threaded throughout this conclusion has been Holloway's (2010) call to action – not through developing more abstract categories, but through revealing interests and power, and from there, the basis of possible struggles. Can we learn to ask more powerful questions about those interests (including our own), and develop a campaign of action? Our capacity to ask strong questions, to demand strong answers, to be open to a range of ways of seeing, and to have the spaces and places for this to happen, is surely what is at the heart of what it means to talk about 'the university' and the part that it, and we, might play, in making future worlds.

◆

Susan L. Robertson is Professor of Sociology of Education at the University of Cambridge, U.K. Susan's main research interests are in global and regional projects, policy formation, cultural political economy of education, state transformation and labour. She has published widely on these issues in leading journals drawing on funded research projects. Susan is founding coeditor of *Globalization, Societies and Education*. Her latest books include *Public Private Partnerships in Education* (2012, Elgar), and *Education, Privatisation and Social Justice* (2014, Symposium).

Notes

1. The member nations are: Antigua and Barbuda, Bolivia, Cuba, Dominica, Ecuador, Nicaragua, Saint Vincent, and the Grenadines and Venezuela.

References

Appadurai A. 1996. *Modernity at Large: Cultural Dimensions of Globalisation*. Minneapolis, MN: University of Minnesota Press.
Bauman, Z. 2000. *Liquid Modernity*. Cambridge: Polity Press.
Beckert, J. 2013. 'Capitalism as a System of Expectations: Toward a Sociological Micro-foundation of Political Economy', *Politics and Society* 4(3): 323–50.
Breneman, D.W., B. Pusser and S.E. Turner. 2006. 'The Contemporary Provision of For-Profit Higher Education: Mapping the Competitive Environment', in D.W. Breneman, B. Pusser and S.E. Turner (eds), *Earnings From Learning: The Rise of For-Profit Universities*. Albany: State University of New York Press.
Browne, J. 2010. Securing a sustainable future for higher education: An independent review of higher education funding and studentfinance. http://www.bis.gov.uk/assets/biscore/corporate/docs/s/10-1208-securing-sustainable-higher-education-browne-report.pdf.
Carney, S. 2009. 'Negotiating policy in an age of globalization: exploring educational policyscapes in Denmark, Nepal and China', *Comparative Education Review*, 53(1): 63–88.

_____. 2011. 'Imagining globalisation: Educational policyscapes', in *World Yearbook of Education*, Gita Steiner Khamsi and Florian Waldow (eds), *Policy Borrowing, Policy Lending*, London and New York: Routledge.

Carpentier, V. 2012. 'Public–Private Substitution in Higher Education: Has Cost-Sharing Gone Too Far?' *Higher Education Quarterly* 66(94): 363–90.

Castells, M. 1999. *The Network Society*. Oxford: Blackwell.

Cerny, P. 1990. *The Changing Architectures of Politics*. London and New York: Sage.

Collinge, C. 1999. 'Self-organisation of Society by Scale: A Spatial Reworking of Regulation Theory', *Environment and Planning D: Society and Space* 17: 557–74.

Dale, R. 2004. 'Forms of Governance, Governmentality and the EU's Open Method of Coordination', in W. Larner and W. Walters (eds), *Global Governmentality: Governing International Spaces*. London and New York: Routledge.

de la Porte, C., and P. Pochet. 2012. 'Why Now (Still) Study the Open Method of Coordination', *Journal of European Social Policy* 22 (3): 336–44.

Docherty, T. 2011. *For the University*. London: Bloomsbury.

Douglass, J.A. 2010. 'Higher Education Budgets and the Global Recession', Working Paper 4.10. Center for Studies in Higher Education.

Elden, S. 2010. 'Land, Terrain, Territory', *Progress in Human Geography* 34: 799–817.

Erturk, I., et al. 2008. *Financialisation at Work*. London and New York: Routledge.

Fielden, J., R. Middlehurst and S. Woodfield. 2010. *The Growth of Private and For-Profit Higher Education Providers in the UK*. London, Universities UK.

Giddens, A. 1987. *The Nation, State and Violence*, Berkeley: University of California Press.

Gibson-Graham, J.-K. 2008. 'Diverse Economies, Performative Practices for Other Worlds', *Progress in Human Geography* 32(5): 613–32.

Gomes, A., S. Robertson and R. Dale. 2013. 'Globalising and Regionalising Higher Education in Latin America', in D. Araya et al. (ed.), *Globalising Higher Education*. London and New York: Routledge.

Hameiri, S. 2013. 'Theorising Regions through Changes in Statehood: Rethinking the Theory and Method of Comparative Regionalism', *Review of International Studies* 39: 313–35.

Hameiri, S., and K. Jayasuriya. 2011. 'Regulatory Regionalism and the Dynamics of Territorial Politics: The Case of the Asia-Pacific', *Political Studies* 59: 20–37.

Harvey, D. 2005. *A Brief History of Neoliberalism*. Oxford: Oxford University Press.

Hentschke, G., V. Lechuga and W. Tierney (eds), 2010. *For-Profit Colleges and Universities*. Virginia: Stylus.

Heyman, J., and H. Campbell. 2009. 'The Anthropology of Global Flows: A Critical Reading of Appadurai's "Disjuncture and Difference in the Global Cultural Economy"', *Anthropological Theory* 9: 131–47.

Holloway, J. 2010. *Crack Capitalism*. New York: Pluto Press.

Holmwood, J. 2011. *A Manifesto for the Public University*. London: Bloomsbury.

Keeling, R. 2006. 'The Bologna Process and the Lisbon Research Agenda: The European Commission's Expanding Role in Higher Education Discourse', *European Journal of Education* 41(2): 203–23.

Kinser, K. 2006. *From Main Street to Wall Street*. New York: AISHE.
Lancrin, S. 2006. 'What is Changing in Academic Research: Trends and Futures Scenarios', *European Journal of Education* 41(2): 169–202.
Marginson, S., and M. Considine. 2000. *The Enterprise University*. Cambridge: Cambridge University Press.
Marginson, S., et al. 2010. *International Student Security*. Cambridge: Cambridge University Press.
McGettigan, A. 2013. *The Great University Gamble*. London: Pluto Press
Miéville, C. *The City and the City*, London: Macmillan.
Middlehurst, R., and J. Fielden. 2011. *Private Providers in UK Higher Education: Some Policy Options*. London: Higher Education Policy Institute.
Muhr, T. 2010. 'Counter-hegemonic regionalism and higher education for all: Venezuela and the ALBA', *Globalisation, Societies and Education* 8(1): 39–57.
Murakami, H. 2011. *1Q84*. London: Vintage.
OECD. 2012. 'Education at a Glance 2012'. Paris.
Olds, K., and N. Thrift. 2005. 'Cultures on the Brink: Re-engineering the Soul of Capitalism on a Global Scale', in A. Ong and S. Collier (eds), *Global Assemblages*. Oxford: Blackwell Publishers.
Ravinet, P. 2008. 'From Voluntary Participation to Monitored Coordination: why European countries feel increasingly bound by their commitment to the Bologna Process', *European Journal of Education* 43(3): 353–67.
Reserve Bank of Australia. 2008. 'Australia's Exports of Education Services'. Retrieved 1 September 2013 http://www.rba.gov.au/publications/bulletin/2008/jun/2.html.
Robertson, S. 2008. 'Embracing the Global: Crisis and the creation of a new semiotic order to secure Europe's knowledge-based economy', in N. Fairclough, R. Wodak and B. Jessop, (eds), *Education and the Knowledge-based Economy in Europe*. Netherlands: Sense Publications.
_____. 2010. *Globalising UK Higher Education*. London: LLAKES.
_____. 2011. 'The New Spatial Politics of (Re)bordering and (Re)ordering the State-Education-Citizen relation', *International Review of Education* 57: 277–97.
Robertson, S., and J. Komljenovic. 2015. 'Forum Shifting and Shape Making in Europe's Negotiations on (Education) Trade in Services Education', presented to the Education and Trade Panel ECPR, 26–28 August, Montreal.
_____. 2016. 'Unbundling the University and Making Higher Education Markets', in A. Verger, C. Lubienski and G. Steiner-Kamsi (eds), *World Yearbook in Education* (Global edu). London: Routledge. Retrieved 10 February 2016 from https://susanleerobertson.files.wordpress.com/2009/10/robertson-and-komljenovic-2016-unbundling-higher-educationfinal.pdf.
Sassen, S. 2006. *Territory, Authority, Rights*. Princeton, NJ: Princeton University Press.
Scott, J.C. 1998. *Seeing Like a State: How Certain Schemes to Improve the Human Condition Have Failed*. New Haven, CT: Yale University Press.
Sirat, M., N. Axman and A. Abu Bakar. 2016. 'Harmonization of Higher Education in Southeast Asia: Regionalism with Politics First and the Education',

in S. Robertson, et al. (eds), *Global Regionalisms and Higher Education*. Cheltenham: Edward Elgar.

United Nations, 1948, *Declaration of Human Rights*, Geneva: United Nations, available at http://www.ohchr.org/EN/UDHR/Documents/UDHR_Translations/eng.pdf

Yang, R. 2010. 'Soft Power and Higher Education: An Examination of China's Confucius Institutes', *Globalisation, Societies and Education* 8(2): 235–45.

Index

academic capitalism, 1, 50, 90
academic freedom, 51, 64, 175, 189, 244, 278, 281–283
  consequences for academic freedom, 186
academic labour, 49, 55, 57–58, 91, 102–103, 325
accountability, 7, 93, 94, 98, 187, 219, 243, 260, 269, 275
actor-network theory, 120
adhocracy, 79
administrators, 5–7, 35, 49, 59, 189, 241, 282, 313
  administeriat, 7
  administrative bloat, 5, 21
affect/affective economy, 139, 144, 148, 150–52
agency, 18, 75, 96, 217, 269, 281, 288, 318
agent, 78
  'free agent', 78
  'principal-agent' theory, 75
alternative university models, 19–20
anxiety, 12, 150, 213–14, 217–18, 221–26, 230, 253
arrhythmia, 157, 161
Asia, 2, 12, 94, 259, 264, 268–69, 316, 321
assessment, 4, 52, 63, 93–94, 102, 104, 118, 144–45, 193, 202, 204–5, 214–16, 230
Association of American Universities (AAU), 258–59, 265
Association of Pacific Rim Universities (APRU), 258–59, 262, 266, 270
Association of Southeast Asian Nations (ASEAN), 259, 316
audit
  auditable, 58
  auditing, 4, 102, 213, 215, 217, 221, 226, 275, 281–82, 288, 290

audit culture, 4–5, 216, 230, 243
Augé, Marc, 158, 168, 308
autonomy, 17–18, 36, 75, 90, 255, 261, 278, 281, 322
  academic autonomy, 47, 106, 269, 326
  institutional autonomy, 51, 281, 283
  political autonomy, 260
  professional autonomy, 102

Barber, Michael, 12, 13
Beck, Ulrich, 168, 213
biotech, 124, 129–34
blended courses; curriculum, 147–48
Boden, Rebecca and Epstein, Debbie, 243, 245, 269–70
Bologna Process, 81, 156–8, 162, 164, 166–7, 168, 182, 316–18
boundary, 79, 316, 318, 326
Brown, Phillip, 10, 82, 84, 93
bureaucracy, 75, 79, 221, 229, 239, 257
bureaucratization, 243

California (state), 3
  University of California, 20, 270
Cameron, Angus and Palan, Ronen, 74, 83
Cerny, Philip, 74–75
Chicago School Economics 3, 9
Chile 3, 17, 317, 324
China, 82, 254, 259, 264, 268, 315, 321
circumvention, 128, 132–34
citizens, 75, 80, 144, 261, 303, 322
  'competition citizens', 84
  consumer citizen, 138–39, 151–52
  critical citizen, 250
  modern citizens, 270
  public citizens, 152
citizenship, 35, 51, 180,
  consumer citizenship, 151
  critical citizenship, 81

democratic citizenship, 280
equal citizenship, 305
civic engagement, 276, 286
class, 33–41, 44, 59, 82, 218, 268, 299, 301, 304, 323–24
collegial/collegiality, 7, 49, 78–79, 97, 100, 282–83, 291
  collegial rule, 78
collective/collectivity, 77, 147, 255, 259, 262, 268, 270, 277, 288, 290–91, 319
commercialization, 8, 49, 51–52, 55–56, 60–63, 95, 98, 117–19, 279
  commercialization offices, 49
  commercialization units, 54–56
commodification, 151, 288, 290, 297
competences, 69, 77, 81, 83–84, 157, 162, 165–66
competition state, 69–70, 73–74, 80–81, 84–85
complexity 125, 159, 317
consent, 220, 231–33, 235, 237–39
Conservative government, 3, 13, 31–2, 39, 73
Cooperative universities, 19
corporatization, 279
cost-sharing, 3, 10, 180
creativity, 83–84, 308
  critical creativity, 308
  intellectual creativity, 269
critic and conscience, 153, 278, 282, 287–90
critique, 18, 64, 119, 196, 218, 221, 256, 267–68, 284, 301, 312–14, 328
  Bourdieu's 'Critique of Scholastic Reason', 307
  'ideology critique', 33
cronyism, 62
cultural cringe, 196–97, 205

democracy, 18, 20, 35, 51, 266, 269, 276–78, 282–85, 287, 290–91, 305
divergence, 133–35
Drucker, Peter, 81–82

ECTS, 156–9, 168
economic outputs, 280, 283, 291

Education Act, 265
  1944 (UK), 34
  1989 (New Zealand), 202, 277–79, 286
efficiency, 4, 73, 92, 147, 160, 180, 197, 284–85, 291, 317–18
elites, 1, 43, 83, 253, 255–57, 262–64, 271, 278, 283, 287, 290–91, 304–5, 323
employability, 81, 162, 164, 168
  graduate employability, 94, 99, 102–103, 165
  student employability, 157, 162
employment practices, 49
  and exceptionalism, 62
enterprise, 42–43, 52, 60, 64, 71, 77, 84, 100, 186
  co-operative enterprise, 304
entrepreneurial university, 8–9, 50, 91, 95, 100, 106, 312
entrepreneurialism, 21, 59, 61, 83, 105
equality, 2, 18, 34, 276–77, 279–80, 285, 287, 291, 305
  gender equality, 108, 124
  social equality, 167
  See also inequality
equity, 15, 92, 94–95, 105, 107, 138, 145, 262, 271, 286, 323
  See also inequity
ethics, 5, 21, 77, 141, 230, 254, 319
  committees, 229, 230–46
  Confucian Ethics, 268
  deontological, 234
ethnographic research, 237, 244–45
European Research Council (ERC), 317
European Union (EU), 178, 316,
export education, 8, 51

'faculty land', 64–65
feminist perspective, 90, 102, 105
feminization, 91, 97, 99, 101, 104, 108
financialization, 5, 313, 319, 324–26
Finland, 214
forecasting, 156, 165
  forecasting techniques 158
foresight, 165, 166
for-profit
  for-profit providers, 3, 13, 17, 327–28

for-profit sector, 13–14
for-profit colleges, 14, 16
free market, 17, 290, 327
free universities, 18, 20–21
freedom of choice, 158, 163–5, 169
Friedman, Milton, 3
funding arrangements, 180
futures, 2, 18, 40, 158, 165, 169, 270
  alternative futures, 2, 271
  competitive futures, 255
  dystopian futures, 253
  leadership futures, 106
  See also university futures

gaming, 200, 202–7
gender, 2, 40, 91–92, 95, 97, 99, 103, 108, 196, 216, 218, 220
  gender studies, 100, 199, 208
Germany, 17, 37, 82, 315
Giddens, Anthony, 218
global impact of research universities, 257
global knowledge economy. *See* knowledge economy
Global Research Council, 265
Global University Leaders Forum, 262
globalization, 2, 13, 47, 74, 83, 92, 175–79, 187, 257–58, 267, 270
  grassroots globalization, 269
governance, 2, 20, 54, 63, 65, 69, 71, 78, 90, 92, 105–6, 159, 177, 180, 183–84, 283, 318, 321, 326
  soft governance, 213
governing, 5, 118, 186, 314, 316–18, 328
  governing board, 75, 79
  governing bodies, 184, 218
  governing class, 7
governmentality, 142, 144, 150, 255, 270
  'authoritarian governmentality', 243
Gumbrecht, Hans Ulrik 168

Huber, Michael and Rothstein, Henry, 219
Human capital theory, 7, 10, 80, 181

India, 82, 254, 315, 321
Indicators, 4, 34, 69, 184–85

performance indicators, 7, 21–22, 65, 95, 182–83, 282, 287, 291
industry university relations, 7–8, 49, 52, 60, 72, 76–80, 84, 95, 97, 99, 117 129–34, 255
inequality, 256, 259–62, 267, 187–88
  See also equality
inequality and risk, 256, 259
inequity, 217. *See also* equity
innovation, 51–53, 57, 60–61, 72, 76, 92, 95–96, 100, 105–8, 120, 145, 165–66, 195, 256, 259, 263, 286, 318
institutional capture, 7, 47
Institutional Review Boards (IRB), 229, 232–34, 237–38, 244
and 'export education', 8, 51
international networks/consortia, 70, 255, 319
international rankings, 258, 269
international relations, 199, 208, 253–254, 271, 333
international students, 8, 15, 99, 187, 266, 320–21, 327
internationalization, 255–56, 266–68, 320
Ireland, 92, 214
Italy, 214, 316

Joyce, Stephen, 195, 281

Keynes, 9, 184
knowledge economy, 138
  global knowledge economy, 1, 49 70, 73, 76, 80–81, 178, 185–86
  knowledge based economy, 95, 181, 197, 313
knowledge work, 73, 82
knowledge worker, 70, 76, 80–84

Labour government, 3, 31, 34
labour market, 74, 80–82, 165, 169, 198, 275, 279, 321, 323
  competitive labour market, 169
  future labour market, 156–58, 169
  global labour market, 1, 10, 74, 83
  international labour market, 106
  iocal labour market, 84

Lash, Scott, 218
Latour, Bruno, 120–21, 125
leaderism, 95, 100
leadership, 60, 65, 76, 78–79, 85, 90, 96, 100, 142, 145, 215, 268, 302
  academic leadership, 48
  executive leadership, 91, 93, 98, 106
  intellectual leadership, 256, 290
  international leadership, 264
  leadership feminization, 97
  leadership framework, 52–3, 55
  'political leadership', 74
  public leadership, 255
lecturing, 20, 101, 205
Lefebvre, Henri, 157, 161
lifelong learning, 80, 165–6
Lupton, Deborah, 218

Malaysia, 315–16
management
  performance management, 79, 107
  research management, 121
manager, 7, 20, 54, 58, 64, 75, 78, 95, 99, 103, 105–8, 117, 122, 125, 129, 146 149
  faculty managers, 306
  university manager, 4, 5, 7, 21, 22, 47, 49–50, 107, 193, 245, 282, 291
managerialism, 5, 18, 21, 50, 65, 93, 275
  'new managerialism', 215
marketization, 90, 93, 139, 289–90
'massification', 92, 94, 101, 179–80
MBIE (Ministry of Business, Innovation and Employment), 56–57, 280
McGettigan, Andrew, 10, 18
mission creep, 232, 234, 327
mixture, 55, 121
mobility, 40, 77, 98, 186, 270, 319
  international mobility, 182
  social mobility, 1, 9 34, 37–39, 179, 305
  student mobility, 156, 159, 317
modularization, 143, 146–47, 156–7, 164, 168
MOOCs, 11, 18, 94

nationalism, 50, 231, 242, 256, 263–4
neoliberalism, 180, 213, 318
neoliberal policies, 92, 194, 260
networking, 77–79, 85, 124
new public management, 73, 78, 180, 189, 258, 260
New Labour, 3, 31, 40, 49, 57
New Zealand
  as small country, 2, 8, 57, 60–61, 193
'non-place', 158, 168, 308
Nowotny, Helga, 167

Occupy Wall Street, 259
Open Method of Coordination (OMC), 317–18
open university, 43, 297
  Really Open University (ROU), 20, 297–98
organizations, 97, 185
  flat, 85
  flexible, 77–78
  international, 178–79, 186
  knowledge, 1–2, 70, 76–78, 81
  low-trust, 21
  philanthropic, 93
  private sector, 271
  public, 51, 57
  risk, 213
  service delivery, 75
  tertiary education, 194, 201–7
Organization for Economic Cooperation and Development (OECD), 1, 10, 70, 72–74, 93, 167, 178–179, 186, 260, 275, 281, 312, 321

'parasite logic', 128, 131, 134
participatory research, 230, 235
Pearson, 12–13, 15, 93, 99, 325, 327
pedagogy, 102, 139–40, 144, 150, 296, 299
  entrepreneurial pedagogy, 59
  outcomes, 140
  post-pedagogy, 308
Pedersen, Ove Kaj, 80
Performance-Based Research Fund (PBRF) 49, 52, 63, 193, 201, 206

performance management. *See* management
personal capital, 84
philanthropy, 40, 324
Porter, Michael, 71
Portugal, 214
power, 10, 14, 31, 38, 90, 101, 107–8, 121–22, 125, 132, 186, 206, 231, 236, 254, 278, 283, 314, 319, 329
  'agent-centred notion of', 286
  brain power, 181
  financial power, 256, 260, 276
  power growth, 11
  power relations, 7, 139–40, 189, 238, 306
  power shift, 82, 94, 99
  soft power, 315
precarity, 218
private good, 195, 287
private providers, 3, 16, 94, 327
privatization, 73, 93, 98, 289
  privatization of universities, 13–15, 16, 17
'project barons', 54, 122–123
productivity, 4, 42, 64, 75, 84, 106, 135, 140, 166, 258, 263, 279
public educational support, 159
public good, 9, 55–56, 74, 277, 280, 285, 320
public university, 1–2, 11, 18, 57, 70, 251
  borders and boundaries of, 49
  meaning of, 85
  mission of, 21, 47
  transformation of, 13

qualifications framework, 81, 162–3
quality assurance, 99, 101–2, 175, 181–83, 185–86, 233, 314
quality indicators and rankings, difference between, 183

real utopias, 275, 277
reflexivity, 217–218, 245
reforms, 1–2, 11, 69–70, 72–73, 75–76, 80, 92, 117, 121, 157–58, 162, 278
  Dawkins Reforms, 91

new public management reforms, 78, 108
  neoliberal reforms, 17
  study progress reform, 159–60, 169
regions
  Mercosur, 316
  ALBA, 317
'regulatory hypervigilance', 234, 238
Reich, Robert, 74, 77, 81–82
Rancière, Jacques, 305–6
Research Assessment Exercise (RAE), 193, 213–14
  RAE-ification, 216, 226
Research Excellence Framework (REF), 4, 213–14
research imagination, 229, 242, 245, 270
research outputs, 51, 193–94, 196, 222, 281, 287
research policy, 117–19, 122–23, 129, 133
restructuring, 11, 36, 92, 95, 97, 104–6, 187, 206, 317
  administrative, 62
  institutional/organizational, 90, 92, 99
  global, 90
  radical, 90, 98
risk
  reputational risk, 175, 184, 186–89, 213, 219, 226, 230
  risk management, 5, 49, 51, 175, 182, 184–88, 218–19, 229–30, 243, 246, 261, 267, 318
  risk organisation, 219
  societal risks, 175, 177
Robins Report (1963), 36
Russia, 254

Sandbrook, Dominic, 43–44
scale, 10, 62, 91, 98, 101, 178, 241, 243, 255–56, 266, 271, 316–19, 327–28
  large-scale, 22, 261
  Likert scale, 149
  rescaling, 266, 319
  'scaled up', 93
  scale jumping, 316, 319
  small scale, 50, 53, 286
  world scale, 182, 258

science-industry collaboration, 56–57, 117
semesterization, 146–47
Sinfield, Alan, 32–34, 38, 45
symbiosis, 117, 128–29, 133–35
skills, 1, 10, 52, 57, 60, 64, 74, 80, 95, 140–41, 157, 194–95, 238, 312
  academic skills, 14
  critical skills, 278
  employability skills, 102, 163
  transferable skills, 152, 166
  'high' skills, 76
  'soft' skills 70
social cohesion, 1, 74, 261
Spain, 19, 92, 214
spin-in and spin-out companies, 56
spin-off, 19, 129–30
standardization, 18, 157, 282
State
  role of, 3, 11, 35–6, 40, 70–71, 73–75, 80, 118, 170, 180–81, 313, 318, 323–24
  competition, 69–70, 73–74, 80–81, 84–85, 181, 313
STEM subjects, 3, 49, 84, 195, 206–8
Stewart, Thomas, 82
student debt, 16, 288, 302, 325
student fees, 10, 322–25
student loans, 4, 10, 14–16, 319–20, 322, 328
  loan book, 323–24
student evaluations of teaching, 149–50
subjectivity, 49, 144, 150
sustainability, 6, 18, 48, 255, 259, 262, 270, 276–78, 284–85, 287
symbolic analysts, 81

Taiwan, 92
techno-globalism, 256, 264, 266–67
techno-nationalism, 256, 263–64
temporality
  in students' study life, 157
  aductive, 162, 165, 168–69
  See also time

territorialization
  de-territorialization, 315
Thatcher, Margaret, 41, 43–44
  Thatcher governments, 31, 39
Third Mission, 47, 53–55, 60, 62–63
  definition, 49–50
  university, 58–59, 61
time
  as condensed future, 167
  standardized policy, 158, 160–61
  subject-oriented, 158, 160–61
  See also temporality
Trust university, 19–20
tuition fees, 3, 8, 14–15, 17, 83

unbundling, 12, 101, 320
UniServices Ltd, 48, 56
United Kingdom, 193, 316, 320
university administration, 269
  growth of, 5–6, 7–8
university futures, 2, 18–20, 22, 47
University of Phoenix, 16–7
university ranking systems, 23, 186, 230
  as 'arms race', 4
universities
  as 'knowledge organizations', 1–2, 70
  expansion of, 32, 34.37, 41–44
  literary representations of, 32, 38
  state disinvestment in, 2–4
Universities New Zealand, 52

value creation, 60, 72, 129–30, 133–34
vice chancellors, 4, 9, 49, 51, 63, 65, 91–93, 98–99, 105, 146

welfare state, 33, 36–7, 39–41, 45, 80, 167
World Bank, 10, 71, 73, 178–80, 260–61
'world class' status, 4
World Economic Forum, 260–162

'zombification', 18

LEARNING AND TEACHING
The International Journal of Higher Education in the Social Sciences

Editors: Penny Welch, University of Wolverhampton

Susan Wright, University of Aarhus

Learning and Teaching (LATISS) is a peer-reviewed journal that uses the social sciences to reflect critically on learning and teaching in the changing context of higher education.

The journal invites students and staff to explore their education practices in the light of changes in their institutions, national higher education policies, the strategies of international agencies and developments associated with the so-called international knowledge economy.

The disciplines covered include politics and international relations, anthropology, sociology, criminology, social policy, cultural studies and educational studies. Recent topics include curriculum innovation, students' academic writing, PhD research ethics, neo-liberalism and academic identity, and marketisation of higher education.

The readership spans practitioners, researchers and students. It includes undergraduates and postgraduates interested in analysing their experience at university, newly appointed staff taking a qualification in learning and teaching, staff of learning and teaching units, experienced teachers in higher education and researchers on university reform.

RECENT ARTICLES

Critical pedagogy and Socially responsible investing (SRI): questioning our post-secondary institutions' investment strategies
  DAVID P. THOMAS

From rite of Passage to a mentored educational activity: fieldwork for master's students of anthropology
  HELLE BUNDGAARD AND CECILIE RUBOW

International learning experiences at home in Japan: the challenges and benefits of taking English-medium courses for Japenese students
  YUKIKO ISHIKURA

Teaching internationalisation? Surveying the lack of pedagogical and theoretical diversity in American International Relations
  CHRISTOPHER R. COOK

---

berghahnjournals.com/latiss

ISSN 1755-2273 (Print) · ISSN 1755-2281 (Online)
Volume 10/2017, 3 issues p.a.

www.ingramcontent.com/pod-product-compliance
Lightning Source LLC
Chambersburg PA
CBHW072143100526
44589CB00015B/2064